D0322270

ACTION DHARMA

Action Dharma charts the emergence of a new chapter in an ancient faith – the rise of social service and political activism in Buddhist Asia and the West. Sixteen new essays, including a critical introduction, and conclusion, treat the historical origins, global range, teachings and practices, and leaders and organizations that make up the latest turning of the Dharma. Environmentalism and peace walks through the minefields of South-east Asia, the future of the 'untouchables' in Japan, and outreach to minorities and inmates of the criminal justice system in the West are some of the challenging topics considered.

Christopher Queen is Lecturer on Religion and Dean of Students for Continuing Education in the Faculty of Arts and Sciences, Harvard University. He is editor of and contributor to *Engaged Buddhism: Buddhist Liberation Movements in Asia* (with Sallie B. King), *American Buddhism: Methods and Findings in Recent Scholarship* (with Duncan Ryuken Williams), and *Engaged Buddhism in the West*.

Charles Prebish is Professor of Religious Studies at the Pennsylvania State University and founding co-editor of the online *Journal of Buddhist Ethics*. He is author or editor of eleven books, including *Buddhist Monastic Discipline, American Buddhism, Historical Dictionary of Buddhism, A Survey of Vinaya Literature, The Faces of Buddhism in America*, and *Luminous Passage: The Practice and Study of Buddhism in America*.

Damien Keown is Senior Lecturer in Indian Religion at Goldsmiths College, University of London, and founding co-editor of the online *Journal of Buddhist Ethics*. His publications include *The Nature of Buddhist Ethics, Buddhism and Bioethics*, and *Buddhism: A Very Short Introduction*.

ROUTLEDGECURZON CRITICAL STUDIES IN BUDDHISM
General Editors:
Charles S. Prebish and Damien Keown

RoutledgeCurzon Critical Studies in Buddhism is a comprehensive study of the Buddhist tradition. The series explores this complex and extensive tradition from a variety of perspectives, using a range of different methodologies.

The series is diverse in its focus, including historical studies, textual translations and commentaries, sociological investigations, bibliographic studies, and considerations of religious practice as an expression of Buddhism's integral religiosity. It also presents materials on modern intellectual historical studies, including the role of Buddhist thought and scholarship in a contemporary, critical context and in the light of current social issues. The series is expansive and imaginative in scope, spanning more than two and a half millennia of Buddhist history. It is receptive to all research works that inform and advance our knowledge and understanding of the Buddhist tradition.

THE REFLEXIVE NATURE OF AWARENESS
Paul Williams

BUDDHISM AND HUMAN RIGHTS
Edited by Damien Keown, Charles Prebish, Wayne Husted

ALTRUISM AND REALITY
Paul Williams

WOMEN IN THE FOOTSTEPS OF THE BUDDHA
Kathryn R. Blackstone

THE RESONANCE OF EMPTINESS
Gay Watson

IMAGING WISDOM
Jacob N. Kinnard

AMERICAN BUDDHISM
Edited by Duncan Ryuken Williams and Christopher Queen

DEVELOPMENTS IN AUSTRALIAN BUDDHISM
Michelle Spuler

THE BUDDHIST UNCONSCIOUS
William S. Waldron

ACTION DHARMA
Edited by Christopher Queen, Charles Prebish and Damien Keown

ACTION DHARMA

New Studies in Engaged Buddhism

*Edited by Christopher Queen,
Charles Prebish and
Damien Keown*

RoutledgeCurzon
Taylor & Francis Group

First published 2003
by RoutledgeCurzon
11 New Fetter Lane, London EC4P 4EE

Simultaneously published in the USA and Canada
by RoutledgeCurzon
29 West 35th Street, New York, NY 10001
RoutledgeCurzon is an imprint of the Taylor & Francis Group
Editorial matter

Typeset in Sabon by Taylor & Francis Books Ltd
Printed and bound in Great Britain by The Cromwell Press,
Trowbridge, Wiltshire

British Library Cataloguing in Publication Data
A catalogue record for this book is available from the British Library

Library of Congress Cataloging in Publication Data
Action Dharma: new studies in engaged Buddhism/ edited by Christopher
Queen, Charles Prebish and Damien Keown. p.cm. -- (RoutledgeCurzon
critical studies in Buddhism) Includes bibliographical references and index.

ISBN 0–7007–1593–2 (hbk)
ISBN 0–7007–1594–0 (pbk)

DEDICATION

This volume is dedicated to Dr. A. T. Ariyaratne, founder of the Sarvodaya Shramadana Movement in Sri Lanka in 1958. Under his leadership, Sarvodaya has followed the Dharma into the world and sought to relieve the suffering of the poorest of the poor. Dr. Ariyaratne has held that the Buddhist teachings of selflessness and interconnection mean that individual liberation cannot be separated from the liberation of society. Working for grassroots development and leading peace marches and public meditations for more than four decades, the Sarvodaya Movement has sought the realization of its name, "Awakening of all."

CONTENTS

Part II Asian Narratives

CONTENTS

CONTRIBUTORS

Leslie D. Alldritt is Acting Vice-President and Dean of the College at Northland College in Ashland, Wisconsin, and Associate Professor in the Religion and Philosophy program. In summer 2001, he continued his field work on the *burakumin* in Japan under a NEH summer stipend. He is at work on a book-length manuscript focusing on the *burakumin* and Japanese Buddhism.

George D. Bond is Professor of Religion at Northwestern University and recipient of the Charles Deering McCormick Professorship of Teaching Excellence. He teaches courses on Buddhism and the history of religion. He is the author of several books including, *The Buddhist Revival in Sri Lanka* and *The Word of the Buddha*, and has also written numerous articles on Theravada Buddhism.

Susan M. Darlington is Associate Professor of Anthropology and Asian Studies at Hampshire College. She received her PhD in anthropology at the University of Michigan, where her research focused on Buddhism and rural development in northern Thailand. Her more recent research, supported by grants from the Social Science Research Council and the National Endowment for the Humanities, explores the relationship between Buddhism and environmentalism, the involvement of Thai Buddhist monks in environmental activism, and the reinterpretation of religion and religious practice in the process. She teaches courses on the anthropology of religion, human rights, environmentalism, culture and religion, and Southeast Asian studies.

James E. Deitrick received his doctorate in Religion and Social Ethics from the University of Southern California, where he was awarded the Yvonne Leonard Dissertation Fellowship for research on engaged Buddhism. He is currently Assistant Professor of Religious Studies and Director of the Interdisciplinary Program in Religious Studies at the University of Central Arkansas. Dr. Deitrick has delivered several papers on engaged Buddhism at academic conferences, including the annual meeting of the American Academy of Religion. He received the

Science and Religion Course Award from the Center for Theology and the Natural Sciences.

C. **Julia Huang** is a Senior Fellow at the Center for the Study of World Religions, Harvard University. She received her PhD in Anthropology from Boston University and completed a postdoctoral fellowship at the Institute for Human Sciences, Vienna, Austria. Her research focuses on religion, charisma, gender, and transnationalism. Since 1993, she has conducted research on the Buddhist Compassionate-Relief Foundation (Tzu-chi) in Taiwan and overseas Chinese communities, and is currently finishing a book on the topic. She has delivered panel presentations on her research at major academic conferences and institutions in the USA, Taiwan, and the People's Republic of China. With Robert P. Weller she co-published the first article in English on Ciji (Tzu-Chi), "Merit and Mothering: Women and Social Welfare in Taiwanese Buddhism" in the *Journal of Asian Studies* (1998). In addition, Huang has authored several book chapters, including "A Case Study of Global Engaged Buddhism in Taiwan: The Buddhist Compassionate-Relief Merit Society" (in *Doing Globalization Justice: A View from the World's Religions*, edited by V. C. Falsina, in press), and "The Compassionate-Relief Diaspora" (in *Buddhist "Missionary Spirit" in the Twentieth Century: Monks, Nuns, and Immigrants in the Era of Globalization*, edited by Linda Learman, forthcoming).

Derek S. Jeffreys teaches religion and philosophy at the University of Wisconsin, Green Bay. He received his PhD in Religious Ethics from the University of Chicago Divinity School in 1998. He has taught at Mahidol University in Bangkok, Thailand, as well as at California State University, Chico. He works on ethics and the philosophy of religion, with particular attention to political ethics. Professor Jeffreys has published articles on John Calvin, euthanasia, and Reformed Epistemology. Currently, he is completing a book on Pope John Paul II's political thought, which considers the relationship between modern phenomenology and Thomism.

Stephen Jenkins is Associate Professor of Religious Studies at Humboldt State University. He received his doctorate from Harvard in 1999. His dissertation was a thematic study of compassion in Indian Buddhist thought. He publishes articles on Buddhist ethics and philosophy and on Vishishtadvaita. He is currently editing a volume on Buddhist violence and co-authoring a work on religion in cinema.

Damien V. Keown is Reader in Buddhism at Goldsmiths College, University of London. His publications include *The Nature of Buddhist Ethics, Buddhism and Bioethics, Buddhism and Abortion, Contemporary Buddhist Ethics*, and *Buddhism: A Very Short*

Introduction. He is a founding co-editor of the online *Journal of Buddhist Ethics*, and co-editor of the Curzon Press "Critical Studies in Buddhism" series.

Harriet Kirkley has taught at the University of British Columbia. She attended Agnes Scott College and Stanford University, and grew up near the site where Sequoyah invented the Cherokee syllabary. She is studying Burmese Buddhism.

Virginia Cohn Parkum received her doctorate, focusing on participatory democracy and voluntarism, from the University of Mannheim, Germany. She helped develop public sector courses for the Yale University School of Organization and Management. She co-authored "The Angulimala Lineage: Buddhist Prison Ministries" with Sensei Anthony Stultz in Christopher S. Queen's *Engaged Buddhism in the West* (Wisdom, 2000) and "Engaged Buddhism in the American Criminal Justice System: Shin Roots, Shin Blossoms," in *The Pure Land* (December 1999). Having received an M. S. in Library Science, she has advised the Buddhist Study Center Library in Honolulu, Hawaii on collection development and future directions. Her art has been featured in gallery shows in the US, Denmark and Germany. She created the art and haiku poetry for *Soul Quest: Zen Lessons for the Journey of Life* (Anthony Stultz, Blue Mountain Lotus Society 2001, and forthcoming in an expanded format). She holds lay ordination in The Blue Mountain Lotus Society, a non-profit organization devoted to sharing the universal teachings of the Buddha in the 21st century within the context of contemporary life.

Charles S. Prebish is Professor of Religious Studies at the Pennsylvania State University. He received his PhD. in Buddhist Studies at the University of Wisconsin in 1971. He is the author or editor of more than a dozen books, the most recent of which are *Luminous Passage: The Practice and Study of Buddhism in America*, and *Westward Dharma: Buddhism beyond Asia* (edited with Martin Baumann). He is a past officer of the International Association of Buddhist Studies, former co-chair of the Buddhism Group of the American Academy of Religion, and former editor of Critical Review of Books in Religion. Along with Damien Keown, he is a founding co-editor of the *Journal of Buddhist Ethics* and co-editor of the Curzon Press "Critical Studies in Buddhism" series.

Christopher S. Queen is Lecturer on Religion and Dean of Students for Continuing Education in the Faculty of Arts and Sciences, Harvard University. He holds degrees in religion from Oberlin College, Union Theological Seminary, and Boston University. His interest in engaged Buddhism arose during his research in the 1980s and 1990s among the

Dalit Buddhists of India, the ex-Untouchable followers of B. R. Ambedkar. He has taught Buddhist social thought, American Buddhism, and World Religions at Harvard since 1992. His publications include *Engaged Buddhism: Buddhist Liberation Movements in Asia* (edited with Sallie B. King); *American Buddhism: Methods and Findings in Recent Scholarship* (edited with Duncan Ryuken Williams); *Engaged Buddhism in the West* (editor and contributor); and entries in the *Encyclopedia of Buddhism* (Macmillan, forthcoming). He is working on a study of Ambedkar and the hermeneutics of Buddhist liberation.

Sharon Smith is an MPhil student in the Historical and Cultural Studies department at Goldsmiths' College, University of London, UK. Her research project is "Sangha, Diversity and Race: Multiculturalism in Western Buddhist Convert Sanghas in Inner London." She has worked as a community worker and as an equal opportunities officer for a local authority in East London. Her interests lie in exploring how issues of multiculturalism, discrimination and social exclusion are being addressed within institutions, particularly faith communities, and how the experience gained in addressing such issues can be more widely disseminated. She is an African-Caribbean woman who has been practicing Buddhism for over twelve years.

Jacqueline I. Stone received her PhD in 1990 from the Department of East Asian Languages and Cultures at the University of California at Los Angeles. Currently she teaches Buddhism and Japanese Religions in the Religion Department at Princeton University. She has served as co-chair of the Buddhism Section of the American Academy of Religion and president of the Society for the Study of Japanese Religions. Her research has focused on Japanese Buddhism in both the medieval and modern periods. She is the author of *Original Enlightenment and the Transformation of Medieval Japanese Buddhism* (1999). Her current research plans include continued work on the Nichiren tradition.

J. Anthony Stultz is Spiritual Director of the Blue Mountain Lotus Society, a non-profit organization devoted to sharing the universal teachings of the Buddha in the twenty-first century within the context of contemporary life. He holds two graduate degrees in theology, including an MA in Pastoral Theology from the Episcopal Divinity School (Cambridge), and has studied for ministry in the Zen and Tibetan traditions. He completed his clinical education at the Pennsylvania State Milton S. Hershey Medical Center and holds a diploma from the American Psychotherapy Association. Sensei Stultz served as Buddhist chaplain in various types of prisons for twelve years as well as in university and hospital settings. His work has appeared in the *Journal of Buddhist Ethics* and *The Pure Land* and been presented at The International Association for Shin Buddhist Studies Conference (1999). He is a contributor to *Engaged Buddhism in the West* (edited by Christopher S. Queen; Wisdom Publications, 2000). Sensei Stultz is co-recipient with Virginia Parkum of a grant from the Pennsylvania Council on the Arts and MetroArts to develop a format for presenting Zen and Shin teachings in a contemporary way, *Soul Quest: Zen Lessons for the Journey of Life* (Blue Mountain Lotus Society, 2001 and forthcoming in an extended format). He is director of the Center for Natural Counseling in Harrisburg, PA.

Frank M. Tedesco earned a doctorate in Buddhist Studies at Dongguk University in Seoul in 1998 on a Presidential Fellowship near the end of fifteen years of residency in Korea. A social activist and anthropologist immersed in Korean Buddhist culture and practices throughout those years, he has been widely quoted in the Korean and international media because of his expertise and candor regarding sensitive cultural issues in Korea. He wrote "Open Mind," a column on spiritual movements in the San Francisco Bay area, for the underground newspaper *The Berkeley Barb* while an honor student at University of California Berkeley (1968–71), and earned an M. A. with distinction at Lancaster, UK (1974). He pursued doctoral research in anthropology and cultural psychiatry at the University of Pennsylvania and Johns Hopkins Medical School (1974–80). He currently teaches anthropology and religious studies at the University of South Florida and Eckerd College in St Petersburg and continues to write about Korea, Buddhism and social engagement today.

Matthew Weiner is an academic fellow at the Interfaith Center of New York, where he coordinates the Urban Program. He is a graduate of Harvard Divinity School. He was the director of Stories for Peace, a children's book and peace project for the Sarvodaya Movement in Sri Lanka. He has worked for the Office of Tibet and the Project on Religion and Human Rights. He has written about Buddhism and interfaith dialogue.

Thomas Freeman Yarnall has been engaged with Buddhist studies for 25 years. After receiving his BA in Religion at Amherst College in 1983, he studied intensively with many Tibetan lamas in the USA, India, and Nepal. In the early 1990s he studied advanced literary Tibetan and Sanskrit at the University of Washington in Seattle, before transferring to the PhD program in Religion at Columbia University in 1993. He has received numerous awards, including the Columbia University President's Fellowship from 1993–98, several Foreign Language and Area Studies (FLAS) awards, and two A.W. Mellon Research Fellowships. He earned an MA at Columbia in 1995, an MPhil in 1997. His doctoral dissertation is on the topic of tantric Buddhist theory and practice, focusing on the role of visualization in the Buddhist path and including an exploration of the social implications of such practices. He has taught numerous courses in Buddhist theory and practice around the Seattle and New York areas, and has been an Adjunct Professor of Religion at Columbia for the last two years. He is currently employed by Tibet House U. S., working with Dr. Robert Thurman to develop a new kind of institute for advanced studies, a "Global Renaissance Institute," dedicated to the advanced study of the inner arts and sciences in the modern university. In conjunction with this he has edited several books on Buddhism, Tibetan art, and Asian religions.

Daniel Zelinski is Assistant Professor of Philosophy of Religion at Richard Bland College of the College of William and Mary. He received his doctorate in Philosophy from the University of California, Irvine, in 1997, with his dissertation, "The Meaning of Mystical Life: An Inquiry into Phenomenological and Moral Aspects of the Ways of Life Advocated by Dogen Zenji and Meister Eckhart." He has since presented papers on "Mysticism and Morality," "Socially Engaged Buddhism," and "Dissolving the Problem of Death;" and he has served as a Visiting Assistant Professor at Kansas State University and Central Missouri State University. For the 2002–3 academic year, he has been awarded a Post-doctoral fellowship at Princeton University's Center for the Study of Religion, where he will assist Professor Christian Wildberg in hosting a seminar and conference on "The Moral Mystic."

PREFACE
Charles S. Prebish

In 1995 when the *Journal of Buddhist Ethics* sponsored its first online conference, devoted to the topic of "Buddhism and Human Rights," the editors had very modest expectations. After all, an online conference in Religious Studies had never been previously attempted, and the journal had a subscriber base of only 800 individuals. Despite the timeliness of the topic, and the quality of the papers presented, prior to the conference, everyone associated with the journal held his or her collective breath. During the actual two-week conference, the journal's homepage was accessed 1,350 times, and over 400 e-mail messages were posted to the journal's listserv. The discussion was lively and the responses productive. Needless to say, the editors were pleased with the overall success of the conference, and encouraged by many participants to publish the conference papers in traditional hard-copy form as a book. In 1998 *Buddhism and Human Rights* appeared as one of the early volumes in the Curzon "Critical Studies in Buddhism" series.

To be sure, planning and executing an online conference is no simple matter, and although the *Journal of Buddhist Ethics* was eager to sponsor a second one, it took several years of discussion and planning to bring the 2000 conference on "Socially Engaged Buddhism" to fruition. Because the *JBE* had grown considerably in size between 1995 and 2000 (to over 3,000 subscribers) it became clear that the conference needed to function as its own entity. In other words, it was neither pragmatic nor fair to forward all conference discussion e-mails to each subscriber. Additionally, in view of the exceedingly busy schedules of prospective participants, reducing the time frame of the conference from two weeks to one made the conference significantly more attractive and manageable.

Since socially engaged Buddhism was rapidly becoming one of the most compelling topics in Buddhist Studies, as well as in the practice of Buddhist communities worldwide, the *JBE* editors felt it would be important to secure guidance and leadership from one of the most established authorities on the topic. In that regard, Dr. Christopher S. Queen of

Harvard University, whose books on engaged Buddhism have been at the very forefront of the topic, and whose ruminations about engaged Buddhism as a potential "fourth *yāana*" in Buddhism have created much interest, was invited to be the honorary chairman and convener of the conference. It was his leadership that was pivotal in creating and structuring the substance and direction of the conference.

More than a year before the actual presentation of the conference, a call for papers was posted on the *JBE* homepage and circulated to various Buddhist online newsgroups. Many proposals were received and evaluated, and by 1 April 2000, all thirteen conference papers were posted for online examination. Wisdom Publications graciously extended permission to the *JBE* to reprint three papers from Queen's *Engaged Buddhism in the West* volume for the conference. Thus, the conference was launched on 7 April 2000, and it continued for one week with discussion assigned to a special listserv created specifically and solely for that purpose. During the week's discussions, more than 200 e-mail notes were posted to the listserv, monitored by the *JBE*'s technical editor Daniel McShane, and with discussion led at various points by Queen, Damien Keown, and myself.

From the outset, Queen and the *JBE* editors planned to issue a volume based on the conference proceedings. However, because the conference papers by Queen, John Powers, and Kenneth Kraft had previously appeared in original form in Queen's *Engaged Buddhism in the West*, and would not be reprinted, it was decided to invite several additional scholars to contribute chapters to enhance the overall usefulness of the published version. In that regard, Jacqueline Stone, Matthew Weiner, George Bond, Frank Tedesco, and Derek Jeffreys joined the project. Enhanced by a new introduction by Queen, the conference volume makes its appearance as *Action Dharma: New Studies in Engaged Buddhism*. As with the first *JBE* conference volume, we have retained the original formatting of each chapter. It is our hope that this book will add to the important, growing literature on engaged Buddhism.

Our dedication of the volume to Dr. A. T. Ariyaratne, founding leader of the Sarvodaya Shramadana movement in Sri Lanka, is offered in token of his pioneering work as an exemplar of socially engaged Buddhism. With its focus on rural economic development, voluntary service, ecumenical cooperation, and nonviolent peacemaking, Sarvodaya, now in its forty-fifth year, epitomizes the social revolution implicit in the Buddha's ancient teachings. May Dr. Ariyaratne and his followers prosper in their peace-work for many years to come.

ACKNOWLEDGEMENTS

The editors wish to thank Dr. George D. Bond for providing the cover photograph and dedication, and David Mumper for his assistance in preparing the manuscript for publication.

INTRODUCTION
From Altruism to Activism

Christopher Queen

A Tathagata fully awakens to this fact ... that all formations
are impermanent, that all formations are subject to suffering,
that all things are not-self.

(Anguttara Nikaya III.134)

This collection of studies on engaged Buddhism is offered to advance our
understanding of the rise and significance of a complex and evolving
movement. The contributors have attempted (1) to trace the historical
roots of Buddhist social engagement; (2) to present actors, movements,
and models that have not been critically studied before; and (3) to question
the viability, novelty, and authority of engaged Buddhism and its scholarly
interpretations to date. In choosing these chapters, the editors have tried to
underscore the fact that socially and politically engaged Buddhism
continues to grow and diversify in Asia and the West, that it continues to
challenge conventional assumptions about the nature and direction of
Buddhism, and, perhaps most importantly, that engaged Buddhist studies
remain at a stage best regarded as exploratory and constructive.

The title of the book, *Action Dharma*, was coined to suggest that
engaged Buddhism, grounded in ethics and morality, is a path of social
action in the world – as opposed to the paths of ritual, knowledge, and
devotion that characterize other, perhaps better known, expressions of
Buddhism. This does not mean that Buddhists who do not participate in
social service or political activism are less committed or compassionate in
their lives or less "active" in their practice of Buddhism. But it does imply
that the moral training (*sila*) featured in the traditional Eightfold Path
(right speech, action, and livelihood), may be of special interest to engaged
Buddhists, informing their choice of public statements, activities, and roles
in ways that meditation training (*samadhi*: right effort, mindfulness,
concentration) and wisdom training (*prajna*: right understanding and
resolve) are not.

Caution is in order here. Just as the Hindu paths of action (*karma
yoga*), knowledge (*jnana yoga*), and devotion (*bhakti yoga*) are likely to

1

crisscross, diverge, and converge in practice, so the strands of cult, creed, and code – devotion to the Buddha, knowledge of the Dharma, and action in the Sangha – are likely to form a colorful, braided pattern in Buddhism.[1] The distinction between *social action* (caring for the sick or joining a peace march, for example), which is typically undertaken to relieve others' suffering, and *ritual action* (meditation and devotional rites, for example), which is typically undertaken to relieve the practitioner's own suffering, is not easy to maintain in Buddhism, where "inner" and "outer" practices are deeply interdependent. Peace marches and political rallies, like meditation itself, are rituals after all, and many Buddhist rites are dedicated to the liberation of all beings. On the other hand, the moral trainings of the Eightfold Path may be interpreted in ways that de-emphasize their utility as programs of action in the social sphere.

Most of the engaged Buddhists profiled in this book insist on the identity of the spiritual and social dimensions of their practice, and they regard service and activism as essential to the Buddhist path. This viewpoint is not shared by all Buddhists, however, or by all scholars of Buddhism. In a volume entitled *Paths of Liberation: The Marga and its Transformations in Buddhist Thought*, Robert Buswell and Robert Gimello argue that Buddhist practice, such as the Eightfold Path, "brings to an end the impulses that sustain one's ties to the phenomenal world of suffering and so engenders the radical renunciation that is nirvana."[2] Accordingly, none of the activities that engaged Buddhists describe as their practice in these pages – activities that, by definition, engaged them in the phenomenal world of suffering – appear as "paths of liberation" in the volume of that title. In their analysis, Buswell and Gimello seem to rule out the impulse behind the fourth precept of Thich Nhat Hanh's Tiep Hien Order of engaged Buddhism:

> Do not avoid contact with suffering or close your eyes before suffering. Do not lose awareness of the existence of suffering in the life of the world. Find ways to be with those who are suffering by all means, including personal contact and visits, images, sound. By such means awaken yourself and others to the reality of suffering in the world.[3]

Not all engaged Buddhists embrace the proposition that spirituality and activism are one. Untouchable Buddhist converts in India – Dalit or Ambedkarite Buddhists – for example, despite their passionate embrace of the Dharma, are often hesitant to sign up for Buddhist meditation training courses that are offered, free-of-charge, at the Vipassana retreat centers of S. N. Goenka. A Buddhist professor at the University of Nagpur, site of the mass conversions in 1956, explained that the equanimity, peace, and tolerance associated with meditation practice would weaken his community's ongoing struggle against caste oppression. Activism is the spirituality of the times, he would say, not the pacifism of the cushion. Meanwhile, the chairman of his department (also a Dalit Buddhist) and many international figures in engaged Buddhism, particularly ordained leaders such as Thich Nhat Hanh, the Dalai Lama, and Maha Ghosananda, hold that spiritual effort, mindfulness, and meditation are the very actions that will decisively shape one's speech, social behaviors, and livelihood – and these will, in turn, have incalculably beneficial ripple effects throughout society.[4]

Thus, defining action dharma as social engagement in the context of more traditional paths of liberation remains an overarching task for scholars of contemporary Buddhism. Each contributor to this collection has identified critical contexts: Buddhist history and literature, e.g. the Mahayana *sutras* and the writings of Dogen Zenji and Nichiren Daishonen in Part I of the book; the geography of engaged Buddhism today – Thailand, Cambodia, Taiwan, South Korea, Japan, Hawaii, Burma, and communities of color and the penal institutions of Britain and the USA – in Parts II and III; and the methodological concerns that occupy the three critics in Part IV. Some solutions to the puzzle of action dharma may be heard in the voices of environmental monks, prison chaplains, peace walkers, and disaster relief workers who act in the name of Buddhism, while others are formulated, however provisionally, by the scholars who listen.

In this Introduction we shall preview the findings of the fifteen chapters that follow, organizing our discussion around the classical teaching of the Three Marks of Existence (Pali *ti-lakkhana*): "A Tathagata fully awakens to this fact ... that all formations are impermanent, all formations are subject to suffering, that all things are not-self," as it is presented in *Sutta 134* of the "Threes" section of the *Anguttara Nikaya*.[5] I hope this device will be as useful to the reader as it has been for me in making sense of the descriptive and interpretive data now at our disposal. Its potential value struck me when I noticed that the three marks were reflected in the three critiques that conclude the volume – James Deitrick's concern with the meaning of suffering (*dukkha*) in engaged Buddhism, Derek Jeffreys' insistence on the importance of the not-self (*anatta*) teaching in Buddhist ethics, and Thomas Yarnall's concern with issues of continuity and discontinuity, identity and impermanence (*anicca*) in the transmission of Buddhist ethics. Further examination of the studies that make up the three central parts of the book reveal that the three marks offer valuable organizing principles there as well.

In considering the historical roots of engaged Buddhism in Part I, Jenkins, Zelinski, and Stone illustrate the evolution of ancient and medieval notions of *suffering* in Buddhist India and Japan. In the Asian narratives that follow in Part II, Darlington, Weiner, Bond, Huang, Tedesco, and Alldritt explore instances of cultural borrowing, globaliza-

3

tion, transnationalism, and marginalization that illustrate the *insubstantiality*, hybridity, or "not-self" of Buddhist thought and practice throughout Asia. And in visiting three of the Western frontiers of engaged Buddhism, the affiliation of Hawaiian and Burmese sanghas, and the adaptation of the Dharma to minority and prison populations in North America, Kirkley, Smith, Parkum, and Stultz in Part III illustrate the dialectics of tradition, innovation, and *impermanence* in Buddhism's transmission to the West.

While it may be said that the use of traditional Buddhist teaching formulae such as the Three Marks, the Three Refuges, the Four Noble Truths, or the Yanas as principles of classification cannot substitute for scholarly methodologies grounded in modern literary criticism, historical analysis, and anthropological description – all of which are used in this volume – I would suggest that the hermeneutical use of Buddhist categories may offer access to levels of understanding not available through the exclusive use of non-Buddhist categories. This is the meaning of *emic* analysis, introduced by Kenneth Pike in 1967, as explained by anthropologist Marvin Harris:

> The test of the adequacy of emic analyses is their ability to generate statements the native accepts as real, meaningful, or appropriate. In carrying out research in the emic mode, the observer attempts to acquire a knowledge of the categories and rules one must know in order to think and act as a native.[6]

Etic analysis, on the other hand, favors the categories of the observer in order to "generate scientifically productive theories about the causes of sociocultural differences and similarities."[7] The reader of *Action Dharma* will find both approaches in regular use throughout the volume.

Suffering in the history of Buddhist engagement

The ancient tradition records the Buddha as saying, "In the past, Bhikkhus, as well as now, I teach only *dukkha* and the utter quenching of *dukkha*."[8] Among the handful of ideas at the center of Buddhist wisdom, *dukkha*, usually translated as "suffering," "unsatisfactoriness," and "ill," is one of the most crucial. It may be regarded as the subjective state of being, or "mark of existence," that flows from the more objective marks of *anicca*, "impermanence," and *anatta*, "insubstantiality" ("not-self" or "hybridity") that characterize all conditioned things. "*Dukkha* and its quenching is a summary of the Four Noble Truths, the framework of Buddhism," writes Santikaro Bhikkhu, the engaged Buddhist scholar-monk. "Here we have the entire scope and range of the Buddha's teachings, although its heights and depths may not be immediately apparent." [9]

As important as the teaching of suffering is in ancient Buddhism and as a motive for social engagement today, James Deitrick, in the first critique in Part IV, argues that engaged Buddhists have misunderstood this critical concept:

> Suffering for Buddhism is not typically equated with physical pain or societal oppression, at least not in the deepest sense of *dukkha*. Rather, it is the sense of unsatisfactoriness that comes with the perverse tendency to cling to the self and other ostensibly illusory objects in an ever-changing world.

Furthermore, such dissatisfaction "cannot be eradicated by eliminating the causes of oppression," thus "work toward creation of a good society ... holds no intrinsic value for Buddhism." Consequently, by viewing the relief of social suffering as its ethical goal, rather than as a means to the goal of personal liberation, Deitrick argues that engaged Buddhists have "mistaken the boat for the shore" – in effect, missing the boat to liberation.

To address Dietrick's charge, we turn to the first three chapters of the book, which take up the historical roots of engaged Buddhism and, in the case of Jacqueline Stone's chapter, three derivative "new religions" in contemporary Japan. Here we may begin to identify the evolving place and meaning of the teaching of suffering in the tradition, and the range of skillful means employed to relieve it.

Stephen Jenkins in Chapter 1 shows that altruistic service to the poor has been a perennial theme in Buddhist literature, and that the *bodhisattva* ideal of the Mahayana, proclaimed in the vow to save all beings and manifested in a wide range of techniques we would call "social action," represents the epitome of engaged Buddhism. Citing a range of Pali and Sanskrit sources, Jenkins details the compassionate actions of bestowing food, shelter, clothing, medicine, and physical protection to those in need. He calls the shift from the Hinayana emphasis on the laity's material support for the ordained *sangha* to the Mahayana emphasis on the *bodhisattva*'s material support for the poor as a "Copernican flip" in Buddhist ethical thought, and concludes:

> Several central Mahayana and mainstream sources define compassion as a kind of action and, in merit making, action is far superior to mere good intentions... In Mahayana sources, there is a great relative preponderance of passages that identify and show

concern for poverty and see relieving it as the role of the ideal practitioner, the *bodhisattva*.[10]

Thus, from the outset, the Buddhist definition of suffering was broad enough to encompass both spiritual disease and material deprivation, and the remedies offered by the tradition included both spiritual exercises and altruistic action. But are these responses to human suffering mutually exclusive?

Daniel Zelinski in Chapter 2 argues that the "ceaseless practice" (*gyogi*) advocated by the Japanese Zen master Dōgen (1200–1253) represents a total fusion of spiritual and social-ethical horizons, as the bare awareness, mindfulness, nonattachment, alertness and equanimity associated with *zazen* are linked to the bodhisattva practices of almsgiving (*fuse*), loving words (*aigo*), beneficial action (*rigyo*), and identification/cooperation with those who need help (*doji*). Thus, the altruistic practices found in the Indian Buddhist record by Jenkins are shown by Zelinski to grow directly from the spiritual cultivation of Buddha-nature and the collapse of inner-outer dualism. "Beneficial action" or *rigyo* "means that we take care of every kind of person, no matter whether of high or low position," according to Dōgen; "*Rigyo* is the one principle wherein we find no opposition between subjectivity and objectivity." This experience of oneness with the other is consummated in the notion of *doji*: "It is not opposing oneself and not opposing others ... When one knows cooperation, self and others are one thusness... After regarding others as self, there must be a principle of assimilating oneself to others" – and illustrated by Kuo-an Shih-yuan's final Zen ox-herding picture, entitled "Entering the Marketplace with Helping Hands," where the marketplace, Zelinski explains, is the social world of suffering.

While Jenkins and Zelinski succeed in demonstrating the presence of social altruism and the relief of material suffering from earlier times, and especially since the dawn of the bodhisattva ideal – thus suggesting a rebuttal to James Deitrick's strict construction of the Buddhist *dukkha* as a purely spiritual malaise – we do not find in their analysis any evidence for another kind of engaged Buddhism that has appeared throughout Asia and the West over the past century, namely the political activism that views the state and other social institutions as agents of collective suffering. For this perspective, we turn to the next chapter.

Jacqueline Stone in Chapter 3 takes a close look at three Japan-based sects that are widely regarded for their peace advocacy and social engagement: Soka Gakkai, Rissho Koseikai, and Nipponzan Myohoji. She notes similarities: veneration of the Lotus Sutra and the Buddhist teacher Nichiren (1222–1282), daily chanting of the *daimoku*, "Homage to the Lotus of the Pure Law" (*Namu-myoho-renge-kyo*), and social activism for world peace, including peace marches, educational campaigns, and building "peace pagodas" around the world. She also notes differences of belief, ritual, and relationship to their founding teacher and scripture. Stone's finely nuanced analysis raises two questions for our purposes: what kinds of suffering are addressed by the Nichiren-inspired sects, and what kinds of remedies are prescribed?

While the Lotus Sutra does not contain an explicit social ethic, according to Stone, its Japanese interpreters, particularly Saicho (767–822), founder of the Tendai school, associated veneration of the Lotus Sutra with national peace and prosperity. This theme was amplified by Nichiren in *Rissho ankoku ron*, "Treatise on establishing the True Dharma and bringing peace to the land," wherein he associated such natural and political calamities as earthquakes, crop failure, famine, and epidemics with the failure of the government and the people to embrace the teachings of the Lotus. Indeed, Nichiren held that all of the depredations of the current "degenerate age of the Dharma" (*mappo*), including domestic political strife and the threat of conquest from the mainland "were due to neglect of the Lotus Sutra in favor of 'lesser,' provisional Buddhist forms, such as Pure Land devotion, Zen meditation, and esoteric ritual practice," according to Stone.

Nichiren cannot be regarded as an "engaged Buddhist" in modern terms, therefore, because he was more concerned with the advancement of Lotus-based spirituality than with any direct eradication of social suffering. *Shakabuku*, vigorous proselytizing on behalf of the Lotus – the chief public activity of Nichirenism – is a far cry from housing the poor or pressuring the government for better distribution of food and medicine. Yet the association of Buddhist practice, however ritualized or magical, with public peace and prosperity takes us halfway to the engaged practice of today – an interpretation of the Dharma grounded in alleviating social suffering in this lifetime, however indirectly. The completion of this transition from sectarianism to active engagement in the specifics of social suffering is accomplished by the Nichiren-inspired sects of the twentieth century.[11]

Soka Gakkai and Rissho Koseikai, representing seventeen million and six million members in Japan alone, exemplify many of the service-oriented practices that have come to be called engaged Buddhism today: peacework in association with the United Nations, and relief programs targeted at the victims of natural and human disasters. Nipponzan Myohoji, a much smaller sect, numbering about 1,500 members, utilizes nonviolent protest and public symbolization – the peace march and the erection of "peace pagodas" – to build public sentiment for the abolition of nuclear weapons, the payment of reparations for the atrocities of war, and the creation of societies based on justice and compassion. In conclusion, Stone emphasizes the creativity with which Nichiren and his heirs have selectively adapted the teachings of the Lotus Sutra to address the challenges of their time:

> Nichiren drew selectively on his Tendai Background in Lotus Sutra studies as well as elements in the broader medieval Japanese religious culture to formulate an interpretation that he saw as answering the needs of his time. And his successors in later ages have done likewise. Exponents of the nationalistic Nichirenism of Japan's modern imperial period reinterpreted his teachings to legitimize their participation in nation-building, imperialism and war, while Nichiren- and Lotus Sutra-based engaged Buddhists in the contemporary period have similarly re-read these teachings in light of their own commitments to non-violence and world peace.

Thus in the opening chapters we learn that some forms of Buddhist social engagement, particularly service to the poor, are attested in the tradition from early times, while others, particularly activism in the society at large, are later in coming. On the other hand, the record of Buddhist engagement *vis-à-vis* government authority remains a mixed one. In the last century, for example, even the Nichiren sects of Japan, now known for associating religious practice with national prosperity, were more likely to support militant nationalism than to pressure their government, or any government, to modify its military or social policies. The public activism of the Nichiren peace sects since 1945 has been more directed to changing public opinion through nonviolent demonstrations and education than through civil disobedience of the Gandhian type, directed toward established authority.

Meanwhile, the definition of suffering has been expanded, particularly in the Mahayana, to include a wide range of social ills, while their remedies have likewise broadened to address the social conditions – not only psychological ones – that give them rise. The connection between social suffering and the behavior of large social, economic, and political entities, and the roles that religious activism might play in shaping the behavior of these entities, are more clearly illustrated in the studies that make up the next part of the book.

Not-self in Asian narratives of engagement

A second characteristic of existence that frequently appears in the Pali scriptures in connection with suffering and impermanence is that of *anatta*, usually translated as not-self, non-self, no-self, selflessness, or insubstantiality. "The Buddha teaches, contrary to our most cherished beliefs, that our personality – the five aggregates – cannot be identified as self, as an enduring and substantial ground of personal identity," writes Bhikkhu

Bodhi, the respected translator and commentator on the *Majjhima Nikaya*. "The notion of a self has only a conventional validity, as a convenient short-hand device for denoting a composite insubstantial situation."[12] Just as personality is traditionally deconstructed into the five "aggregates" (Pali *khandhas*: form, feeling, perception, disposition, and consciousness), none of which can be identified as "I, mine, or myself," so, even gross phenomena, such as earth, air, fire, and water may be characterized as *anatta* because they are composite and impermanent, made up of different constituents at different times.[13] If *anatta* may be seen to cover such complex phenomena as personality and the elements of the natural world, how much more might it be employed in the analysis of complex, cultural evolution, such as the international history of Buddhism? Here we shall employ the terms *hybrid* and *insubstantial* to express the notion of "not-self" in the emergence of engaged Buddhism.

Derek Jeffreys, in Chapter 14, the second critique of engaged Buddhism, has placed the concept of not-self at the center of his dismissal of human rights language in current Buddhism. Drawing on the writings of the eminent Thai scholar-monk, Prayudh Payutto (Ven Dhamma-pitaka), Jeffreys argues that engaged Buddhists and scholars of Buddhist ethics (particularly Damien Keown), besides failing to address recent criticisms of the human rights tradition by Western thinkers, seem to presuppose the existence of a self, "a stable agent who possesses rights." Yet such a presupposition would require the abandonment of the Buddhist *anatta*; for a "rights-holder," a person who endures over time and may sue in court to recover his or her rights, is not possible in Theravada Buddhism. Like Deitrick, Jeffreys wants to restrict the meaning of traditional concepts in the face of new interpretations generated by the practice of engaged Buddhism and by cultural values and patterns of action arising outside the tradition. We shall return to comment on Jeffreys' critique after considering the pervasive hybridity of engaged Buddhist institutions and ideologies in Asia.

Susan Darlington's first-hand account of the rise of Buddhist environmentalism among a small circle of activist monks in Thailand in Chapter 4 is compelling at many levels. Certainly the poignancy of the rapid and extensive loss of forests to the state-sponsored logging industry – from 72 per cent of the land in 1983 to 15 per cent today, in a country that has honored the "forest tradition" of Buddhist monasticism for over two thousand years – is matched only by the courage of the monks who confront the state-sponsored Buddhist hierarchy that opposes reform. The innovation of new rituals and temple practices on behalf of the environment – tree ordinations, rice and buffalo banks, alms rounds for land donation, sustainable farming on temple grounds, and meditation walks for eco-tourists – suggest both the creativity of the ecology monks and their openness to non-Buddhist influences. In her conclusion, Darlington highlights neither the personalities of the ecology monks nor their specific innovations, but the confluence of cultural elements and motives that shaped each local campaign. "As Buddhists have done since the Buddha's time, [the Thai ecology monks and their lay supporters] adapt their interpretations and practices of the religion to fit a changing sociopolitical – and natural – environment, in this case, a result of modernization."

In Chapter 5, Matthew Weiner offers a similar interpretation of Maha Ghosananda and the annual *Dhammayietra* peace walks through war-torn and landmine-infested Cambodia, arguably "the most devastated Buddhist country in modern times." Again, we find a reinvented Buddhism, directed at psychological and political change in a time of great social instability, following the Khmer Rouge's murder of more than two million Cambodians and their attack on Buddhist institutions and leaders. Noting parallels with the Vietnamese Thich Nhat Hanh, the Dalai Lama of Tibet, and the Burmese opposition leader Aung San Suu Kyi, Wiener writes that "Ghosananda's activism began with the rebuilding of Cambodian Buddhism, teaching peace through example, and being completely nonpartisan, successfully offering his peace ministry even to members of the Khmer Rouge." For his quiet courage, "the Cambodian Gandhi" has received five nominations for the Nobel Peace Prize.

Maha Ghosananda manifests the Buddhist *anatta* in extraordinary ways. The quiet monk exemplifies selflessness in his dedication to the cause of peace, no matter what the risks, and in his unique cultivation of personal invisibility. Theravada monks traditionally cover their faces with a bamboo fan when giving *dhamma* talks to the community, a symbolic expression of the Buddha's subordination of teacher to teaching. Ghosananda finds ways to extend this practice to other areas of public communication: from the benevolent, even joyful silence he generally practices in groups to his gnomic utterances ("Here. This. Now.") and lapidary responses to the interviewer (Question: "You have been criticized by some as an activist." Answer: "Yes. We walk for peace and plant trees."). Like a powerful gravitational field, Ghosananda's quiet presence attracts talented planners and activists to carry out the details of grass-roots organizing. Finally, Wiener shows how the social *anatta* of the Cambodian *Dhammayietra* movement is manifested in the hybridity of its central practices: the nonviolent activism of the peace march is inspired by Mahatma Gandhi's *satyagraha* campaigns during the Indian independence struggle, and the determination to "speak truth to power" is inspired by nonviolent Quaker activism for human rights throughout the world.

Like the Cambodian Dhammayietra movement, the Sarvodaya Shramadana movement of Sri Lanka draws upon Gandhian principles and a deep belief in interfaith cooperation. Since its foundation in 1958 as a network of summer work camps for college students, the organization has mushroomed to more than 10,000 villages and two million volunteers. Dr

A. T. Ariyaratne, the visionary founder, conceived the movement in Buddhist terms from the start, drawing out the social implications of traditional teachings, such as the Four Noble Truths, the Five Precepts, selflessness (*anatta*) and interdependence (*paticcasamuppada*).[14] In recent years, however, according to George Bond, the influence of Hindu social activists M. K. Gandhi and Vinoba Bhave has grown increasingly prominent. Such Gandhian teachings as nonviolence (*ahimsa*), self-realization (*swaraj*), truth-force (*satya-graha*) and the contributions that all religions may make to the building of a culture of peace have been consciously embraced by the Sarvodayans. The result has been a growing focus on building a national interfaith coalition for a nonviolent end to Sri Lanka's devastating civil war. This new emphasis has been expressed in a tradition of massive peace walks, begun in 1983 and culminating most recently in March 2002, when 650,000 marchers converged on the holy city of Anuradhapura for a day of silence. Meanwhile, Dr. Ariyaratne has opened dialogues with such disparate groups as the ultra-nationalist Janatha Vimukthi Peramuna party (JVP), the violent separatist Liberation Tigers for Tamil Eelam organization (LTTE), and a wide range of Buddhist, Tamil, and Muslim communities from all social strata. In the end, said Ariyaratne, "It is only by the turn of the wheel of righteousness consisting of justice and nonviolence that the vicious circle of violence and injustice can be broken."[15]

The Buddhist Tzu-Chi (*Ciji*) Foundation of Taiwan, founded in the 1960s to provide medical services to the poor, today boasts five million members in twenty-eight countries and a US$600 million budget supporting two modern hospitals, a university, a high school, TV and other media outlets, and a range of global programs for public health and disaster relief. Founded by the Ven. Cheng-yen, a nun in the Taiwanese Pure Land tradition, Tzu-Chi manifests the hybridity of any well-established transnational, globalized non-governmental organization (NGO). Among the many culturally hybrid elements of Tzu-Chi analyzed in Julia Huang's field-based research are the founder's adaptation of Roman Catholic social-service and multinational business management practices, state-of-the-art medical technology, such as bone marrow collection, and the sophisticated use of telecommunications, including TV and Internet programming. Balancing the local adaptation of East Asian Buddhist values in places like New York, Boston, Tokyo, and Malacca are universal elements in the rapid growth of Tzu-chi in the 1990s, according to Huang: the charismatic appeal of Ven. Cheng-yen and her quintessentially Buddhist message:

> In contrast to the American idea of well-being, Tzu-chi followers are people who look for misery. Devotees tirelessly endeavor to carry out their mission across ethnic boundaries, for example, by

working among the Christian missionaries for the homeless, caring for the elders at nursing homes, and serving the local poor and non-Chinese refugees. Behind this engaged Buddhism lies the emotion of charity and compassion – an emotional commitment triggered by the personal appeal of their charismatic leader, and rooted in the Bodhisattva's compassion for all living things.

In Chapter 8, Frank Tedesco describes a much different scenario in South Korea at the beginning of the new millennium: the stirring of a handful of socially engaged revitalization movements within Buddhism, after centuries of decline. Following strong opposition to Buddhism by Confucian, Shinto, Marxist, and Christian forces in the twentieth century, Tedesco reports that only a quarter of the population remained Buddhist in 2000, with 19,000 temples competing for membership with 62,000 Christian churches. The majority of lay practitioners of this "low-status religion" are elderly women seeking success and happiness (*kipok pulgyo*), in contrast to the membership of the dominant Christian churches, made up of South Korea's leading professionals in law, medicine, education, and commerce. Social services in South Korea are provided by the national government and religious groups, with Christianity again leading the non-government sector.

Against this backdrop of steady retreat, the vitality of such groups as the Buddhist Coalition for Economic Justice, the JungTo Society, Buddhist Solidarity for Reform, and the Indra Net Life Community offers hope for the future. Addressing a wide range of social, institutional, and environmental issues, these organizations also illustrate the cultural hybridity that we see elsewhere in the world of engaged Buddhism. Such issues as fair elections, sexual equality, human rights, aid to developing countries, and environmental protection read like the agenda of hundreds of non-Buddhist NGOs outside of South Korea, both religious and secular, that seek international support for local initiatives, and local support for global engagement. On the other hand, these groups find distinctively Buddhist ways of interpreting the challenges they face and the solutions they offer. The JungTo Society, for example, consisting of ninety full-time activists, sees itself as "a community to realize 'JungTo' or *Sukhavati*, a Land of Bliss in the world, here and now." This Pure Land is further defined as the social manifestation of *anatta*, a not-self or hybrid reality:

> By understanding that myself, society, and nature are parts of one existence, interrelated with one another (non-ego) through the law of cause and effect, we can discard the concept of "mine" (non-possession) and "my thought" (non-self-assertion). Then, we may set ourselves free from any dogma, keeping our minds peaceful, consuming the least amount of resources, and sharing with others.

Therefore we are able to form a peaceful community with good relations among people, and create a world with harmony and balance between human beings and nature.

Finally, among the Asian narratives of engaged Buddhism, in Chapter 9, Leslie Alldritt's account of recent efforts to rehabilitate Japan's untouchables, the Burakumin, makes a sobering footnote. Called "polluted' (*eta*) "village people" (*burakumin*), members of the Japanese underclass are treated in many quarters as "non-persons" (*hinin*) and "animals" (*yotsu*). Paradoxically, the oppression of the Burakumin, who are traditionally Buddhist, may date back to the introduction of Buddhist vegetarianism to Japan in the sixth century, the subsequent rise of social discrimination based on notions of dietary and ritual purity, and the introduction of Indian Mahayana literature depicting a class of people called "hedonist" (Sanskrit. *icchantika*, Japanese *issendai*), perverse libertines who transgress the ten perfections and practice the ten evils. By 1868, as Japan emerged from international isolation, Buddhist temples perpetuated the inferiority of the Burakumin through discriminatory temple rituals, ancestor registries and tomb inscriptions. While the government took action in 1871 to outlaw discrimination (*sabetsu*) and to rename the Burakumin *shin heimin* ("new common people"),[16] the Buddhists have taken longer to acknowledge and reverse centuries of oppressive treatment. Alldritt believes that hybrid models from outside Japan, such as the liberation theologies of Latin American Catholicism, the African-American civil rights movement in the United States (inspired by evangelical Christianity), and the Dalit liberation movement in India (inspired in part by Ambedkar's engaged Buddhism) may be needed to jump-start the nascent Burakumin movement. Yet indigenous resources, such as the Buddhist teaching of Original Enlightenment (*hongaku*), and the Pure Land emphasis on Amida's divine compassion for the lowest persons may be sufficient to inspire and motivate a new generation of activists.

In these reports of recent Asian Buddhist social engagement, we see abundant traces of what I have called *social anatta*: the near-universal cultural hybridity that has resulted from the globalization of ideas and values, particularly those associated with civil society, human rights, and environmentalism. We thus encounter a paradox in Derek Jeffreys' argument for the centrality of the not-self teaching in Buddhist ethics. While human rights cannot be ascribed as a fixed possession or attribute to an abiding, essential self, as the Ven. Payutto maintains, neither can Buddhism itself be fixed and essentialized in time and space with respect to the moral and ethical teachings that Buddhists practice. Rather, engaged Buddhism, like the myriad Buddhisms of the past, is being reconstructed of *non-Buddhist* elements, drawn from local customs and practices and from the increasingly borderless flow of information and lifestyles. Thus human rights, civil society, democratic due process, gender equality and environmental sustainability are now believed to be compatible with Buddhist teachings.[17] Yet the interweaving of these ideas and actions into the fabric of the Buddhist symbol system requires creativity and courage – the courage to carry the Dharma into situations formerly dominated by secular or non-Buddhist sectarian interests.

Impermanence and creativity: engaged Buddhism in the West

The third mark of existence in the traditional formulation of the *ti-lakkhana* – and the master principle of Buddhist metaphysics – is the law of universal flux, change, and impermanence, *aniccata* (adjective: *anicca*). Illustrating the pervasiveness of this teaching in the Middle Length Sayings (*Majjima Nikaya, MN*) of the Buddha – and its application in all realms and levels of experience – Bhikkhu Bodhi writes:

> Impermanence, in the Buddhist view, comprises the totality of conditioned existence, ranging in scale from the cosmic to the microscopic. At the far end of the spectrum the Buddha's vision reveals a universe of immense dimensions evolving and disintegrating in repetitive cycles throughout beginningless time – "many aeons of world-contraction, many aeons of world-expansion, many aeons of world-contraction and expansion" (*MN* 4.27). In the middle range the mark of impermanence comes to manifestation in our inescapable mortality, our condition be being bound to ageing, sickness, and death (*MN* 26.5), of possessing a body that is subject "to being worn and rubbed away, to dissolution and disintegration" (*MN* 74.9). And at the close end of the spectrum, the Buddha's teaching discloses the radical impermanence uncovered only by sustained attention to experience in its living immediacy: the fact that all the constituents of our being, bodily and mental, are in constant process, arising and passing away in rapid succession from moment to moment without any persistent underlying substance. In the very act of observation they are undergoing "destruction, vanishing, fading away, and ceasing" (*MN* 74.11).[18]

This Buddhist process philosophy may be favorably compared in its breadth and depth to counterparts in Western philosophy and science, notably the teachings of Heraclitus (a contemporary of the Buddha) and Aristotle, the Neoplatonists of the early Common Era, and, in modern times, the intellectual heirs of Charles Darwin, Alfred North Whitehead and John Dewey. But Buddhism may be distinguished from these systems by the perennial *narrowness* of its soteriological project: not merely to account for the nature and dynamics of what Whitehead called "process and reality," but to relieve the suffering of living beings by pointing the way through the flux of existence. A paradoxical, but powerful, formulation of this Buddhist goal is offered by Peter Harvey:

> While impermanence often leads to suffering, it also means that people, having no fixed Self, are always capable of change for the better, and should be respected accordingly, rather than dismissed as unworthy by saying, for example, "Oh, *he's* a thief".[19]

For engaged Buddhism, Harvey's insight may be enlarged: "While impermanence often leads to suffering, it also means that *societies*, having no fixed character, are always capable of change for the better, and should be respected accordingly." And for the study of the history of religions, including Buddhism, the formula might be enlarged again: "While impermanence often leads to suffering, it also means that *religious traditions*, having no fixed character, are always capable of change for the better, and should be respected accordingly."

This is precisely the issue that Thomas Yarnall raises in the final critique in this volume, "Engaged Buddhism: New and Improved?" In Chapter 15, Yarnall divides commentators on the history of engaged Buddhism into those who stress its continuity with Buddhist teachings and practices of the past (the "traditionists") and those who find significant innovation, creativity, and hybridity in its mix of Buddhist and non-Buddhist elements (the "modernists"). He sums up the position of the modernists in five points: (1) traditional Buddhism has not been socially engaged; (2) the modern world faces unprecedented socio-political problems; (3) western socio-political theory presents new solutions that "must" be adopted by engaged Buddhism; (4) traditional Buddhism does not offer viable models for engagement; and (5) Buddhism's latent potential for social engagement is activated by its accommodation to modern ideas.

Yarnall's profile of the modernist commentators on Buddhism is richly illustrated by the three chapters in our "Western Frontiers" section. While not all of the contributors would agree with every point in his profile (modern ideas are certainly not obligatory for Buddhist engagement, as we have seen), most would be comfortable with the general contours of Yarnall's picture. Here *anicca* may be seen in the adaptations which engaged Buddhists have wrought in the face of globalization, racism, and the brutality of prison life. We see the "parallel worlds" of a western dharma center and a traditional monastery in central Burma, collaborating on the meaning of "suffering," "development," "engagement," and "community" (Kirkley); the struggle of Western convert *sanghas* in Britain and the United States to meet the cultural and social needs of minority communities with ties to Asia, Africa, and the Caribbean (Smith); and the conscious adaptation of traditional Buddhist symbols and narratives by prison chaplains in the criminal justice system in the USA. In each case the Buddhist actors find a balance – reminiscent of the founder's Middle Way – between accommodation to and initiation of novelty in a fluid social environment.

Harriet Kirkley grounds her discussion of the collaboration of Vipassana Hawaii and Kyaswa Monastery in the Sagaing Hills of central Burma by defining Buddhism as a technique for quenching *dukkha* (following Santikaro Bhikkhu), and Buddhists as those who act in the spirit of the three refuges. This stipulation makes it possible to consider the creativity and hybridity that result when "parallel worlds" (Paul Numrich's term for East–West co-existence in Buddhism)[20] collide and interpenetrate. Kirkley describes MettaDana, an American-funded, socially engaged Buddhist development program offering medical, educational, and economic assistance to the hill people served by the monastery. The services include a fifty-bed hospital and outpatient clinic for monks, nuns and villagers, a nurses-aid training program and an American acupuncturist (a wildly popular example of "pizza-effect" hybridity);[21] a TB control project targeting 3,000 villagers and 7,000 monks and nuns; a primary school serving 250–300 students; road construction and water purification projects; and monument preservation and restoration. In exchange, the Burmese provide meditation instruction and spiritual guidance for Western students and retreatants in Hawaii and the Sagaing Hills. Lest the bargain seem unequal, Kirkley stresses the interdependence of the Burmese and American contributions, taking their synergy as axiomatic for engaged Buddhism:

> As actively engaged Buddhists know too well, Western ideology and social visions have no corner on the issues of modernity that face the entire planet. Still less does Western ideology have solutions to problems that we, in large measure, have created. The attempt to respond to modernity in all its protean forms affects us all, West and East alike. Indeed, socially engaged Buddhism as it exists in the West at present seeks either to act locally (somewhere on the planet) within a Buddhist framework and/or to bring Buddhist perspectives to bear on the problems created by a predominantly Western ideology of technology and secularism.

In her study of African, Caribbean, and Asian diasporas in the English-speaking West, Sharon Smith, in Chapter 10, explores possible causes of their under-representation among the predominantly white Buddhist convert sanghas that have emerged since the middle of the last century. In order to demonstrate the complexity of the problem, she reviews several intersecting historical trajectories: the transmission of Asian Buddhism by Asian missionaries and immigrants since the nineteenth century; the emergence of a distinctive Western Buddhism emphasizing Euro-American values of individualism (the Reformist Luther), autonomy (the Enlightenment Kant), and self-reliance (the Romantic Emerson); and the rising awareness of diaspora communities of African, Caribbean, and non-Buddhist Asian descent, who emphasize the experience of self not in reaction to society, but as "a nexus of social relations." The prominence of family and community values within minority communities of color contrasts with the eccentricity and alienation that social surveys have found among converts to Asian and New Age religions.[22] Furthermore, the issues that motivate engaged Buddhists in the West – who are largely of Euro-American ethnicity – such as human rights, ecology, and peace, contrast with the political passions of the minority communities, such as criminal justice, community safety, education, and access to healthcare and employment.

To address the cultural mismatches and disconnects experienced by communities of color and the new Buddhisms of the West, Smith suggests four approaches to diversity: (1) education to raise awareness of differences and commonalities among the groups in question, including informed and balanced reporting in the media; (2) peer support for people of color within Buddhist sanghas, where, in the words of Lewis Woods of the Buddhist Peace Fellowship, "black folks can go to study and practice the dharma without having to deal with racism and Eurocentric assumptions, attitudes, and behaviors"; (3) outreach initiatives such as the London-based orientation sessions for black people (particularly popular among African-Caribbean women and South Asian men) sponsored by the Friends of the Western Buddhist Order (FWBO), and the numerous overtures to members of the African-American and Latino communities by Soka Gakkai International in the United States (SGI-USA); and (4) social action programs targeted to minorities, such as clinics and counseling services for Latina women, and public school programs dealing with issues of diversity, social equity, and race, sponsored by the Buddhist Peace Fellowship (BPF) and its affiliate, the Buddhist Alliance for Social Engagement (BASE).

The Buddhist prison ministries documented by Virginia Cohn Parkum and J. Anthony Stultz in Chapter 12 might well be added to Smith's list of initiatives to the minority communities of Britain and North America, given the over-representation of minority men serving prison sentences in both societies. Again we witness the innovation, adaptation, and creativity of engaged Buddhism in a context of rapid social change and harsh suffering, and in so doing we confront a question that Kenneth Kraft posed at the end of *Engaged Buddhism in the West*, "When do fresh interpretations, often in the service of engagement, distort Buddhism's past inauthentically?"[23] Parkum and Stultz argue that this question must be applied to the rereadings of traditional Buddhist figures invoked in prison rituals and meditations today, including the serial killer Angulimala, the misguided Prince Ajatasatru, the falsely incarcerated Queen Vaidehi, the sorcerer-turned-saint Milarepa, and the wrathful deity Fudo. To the guidelines offered by other practitioners of the new Buddhist homilitics, or theory of preaching, Parkum and Stultz offer two of their own: "(1) Is the use of hellish-looking images and stories about criminal behavior effective in the prison setting?" and "(2) Are they used in ways that are faithful to their content and intent: are the translation and re-telling accurate and are they used in a way consistent with the Buddha's teaching methodology?" Following their participant-observer accounts of prison hermeneutics-in-action, the authors conclude that:

> [using] stories of people with criminal histories or those affected by crime goes back to the very roots of Buddhism, the original sangha and the Buddha's teachings and teaching methodology. These narratives are as forceful now as they were when they were first told in the various traditions.

In a final example of the freedom with which engaged Buddhists reinvent their tradition, we note that these Buddhist chaplains have adapted their stories to serve a population that was expressly excluded from the community of monks by the ancient Vinaya code: persons convicted of violent crimes, including those who were disfigured by physical punishments and those who had escaped their confinement. Along with debtors, slaves, children, pregnant or nursing women, and persons with physical and mental disabilities, the ancient sangha considered criminals unfit for advanced Buddhist practice because their presence might disrupt or endanger the sangha or place it at odds with political authorities. Here again we witness the inventiveness of engaged Buddhists – their embrace and transformation of impermanence – as a marginalized and disempowered group cited for exclusion from the ancient sangha is now the object of intense interest by Buddhist social workers and political activists. And here again we find a new focus for Buddhist soteriology: compassion for those whose humanity is systematically abridged by conditions and forces that lie outside their control.[24]

Tradition and modernity

In the final critique of this volume, Thomas Yarnall reflects on the challenges of history and methodology confronting interpreters of engaged Buddhism. As we have seen, Yarnall terms those who hold that Buddhism has always been engaged with social and political realities "traditionists." For them, Buddhist engagement flows from the Buddha's teachings on poverty and caste in society, from the early sangha's experience as a social institution, and from the later Mahayana's ethical universalism, exemplified in the bodhisattva's vow to save all beings. For the traditionists – activists such as the Dalai Lama, Thich Nhat Hanh, Sulak Sivaraksa, Joanna Macy, and Bernard Glassman, and academics such as Robert Thurman of Columbia University and Yarnall himself – engaged Buddhism is not "new and improved," but consistent with its long history as a comprehensive path of liberation, open to all who would participate.

One the other hand, Yarnall describes as "modernists" those who argue that the patterns of service and activism we call engaged Buddhism today are indeed "new and improved," responsive to unprecedented historical conditions, and arising from global interactions that have blended material, political, and cultural values of Asian and Western societies in modern times. This construction is not altogether harmless, Yarnall warns, for these modernists – practitioners and academics such as Gary Snyder, Joseph Kitagawa, Richard Gombrich, Cynthia Eller, Kenneth Kraft, and myself – may be guilty of unconscious, if not intentional "orientalism" and "neo-colonialism," sharing the assumptions that Asian Buddhists are incapable of navigating social change without help from the West, and that notions such as "social suffering," "human rights," and "civil society" are un-Buddhist ideas that must be credited to Western thinkers.

Among the scholars whom Yarnall cites in favor of traditionism is Bardwell Smith, a respected historian of Buddhism and politics in Theravada societies. In a review of *Engaged Buddhism: Buddhist Liberation Movements in Asia*, Smith questions:

> the overly sharp distinction that is made between modern forms of Buddhist engagement, however unprecedented many of their features may be, and those that have occurred over the centuries, almost as if there were no prophetic or deeply engaged precursors in Buddhist history.

He wishes that scholars of engaged Buddhism would offer "serious, even if brief, attention to a few major examples of premodern Buddhists whose involvements with the social order was a protracted concern with issues of social justice."[25] Like Yarnall, Smith does not indicate who he may have in mind – other than Nichiren, whose career and legacy were treated in the earlier book, and who, we learn in Stone's chapter below, was not interested in social justice.

It is true that few scholars have taken up Yarnall's and Smith's challenge to find ancient precursors of contemporary Buddhist service and activism. The opening chapters of this volume were solicited in hopes that examples of premodern Buddhist voices for peace, justice, and freedom – today's universal ideals, shared by engaged Buddhists – may be found. As we have seen, Jenkins, Zelinski, and Stone find rich examples of compassionate altruism in ancient India and medieval Japan, where poverty, disease, and disaster were at least as common as they are today. But the kinds of circumstances that mobilize modern-day engaged Buddhists did not preoccupy the writers of canonical Buddhist literature: struggles against commercial and political adversaries (Thailand and Cambodia), against widespread economic and social injustice (Taiwan, South Korea and Japan), and against racism, classism, and war (the Western studies). Furthermore, the collective methods, strategies, and technologies employed to relieve social suffering by engaged Buddhists in the Asian and Western studies presented here are seldom if ever attested or prefigured in traditional Buddhist literature: boycotts and peace marches, tree ordinations and farmer collectives, medical and educational systems, and direct challenges to official policy and state power. In the end we must conclude, paradoxically, that Bardwell Smith was correct in 1972 when he wrote:

> The primary goal of Buddhism is not a stable order or a just society but the discovery of genuine freedom (or awakening) by each person. It has never been asserted that the conditions of society are unimportant or unrelated to this more important goal, but it is critical to stress the distinction between what is primary and what is not. For Buddhists to lose this distinction is to transform their tradition into something discontinuous with its original and historic essence. Even the vocation of the bodhisatta is not as a social reformer but as the catalyst to personal transformation within society.[26]

Here Smith clearly supports the position of the modernists in identifying personal awakening, in contrast to social change, as the principal goal of traditional Asian Buddhism. By this reading, the engaged Buddhism manifested in the case studies in this volume and its predecessors, is indeed a transformation of the tradition "into something discontinuous with its original and historical essence." The shift is so palpable – like Jenkins' "Copernican flip" from Hinayana individualism to Mahayana altruism – that Smith's observation about traditional Buddhism might be reworded to reflect the emergent world-view of engaged Buddhism. The primary goal of engaged Buddhism today *is* a stable order and a just society, seen as *necessary or prior conditions* for the discovery of genuine freedom (or awakening) by each person. It is never asserted by engaged Buddhists that individual freedom and awakening are unimportant or unrelated to social justice, human rights, and environmental protection, but it is critical to stress the distinction between immediate and long-term objectives.

It is here that the classical teaching of the three marks of existence, applied reflexively to the tradition itself, offers further guidance. For the characteristic elements of Buddhism, present in both traditionist and modernist readings of socially engaged practice, mirror more general patterns of experience: the focus on suffering wherever it may be found (in oneself, in one's community, and throughout society and the world); the inventiveness of crafting skillful means to meet the changing conditions of time and place; the hybridity of cultural borrowing, mutual assimilation, and adaptation that occurs when the Dharma is transported, transmitted, and transposed from one society to another; and the sense of dislocation, alienation, and groundlessness that follows as Buddhist immigrants, converts, pilgrims, refugees, missionaries, deposed leaders, reformers, scholars, exiled teachers, and simple practitioners attempt to practice or to interpret the ancient teachings in new circumstances. In all of these we find eloquent testimony to the truths of impermanence, suffering, and not-self.

In writing about the emergence and phenomenology of engaged Buddhism, I have attempted to introduce a number of critical definitions, frames of reference, and historical constructions. In the Introduction to *Engaged Buddhism: Buddhist Liberation Movements in Asia* (1996), I examined transformations of leadership, ideology, and institutionalization (under the rubrics of Buddha, Dharma, and Sangha), as exemplified in the book's nine case studies, and argued that patterns of social engagement have emerged since the late nineteenth century as a result of the vigorous interaction of Asian, European, and American values in the post-colonial era. Similarly, I argued that engaged Buddhism cannot be traced to a primitive counterculture committed to social reform from below (which never existed), nor to the power politics of a Buddhist state committed to social change from above (which has existed for centuries in Asia). Rather, the engaged Buddhism of the twentieth and twenty-first centuries has taken the form of an unprecedented counterculture: local, voluntary associations, regional and international networks, and globalized NGOs committed to service and activism. These agencies have sometimes existed apart from mainstream Buddhist sects, temples and associations, which remain committed to "personal transformation," or they have remained within the fold, seeing the personal and the social as deeply interconnected.

In *Engaged Buddhism in the West* (2000), I argued that social transformation is a relatively new objective for Buddhism, while it has been central to other religious traditions for millennia. I presented several ways of classifying the activities and attitudes of engaged Buddhist leaders and groups, including Ken Jones's contrast of the *soft-enders* who trust in the ripple effects of one-to-one influence in launching a peaceful society, and the *hard-enders* who are committed, quietly or militantly, to "influencing public policy and establishing new institutional forms." I proposed four emergent and cumulative styles of Buddhist ethics (discipline, virtue, altruism, engagement), and speculated that engaged Buddhism may represent the appearance of a *fourth yana* – a practice vehicle of service and activism – in contrast to the three earlier *yanas* based on monastic renunciation (Hinayana), lay-based altruism (Mahayana), and priest-based ritualism (Vajrayana).[27]

While these formulations may be useful to some readers in interpreting the growing record of engaged Buddhism, I suspect that an important point may have been lost in a thicket of distinctions (one reviewer called my analysis "three of this and four of that," an observation that might be made of traditional Buddhist exposition). The point is this: while political activism – not social service – is, in my view, the distinctive innovation of engaged Buddhism in the twentieth century (Jenkins traces altruistic service all the way back, as we have seen), the term "engaged Buddhism" makes the most sense when applied to both categories, activism and service. I still hold that the ethics of altruistic service is different from the ethics of engagement, manifested in activism to reform or abolish the social systems that cause suffering. But by excluding altruistic service from the definition of engaged Buddhism – and by stressing political over social forms of engagement – I was perhaps too hasty in speculating that engaged Buddhism, *tout court*, first appeared in the religious activism of Henry Steel Olcott and Anagarika Dharmapala in the late nineteenth century.[28] And by presenting Olcott, Dharmapala, and the later Ambedkar as harbingers of the prophetic and reformist activism of Thich Quang Duc and the other clergy who immolated themselves for peace in Vietnam – the activism that prompted Thich Nhat Hanh to coin the expression "engaged Buddhism" in the 1960s – I may have under-estimated the scope of public activities that contemporary Buddhists included in their notion of spiritual practice.

Orientalism and the Fourth *Yana*

In his detailed critique of recent studies of the history and practice of engaged Buddhism, Yarnall argues that modernists exhibit what may be an unconscious "Theravadin" bias toward Buddhist history, seeing only the personal striving of the "individual vehicle" (the Hinayana), and not the social implications of the "universal vehicle" (the Mahayana) and its vow to save "all beings." Yet I and others he cites in this discussion have regularly and impartially scanned the Theravada, Mahayana, and Vajrayana traditions for examples of engagement in the past as well as the present. We have found that past examples are as scarce as recent examples are abundant, from Dr. Ariyaratne's Sarvodaya Shramadana movement in Sri Lanka (Theravada), to the Nichiren and Pure Land reformist and service organizations in Japan, Taiwan, and Korea (Mahayana), to the Dalai Lama and the Tibetan struggle in Asia and the West (Vajrayana).

Moreover, by arguing that the new Buddhism entails a shift from other-worldly values ("enlightenment," "buddhahood," a better rebirth or no rebirth, for example) to the mundane values of clean water and air, death with dignity for AIDS patients, or a political system in which citizens can vote for their leaders (an oft-stated goal of such disparate figures as Ambedkar, the Dalai Lama, Daisaku Ikeda, and Aung San Suu Kyi), I do not side with one kind of Buddhism over another, or promote any sectarian expression of Buddhist engagement over another. I and others have suggested, rather, that an unprecedented Buddhism, in which collective goals are considered to be as important or more important than personal transformation, is at hand. This is Fourth Yana Buddhism, spontaneously named the *Navayana* or "new vehicle" by Ambedkar in answer to a reporter's question in 1956, but generally called "engaged Buddhism" today.

In a serious charge, Yarnall compares the modernist interpreters of engaged Buddhism with orientalists and post-colonialists who in the past have viewed Asians as culturally inferior and dependent upon the West. He disparages the "entrenched neo-colonial, neo-Orientalist bias among Buddhologists" who are overly concerned with textual exegesis (over other kinds of evidence), who privilege ancient texts over "living oral interpretations ... disregarding contemporary Asian Buddhists' own understandings of their texts (let alone their overall tradition)," and who place philosophy over the ritual and (by extension) social-political activities of Buddhists. Furthermore, modernist western interpreters "have constructed a disengaged history for Buddhism in order to appropriate for themselves the title of 'inventor of engaged Buddhism.'" This "unavowed colonial stance" often involves a three-fold process of recognizing and appropriating selected elements of Buddhist history for their arguments, and then "distancing" themselves from the Buddhist "other" by claiming superior learning. Such interpreters conclude that:

> the socially transformative power potentially *latent* in Asian Buddhism can only transform society when mediated through the Western modernists' socio-political theories, with the Western modernist serving as the intermediary between East and West, both as strategist and social activist.[29]

I believe that readers of this volume and its predecessors will encounter western scholars who have approached the study of Buddhism, ancient and modern, with sincere interest, respect, and – a word not often used in the study of religion – *appreciation*. Professional students of Buddhism, it seems to me, are not unlike most other scholars of religion: they are not neutral in their approach to their subject, but neither are they blinded by prejudice or by feelings of superiority. In a lead article in the *Journal of the*

American Academy of Religion, Thomas A. Tweed argues that religion scholars may be compared to transnational migrants – such as the immigrants and missionaries that carried Buddhism from India to South-east, Central, and East Asia in ancient and medieval times, and to the West in modern times. Religion scholars "cross over" to the perspectives of their subjects in their efforts to understand their unfamiliar cultural languages and practices. Then they cross back to their own assumptions and categories in their efforts to communicate what they have experienced. (Or, as in the case of our use of the "marks of existence" and other traditional formulae, they may attempt to find felicitous use of their subjects' own categories.) Tweed argues that scholars cannot be "everywhere and nowhere," disembodied God's eyes in the sky. On the other hand, their location, their situatedness, cannot be fully pinned down: they are always moving back and forth in their quest for understanding. He summarizes his "translocative theory of interpretation" as follows:

> First, religion scholars, when they generate theory and when they write case studies, are situated. Second, we usually stand in an epistemologically and morally ambivalent site. Third, any theory of interpretation that stills the ongoing process by locating the scholar in *any* fixed position – here or there, inside or outside, even between – misrepresents scholarly practice. Finally, by studying transnational migration and diasporic religion we learn more than we might have imagined. Transnational migrants, who use religious symbols to continually transport themselves back and forth, offer us some illuminating hints about where we are when we do our work.[30]

Of the dozens of scholars who have written on engaged Buddhism in recent years, many have lived abroad, some were born abroad, and some have participated as Buddhists in the activities that they chronicle in their work. They know better than to feel superior to their subjects, for they have confronted their own ignorance in attempting to grasp the ideas and events they witness. On the other hand, many engaged Buddhists, of both Asian and Western descent, perfectly exemplify the cultural hybridity that Tweed has written about and that I have attempted to highlight here and in earlier accounts. My favorite paradigm in this regard is that of Dr. B. R. Ambedkar (1891–1956), the Dalit ("untouchable") leader, who was appointed as law minister to Nehru's first cabinet and served as the principal draftsman of the Indian Constitution. As a convert to Buddhism, Ambedkar freely chose to read his studies under American philosopher and Columbia professor John Dewey – as well as other Western and Indian writers – back into his account of Buddhism. In so doing, he consciously formulated a new, pragmatic and socially engaged Buddhism, one that has resonated powerfully with the sensibilities of millions of his Dalit followers, the largest group of converts to Buddhism in the twentieth century.[31]

Similar examples of Asian Buddhist leaders who have chosen – again freely, not at neo-colonialist gunpoint – to integrate elements of social and political thought, historical analysis, and scientific theory from many sources, Western as well as Asian, may be readily found. We live in a globalizing world in which the old charges of orientalism and neo-colonialism break down precisely because the "others" – Asians, Africans, Latinos, women, gays, lesbians, transgendered persons, the disabled and the incarcerated – are not passive subjects of the white, male, western gaze, but actors who *look back*. They also *talk back* and *act back* by appropriating and adapting the products and services of the West that suit their purposes – technology, political alliances, business partnerships, manufactured goods, and, most critically for our purposes, the "intellectual property" of Western scholars of history, literature, science, and religion.

In this light it is fitting to propose that modern engaged Buddhism began, not when the American Colonel Olcott and the European Madame Blavatsky arrived in Columbo on May 25, 1880 to support the Singhalese Buddhist struggle against Protestant missionaries (as I have previously suggested) – but seven years earlier, in 1873 at Panadura, when the eloquent Ven. Mohottivatte Gunananda defeated the white evangelists in a two-day, open-air debate before an audience of ten thousand Buddhist laymen and women. But in suggesting such a birth scenario, it must be recalled that the story did not end there, for the Buddhist activists went on to embrace the Theosophists from New York. Within a year of Olcott's arrival, another lineage head of the Sinhalese Sangha, Hikkaduve Sumangala, had given his imprimatur to Olcott's *Buddhist Catachism*, a boldly modernist reading of the Dharma.[32] So the questions arise: who embraced whom, who exploited whom, and who manipulated whom in the Sinhalese struggle for hearts, minds, and social progress? Do the school children who honor Olcott and his Sinhalese protégé, Anagarika Dharmapala, as national heros in the annual school holidays that bear their names, see them as cultural exploiters, manipulators or victims? As Thomas Tweed wrote in 1999 with specific reference to the globalization of Buddhism, the history of religion manifests "hybridity all the way down."[33]

Whither engaged Buddhism?

In his Introduction to *Buddhism and Politics in 20th Century Asia*, Ian Harris offers a framework for our final observations regarding the prospects of engaged Buddhism:

It is difficult to point to any part of the contemporary Buddhist world that has not been massively transformed by at least one aspect of modernity, be it colonialism, industrialization, telecommunications, consumerism, ultra-individualism, or totalitarianism of the left or right. In this radically new situation Buddhists have been forced to adapt or risk the possibility of substantial decline. There is plenty of evidence ... of significant Buddhist involvement in anti-colonial movements, particularly since the Second World War. Similarly, new or revamped Buddhist organizations with strongly nationalist, reformist, social-activist, therapeutic or reactionary-fundamentalist character are much in evidence throughout the 20th century.[34]

In this snapshot of the struggle between tradition and modernity, we can see the stark options that Buddhism faces – adaptation or decline – and the great range of adaptations or "involvements" that the struggle has generated. These tend to move in a great circle from anti-colonial and nationalist (conservative) movements, to reformist (liberal) and social-activist (radical) movements, back around to therapeutic (individualist/libertarian) and fundamentalist (reactionary) movements. It will be immediately apparent that not all of these "involvements" qualify as "engagement" by our definition. Indeed, Harris's collection focuses on the complex evolution and interaction of large-scale religious and state institutions in ten historically Buddhist countries – what Buddhist activist Sulak Sivaraksa calls "capital-B Buddhism."[35] Nevertheless, the snapshot paragraph above serves equally well to locate the world of the "small-b" Buddhist movements that we have studied, from local and regional dharma organizations to international NGOs that struggle "from below" for peace, justice, freedom, and environmental sustainability.

What will become of these groups and movements in the coming years? The present book, *Action Dharma*, grew out of an innovative technology for revealing and advancing the study of contemporary life – the Internet-based online conference. As a virtual meeting place for scholars, Buddhist practitioners, and laypersons who have reflected on the state of Buddhism today, the conference may be considered a barometer of the global discussion on engaged Buddhism that was underway at the turn of the twenty-first century. It may also be thought of as a way of forecasting some of the themes and issues that will most likely dominate the discussion, if not the practice, of engaged Buddhism in the future. Thus in closing with reflections on the prospects of engaged Buddhism, let us draw upon some of the electronic messages ("posts") that enlivened the week of the conference, April 7–14, 2000.

The challenge of engaged Buddhism and its interpretation begins with the problem of definition. Which Buddhists are "engaged" and how do their attitudes and actions differentiate them from other Buddhists who are, shall we say, "involved" or "devoted"? I have argued that "action dharma" is the dharma of social service and activism, premised on the belief that suffering is not only the result of individual karma, and that its remediation requires collective effort. In an early post to the conference, Scott C. Hurley called engaged Buddhism "a vibrant and thriving movement in which social action is not defined in terms of Buddhist concepts and practice, but instead just the opposite applies: Buddhist doctrine and praxis are reconceptualized in terms of social action." As an example, Hurley recommended consideration of the Tzu Chi (*Ciji*) Compassionate Relief Foundation of Taiwan (a recommendation that led to our discovery of Julia Huang's just-completed doctoral work on Tzu Chi at Boston University, and her agreement to contribute to this book). Behind Tzu Chi, according to Hurley, is the thought of the Chinese scholar-monk Yin Shun (b. 1906 and active in the 1950s), who emphasized the notions of *renjian fojiao*, "Buddhism in the human realm," and *renjian jingtu*, "founding the Pure Land in the human realm."

> Both of these ideas were an attempt to rationalize Buddhism by bringing the focus away from rebirth in the other realms and from rebirth in a transcendent Pure Land and instead placing it within the "here and now" – the human realm.

This immanentist soteriology is perfectly captured in the popular saying of Tzu Chi's founder, the nun Cheng-yen, "Just do it!" – that is, in every situation, practice the ancient Mahayana virtue of generosity (*dana*), "the most fundamental form of Buddhist practice."[36]

A number of participants echoed Hurley's notion of the primacy of activism over traditional Buddhist doctrines and rituals. Susan Darlington, epitomizing her study of the environmental monks in rural Thailand, wrote:

> [activist monks] rarely stop to think through in depth the philosophical or scriptural bases of their work ... [They] are not really concerned with the question of tradition versus innovation. They are, rather, concerned with the suffering people face in their lives today.[37]

Harriet Kirkley, another author at the conference and in this volume, wrote, "In my case, meditation came second. As a frontline HIV volunteer in the 1980s, I learned samadhi meditation from a Hindu lineage taught by a western hospital psychiatrist as part of teaching, yes, stress management!" Eventually, she discovered Buddhist meditation and found that it strengthened her effectiveness as a health care worker.[38] Dr. Colin Butler, co-founder of the Benevolent Organization for Development, Health, and Insight (BODHI), a Buddhist-inspired grant-maker in Tasmania, Australia, asks:

> What is mindfulness? Is it just taste and sensation? If I eat at McDonald's or purchase Nestlé's chocolate, am I mindful of the McLibel case or the shameless exploitation by Nestlé of breast-feeding mothers in poor countries? Go deeper. If I eat a banana grown in the Caribbean am I aware of the struggle for better working conditions by Caribbean workers against the fruit cartels? Do I reflect on the way American and Caribbean economic development, which also helped fuel the industrial revo-lution in Britain, was in large part based on the trans-Atlantic slave trade?

Once a Buddhist recognizes that "the suffering embedded in most products and technologies illustrates the first noble truth," writes Dr. Butler, "an appropriate response means engaging in political action," adding that "to refrain from political action is itself, in a way, to be political, because passivity enables those with power to act with impunity."[39]

Not all conferees concurred with Butler and the activists who stressed political engagement first – or on the nature of the problems to be engaged. John Foster wrote:

> If the base reality of the world we perceive around us is blank (read empty) and our minds are "projecting" onto this blankness on the basis of our past actions (karmic seeds), then there can never be a clear division between things inside and things outside.

Consequently, "daily private meditation (especially on compassion for others), harmony with people immediately around me, and checking up on my own motivation, are all a foundation for socially active work on bigger issues. Yes, the balance is very important."[40] Michele Daniel added that "seeing both personal practice and social engagement as *metta* or *maitri* [loving-kindness] practice ... it becomes much clearer that the dividing line between the two is not only blurry, but in fact, has only an illusory exis-tence."[41] Steven Evans agreed that the line between personal devotion or ritual, particularly chanting practice, and social action cannot be easily drawn. Chanting for loving-kindness, for example, is "calling forth the magic power of benefit for all ... to recite and to act are one as well." Even those "who recite and do not act" may be shaping communal structures and awareness by their piety.[42]

Perhaps the strongest advocate of a non-material interpretation of Buddhist suffering and engagement was Peter D. Hershock, the author of a conference paper, "Changing the Way Society Changes: Transposing Social Activism into a Dramatic Key," and two related books, *Liberating Intimacy: Enlightenment and Social Virtuosity in Ch'an Buddhism* (1996) and *Reinventing the Wheel: A Buddhist Response to the Information Age* (1999). Hershock regards the Buddhist *dukkha* and its quenching as profoundly spiritual and profoundly communal:

> The individual body suffers pain and death only in a metaphorical sense. It is always directly in the patterns of relationship character- ized, for example, as familial, as communal, or as friendly that suffering arises and, hopefully, is resolved... Tripping and falling down is painful. But if we're tripped by a "best friend," skinned knees are not the real problem. Suffering occurs because the *meaning* of our friendship is thrown into doubt and we are not sure why or what to do about it... If Buddhist practice aims, then, at opening meaningful pathways around narrative impasses, whenever and wherever they occur, it consists most centrally of cultivating *dramatic virtuosity*: skill in improvising meaningful – and not merely factual – solutions to problems.[43]

Hershock's interactionist model resonated for many conference partici- pants who, like Mushim Ikeda-Nash, a frequent contributor to *Turning Wheel: The Journal of Socially Engaged Buddhism* (published by the Buddhist Peace Fellowship in Berkeley, California), found his use of the terms "attention," "appreciation," "creativity," and "uniquely realized and meaningful virtuosity" instrumental in "bridging scholarly analysis, practice-based experience, and social engagement."[44]

Other observers, however, worried that overly spiritualized or intellec- tualized readings of suffering and its cure missed the essence of the new Buddhism. Santikaro Bhikkhu, the American monk and activist who was trained and lived in Thailand for twenty years, distinguished *metta* cultiva- tion through chanting, reflection, and visualization and *metta* cultivation through direct service and activism, recommending "a harmonious mix of the two." But he went on to warn that social engagement often incurs dangers more severe than a skinned knee and hurt feelings. Recalling Susan Darlington's post on the political repression of environmental monks and lay activist Sulak Sivaraksa's periods of incarceration and exile for criticizing the Thai government, Santikaro reminded the conference:

> Many monks – perhaps as many as 1,000 – were killed by the Thai government in the 1970s for suspected communist sympa- thies. Grassroots monks remember these facts. There is still much

fear in the Thai Sangha. Powerful politicians, who are often inseparable from organized crime, can have people killed quite easily.[45]

Engaged Buddhism, in other words, cannot be reduced to a series of social propositions, spiritual exercises, or personal feelings.

Some participants chose to address historical and ideological problems related to the evolution of Buddhist ethics. Co-editor Damien Keown, an organizer of the conference and an authority on Buddhist social ethics (*The Nature of Buddhist Ethics*, 1992; *Contemporary Buddhist Ethics*, 2002), noted that the case for a Buddhist ethic of engagement is not easy to make "because it is something relatively new and unfamiliar." He explains:

> Traditional Buddhist texts do talk about this sort of thing, for example, when they say that the ideal ruler should rule justly and distribute goods to those in need ... However, these ideas are not very clearly worked out beyond a rather rudimentary level, so how these principles should operate in practice in complex modern societies is a job that socially engaged Buddhism needs to tackle. It is true that justice cannot be reduced to the altruistic ideal of selfless, compassionate action, but I would suggest that Buddhism in fact has a broader ethical base in which the principle of justice has a place, albeit not very clearly spelled out so far.[46]

Thus scholars as well as practitioners still have important work to do in finding the rationale and the skills for social engagement in a tradition which viewed the mind, not society, as the source of all experience.

Many conferees took up the challenge of imagining the future shape and content of Buddhist engagement in the settings where social suffering is the most acute, from prisons and AIDS hospices at home to refugee camps and war zones in other parts of the world. In these settings, the stark alternatives outlined by Ian Harris – adaptation or decline – seem to motivate much of the discussion. As Buddhists confront conditions and values that are not encompassed in the classical teachings of the dharma, Ken O'Neill predicts:

> We'll come to learn more of the organic nature of Buddhism by virtue of how it reviews itself in new times and circumstances; with a sense of its adaptive fitness, we should come to gain a sense of its principles and how Buddhists creatively apply them. Or, as with fundamentalists we read about in the daily news, we may just as easily argue for rigid adaptation of ancient rules at all costs. In that respect I always think of the Buddhist monks who held fast to

the rules about light cotton robes, living "righteously" by them as they no doubt froze to death in Tibet.

In this connection it was fitting for Thomas Yarnall to remind the conference that his teacher, Tibetologist Robert Thurman, called Buddhism a "tradition of originality" for its myriad adaptive innovations through the ages. For the mountain Buddhists of Tibet did indeed adopt woolen robes and eat meat, innovations that would have been anathema to the earliest Buddhists – and in the process, they survived to create a glorious new civilization.

Speaking for many who participated in the JBE conference and in this collection, David R. Loy, a professor in the faculty of international studies at Bunkyo University in Japan, a founding member of the "Think Sangha" online discussion group of the International Network of Engaged Buddhists, and author of *A Buddhist History of the West: Studies in Lack* (2002), offered these thoughts:

> We cannot escape this task of reconstructing Buddhism to make it meaningful for us and our culture, so that it best addresses the ways that we experience and understand our most oppressive forms of *dukkha*. In that fashion, making a new Buddhism that works for us is itself a traditional, indeed inescapable task that Buddhism requires of us Western Buddhists... There is no alternative to reconstructing Buddhism in the West. The question is whether we will do it poorly, because largely unconsciously, or better, because [we are] more conscious of what we are doing. It is becoming clear that our Buddhism must be and will be socially engaged – not as a replacement of earlier teachings, but as a supplement to and development of them.[47]

Inasmuch as engaged Buddhism is a movement that began in Asia and has been articulated and embodied most visibly and compellingly by Asian Buddhist actors and thinkers, I would close by suggesting that Professor Loy's remarks on the inevitability of the reconstruction and engagement of Buddhism in the West might be extended to all – practitioners and observers, traditionists and modernists, in Asia, Africa, Latin America, and all the countries of the West. And through the innovations and complications that engaged Buddhists meet in their quest to heal the hurts of our time, I believe that the Buddha's ancient teachings on suffering, impermanence, and selflessness will continue to shine.

Notes

1 The Hindu scripture, *Bhagavad Gita*, illustrates the three paths as follows: *Karma Yoga*: "Perform necessary action; it is more powerful than inaction;

without action you even fail to sustain your own body" (3.8). *Jnana Yoga*: "Sacrifice in knowledge is better than sacrifice with material objects; the totality of all action culminates in knowledge" (4:33). *Bhakti Yoga*: "The leaf or flower or fruit or water that he offers with devotion, I take from the man of self-restraint in response to his devotion" (9:27). From Barbara Stoler Miller, trans., *The Bhagavad-Gita: Krishna's Counsel in Time of War* (New York: Bantam Books, 1986).

2 Robert E. Buswell and Robert M. Gimello, "Introduction," in Buswell and Gimello (eds.), *Paths to Liberation: The Marga and Its Transformations in Buddhist Thought* (Delhi: Motilal Banarsidass, 1994), p. 7. The editors of this conference volume suggest that the soteriological path (*marga*) of individual effort is "the fundamental assumption from which all Buddhist soteriological speculation derives," and that the solitary path of practice and realization may further be "taken out of the realm of the practical and the immediate and exalted to the status of a dramatization, or mythic recapitulation of the process by which such ideal persons [as the Buddha and his disciples] are said to have achieved enlightenment",p.10) In a note, the editors "very much regret the fact that Pure Land Buddhism, consideration of which is essential to any full treatment of marga [but which does not support the author's conclusions, as it is based on faith in Amida's saving action] is glaringly absent from this volume", p.33,n.25) On the other hand, they do not comment on the absence of any discussion in the volume of the claim – common among engaged Buddhists today – that social action (as opposed to ritual action) is a Buddhist "path to liberation."

3 Thich Nhat Hanh, *Being Peace* (Berkeley, CA: Parallax Press, 1987), p. 91.

4 Prof. N. V. Dhoke, Dept. of Dr. Ambedkar Thought, University of Nagpur expressed reservations about the efficacy of meditation for engaged Buddhism, while Prof. Bhao Lokhande, chairman of the department, argued for the mutual benefit of mindfulness and activism. Both members of the faculty are active in the Dalit Buddhist community in Nagpur. Personal communication, January 2001.

5 Nyanaponika Thera and Bhikkhu Bodhi, trans. and eds, *Numerical Discourses of the Buddha: An Anthology of Suttas from the Anguttara Nikaya* (Walnut Creek, CA: AltaMira, 1999), p. 77. This formulation of the *ti-lakkhana* or "three marks" of existence – *Sabbe sankhara anicca, sabbe sankhara dukkha, sabbe dhamma anatta* – differentiates the first two, impermanence and suffering, which characterize all "formations" or "conditioned phenomena" (*sankhara*), from the third, not-self, which encompasses all "things" (*dhamma*), whether conditioned or unconditioned, implying that even *Nirvana*, the unconditioned state of peace and freedom that is the goal of the Buddhist path, is "not-self," i.e. unlimited by the personal experience of a subject. Ibid., p. 279, notes 19–20.

6 Marvin Harris, *Cultural Materialism: The Struggle for a Science of Culture* (New York: Vintage-Random House, 1980), p. 32. Cf. K. L. Pike, *Language in Relation to a Unified Theory of the Structure of Human Behavior*, 2nd edition (The Hague: Mouton, 1967).

7 Ibid.

8 *Alagaddupama Sutta (22), Majjhima Nikaya i.140.*

9 Santikaro Bhikkhu, "Buddhadasa Bhikkhu: Life and Society through the Natural Eyes of Voidness," in Christopher S. Queen and Sallie B. King (eds.), *Engaged Buddhism: Buddhist Liberation Movements in Asia* (Albany, NY: State University of New York Press, 1996), p. 157.

10 This is not to say that Mahayana sources do not provide ample support for Deitrick's view that Buddhist suffering is primarily psychological – a perception of the world, and not an intervention. In the metaphor of "Santideva's sandals," with which Jenkins begins his analysis, the Buddhist philosopher likens the focus on mental transformation ("But should I restrain this mind of mine, What would be the need to restrain all else?") to wearing leather sandals – far more practical than attempting to cover the surface of the Earth with leather. On the other hand, Jenkins shows that the Pali/Sanskrit term *karuna*, "compassion," might be derived from the roots *kr*, meaning to make, cause, or act; *krt*, meaning to cut or break, and *krr*, meaning to disperse or spread – all "give an active and materially effective meaning to compassion."

11 For the concept of "social suffering" and its emergence in the history of religions, see my "Introduction: A New Buddhism," in Christopher S. Queen (ed.), *Engaged Buddhism in the West* (Somerville, MA: Wisdom Publications, 2000), pp. 1–39.

12 Bhikkhu Bodhi, "Introduction" to *The Middle Length Discourses of the Buddha: A New Translation of the Majjhima Nikaya*, trans. and ed. Bhikkhu Nanamoli and Bhikkhu Bodhi (Boston: Wisdom Publications, 1995), p. 28.

13 See the *Mahahatthipadopama Sutta*, in Nanamoli and Bodhi, op. cit., pp. 278–285.

14 For a brief history of the Sarvodaya movement, see Joanna Macy, *Dharma and Development: Religion as Resource in the Sarvodaya Self-Help Movement* (West Hartford, CT: Kumarian Press, 1983); and George D. Bond, "A. T. Ariyaratne and the Sarvodaya Shramadana Movement," in Queen and King (1996), op. cit., pp. 121–146.

15 For a study of the metaphor of the "wheel of righteousness" in Buddhism, see Christopher S. Queen, "The Peace Wheel: Nonviolent Activism in the Buddhist Tradition," in Daniel L. Smith-Christopher (ed.), *Subverting Hatred: The Challenge of Nonviolence in Religious Traditions* (Maryknoll, NY: Orbis Books, 1998), pp. 25–48.

16 Compare Gandhi's introduction of the term *harijan*, "god's people," as a way to garner Untouchable support for his Congress Party. Most "ex-Untouchables" (the practice was formally outlawed by Article 11 of the Indian Constitution, drafted by Ambedkar, the Untouchable leader) who have converted to Buddhism prefer the terms *Dalit*, meaning "oppressed," or *Bauddh*, "Buddhist."

17 In the case of human rights, arguments for and against such compatibility are collected in the predecessor to this volume, also the result of an online conference sponsored by the *Journal of Buddhist Ethics*, entitled *Buddhism and Human Rights*, edited by Damien V. Keown, Charles Prebish, and Wayne R. Husted (Surrey: Curzon Press, 1998).

18 Nanamoli and Bodhi, op. cit., p. 26.

19 Peter Harvey, *An Introduction to Buddhist Ethics* (Cambridge: Cambridge University Press, 2000), p. 34.

20 Paul Numrich, "Local Inter-Buddhist Associations in North America," in Duncan Ryuken Williams and Christopher S. Queen (eds.), *American Buddhism: Methods and Findings in Recent Scholarship* (Surrey: Curzon Press, 1999).

21 The term "pizza effect" was coined by the anthropologist Agehananda Bharati to describe cultural exports (such as pizza and acupuncture) that are transformed and reimported to the culture of origin. The naming example is that of American-style pizza, which has reportedly become popular in parts of Italy (even before the globalization of the Pizza Hut franchise). A more complex

example is the influence of Western Buddhist studies and Western styles of Buddhist practice on Asian Buddhists, such as B. R. Ambedkar, A. T. Ariyaratne, and the Ven. Cheng-yen.

22 See James Coleman, "The New Buddhism: Some Empirical Findings," in Williams and Queen, op. cit., pp. 91–99; and James Coleman, *The New Buddhism: The Western Transformation of an Ancient Tradition* (Oxford: Oxford University Press, 2000).

23 Kenneth Kraft, "New Voices in Engaged Buddhist Studies," in Christopher Queen (ed.), *Engaged Buddhism in the West* (Boston: Wisdom Publications, 2000), pp. 485–511.

24 For a discussion of the rules of admission to the ancient *sangha*, see Mohan Vijayaratna, *Buddhist Monastic Life According to the Texts of the Theravada Tradition* (Cambridge: Cambridge University Press, 1990), pp. 117–122.

25 Bardwell L. Smith, review of *Engaged Buddhism: Buddhist Liberation Movements in Asia*, Christopher S. Queen and Sallie B. King, eds. (Albany, NY: State University of New York Press, 1996), in *Journal of the American Academy of Religion* 67, 2 (June 1999): 500–501.

26 Bardwell L. Smith, "Sinhalese Buddhism and the Dilemmas of Reinterpretation," in B. L. Smith *et al.* (eds.), *The Two Wheels of Dhamma: Essays on the Theravada Tradition in India and Ceylon* (Chambersberg, PA: American Academy of Religion, 1972), p. 106. In his *JAAR* review (1999), Smith expresses disapproval of my use of this passage in Queen and King (1996) to make the same point, i.e. Buddhism's focus on individual liberation at the expense of social reform – surely the point he intended to make in 1972.

27 Queen (2000), "Introduction: A New Buddhism."

28 Queen and King (1996), op. cit., p. 20.

29 Yarnall, like Smith, implies here that "modernist" interpreters ignore salient examples of engaged Buddhism in the premodern period, yet offers no examples of his own.

30 Thomas A. Tweed, "On Moving Across: Translocative Religion and the Interpreter's Position," *Journal of the American Academy of Religion*, 70, 2: 272.

31 See Christopher S. Queen, "Dr. Ambedkar and the Hermeneutics of Buddhist Liberation," in Queen and King (1996), op. cit., pp. 45–71.

32 For a range of interpretations, see George D. Bond, *The Buddhist Revival in Sri Lanka: Religious Tradition, Reinterpretation and Response* (Columbia, SC: University of South Carolina Press, 1988); Gananath Obeyesekere and Richard Gombrich, *Buddhism Transformed: Religious Change in Sri Lanka* (Princeton, NJ: Princeton University Press, 1988); and Stanley J. Tambiah, *Buddhism Betrayed? Religion, Politics, and Violence in Sri Lanka* (Chicago: University of Chicago Press, 1992).

33 Thomas A. Tweed, "Night-stand Buddhists and Other Creatures: Sympathizers, Adherents, and the Study of Religion," in Williams and Queen (eds), (1999), op. cit., p 73.

34 Ian Harris (ed.), *Buddhism and Politics in 20th Century Asia* (London: Cassell Academic, 2001), p. 19.

35 Sulak Sivaraksa, "Buddhism with a Small 'b'," in Sulak Sivaraksa, *Seeds of Peace: A Buddhist Vision for Renewing Society* (Berkeley, CA: Parallax Press, 1992), pp. 62–72.

36 Scott C. Hurley, post to jbe-conf@jbe.la.psu.edu on April 9, 2000. During a "right brain" session at the annual meeting of the International Network of Engaged Buddhists, held in Nakorn Nayok, Thailand in February 1994, participants were asked to visualized engaged Buddhism in three dimensions, as a

cartoon or diagram. The result was a picture of lassos thrown up into the sky by common people, pulling a large, floating temple down from the clouds to anchor it to the earth, where everyone could enter freely.

37 Susan Darlington, post to jbe-conf@jbe.la.psu.edu on April 10, 2000.

38 Harriet Kirkley, post to jbe-conf@jbe.la.psu.edu on April 11, 2000.

39 BODHI may be reached via e-mail at <csbutler@tassie.net.au>. The website is <//www.angelfire.com/on/bodhi>.

40 John Foster, post to jbe-conf@jbe.la.psu.edu on April 9, 2000.

41 Michele Daniel, post to jbe-conf@jbe.la.psu.edu on April 9, 2000.

42 Steven Evans, post to jbe-conf@jbe.la.psu.edu on April 9, 2000.

43 Peter D. Hershock, post to jbe-conf@jbe.la.psu.edu on April 13, 2000 (emphasis added). For an elaboration of this position, see P. D. Hershock's *Liberating Intimacy: Enlightenment and Social Virtuosity in Ch'an Buddhism* (Albany, NY: State University of New York Press, 1996) and his *Reinventing the Wheel: A Buddhist Response to the Information Age* (Albany, NY: State University of New York Press, 1999).

44 Mushim Ikeda-Nash, post to jbe-conf@jbe.la.psu.edu on April 13, 2000.

45 Santikaro Bhikkhu, post to jbe-conf@jbe.la.psu.edu on April 11, 2000.

46 Damien Keown, post to jbe-conf@jbe.la.psu.edu on April 9, 2000. See also Damien V. Keown, Charles S. Prebish, and Wayne R. Husted, *Buddhism and Human Rights* (Surrey: Curzon Press, 1998).

47 David R. Loy, post to jbe-conf@jbe.la.psu.edu on April 9, 2000. See his *A Buddhist History of the West: Studies in Lack* (Albany, NY: State University of New York Press, 2002).

I

HISTORICAL ROOTS

1

DO *BODHISATTVAS* RELIEVE POVERTY?

Stephen Jenkins

Occasionally, Buddhists have considered the question of how poverty could continue in a world that is cultivated by celestial *bodhisattvas*. This chapter considers the question of whether Indian Buddhist texts "identify and address sources of human suffering outside of the cravings and ignorance of the sufferer – such as social, political, and economic injustice" – an often-cited criterion of contemporary "engaged Buddhism." Focusing on poverty, it concludes that these sources distinguish between compassionate intentions and action and between material and moral benefit. Furthermore, relief of poverty is seen as a prerequisite for moral development and its neglect is seen as a cause for social degeneration. Therefore, in order to prepare the conditions necessary for teaching the *Dharma*, the *bodhisattva* is called in to relieve these material wants, not only through moral leadership, but also through direct action. The strongest conclusions here are made in reference to the *Large Sūtra on Perfect Wisdom*, with cross-referencing and support from a broad range of other Indian sources.

The call for papers for the *Journal of Buddhist Ethics* online conference states that engaged Buddhism is:

> characterized by a reorientation of Buddhist soteriology and ethics to identify and address sources of human suffering outside of the cravings and ignorance of the sufferer – such as social, political, and economic injustice, warfare, violence, and environmental degradation.[1]

This chapter addresses the question of whether this thesis, that concern to identify and address modes of suffering "outside of the cravings and ignorance of the sufferer" amounts to a reorientation, can be challenged on the basis of Indian Buddhist literature.

Because of the paucity of resources for study, particularly in comparison to East Asia, it is very difficult to say in regard to India how, or to what degree, Buddhism in practice was "socially engaged." However, we do know that in the more historically clear environments of China and Japan, Buddhist activities included road and bridge building, public works projects, social revolution, military defense, orphanages, travel hostels, medical education, hospital building, free medical care, the stockpiling of medicines, conflict intervention, moderation of penal codes, programs to assist the elderly and poor including "inexhaustible treasuries" to stockpile resources for periods of hunger and hardship, famine and epidemic relief, and bathing houses.[2] Perhaps this was purely the unique response of East Asian culture to Indian Buddhism, but we can at least make the weak initial observation that it is reasonable to speculate that East Asians were following Indian models of Buddhist activity.

This chapter seeks to show the types of Buddhalogical resources that were available in Indian Buddhist texts to support such activity. Were these conceptual resources strictly metaphorical, as when the Buddha is described as the physician of the world? Are they merely intentional, that is, is their main purpose to generate character qualities that are conducive to the spiritual liberation of those who have them? If there is concrete action intended, then what kind of action? Are the texts merely concerned with activities of conveying the *Dharma* or do they enjoin the reader to activities that we would recognize as social action? If there is a distinction between spiritual and material benefit, then what is their relationship? Finally, do the textual resources support the idea that, even in India, social activities similar to those in East Asia occurred?

These questions open up a variety of issues that merit independent study. It would be possible to focus the topic here on a variety of types of action. The variety of justifications in Buddhist literature for compassionate violence, from political revolution to capital punishment, are fascinating, and the materials regarding the practice, teaching, manufacture, and science of medicine would also make an excellent example. Here I will focus on the provision of concrete material life support including food, shelter, and clothing.[3]

Sources are cited broadly here for their general support and interest for the subject. However, strong and specific conclusions are made in regard to the *Large Sūtra on Perfect Wisdom*, where there is a clear identification and concern for material modes of suffering, a definite distinction between material and spiritual benefit, an understanding that material support is a prerequisite for moral and spiritual development, and where *bodhisattvas* are enjoined to actively create the material conditions necessary for the spiritual development of sentient beings.

Śāntideva's sandals

It is significant to ask whether the questions raised here about the relationship between compassionate intentions and the concrete relief of suffering were asked by the ancient Buddhists themselves. In at least two disparate but important sources, the *Saṃdhinirmocana Sūtra* and the *Bodhicaryāvatāra*, there are passages that show that they did. In the *Saṃdhinirmocana Sūtra* we find the following fascinating question that shows a concrete distinction between spiritual and material assistance and that relief of poverty was expected from the activity of *bodhisattvas*.

> *Bhagavan*, if the resources of *bodhisattvas* are inexhaustible and if they have compassion, why are there poor people in the world? Avalokiteśvara, that is solely the result of the *karma* of those sentient beings themselves... The fact that hungry ghosts, whose bodies are pained by thirst, perceive the watery ocean as dry is not the ocean's failing... Similarly, the absence of good results is not a failing of the ocean-like generosity of *bodhisattvas*.[4]

If there were no expectation of the actual relief of material suffering this objection could not arise. But, the fact that the outcome does not match the intention shows that the content of intentions may be quite different from their practical outcomes.

Śāntideva, responding to the question of why, if there have been countless *bodhisattvas* who have vowed to save the endless numbers of sentient beings, does the world continue to be filled with suffering, answers that it is in fact not possible to change the world and that generosity is merely a state of mind.

(9) If the perfection of generosity
Were the alleviation of the world's poverty,
Then since beings are still starving now,
In what manner did the previous Buddhas perfect it?

(10) The perfection of generosity is said to be
The thought to give all beings everything,
Together with the fruit of such a thought,
Hence it is simply a state of mind. ...

(12) Unruly beings are as (unlimited) as space:
They cannot possibly all be overcome,
But if I overcome thoughts of anger alone,
This will be equivalent to vanquishing all foes.

(13) Where would I possibly find enough leather
With which to cover the surface of the Earth?
But (wearing) leather just on the soles of my shoes

Is equivalent to covering the earth with it.

(14) Likewise it is not possible for me
   To restrain the external course of things;
   But should I restrain this mind of mine,
   What would be the need to restrain all else?[5]

The continuation of the suffering in the world despite the past vows of countless Buddhas is explained as only natural, since the vow of *bodhisattvas* to relieve all suffering is pragmatically impossible because sentient beings are limitless. Just as one can cover one's own feet with leather, but not the whole world, the vow of the *bodhisattva* perfectly purifies their mind, but not the minds of all sentient beings. In Buddhist practice, molding compassionate intentions in itself is beneficial for the practitioner. Generating compassion is good for everything from snakebite protection to attaining heavenly realms.[6] Here there is a disjunction between the aspiration and its end, which is considered impossible.

So are the intentions to feed the hungry or heal the sick only sublime inspirations? It seems quite reasonable to ask, as Buddhists have above, what relationship compassion really has to the relief of material suffering. Is compassion in Buddhist practice active or is it merely a matter of shaping a character that is most conducive toward spiritual goals? In what sense does it actually get down to relieving the suffering of others?

Buddhist definitions of *karuṇā*

Buddhaghosa, whose commentaries are the central authority for the interpretation of the Pāli scriptures for Theravāda Buddhism, gives an analysis of the word *karuṇā;* that shows that in mainstream Buddhism the concept of compassion calls for aggressive action for the relief of the suffering of others:[7]

> When others suffer it makes the heart of good people tremble (*kampa*), thus it is *karuṇā* it demolishes others' suffering, attacks and banishes it, thus it is *karuṇā;* or it is dispersed over the suffering, is spread out through pervasion, thus it is *karuṇā.*[8]

Buddhaghosa is implicitly giving a philological analysis (*nirutti*) here. What is important here is not the actual etymology, but the meanings presented through this traditional analysis. The fact that the actual etymology of the word *karuṇā* is obscure allows a variety of creative suggestions. Here he suggests three verb roots that may be the basis of the noun *karuṇā kṛ*, meaning to make, cause, or act; *kṛt*, meaning to cut or break; and *kṝr*, which can mean to disperse or spread. It is notable that the second of Buddhaghosa's roots, *kṛt*, meaning to cut or break, gives an even more explicitly active meaning to compassion which is not merely affective, but actually removes the suffering of others.

The first of these verbal roots, kṛ, whose basic meaning is action, is also identified as a base of the word karuṇā in Mahāyāna sources. Another philological analysis from the Akṣayamatinirdeśa Sūtra, one of the earliest and most broadly cited Mahāyāna Sūtras, also gives a definition of karuṇā as action, translated here as "work." As did Buddhaghosa, it plays on the similarity in Sanskrit and Pāli of the words for action, araṇa, and compassion, Karuṇā.[9]

> As for this great compassion, reverend Śāradvatīputra [the meaning of the word compassion is "work"... and all the roots of the good are] work performed by oneself... [Even if it is for the sake of both others and oneself] it is one's own work, thus it is called great compassion.[10]

These definitions give an active and materially effective meaning to compassion.

Material and spiritual benefit and their interrelation

Mainstream sources

Regarding the question of whether compassion is meant to be active or merely meditative, the Abhidharmakośa, a touchstone for mainstream Abhidharma Buddhism and the primary text for Abhidharma studies in Mahāyāna Buddhism, says that the meditation on compassion gains merit from the compassion itself, even though there is no other beneficiary of the compassion:

> Objection: If indeed there is only merit from benefiting others, [then] there is no [merit] in mentally cultivating maitrī and the other immeasureables and in cultivating the right viewpoint ...

> Answer: As in regard to maitrī, et cetera, even without a recipient or benefit to another, merit is produced, arising from one's own thoughts.[11]

However, the text goes on to ask "Are material offerings then superfluous?" The answer is, "No, material offerings gain more merit than mere intentions, just as acting on a bad intention produces more demerit."[12] Clearly, if material gifts were not more efficacious in producing merit than good intentions alone, the result would be potentially disastrous for the monastic community which depends on the material support of the laity.

By the definitions we have examined compassion is active and, even from a self-interested merit-making perspective, it should be concretely effective.

The relationship between government welfare programs and moral development can be seen in the advice to kings. Here there is a distinction between material and moral benefit and the former is a prerequisite for the latter. The government of a model king should establish charitable posts, and give food, money, drink, clothes, and shelter.[13] The downfall of a great king is based on his failure to provide for the poor that leads to violent social degeneration:

> Thus from the not giving of property to the needy, poverty became rife, from the growth of poverty, the taking of what was not given increased, from the increase of theft, the use of weapons increased, from the increased use of weapons, the taking of life increased.[14]

This shows early recognition of the relationship between material and moral well-being. Material well-being is a prerequisite for moral development and its absence leads to social disaster. There is the basis for a critique of government here that will be shown below in the Mahāyāna sources.

In early sources there is a natural logic and motivation for compassionate service on the part of the laity. Material giving is an important form of merit making. However, this does not hold for renunciants. According to Aronson:

> In the discourses loving activities as a group are discussed only in terms of being extended to the religious practitioners... The primary recipients of the loving activities discussed in the discourses are the monks. It must also be understood that the populace at large would benefit from the monk's correct conduct and their teaching.[15]

Although service is part of both the monk's and layperson's practice, it is more passive on the part of the monk and less in the modes of material service that are associated with the modern concept of social action. Receiving alms itself is a compassionate act for a monk, because they themselves act as a merit field for the lay donor. In some understandings, the purer the monk, the more fruitful they are as a merit field; so the very extremity of their seclusion in socially disengaged meditation makes them all the more beneficial to others. In this view, effective compassionate action for others, including their social well-being, need not include anything that in present times would be regarded as social activism. However, the monk's role in moral leadership and the moral impact of renunciation on lay communities should not be discounted.

43

Mahāyāna sources

In the course of my dissertation research on *karuṇā* in Indian Buddhist texts, I found myself unexpectedly, but consistently, revising preconceptions about differences between the Mahāyāna and mainstream Buddhism. The vast majority of these preconceptions are merely the effect of Mahāyāna hermeneutics on the hermeneutics of Buddhist Studies. However, on this topic more than any other, there are striking differences between the two families of textual materials. The first is the enormous relative preponderance of passages in Mahāyāna texts that express concern for the broader physical and material benefit of sentient beings. In the limited literature we have access to in the vast scope of Mahāyāna scriptures, the presence of this concern is so strong that it is very unlikely that this pattern will change as more textual research develops.

The following passage from the *Suvarṇaprabhāsa Sūtra* is typical:

> May those who are in danger of being threatened or killed by kings, thieves, or scoundrels, who are troubled by hundreds of different fears, may all those beings who are oppressed by the advent of troubles be delivered from those hundreds of extreme very dreadful fears. May those who are beaten, bound, and tortured by bonds ... distracted by numerous thousands of labors, who have become afflicted by various fears and cruel anxiety... may they all be delivered; may the beaten be delivered from the beaters, may the condemned be united with life... May those beings oppressed by hunger and thirst obtain a variety of food and drink.[16]

The possibilities for further citation from the *sūtras* are abundant and pervasive.[17] The assertion that these texts are not concerned with identifying material sources of suffering simply will not hold. The issue of whether these sources of suffering are actually addressed is discussed further below.

In the course of further research, I expect to show that this first major difference is based on a second, which is a Copernican flip of the mainstream perspective that focuses on merit-making material service as something done for ideal practitioners by the laity. In Mahāyāna sources there is an inverse emphasis on *bodhisattvas'* merit-making actions for the sake of all sentient beings. The ideal practitioner should materially support others. The *bodhisattva* views the laity as a merit field. This change in perspective seems to be the result of the difference in attitude toward the *bodhisattva* path. In mainstream sources the *bodhisattva* path, in which the *bodhisattva* accumulates massive amounts of positive merit through aeons of service to sentient beings, is an object of awe and reverence. For

Mahāyāna practitioners that view themselves as *bodhisattvas*, the *bodhisattva* path is an object of imitation. The actions of Buddhas in past lives really are models for the *bodhisattva* whose whole practice is an imitation of the Buddhas.

In Mahāyāna sources as well, the moral leadership alone of *bodhisattvas* is credited with producing general social welfare:

> Wherever there appear in the world the worldly means of life – food, drink, clothes, dwelling places, medicinal appliances for sickness, ... etc. to: all that bestows ease in the realms of gods and men, and the ease of Nirvāna – that everywhere is due to the *Bodhisattvas*. And why? Because the *Bodhisattva* coursing on his course, enjoins the six perfections on beings – causes gifts to be given and morality to be undertaken, establishes them in patience and enjoins vigor, establishes them in trance and enjoins wisdom.[18]

Even in the modes of teaching and leadership there is a concern not just for transmitting the *Dharma*, but for improving material conditions.

The same positive evaluation of government concern for the welfare of the people, including relief of hunger, found in the Pāli sources is also found in Mahāyāna *Sūtras*. According the *Large Sūtra on Perfect Wisdom*:

> There are *Bodhisattvas* who... have become Universal Monarchs. Having taken the perfection of giving for their guide they will provide all beings with everything that brings ease – food for the hungry, drink to the thirsty... until, having established beings in the ten ways of wholesome action, they ... know full enlightenment.[19]

Here again, material support precedes successful moral leadership, because it eradicates the immoral environments and poverty that are obstructions.[20] The same argument seen in the *Nikāyas*, that immorality is produced by poverty, is found here also:

> The *bodhisattva*, who courses in the perfection of giving, and who has seen beings who are helpless, suffering and without food or shelter, matures them in this way: "Come here, you sons of good family, take from me food etc. to: the seven treasures, and let me thus help beings. And all that will contribute to your welfare, weal and happiness for a long time..." Moreover the *bodhisattvas* should mature beings as follows: "It is through the lack of necessary conditions that you are immoral, but I will bestow those necessary conditions on you, i.e. food etc. to: anything that may

be useful to you."... He helps beings in this manner with the result that they conform to the ten wholesome ways of action.[21]

This clear distinction between material and spiritual benefit with attention to their interrelationship clearly shows that this discourse is not merely eulogizing positive sentiments.

The *Saṃdhinirmocana Sūtra*, while warning that ultimately suffering cannot be relieved by material benefits alone, calls for *bodhisattvas* to provide the poor with material goods. Again, there is a clear distinction between material and spiritual benefit and attention to providing concrete relief in the form of material goods.[22] The same correlation between improving physical well-being and subsequently attending to spiritual teaching is found in the vows of Bhaiṣajyaguru to provide all beings with the necessities of life and to relieve the hungry and the desperately famished that they might later hear the teachings.[23] There is a correlation here between material support and proselytization, but the reasoning is always that in order to create the conditions necessary for benefiting people spiritually, one must first attend to their material needs. The *Vimalakīrtinirdeśa Sūtra* lauds the giver who gives to the lowliest poor of the city, considering them as worthy as the *Tathāgata* himself, and depicts the poor of the city subsequently conceiving *bodhicitta*.[24]

Conclusion

Occasionally Buddhists themselves considered the question of how poverty could continue in a world that is cultivated by celestial *bodhisattvas*. The benefits of compassion in itself for the compassionate are so strong that it is worth considering whether actual material support for others is necessary. However, this is clearly the case. Several central Mahāyāna and mainstream sources define compassion as a kind of action and, in merit making, action is far superior to mere good intentions. In mainstream sources, giving material support is clearly recognized as an important activity for the laity. However, the monks tend to be recipients of this support and do not play a role in materially relieving the poverty of the poor. The role of the ideal government is to prevent social degeneration by attending to the needs of the poor. This shows a distinction and relation between material and moral goods, where material goods have priority as a prerequisite for moral well-being.

In Mahāyāna sources, there is a great relative preponderance of passages that identify and show concern for poverty and see relieving it as the role of the *bodhisattva*, the ideal practitioner. As in *Pāli* sources, the satisfaction of material needs is seen as a prerequisite for moral development and its absence is seen as the cause of moral decay. The role of the *bodhisattva* is to relieve these material needs, not only through moral leadership but through direct action, in order to prepare the conditions necessary for teaching the *Dharma*. These points are made most strongly in regard to *The Large Sūtra on Perfect Wisdom*, with secondary reference to several other major *sūtras*. If the general preponderance of *sūtra* passages showing concern for poverty can be read in light of those *sūtras* which speak directly on the relationship between material and moral well-being, then it is a reasonable generalization that in Mahāyāna scriptures there is a broadly attested concern for poverty as an obstruction to spiritual progress and a clear mandate for its direct relief as a prerequisite for addressing the more subtle roots of *saṃsāra*.

Notes

1 Call for papers, *Journal of Buddhist Ethics* online conference on "Socially Engaged Buddhism," April 7–14, 2000, http//jbe.la.psu.edu/online.html
2 Luis O. Gomez, "From the Extraordinary to the Ordinary: Images of the Bodhisattva in East Asia," in *The Christ and the Bodhisattva* (Albany, NY: SUNY, 1992). Arthur F. Wright, *Buddhism in Chinese History* (Stanford, CA: Stanford University Press, 1959), pp. 58, 75, and 93–94.
3 This chapter draws on the author's recent doctoral dissertation and is a preliminary study in support of a chapter to be part of a book developed from the dissertation.
4 *Wisdom of Buddha: The Saṃdhinirmocana Sūtra*, trans. John Powers (Berkeley, CA: Dharma Publishing, 1995), p. 261.
5 *Guide to the Bodhisattva's Way of Life*, trans. Stephen Batchelor (Dharamsala: Library Tibetan Works Archives, 1987), V.9–14, pp. 45–46.
6 Stephen Jenkins, "The Circle of Compassion: An Interpretive Study of *Karuṇā* in Indian Buddhist Literature" (PhD dissertation, Harvard University, 1999), pp. 47–54.
7 In this chapter, the expression "mainstream Buddhism" will be used to designate the schools generally referred to as the *"hīnayāna."* These schools remained in the majority throughout Buddhism's history in India and use of the pejorative term *"hīnayāna"* merely reflects the assimilation of Mahāyāna hermeneutics into Buddhist Studies.
8 *Paradukkhe sati sādhūnan hadayakampanan karoti iti karuṇā kiṇāti vā paradukkhan, hiṃsati vināseti iti karuṇa; kiriyati vā dukkhite·u, pharaṇavasena pasāriyati iti karuṇā. Visuddhimagga of Buddhaghosācariya*, Harvard Oriental Series, vol. 41, ed. Henry Clarke Warren, revised Dharmananda Kosambi (Cambridge, MA: Harvard University Press, 1950), chapter IX, verse 92, p. 263.
9 *Karuṇam* occurs in the Vedas as action; *karuṇā* may have actually derived from this root. Monier - Williams, *A Sanskrit English Dictionary*, (Oxford: Oxford University Press, 1979 [first edition 1899]), s.v. "karuṇā".
10 *Akṣayamatinirdeśasūtra: The Tradition of Imperishability in Buddhist Thought*, trans. Jens Brārvig, (Oslo: Solum Forlag, 1993), p. 354. The commentary adds directly that the meaning of compassion, *karuṇā*, is action, *karuṇā*; See also p. 411: "Conduct with purpose is effort by one who has generated an intention purified by great compassion in whatever needs to be done for all sentient beings"; see also p. 356: "Great compassion is regard *[āpekṣā]* for the poor, suffering, and the unprotected, because it has its origin in removing the suffering of all sentient beings."

11 *Abhidharmakośa and Bhāṣya of Ācārya Vasubandhu with Sphuṭārthā Commentary of Ācārya Yaśomitra,* 4 vols, Bauddha Bharati Series 9, ed. Swami Dwarikadas Shastri (Varanasi: Bauddha Bharati, 1973), vol. 2, p. 548.
12 Ibid.
13 *Thus Have I Heard: The Long Discourses of the Buddha,* trans. Maurice Walsh (London: Wisdom, 1987), p. 284.
14 Ibid., p. 398.
15 Harvey Aronson, *Love and Sympathy in Theravāda Buddhism* (Delhi: Motilal Banarsidass, 1980), p. 37.
16 *The Sūtra of Golden Light,* trans. R.E. Emmerick (London: Luzac and Co. Ltd., 1970), p. 15. See also pp. 2, 4, 9, 14, 19, 24.
17 For passages related to poverty, see the *Akṣayamatinirdeśa Sūtra,* p. 358, on "giving to beggars," p. 459 on "providing food for the poor," and p. 410, on "pleasing, not deriding, fulfilling beggars"; "Tathāgata Ak·obhya's Merits," *A Treasury of Mahāyāna Sūtras,* ed. C.C. Chang (London: Penn State, 1983), p. 318, on giving material things; "The Ten Stages," in *The Flower Ornament Scripture,* trans. Thomas Cleary (Boston: Shambhala, 1993), p. 805, on protecting beings by providing what they require; *Entry Into the Realm of Reality,* trans. Thomas Cleary (Boston: Shambhala, 1989), pp. 290–291, "put an end to poverty for all sentient beings, satisfy all sentient beings with gifts of food and drink, satisfy all beggars by giving away all goods"; *Kāruṇāpuṇḍarīka-sūtra,* trans. Isshi Yamada (London: School of Oriental and African Studies, 1968), vol. I, p. 110, "*praṇidhāna* to become a merchant and shower jewels on many poverty stricken worlds"; *The Perfection of Wisdom in Eight Thousand Lines,* trans. E. Conze (Bolinas, CA: Four Seasons, 1973), p. 218, "that all beings, ... should not go short of the requirements of life"; *Saṃdhinirmocana Sūtra,* p. 239, "Bodhisattvas benefit sentient beings by giving them material goods," p. 245 "giving material things"; "*Tathāgataguhya Sūtra,*" in *Śikṣāsamuccaya,* trans. Cecil Bendall and W.H.D. Rouse (Delhi, Motilal Banarsidass, 1971), pp. 251–252, "When any are hungry he gives them the best food ... The poor he rejoices with plenty ... He goes share for share with those afflicted with poverty"; *The Lion's Roar of Queen Śrīmālā,* trans. Alex and Hideko Wayman (Delhi: Motilal Banarsidass, 1990), pp. 64–65, "I shall not accumulate wealth for my own use, but shall deal with it to assist the poor and friendless ... liberate them from each of those sufferings; having conferred goods upon them"; "On the *Pāramitā* of Ingenuity," *Treasury,* p. 429, "be generous to beggars," p. 430, "give food, drink and medicine"; *The Question of Rāṣṭrapāla,* trans. Jacob Ensink (Zwolle: J.J. Tijl, 1952), p. 26, shelter from the snow. "Samādhirāja Sūtra," in *Studies in the Literature of the Great Vehicle: Three Mahāyāna Buddhist Texts,* eds. Luis O. Gomez and Jonathon A. Silk (Ann Arbor, MI: Center for South and South East Asian Studies, University of Michigan, 1989), p. 58, "[This samādhi] is not humiliating those who suffer, but offering material assistance. It is not disappointing the poor." For further citations from the *Large Sūtra on Perfect Wisdom, Vimalakīrtinirdeśa,* and *Bhaiṣajyaguru Sūtras,* see the main text.
18 *The Large Sūtra on Perfect Wisdom,* trans. Edward Conze (Berkeley, CA: University of California, 1975), p. 86.
19 Ibid., p. 138.
20 The *Sūrataparipīcchā Sūtra* shows the possibilities for a social critique: "You levy taxes and punish the innocent for no reason, infatuated with your sovereignty, you do not protect your subjects and have no pity for the poor and suffering" (*Treasury*), p. 249.

21 *The Large Sūtra*, p. 614.

22 *Saṃdhinirmocana Sūtra*, see p. 249, for the warning that merely providing material goods is not skillful, sentient beings cannot be made happy by any means that benefits them through material goods alone.

23 Raoul Birnbaum, *The Healing Buddha* (Boston: Shambhala, 1989), p. 62 on the twelve vows of Bhaiṣajyaguru: vow number eleven: "May the desperately famished be given food and may they ultimately taste the teachings," vow number three: "may I enable all to obtain necessities of life," and vow number twelve: "May the destitute of clothes obtain attractive garments."

24 *The Holy Teaching of Vimalakīrti*, trans. R. Thurman (London: Penn State, 1976), p. 41. See also p. 70 on treasure and food for the poor, p. 20 on wealth for the poor, and p. 55 on the idea that beggars are usually *bodhisattvas* testing us.

2

DŌGEN'S "CEASELESS PRACTICE"

Daniel Zelinski

The ever-increasing number of articles on socially engaged Buddhism offers a perspective in sharp contrast to the common conception of Buddhism as a tradition that advocates spiritual awakening at the expense of affective connections within the social world. This conception is not without *some* validity. Many Buddhist monks have separated themselves from their larger society for significant periods, and Buddhist teachers have spoken of the need to transcend all duality, including notions of "good/evil" and "right/wrong," which rest on social convention. However, a repudiation of social norms is far from a rejection of all morality. *A fortiori*, moral apathy is far from an essential corollary of Buddhist Dharma.

While the specific connection between Buddhism and morality has not been afforded much analytic philosophical attention in the West, some philosophers have argued that all of the major Asian traditions are necessarily amoral, claiming that they essentially involve attitudes or forms of awareness inconsistent with any notion of morality. One such line of thought insists that adopting an attitude of nonattachment, a trait seemingly essential to all branches of Buddhism, is to cut oneself off from any concern for others and thus from any sense of morality. Instances of this argument have been advanced by Arthur Danto in his book *Mysticism and Morality*.[1]

I propose that these accusations are in error when offered as blanket generalizations. Many, perhaps most, Buddhist teachers have emphasized moral teachings. Moreover, far from being tangential, these teachings are often essentially linked to their mysticism – that is, to their espousal of an attitude of nonattachment. For brevity, I will focus on "ceaseless practice in the Buddha-mind," the way of life advocated by Dōgen Zenji (1200–1253), the founder of Japanese Sōtō Zen Buddhism. I take Dōgen to be describing a *mystical* way of being, inasmuch as the ideal spiritual life he describes involves the maintenance of an attitude of nonattachment and a continuous awareness of the Divine (that is, Buddha-nature) as a pervasive unity encompassing all things. I hope to reveal that for Dōgen these purely phenomenological features are essentially linked with a new way of relating to others, which may be characterized as exhibiting the virtues of humility, respect, and compassion.[2]

Beyond *satori*

The attainment of a particular unitive mystical state of consciousness, a *satori* experience, has always played a major role in Zen. Broadly, *satori* is a conscious insight or realization into the essential nature of the universe. The exact characteristics of this experience are, however, a matter of some dispute among scholars of Zen.[3] Even though there may be no phenomenologically unique experience correctly identified by the term, *satori* has often been regarded as the *telos* of monastic mystical achievement in both the Sōtō and Rinzai branches of Zen. However, the *satori* experience has generally not been held to be the pinnacle of Zen practice, at least not in the Sōtō tradition. Dōgen wrote:

> To think practice and realization are not one is a heretical view. In Buddhism, practice and realization are one equivalence... Being the realization of practice, there is no boundary of realization, being the practice of realization, there is no beginning of practice.[4]

This was Dōgen's (dis)solution to the question that plagued him from his beginnings as a Tendai initiate: "Why must we practice to obtain enlightenment, if we all are innately enlightened?" Practice is not merely a *means* to the goal of enlightenment; when viewed correctly it *is* enlightenment. "Practice," and hence "realization" along with it, should here be seen as referring to all of a Zen practitioner's activities and not merely times of formal meditation. But in what sense are all of one's activities *practice*? Surely not everyone's activities count as practice – so what is the distinction? For Dōgen, the difference lay in the attitude of the Zen practitioner. Zen practice, which Dōgen referred to as "ceaseless practice" (*gyoji*), is primarily the continuous maintenance of a specific frame of mind.

This is not to suggest that Dōgen rebuked formal meditation. In fact, he insisted that *zazen* (sitting meditation) was the most important aspect of Zen training.[5] Given this emphasis on *zazen*, and since, according to Zen accounts, steadfast *zazen* results in a *satori* experience, why didn't Dōgen praise *satori* as the ultimate *telos* of Zen training? The answer must be that he felt that Zen practice was concerned with something more than the attainment of any transitory mystical state. He wrote, "It is said, 'even a thousand acres of clear fields is not as good as a bit of skill that you can take around with you.'"[6] Given that "a thousand acres of clear fields" plausibly refers to the state of consciousness during a *satori* experience, Dōgen is here admonishing that no transitory experience should be considered the final culmination of one's practice. He insisted, "Enlightened vision does not only occur in an instant [as in *satori* experiences], but is constantly active at all times."[7] True, or complete, realization is not transitory; it involves a fundamental and permanent alteration of one's perception of reality, and it is the cultivation of *this* awareness that Dōgen instructed should be a Zen student's main direction.

Bankei, the seventeenth-century wandering Zen master who extended Dōgen's call to "instruct all who would listen" into a repudiation of the rigid monastic system, clearly echoed Dōgen's insistence that ultimate realization in Zen requires the maintenance of a specific quality of consciousness throughout all of one's activities, the realization that "everyday life is meditation": "At all times he [the fully awakened individual] abides continually in the Buddha Mind, and there's not a single moment when he's not in the Buddha Mind."[8] The notion of Buddha Mind that Bankei uses here, and that was also employed by Dōgen, is crucial because it does not denote the state of consciousness during any transitory experience (including *satori*), but a permanent frame of mind. In Sōtō Zen, the realization of this consciousness is associated with *mujodo no taigen*, which Hakuun Yasutani described as "the actualization of the Supreme Way throughout our entire being and daily activities."[9]

For Dōgen, and the Sōtō tradition that followed him, enlightenment involved an integration of one's perception of the world and one's actions in it: "*Acting on* and *witnessing* oneself in the advent of myriad things is enlightenment."[10] Let me attempt to elucidate the Sōtō Zen picture within each of these two realms in greater detail.

Nonattachment

What is this "bit of skill" that Dōgen praised above *satori*, that he maintained could be employed continuously, and that he claimed was instrumental in instilling this perception of unity? He most certainly held it to be an extension of the attitude of nonattachment that is cultivated in *zazen* practice. In *zazen*, the practitioner cultivates a form of consciousness wherein all thoughts, concerns, desires, and so forth are ineffective at capturing one's attention. In beginning *zazen* practice, these thoughts inevitably arise, but the practitioner's conscious attention always returns to his or her focus, either to his or her breathing or to nothing at all (that is, to an "open" alertness without any specific object of attention).

This attitude of nonattachment toward all one's thoughts during *zazen* is the Zen vehicle to the Buddhist ideal of transcending all strong desires, or cravings, which are seen as the root of all suffering. It is the key to the Eightfold Path, the middle way between the extreme self-denial of asceticism and the suffering inherent in craving.[11] One who is nonattached is beyond craving, which is not to say that such individuals have no desires or interests. While the nonattached individual may be said to maintain interests in the prerequisites for a healthy life (food, shelter, and so forth) as well as personal interests (for example, gardening or painting), he or she is not obsessed with these ends.

This attitude represents a drastic phenomenological shift in one's entire conscious life, but its affective quality is perhaps most apparent in the nonattached person's equanimity in the face of loss. For example, a famous Zen story tells of a monk who, upon returning to his hut to discover that all his possessions have been stolen, remains undisturbed: "The thief left it behind – the moon in the window."[12] The monk's response stands in sharp contrast to that of an attached individual, who, we can imagine, craving to maintain his or her possessions, would be crushed by such a discovery.

Dōgen repeatedly made "nonattachment" a central theme of his lectures.[13] He spoke against all forms of attachment, but most commonly referred to the difficulty and necessity of freeing oneself from attachment to one's self. He often described this conception of nonattachment to self as a transcendence of the craving for individual immortality, as well as cravings for self-centered objectives such as "fame or fortune."[14] Further, he insisted that such an attitude, thoroughly practiced both during and outside of formal meditation, would result in a pervasive mood of serenity or contentment and even extreme joy in all situations.[15]

Every form of attachment, including attachment to *satori* experiences, has always been regarded as a danger within Sōtō Zen.[16] Most Sōtō Zen masters who followed Dōgen agreed that *satori* experiences foster a false sense of pride and a desire for repeated experiences, both of which were viewed as impediments to spiritual growth. This concern is clearly behind the following admonition given by Bankei: "Since your Unborn Buddha Mind hasn't been realized, you can't manage smoothly in your daily affairs. In exchanging it for something like 'the empty sky,' you're *obscuring* the marvelously illuminating Buddha Mind."[17] Here, "the empty sky" refers to the state of consciousness in a *satori* experience, while "the Unborn Buddha Mind" denotes a mystical type of awareness that may be maintained continuously and the attainment of which was, according to Bankei, *the* goal of Zen.

Satori experiences are generally described as incredibly blissful states of consciousness, and it is understandable how one, upon having achieved such a state, might long to experience it again. However, should such a desire become a craving, it threatens to destroy the attitude of nonattachment deemed so vital to Zen practice and, ironically, to the very attainment of such states of consciousness. More importantly, it blocks the shift in one's perception Dōgen insisted results from the cultivation of nonattachment.

The unity of the Buddha-nature

Perhaps the most striking quality of nonattachment in Dōgen's account is its ability to fundamentally alter one's perception of reality.[18] Within the Sōtō tradition this altered perception is taken as carrying metaphysical import (that is, as an unveiling of the truly real) and is characterized as an awareness of Buddha-nature or the Buddha-seal, as immanent in all things:

> If someone, even for one period of time, shows the Buddha-seal in physical, verbal, and mental action, and sits straight in concentration, the whole cosmos becomes the Buddha-seal, all of space becomes enlightenment.[19]
>
> [T]he Buddha, the Blessed One, is transcendent wisdom. Transcendent wisdom is all things ... The manifestation of this transcendent wisdom is the manifestation of the Buddha.[20]

These passages convey a central tenet in Dōgen's teaching, that enlightenment consists in a sensual recognition that all things are intimately connected through a fundamental unity, which is Buddha-nature.

The perception of Buddha-nature as a fundamental unity immanent in all things is also apparent within Dōgen's famous interpretation of the Buddhist teaching "all beings *have* Buddha-nature" as "all being *is* Buddha-nature."[21] Here he insists that the Buddha-nature is a pervasive unity rather than an individually distinct soul. He wrote, "[T]o see mountains and rivers is to see Buddha-nature. To see Buddha-nature is to see a donkey's jaw or a horse's mouth."[22] In other words, Buddha-nature is all around us – everywhere.

This altered perception clearly involves a new awareness of one's own relation to everything, everything perceived, and beyond. Hence, enlightenment, according to Dōgen, also involves transcending, at least phenomenologically, the dichotomy between self and others:

> To learn the Buddhist Way is to learn about oneself. To learn about oneself is to forget oneself. To forget oneself is to perceive oneself as all things. To realize this is to cast off body and mind of self and others. When you have reached this stage you will be detached even from enlightenment but will practice it continually without thinking.[23]

> "In the entire universe everything has self." The entire universe is myself-as-it-is, myself as myself, yourself as myself, myself as

yourself. Myself-is-yourself, yourself-is-myself and the entire universe form one unity.[24]

There is a clear breakdown here of a sense of reality as composed of metaphysically distinct entities, including one's sense of oneself as an essentially separate individual in the world.[25]

No-self

We have seen that both the enlightened Zen practitioner's attitude of nonattachment and his or her perception of the unity of the Buddha-nature, given that it is perceived as having metaphysical legitimacy, have implications for both the subject's sense of him or herself and his or her relation to others and the world. "Selflessness," the doctrine that there is no permanent substantial subject, is a main tenet of Buddhism in general. In Zen this dogmatic ontological position is held to have clear phenomenological grounding. According to Dōgen, enlightenment results in a distinct perceptual sense that there is no enduring substance with which one may identify one's "self," including the physical body:

> The foremost concern of the student is to detach from the notion of self. To detach from the notion of self means that we must not cling to this body... [I]f you are attached to this body, and do not detach from it, you could not find the Way of the Buddhas even in ten thousand eons ... if you do not leave off your feeling of attachment to your body, you are idly counting the treasures of others without having a halfpenny of your own ... that neither the beginning nor end of one's body can be grasped is the essential point to be aware of in practicing the Way.[26]

Joko Beck, a contemporary American Zen teacher, has reiterated this focus: "Zen practice is about being selfless, about realizing that one is no-self."[27]

What is this realization like phenomenologically? A clue is afforded by an explication of the concept of "self" that is claimed to be lost. Clearly, the *idea* of the self as a permanent entity, fundamentally separated from others and the world, is part of what is referred to as lost here. This seems to follow from Dōgen's admonitions regarding attachment to one's body. However, there is also a sense of "self" in the tradition that is associated with the sum total of all of one's cravings. According to Dōgen, an ordinary (that is, unenlightened) individual's sense of herself is intimately connected with his or her cravings. Hence, Dōgen maintained that this no-self-awareness involved, in addition to a perceptual awareness of oneself as intimately connected with everything through the unity of Buddha-nature, an absence of any form of craving, together with an absence of any conception of oneself as essentially defined through one's desires.

Engaged nonattachment

In spite of this attitude of nonattachment, and the absence of a sense of self and the presence of an unshakable sense of serenity that accompany it, Dōgen insisted that enlightenment did not result in inactivity or apathy. He held that nonattachment was consistent with intentional (that is, purposeful) action. In other words, nonattachment did not mean having no goals or ends. According to Dōgen, the real problem was attachment to one's goals, not goals in themselves (except for purely selfish ends). In fact, Dōgen's admonitions against *satori* experiences can be seen as warnings against attachment to (the goal of) nonattachment. This position is apparent in passages that we have already seen, wherein Dōgen insisted that one's awareness in the Buddha-mind must be maintained continuously. Perhaps more than any other Sōtō teacher, Bankei reiterated this point, noting that one's particular activity is unimportant as long as one remains in the Buddha-mind (that is, nonattached):

> Once you've affirmed the Buddha Mind that everyone has innately, you can all do just as you please: if you want to read the sutras, read the sutras; if you feel like doing *zazen*, do *zazen* ... or simply performing your allotted tasks – whether as a samurai, a farmer, an artisan or a merchant – that becomes your *samadhi* [your *practice*] ... What's essential is to realize the Buddha Mind each of you has, and simply abide in it.[28]

While Bankei is insisting that one's particular form of practice is unimportant, he is not advocating pure subjectivism. The important point to note here is the insistence on the need to act in accord with one's "realization of the Buddha Mind." It is not subjectivism, because Bankei insists that it is always necessary to "*abide* in the Buddha Mind" and, as may be becoming clear, this frame of mind and the altered perspective of reality that accompanies it have dramatic effects upon how one relates to others and the world.

The Taoist ideas of *wu wei* (literally "nondoing" or "nonaction") and *wei wu wei* ("acting through nonaction"), which were deeply integrated into Zen thought, express this same possibility of acting from an attitude of nonattachment through an absence of any concern for the actual result. Note the following passage from the *Tao Te Ching*: "The sage dwells in affairs of nonaction [*wu wei*]... He acts but does not presume; he completes his work but does not dwell on it."[29]

There is work to be done, legitimate ends to pursue, but the emphasis always lies in the action itself. To attempt to convey this shift in emphasis, Dōgen insisted that the Buddha would still have practiced his meditation and teaching even if all sentient beings were already saved.[30] Nonattachment is revealed not by the absence of goals but rather by the absence of any *mental preoccupation* with one's goal during the activity or after the attempt to realize it is complete, whether or not the goal has been successfully realized. Moreover, whether or not the end toward which the activity is directed is realized has no bearing on such an individual's sense of self-esteem. However, this does not mean that the Zen master did not take the activity seriously. Action is important as it is seen as an expression of the *Tao* ("the flow of life") or the Buddha-nature, but its value lies completely within itself.

We have seen that Dōgen insisted that the attitude of nonattachment could be (and indeed should be) continuously maintained. Hence, he clearly held it to be consistent with intentional activity. In a major lecture titled "Ceaseless Practice" (*Gyoji*), he instructed:

> If we wish to build a temple [that is, engage in any intentional activity], we must remember that the main purpose is not form, fame and fortune, but it is rather the ceaseless practice of the Buddha Dharma which is most important.[31]

Here Dōgen insists that the value of any action lies not in the contingent realization of one's end but in the activity itself as a moment of practice of nonattachment and its accompanying perceptions and feelings. D. T. Suzuki, a pioneer in bringing Zen to the English-speaking world early in the twentieth century, concurred: "Zen emphasizes the purposelessness of work or being detached from teleological consciousness."[32] Beck has described this attitude as a way of "living without hope," since "hope" entails a strong attachment to an intentional objective.[33]

Finally, note that this sense of *engaged nonattachment* involves not seeking or desiring any thanks or praise for one's acts. For example, Dōgen wrote, "When one [who is enlightened] has seen an exhausted turtle or an ailing sparrow, one doesn't want their thanks – one is simply moved to helpful action."[34] But if one is nonattached, why is one "moved toward *helpful* action" as opposed to harmful action? Why is an unattached individual moved toward any action at all? I believe that we are now in a position to appreciate Dōgen's response to this worry.

The *bodhisattva* virtues

The scope of nonattachment is generally recognized in Zen as including normative rules or conventions. However, Dōgen often spoke of the need for diligence to do good.[35] Moreover, within Dōgen's "ceaseless practice," the actions of an enlightened individual were clearly expressive of specific moral virtues that flowed out of the Buddha-mind (that is, from the maintenance of an attitude of nonattachment). These virtues are evident in Dōgen's explication of "the four ways a Bodhisattva acts to benefit human beings": *fuse* (almsgiving), *aigo* (loving words), *rigyo* (beneficial action), and *doji* (identification with the beings that are to be helped, or cooperation).[36]

The virtue of humility is clearly expressed in his explication of *fuse* (almsgiving): "*Fuse* ... is not to covet or be greedy, not to flatter, adulate, nor curry favor. [Regardless of the gift or receiver, it] is the same as offering a flower that blooms in the far mountains to Buddha."[37] The absence of selfish traits such as coveting or greed expresses a *moral* sense of selflessness (nonselfishness) and is a direct result of the attitude of nonattachment. The regarding of every gift as both precious as well as an extension of what one considers to be a gift reveals a sense of gratitude and humility that is no doubt connected with the perception of all things as Buddha-nature.

Aigo (loving words) and *rigyo* (beneficial action) express a deep sense of compassion that Dōgen noted arises naturally within an enlightened individual:

> *Aigo* means that whenever we see sentient beings, our compassion is aroused naturally and we use loving words ... To become friends with the enemy and to reconcile enemy kings should be the root of *aigo* ... We should realize that *aigo* comes from *aishin* [the mind of love] and that *aishin* is based on compassion.[38]
>
> *Rigyo* means that we take care of every kind of person, no matter whether of high or low position ... *Rigyo* is the one principle wherein we find no opposition between subjectivity and objectivity.[39]

Note that this compassion extends to all sentient beings, including one's enemies. Furthermore, the lack of "opposition between subjectivity and objectivity" suggests that this consideration and love for others are the result of a sense of connection that comes from the enlightened perception of unity of all things within Buddha-nature. This idea that the perception of unity leads directly to a moral regard for others is directly apparent in *doji*. "[*Doji*] means nonopposition. It is not opposing oneself and not opposing others ... When one knows cooperation, self and others are one thusness ... After regarding others as self, there must be a principle of assimilating oneself to others."[40] Here, the sense of all things as Buddha-nature is expressed through a perceived connection between oneself and others, and this connection is seen as resulting in a sense of respect expressed through non-opposition, or non-harming.

In sum, these passages elucidate that the virtues of humility, respect, and compassion are infused within a practitioner of ceaseless practice via a sympathetic union with others, which results from the enlightened perception of reality as Buddha-nature discussed above. Given that "respect" may be identified with the absence of any disposition to harm others and "compassion" with a disposition to help others, this connection seems natural enough; if one feels fundamentally unified with others, one would be inclined to refrain from injuring them and, in fact, come to their aid.

The espousal of these virtues is far from unique to Dōgen. They are present throughout the Zen, Buddhist, and Taoist traditions. For example, this same notion of respect is reflected in Chuang Tzu's claim, "The man in whom the *Tao* acts without impediment harms no other being."[41] Kuo-an Shih-yuan's additions to the Zen ox-herding pictures suggest that a clear sense of compassion accompanies complete enlightenment. The final picture in Kuo-an's sequence, which represents the culmination of Zen practice, is titled *Entering the Marketplace* [that is, the social world] *with Helping Hands*.[42] Yasutani also clearly echoed Dōgen's contention that a perception of the unity of Buddha-nature would result in one's actions toward others being based on both respect and compassion:

> When you truly realize the world of oneness, you could not fight another even if he wanted to kill you, for that person is nothing less than a manifestation of yourself. It would not even be possible to struggle against him. One who has realized the world of equality will regard with compassion even people who have homicidal intentions, since in a fundamental sense they and oneself are of equal worth.[43]

Note Yasutani's insistence on a causal relationship here; he claimed an awakened individual "*could* not fight another" He was not advocating a moral rule against harming, but rather insisting that enlightenment shapes one's moral character as much as one's perception. Indeed, he said, one's character is shaped in proportion to one's "realization of the world of oneness [that is, Buddha-nature]." Whether or not the realization of Buddha-nature instills such a stringent adherence to nonviolence as to preclude all possible self-defense, as Yasutani appears to suggest, its connection to a morally significant sense of concern for the well-being of others is undeniable.

Conclusion

I realize the above abbreviated account falls short of doing justice to the depth of Dōgen's thinking regarding "ceaseless practice in the Buddha-mind." I do, however, hope to have provided a portrait of "ceaseless practice" that reveals Dōgen's conception of nonattachment to be not only consistent with moral concerns but in fact foundational for cultivating genuinely moral virtues. Far from being morally indifferent, Dōgen's ideally nonattached individual is a humble agent in the world whose perceived sense of a pervasive interconnected unity of all things through Buddha-nature instills a sympathetic connection to others within him or her, which in turn results in his or her projects and actions expressing both respect and compassion. Dōgen eloquently summarized this integrated ideal:

> There is a very easy way to become a Buddha: not doing any evil, having no attachment to birth and death, sympathizing deeply with all beings, respecting those above, sympathizing with those below, not feeling aversion or longing for anything, not thinking or worrying – this is called Buddha. Don't seek it anywhere else.[44]

Notes

1 Arthur Danto, *Mysticism and Morality* (New York: Columbia University Press, 1987).
2 I offer a fuller account of this way of being in my dissertation, "The Meaning of Mystical Life: An Inquiry into Phenomenological and Moral Aspects of the Ways of Life Advocated by Dōgen Zenji and Meister Eckhart" (PhD dissertation., University of California at Irvine, 1997).
3 See, for example, Roshi Philip Kapleau, *The Three Pillars of Zen* (New York: Anchor Books, 1989); Paul Reps, *Zen Flesh, Zen Bones* (New York: Anchor Books, 1970); Walter Stace, *The Teachings of the Mystics* (New York: Mentor Books, 1960); D. T. Suzuki, *Essays in Zen Buddhism: Selected Writings of D. T. Suzuki*, ed. William Barrett (Garden City, NY: Doubleday Anchor, 1956); Alan Watts, *The Way of Zen* (New York: Vintage Books, 1957).
4 Thomas Cleary, trans., "Bendowa" ("A Story of Buddhist Practice"), in *Shobogenzo: Zen Essays by Dōgen* (Honolulu: University of Hawaii Press, 1986), p. 15. Also see Kosen Nishiyama and John Stevens, trans., *A Complete English Translation of Dōgen Zenji's Shobogenzo*, vol. I, "Ippyaku-hachi Homyo-mon" ("The 108 Brilliant Teachings of the Dharma") (San Francisco: Japan Publications Trading Company, 1975), no. 8, pp. xv and 157.
5 Thomas Cleary, "Zuimonki," in *Shobogenzo*, p. 14; also see pp. 9, 13, 18, 19, and 39.
6 Ibid., p. 15.
7 Kosen Nishiyama and John Stevens, *A Complete English Translation*, vol. II, "Shoakumakusa" ("Refrain from all evil"), p. 172. Also note the following poem of Dōgen's from his Waka collection: "Day and night / Night and day, / The Way of the Dharma as everyday life; / In each act our hearts / resonate with the call of the sutra" (Steven A. Heine, *A Blade of Grass* [New York: Peter Lang, 1989], no. 3, p. 87).
8 Peter Haskel, *Bankei Zen: Translations from the Record of Bankei* (New York: Grove Press, 1984), p. 92; also see pp. 21, 37–38, 59, and 67.
9 Kapleau, *The Three Pillars of Zen*, p. 51; also see p. 48. This integration between religious conscious and everyday life has been at the heart of Zen at

least since Kuo-an Shih-yuan's account of the ox-herding pictures in the twelfth century; Kapleau, section VIII, pp. 313–325.

10 Thomas Cleary, "Genjokoan" ("The Issue at Hand'), in *Shobogenzo*, p. 33; my emphasis.

11 The Eightfold Path comprises right views, right intent, right speech, right conduct, right livelihood, right endeavor, right mindfulness, and right meditation.

12 Reps, *Zen Flesh, Zen Bones*, p. 12.

13 For example, see Nishiyama and Stevens, *A Complete English Translation*, vol. III, "Ippyyaku-hachi Homyo-mon," pp. 117f.

14 Nishiyama and Stevens, *A Complete English Translation*, vol. I, "Daigo" ("Great Enlightenment"), p. 34.

15 Nishiyama and Stevens, *A Complete English Translation*, vol. IV, "Hachi Dainin-Gaku" ("The Eight Means to Enlightenment"), p. 34. Also see vol. I, "Bendowa," p. 154, and vol. III, pp. 117f. (nos 3, 16, 71, and 98).

16 Indeed, this is a common concern throughout most Buddhist traditions.

17 Haskel, *Bankei Zen*, p. 74. Also see Nishiyama and Stevens, *A Complete English Translation*, vol. II, p. 64.

18 The specific connection between the attitude of nonattachment and this altered perception is in need of fuller phenomenological analysis.

19 Nishiyama and Stevens, *A Complete English Translation*, vol. II, "Bendowa," p. 16. Also see Kapleau, *The Three Pillars of Zen*, p. 310 ("Uji" ["Being Time"]).

20 Nishiyama and Stevens, *A Complete English Translation*, vol. II, "Makahannyaharamitsu" ("Great Transcendent Wisdom"), p. 27; also see p. 20.

21 Nishiyama and Stevens, *A Complete English Translation*, vol. I, p. xx, and vol. IV, p. 134; my emphasis. Also see the following poems from the Waka [Heine, *A Blade of Grass*]: nos. 6 (p. 88), 10 (p. 92), 48 (p. 116), and A3 (p. 121).

22 Nishiyama and Stevens, *A Complete English Translation*, vol. IV, p. 123; also see vol. I, pp. 105 and 150.

23 Nishiyama and Stevens, *A Complete English Translation*, vol. I, "Genjokoan," p. 1. For a different translation of this famous passage, see Cleary, p. 32.

24 Nishiyama and Stevens, *A Complete English Translation*, vol. I, p. 105.

25 These views were far from unique in Zen/Ch'an thought; see, for instance, Kapleau, *The Three Pillars of Zen*, pp. 51 and 62, and Sengstan, *Hsin Hsin Ming*, trans. Richard Clarke (Virginia Beach: Universal Publications, N.D.).

26 Cleary, "Genjokoan," pp. 16–17. Also see Nishiyama and Stevens, *A Complete English Translation*, vol. IV, p. 128.

27 Charlotte Joko Beck, *Everyday Zen: Love and Work* (New York: HarperCollins, 1989), p. 96.

28 Haskel, *Bankei Zen*, p. 49; also see pp. 142–143. Bankei's mention of samurai here does present some difficulty for the analysis that I am here attempting; for attempts to respond to this and other challenges, see my dissertation, Chapter IX.

29 *Tao Te Ching*, Victor H. Mair, trans. (New York: Bantam Books, 1990), Chapter 2, p. 60; also see Chapter 67.

30 Nishiyama and Stevens, *A Complete English Translation*, vol. I, "Nyoraizenshin" ("The Entire Body of the Tathagata"), p. 123. Remember, saving all sentient beings is the goal of Mahāyāna Buddhism.

31 Nishiyama and Stevens, *A Complete English Translation*, vol. III, "Gyoji," p. 33.

32 Suzuki, *Essays in Zen Buddhism*, p. 264. See also Kapleau, *The Three Pillars of Zen*, p. 51.
33 Beck, *Everyday Zen*, p. 69.
34 Thomas Cleary, "Bodaisatta Shishoho" ("The Four Integrative Methods of Bodhisattvas"), in *Shobogenzo*, p. 119. See also Nishiyama and Stevens, *A Complete English Translation*, vol. III, p. 117 (no. 11).
35 Nishiyama and Stevens, *A Complete English Translation*, vol. IV, "Hachidai Ningaku" ("The Eight Means to Enlightenment"), p. 34.
36 Nishiyama and Stevens, *A Complete English Translation*, vol. III, "Bodaisatta shishoho," pp. 124–128. "Doji" is translated as "identification with the beings that are to be helped" by Nishiyama and Stevens, and as "cooperation" by Cleary. In the Mahāyāna Buddhist tradition, the ideal of the *Bodhisattva* represents an enlightened being who chooses to stay and act in the world out of compassion, helping others to realize enlightenment.
37 Ibid., p. 124.
38 Ibid., p. 126.
39 Ibid., pp. 126–127.
40 Cleary, "Bodaisatta Shishoho," pp. 119–120.
41 Thomas Merton, *The Way of Chuang Tzu* (New York: New Directions, 1965), p. 91. Also see the *Tao Te Ching*, Chapters 13 and 30.
42 Kapleau, *The Three Pillars of Zen*, p. 323.
43 Ibid., p. 62. For similar remarks by Bankei, see Haskel, *Bankei Zen*, p. 40.
44 Cleary, "Shoji" ("Birth and Death"), p. 123.

3

NICHIREN'S ACTIVIST HEIRS
Sōka Gakkai, Risshō Kōseikai, Nipponzan Myōhōji

Jacqueline I. Stone

Three religious movements founded in the twentieth century – Sōka Gakkai, Risshō Kōseikai and Nipponzan Myōhōji – are often singled out as examples of contemporary Japanese socially engaged Buddhism. All three stand in the tradition of the *Lotus Sūtra* and the Buddhist teacher Nichiren (1222–1282); their members, as a primary practice, regularly recite the sūtra and chant its title or *daimoku* in the formula Namu-myōhō-renge-kō, as Nichiren advocated.[1] All three, on the basis of these explicitly religious practices, undertake additional efforts in society aimed at the achievement of "world peace." But it would be too simplistic to view these contemporary movements as emanating in a straight, unproblematic line from either Nichiren or the *Lotus Sūtra*, as introductory presentations often do. Despite their shared Buddhist heritage, their readings of the *Lotus Sūtra* and of Nichiren's teachings are not the same, nor does Nipponzan Myōhōji's style of social engagement resemble that of Sōka Gakkai or Risshō Kōseikai. In what sense does the commitment to peace shared by these three movements derive from Nichiren's teachings? How, and to what extent, have their specific forms of activism been shaped by other, more recent cultural and historical influences? And what is the role of the *Lotus Sūtra* in their social engagement?

These are the sorts of issues I have been invited to address in this chapter. Obviously these are huge questions, not amenable to resolution in a short article. My aim, therefore, will simply be to raise them for discussion and to suggest – in hopes of encouraging further study – how these three movements have variously reinterpreted a common heritage.

Society, the *Lotus Sūtra* and Nichiren

The *Saddharma-puṇḍarīka-sūtra* (Chinese *Miaofa lianhua jing*; Japanese *Myōhō-renge-kyō*) or *Lotus Sūtra*, thought to have been compiled roughly around the beginning of the common era, numbers among the historically most influential Buddhist texts in East Asia. Rather than a discursive presentation of doctrine, the *Lotus* is a mythic text, unfolding in parables and extravagant imagery its message of a Buddha, awakened since the remotest past, who in countless guises and by innumerable "skillful means" works tirelessly to lead all beings to the same enlightenment as himself. In China, the *Lotus Sūtra's* teaching of the "one Buddha vehicle," in which the disparate paths of the *śrāvaka* and the *bodhisattva* are ultimately resolved, was highly valued as a hermeneutical device for reconciling disparate doctrines. In the Tiantai (Japanese Tendai) school, the *Lotus* served as the foundation for a highly sophisticated system of doctrine and meditative practice. It was also revered across sectarian lines for its perceived magical powers to bring about healing and ensure good fortune and protection in this life and the next.

What the *Lotus Stra* does not contain is an explicit social ethic. This does not mean, of course, that it could not serve as a basis for constructing one. Indeed, the mythic quality of the sūtra, and the ambiguity surrounding its presentation of the "one vehicle" – extravagantly praised but ultimately never explained – have over the centuries enabled an astonishing range of interpretations, prompting one scholar to speak of the *Lotus* as an "empty" text into which generations of exegetes have poured their own meanings.[2] It is in this history of *Lotus Sūtra* interpretation, rather than in the *Lotus* itself, that we find clear associations drawn between the sūtra and the welfare of society. This interpretive move seems to have been particular to Japanese Buddhism and has remote roots in the writings of Saichō (767–822), founder of the Japanese Tendai sect, and in the copying, reciting, and explicating of the *Lotus* in court-sponsored rituals of the Heian period (794–1185) as a "nation - protecting sūtra," believed able to ensure the country's safety and well-being. This link between the *Lotus Sūtra* and the peace and prosperity of the land would become solidified in the thought of Nichiren.

A monk of humble origins, Nichiren first drew public attention when he remonstrated with authorities of the *bakufu* or military government in 1260, submitting a memorial to the shogunal regent titled *Risshō ankoku ron*, or "Treatise on establishing the true [Dharma] and bringing peace to the land." For Nichiren, a follower of the Tendai sect, the "true Dharma" was none other than the *Lotus Sūtra*, revered in Tendai circles as the perfect and ultimate teaching of Shakyamuni Buddha, the one vehicle in which all other, partial truths are united. As indicated by the phrase "peace of the land" (*ankoku*) in his title, Nichiren was from the beginning concerned with the impact of Buddhist faith and practice on the larger society. He wrote his treatise in an attempt to make clear, in the light of Buddhist sūtras, the causes of recent disasters, including earthquakes, crop failure, famine and epidemics, as well as the means of their solution. While it remains an open question whether Japan in the the mid-thirteenth century was really more plagued by calamities than in other eras, there is no doubt that Nichiren, like many of his contemporaries, believed he was living in a uniquely troubled time, coinciding with Buddhist scriptural predictions of the degenerate Final Dharma age (*mappō*) when the Buddha's teachings would become obscured, and enlightenment would be difficult to achieve.[3] Throughout his life, he would assert that the troubles besetting the country – not only natural disasters but internecine political strife and the threat of Mongol conquest – were due to neglect of the *Lotus Sūtra* in favor of "lesser," provisional Buddhist forms, such as Pure Land devotion, Zen meditation, and esoteric ritual practice. Thus he urged:

> Now with all speed you must simply reform your faith and at once devote it to the single good of the true vehicle [i.e., the *Lotus Sūtra*]. Then the threefold world will all become the Buddha land, and could a Buddha land decline? The ten directions will all become a treasure realm, and how could a treasure realm be destroyed?[4]

In claiming that faith in the *Lotus Sūtra* would realize the Buddha land in the present world, Nichiren drew both on perceptions of the *Lotus*'s magical power as a "nation-protecting sūtra" and on traditional Tendai doctrine, which asserts the nonduality of subjective and objective realms (*eshō funi*) and the identity of the present, *sahā* world with the Buddha's Land of Tranquil Light (*shaba soku jakkōdo*). Nichiren made clear that the nonduality of the self and its environment, or the immanence of the Buddha in the present world, was not a mere matter of metaphysical asser- tion or even of subjective, personal insight; where people embraced the *Lotus Sūtra*, the outer world would actually be transformed:

> When all people throughout the land enter the one Buddha vehicle, and the Wonderful Dharma [of the *Lotus*] alone flour- ishes, because the people all chant Namu-Myōhō-renge-kyō, the wind will not thrash the branches, nor the rain fall hard enough to break clods. The age will become like the reigns of [the Chinese sage kings] Yao and Shun. In the present life, inauspicious calami- ties will be banished, and people will obtain the art of longevity. When the principle becomes manifest that both persons and dharmas "neither age nor die," then each of you, behold! There can be no doubt of the sūtra's promise of "peace and security in the present world."[5]

Thus in Nichiren's teaching, the possibility of realizing the Buddha land in the present world was welded to an exclusive truth claim. Only faith in the *Lotus Sūtra*, the one vehicle of the perfect teaching, could bring about the peace of the land. In his estimation, however, his contemporaries had rejected the *Lotus Sūtra* and instead embraced incomplete, provisional teachings – an act of "slander of the Dharma" that would bring ruin to the country and drag individuals down into the painful realms of rebirth. Therefore he urged his followers not only to embrace undivided faith in the *Lotus Sūtra* themselves but to spread that faith to others, assertively rebuking adherence to other, "inferior" teachings. This is known as *shakubuku*, the stern method of teaching the Dharma by explicitly denouncing "wrong views."[6] Nichiren's outspoken criticism of other Buddhist teachings provoked hostility and even persecution from the authorities; he was exiled twice and once nearly executed, while his followers were on occasion imprisoned or banished, had their lands seized, or in some cases were even killed. Since the *Lotus Sūtra* itself predicts that its devotees will meet persecution "in the evil age after the Buddha's *nirvāṇa*," such trials only served to affirm for Nichiren the validity of his course. Thus we find in his writings strong claims about the soteric value of meeting persecution for the sūtra's sake, especially from the worldly authorities. Such hardships, he taught, affirm the correctness of one's faith, serve to expiate one's own past sins of "slandering the Dharma," and guarantee one's eventual achievement of Buddhahood. He also asserted that the truth of the *Lotus Sūtra* transcended worldly authority, and thus, should one's devotion to the sūtra come into conflict with the demands of ordinary social loyalties – of children to parents or of subjects to sovereign – one should defy conventional loyalties and uphold the *Lotus*, even at the the cost of one's life. While it falls short of a critique of political power *per se*, Nichiren's establishing of the *Lotus Sūtra* as a source of transcendent authority made possible, at times even mandated, resistance to worldly rule. This element in his teaching was occasionally invoked by monks of the medieval Hokkeshū or Lotus sect, as Nichiren's later followers were called, to assert the independence of their sangha from the ruler's authority.[7] With a few notable exceptions, however, it has rarely been been emphasized in the modern period and would seem to represent an untapped resource for the construction of a possible Nichiren Buddhist social ethic.

Was Nichiren himself a "socially engaged Buddhist"? Not, one would have to say, in the modern sense of the term. He did not argue that working for social betterment in and of itself constitutes an essential part of Buddhist practice. He displayed no interest in building bridges, digging wells or caring for the sick, the traditional charitable projects of medieval Buddhists. Rather, Nichiren deemed bodhisattva practice for others' sake to be something more fundamental – the spread of exclusive faith in the *Lotus Sūtra* and the denouncing of false attachments to other teachings. And yet his teaching does have a distinctive "social" orientation, in his claim that individuals' faith and practice were not merely a matter a matter of personal liberation but carried profound consequences for the larger world. Now in the Final Dharma age, he wrote, it was no longer appropriate for practitioners to seclude themselves in the mountains to cultivate meditation or to recite the *Lotus Sūtra* in solitude; rather, the times demanded *shakubuku*, the refutation of provisional teachings. Nichiren's linking of faith in the *Lotus Sūtra* to the realization of the Buddha land in this world, and his call to followers to commit themselves to active proselytizing, have been adapted by some modern Nichiren Buddhists as key elements on which to model their social engagement.

Two lay Buddhist movements: Sōka Gakkai and Risshō Kōseikai

Observers of contemporary Japanese religion sometimes speak of the lay movements Sōka Gakkai and Risshō Kōseikai as embodying a "revitalization" or "reformation" of modern Buddhism. Founded in the pre-war years, both have weathered numerous trials, undergone some major self-redefinitions, and have now become well established as the largest of Japan's numerous "New Religions." Sōka Gakkai claims more than seventeen million members, and Risshō Kōseikai, more than six million; both have followings outside Japan.[8] Despite their vast size, the basic activities of both organizations are structured around small gatherings in which members share testimonials, introduce newcomers, and receive instruction and encouragement. The local discussion meeting (*zadankai*) has always been the primary forum for the Sōka Gakkai's proselytizing efforts, while Risshō Kōseikai has emphasized the "Dharma circle" (*hōza*) or group counselling for problem-solving based on Kōseikai teachings. The importance of one-on-one guidance from leaders is also stressed. In addition, larger organizational units are formed at the ward, prefectural and national levels, and members have many opportunities to participate with peers in the activities of youth groups, women's groups, professional divisions, and the like.

Sōka Gakkai

Sōka Gakkai dates its founding from 1930, when the educator Makiguchi Tsunesaburō[9] (1871–1944) launched publication of his lifework, *Sōka kyōiku taikei* (System of Value Creating Education). In 1937, he inaugurated the Sōka Kyōiku Gakkai (Value Creation Educational Society), a group of about sixty teachers and educators committed to his progressive ideals. In 1928, Makiguchi had embraced the teachings of Nichiren Shōshā, a small sect in the Fuji lineage of Nichiren Buddhism, and with time, the society's focus shifted gradually from education to religion. The society was nearly destroyed during the Pacific War, when Makiguchi and other leaders were imprisoned under the Public Security Preservation Law for refusing to have their members enshrine the talismans of the imperial Ise Shrine, as mandated by government religious policy. Among those imprisoned was Makiguchi's disciple Toda Jōsai (1900–1958), who revived the society after the war and established it on a broader basis as a lay organization of Nichiren Shōshū, open to people in all walks of life. It was renamed Sōka Gakkai at that time, to reflect this new orientation. Toda organized and led an intensive proselytization campaign that raised membership to 750,000 households by 1957, the year before his death. Under its third president, Ikeda Daisaku (1928-), the organization continued its phenomenal growth but also expanded its emphasis on proselytizing to include a range of cultural, educational and social welfare activities. (Ikeda retired from the presidency in 1978 but, as honorary president of Sōka Gakkai and president of Sōka Gakkai International, is still the organization's *de facto* leader.) Conflict over who would define the sources of religious authority led in 1991 to a schism with Nichiren Shōshū, and Sōka Gakkai is now undergoing a process of self-redefinition independent of any Nichiren temple denomination.[10]

The broader range of activities inaugurated in the 1960s and 1970s included formal entry into the world of politics. The Sōka Gakkai had begun to sponsor candidates for local offices in the mid-1950s, and in 1964 took the controversial step of inaugurating its own party. The Kōmeitō or Clean Government Party espoused the broad ideals of "human socialism," combining the individual freedom of capitalism with the egalitarian concerns of socialism, and "Buddhist democracy," in which government structures would be informed by Buddhist compassion. Though the Sōka Gakkai and Kōmeitō have been officially separated since 1970, the party remains dependent on Gakkai membership for its electoral base and constitutes something of a lightning rod for periodic disputes over the proper relationship of religion and government.[11] The same period also saw the beginnings of active Gakkai participation in a movement to ban nuclear arms, when youth division members gathered more than ten million signatures on a petition against such weapons and presented them to the United Nations in 1975. Since its early post-war years, Sōka Gakkai has always equated the spread of Nichiren's teaching with peacemaking. As Ikeda writes:

> The core of the message of [Nichiren's] *Rissho ankoku ron* is this: On a national, international, or worldwide scale the only way to bring about lasting peace is to establish the reign of the true Buddhist Law … . War strips loftiness and respect from humanity and, through its wicked actions, covers man with filth. It is only natural that Buddhism, the aim of which is to guide all people to the highest, purest realms, is bound to oppose war directly. By a

like token, the Buddhist believer who is eager to practice his faith in the truest way regards it as his mission to pour his entire soul into the task of building peace.[12]

Risshō Kōseikai

Risshō Kōseikai was founded in 1938 by Niwano Nikkyō (1916–1999) and Naganuma Myōkō (1889–1957). The year before, both had left the Reiyūkai, another Nichiren-based new religion, to which they had belonged. Niwano wrote that they were dissatisfied with what they saw as Reiyūkai's excessive emphasis on organizational expansion and also wished to see more energy devoted to study of the Lotus Sūtra.[13] Unlike the Sōka Gakkai, which followed the purism of Nichiren Shōshū in repudiating all religious elements apart from Nichiren's teaching as "slander of the Dharma," Risshō Kōseikai was at the outset deeply rooted in folk religious traditions. Myōkō Sensei, as Naganuma was often called, possessed considerable shamanistic powers. Oracles she received from the kami or local deities played a key role in directing the organization in its early days. After her death, under Niwano's leadership, the group gradually distanced itself from shamanistic and divinatory practices and has increasingly defined itself in Buddhist terms. This shift in orientation coincided with Kōseikai's increasing involvement in ecumenical activities for peace, beginning in 1963 when Niwano traveled to ten nations as part of an eighteen-member Japanese delegation of religious leaders committed to the banning of nuclear weapons.[14] Since then, Risshō Kōseikai has constructed itself as a socially engaged Buddhism, based on Niwano's hermeneutical perspective that "the whole Lotus Sūtra embodies an ideology of peace."[15] In his popular commentaries, Niwano read specific passages and parables of the sūtra as teaching how peace is to be achieved. For example, Śākyamuni Buddha's gratitude toward his vindictive cousin Devadatta for favors in a prior life teaches one to break the cycle of enmity by refusing to bear grudges. The parable of the medicinal herbs that receive the same rain but grow to different heights in accord with their capacity teaches that differences among nations must be respected; developing nations must not be arbitrarily expected to emulate the industrial model of developed nations. In the parable of the magically conjured city, the long steep path represents "the long history of mankind's suffering caused by war, starvation, poverty and the violation of human rights." The conjured city itself represents temporary peace – the physical cessation of war. The place of treasure, the real goal of the journey, is "the reformation of one's mind by religion" that must underlie lasting peace.[16] Niwano discusses his idea of what this "reformation of the mind" will bring about in interpreting the Buddha's ten supernatural powers displayed in Chapter 21 of the Lotus Sūtra, where passage among the worlds in the ten directions becomes unobstructed, "as though they were one Buddha land." This indicates, Niwano writes, that:

> a world of great harmony will appear when all nations, all races, and all classes come to live in accordance with the one truth, so that discrimination among them vanishes, discord and fighting do not occur, and all the people work joyfully, enjoy their lives, and promote culture. In short, the whole world will become one buddha-land. Organizationally speaking, it can be said that the buddha-land means the formation of a world federation.[17]

Doctrinal approaches: a diametric opposition

In terms of how they understand both Nichiren and the *Lotus Sūtra*, Sōka Gakkai and Risshō Kōseikai contrast sharply, so much so that one wonders whether their historical rivalry may not have helped to define them over and against one another.[18] Sōka Gakkai, more than almost any other Nichiren Buddhist organization, has upheld Nichiren's stance of exclusive devotion to the *Lotus*, and it is Nichiren's writings, rather than the text of the *Lotus Sūtra* itself, that hold normative authority for members. During the "great march of *shakubuku*," the massive proselytization effort spearheaded by Toda in the 1950s, Sōka Gakkai rhetoric appropriated Nichiren's claim for the exclusive truth of the *Lotus Sūtra* to explain the recent horrors of the Pacific War and its aftermath. In Nichiren's view, it was "slander of the Dharma" – rejection of the *Lotus Sūtra* – that had brought Japan to the brink of destruction by the Mongols; now, the sufferings and devastation resulting from the war, including the atomic bombings, were construed in the same way as "collective punishment" for having ignored Nichiren's teaching.[19] This mono-causal account of Japan's misery and defeat proved compelling, not only in its simplicity of explanation but in the empowerment it offered. If the sufferings of the war and Occupation stemmed from slander of the Dharma, then it was ordinary Gakkai members who, through their proselytizing efforts, were rectifying this fundamental evil once and for all:

> You should realize that you were born into the Final Dharma age with this mission [to save all people through *shakubuku*]... If we really desire to rebuild a peaceful Japan and establish peace throughout the world, then, without begrudging our lives, we must advance *shakubuku* to convey the Wonderful Dharma [to all] as soon as possible, by even a single day or hour.[20]

An exclusivistic stance, however, is extremely difficult to maintain in an atmosphere increasingly committed to pluralism. In the 1960s and 1970s,

Sōka Gakkai came under scathing media criticism for its aggressive prose-lytizing and is still battling to overcome the negative images created during that time. As the organization grew increasingly large and well established, religious debate and denunciation of other teachings gave way to the cultural and peace education activities promoted under Ikeda's leadership. This trend toward moderation seems to have progressed by a quantum leap since the break with Nichiren Shōshū, and the Gakkai at present even engages in ecumenical endeavors. Article 7 of the 1995 Sōka Gakkai International Charter announced a commitment to "the Buddhist spirit of tolerance," interfaith dialogue, and cooperation with other religions toward the resolution of humanity's problems.[21] This shift in orientation, while providing entrée into global ecumenical networks of socially engaged religionists, would nevertheless seem (at least from an outsider's perspec-tive) to involve Sōka Gakkai in a certain theological inconsistency. To my knowledge, the organization has yet to reconcile its new interfaith cooper-ation at a theoretical level with its espousal of Nichiren's claim that only faith in the *Lotus Sūtra* leads to enlightenment in the *mappō* era.

Risshō Kōseikai, for its, part, has been inclusive all along. In his lectures on the *Lotus Sūtra*, Niwano Nikkyō writes:

> When seeking the origin of this great universe and the various elements and living things that exist therein, we come to see the one and only energy... Buddhism calls this fundamental energy 'the void,' while some scientists call it "Planck's constant"... Christianity calls it "God"; Judaism, "Yahweh"; Islam, "Allah."

The conviction that all the "great" religions share a single essence (Niwano excepts "low religions that deal with fetish or idol worship") leads him to conclude that the "*Lotus Sūtra*" and "Śākyamuni Buddha" are not proper nouns, but the one truth underlying all phenomena and to which all systems tend.[22] Differently stated, all great religions teach the *Lotus Sūtra* and revere the eternal Buddha; religious pluralism is itself an instance of "all dharmas manifesting the true aspect" (*shohō jissō*). This conviction informed Niwano's lifelong commitment to interfaith coopera-tion. He served, for example, as chairman of the Japan Religions League and of the World Conference on Religion and Peace (WCRP) and played a key role in organizing a number of international ecumenical peace confer-ences.

As might be expected, in a reading of the *Lotus Sūtra* as teaching the essential unity of all faiths, Nichiren's exclusive truth claim does not figure prominently. One of Niwano's sūtra commentaries makes a brief attempt to assimilate Nichiren to his inclusive position by suggesting that Nichiren's criticism of other sects was aimed at their mutual antagonism and attachment to their own teachings, at the expense of the Buddha's unifying intent.[23] However, from the very beginning, it was the *Lotus Sūtra*, rather than Nichiren's teachings, that has served as the basis for Kōseikai teachings. It is also my impression, to be tested by further research, that Nichiren came to be de-emphasized in Risshō Kōseikai with the organization's growing commitment to interfaith endeavors.[24]

Sōka Gakkai, as we have seen, incurred widespread hostility for what many perceived as dogmatic self-righteousness in its claim to exclusive possession of religious truth – something Risshō Kōseikai, with its thorough-going ecumenical stance, has avoided. However, Niwano's claim that "all religions are the same in their essence" would seem to risk obscuring very real differences in the doctrines and practices of individual religious traditions, differences which the members of those traditions might not deem superficial at all but constitutive of their religious identity.[25] The claim to religious unity also raises the question of how Kōseikai members understand the particular identity of Buddhism and their place within it. One cannot but wonder (again, speaking as an outsider) about the danger here of what Robert Bellah has termed "over-tolerance," a too ready acceptance of heterogenous elements that allows the distinctive message of one's own tradition to be overwhelmed.[26]

Although it remains to be seen where Sōka Gakkai's recent ecumenical interests will lead, the social engagement of these two organizations was for a long time rooted in almost diametrically opposed readings of the *Lotus Sūtra* and Nichiren. For Sōka Gakkai, the *Lotus* has been the one true teaching whose propagation alone can bring peace to the world; for Risshō Kōseikai, it is the shared truth inherent in all things, an awakening to which, it is said, will give rise to a sense of universal brotherhood and mutual respect. These contrasting orientations also shaped the way that the two organizations sought in the post-war years to secure their position in a society often hostile to New Religions. Risshō Kōseikai joined forces with other such movements in establishing the Union of the New Religious Organizations in Japan (Shin Nihon Shūkyō Dantai Rengōkai), which claimed sixty member organizations by 1952.[27] Sōka Gakkai, as already noted, established its own political party. Sōka Gakkai and Risshō Kōseikai may perhaps be seen as contemporary representatives of a very old controversy in *Lotus Sūtra* interpretation over whether all teachings and practices, correctly understood, should be seen as expressions of the one vehicle just as they are, or whether the one vehicle is a truth apart, transcending all other forms, which must then be discarded in its favor.[28]

A shared ethos and style of engagement

Despite their radically different understandings of the *Lotus Sūtra*, Sōka Gakkai and Risshō Kōseikai nonetheless exhibit some remarkable similarities in their forms of social engagement and in the ethos underlying that engagement. Both groups support the United Nations as affiliate nongovernmental organizations (NGOs) and also mobilize their members for grassroots volunteer work, including aid to refugees and famine and disaster relief. Only a few of their many projects can be enumerated here. Risshō Kōseikai was instrumental in the founding, in 1969, of the Brighter Society Movement, a civic movement designed to "widen the circle of interreligious cooperation and call forth citizens' goodwill (Buddha nature)."[29] Members promote greening campaigns, visit the elderly and bedridden, and perform other acts of service and citizenship. Kōseikai's Youth Division received the United Nations Peace Prize in 1988 for its work on behalf of UNICEF and its "Donate One Meal" campaign, in which participants skip one meal a month and donate the cost to the Kōseikai Fund for Peace. Risshō Kōseikai also aided Vietnamese refugees through its Boat People Project and, more recently, has done refugee work in Somalia and the former Yugoslavia. Sōka Gakkai, for its part, has launched a grassroots movement for "peace education," sponsoring numerous exhibitions on the destructive potential of nuclear weapons and gathering and publishing multi-volume collections of oral histories of individual experiences from the war. The object of these endeavors is one of consciousness-raising. Keeping alive the memory of war's horror and brutality may help engender a repugnance toward war in those younger generations who have never experienced it personally.[30] Sōka Gakkai has also founded the Toda Institute for Global Peace and Policy Research to promote international collaboration among peace researchers, policymakers, and activists, and to help coordinate the peace efforts of such individuals with those of research centers and NGOs.[31] Rank and file members also initiate their own programs. Inspired by the slogan "think globally, act locally," barbers and hairdressers belonging to Sōka Gakkai have in recent years launched the "Charity Cut," offering free haircuts in exchange for a thousand-yen donation. Money collected has gone to UNICEF; for disaster relief following the 1995 Kobe earthquake; and to the International Organization for Migration, to help repatriate young Vietnamese women.[32]

These very similar efforts of Risshō Kōseikai and Sōka Gakkai also are supported by a shared ethos, in which all social improvement must, ultimately, be grounded in an inner personal transformation – the "human revolution" (*ningen kakumei*), as Gakkai members call it, or "reformation of the mind" (*kokoro no kaizō*), in Kōseikai terms. Since war, strife, and injustice are seen as fundamentally rooted in the three poisons – greed, anger, and delusion – in the hearts of individuals, it is only by individual self-purification that a lasting foundation for peace can be established. Based on faith in the *Lotus Sūtra*, all ordinary activities, at home, at school or in the workplace, are themselves seen as Buddhist practice and as an opportunity to polish one's character. This ethos of "Buddhism is daily life" promoted in both groups entails striving cheerfully and to one's utmost wherever one may be; cultivating gratitude for one's circumstances, even adverse ones, as opportunities for personal growth and self-challenge; and reflecting on oneself before criticizing others. Moreover, since all things are interconnected, such quotidian efforts in effect constitute a unique personal mission to spread the blessings of the *Lotus Sūtra*. To quote Ikeda Daisaku:

> Within all the realms pertaining to you, whether in your family, workplace, or neighborhood, you are the one who holds full responsibility there for the spread of the Wonderful Dharma. Don't forget that true Buddhism and the spread of the *Lotus Sūtra* lie in the most immediate, even humble activities. You should have the self-awareness that you are here [in those circumstances] now as an envoy of the true Buddha, Nichiren Daishōnin.[33]

Given their radically different, even opposed understandings of the the *Lotus Sūtra* and of Nichiren, why do Sōka Gakkai and Risshō Kōseikai display such similar forms of social engagement and embrace so similar an ethos? The short answer is that their style of social engagement and its supporting rationale may owe less to Nichiren and the *Lotus Sūtra* than to the broader religious culture of modern Japan. Let us briefly consider some of the larger trends in which their common ethos is grounded.[34]

Both Sōka Gakkai and Risshō Kōseikai participate in what scholars have termed the "vitalistic theory of salvation" found in a number of Japanese New Religions of both Buddhist and Shinto derivation and having remote roots in agrarian religion.[35] According to this theory, all phenomena in the universe are expressions of a "great life" (*daiseimei*) or "life force" (*seimei-ryoku*) and are therefore all interrelated. Human ignorance of or disconnection from this fundamental life force is deemed responsible for discord, sickness and misfortune, while "salvation" entails bringing oneself into harmony with this life force, resulting in improved health, prosperity, harmonious family relations, and, on a broad scale, a brighter, happier world. Thus achievement of this-worldly benefits, individual salvation, and the realization of an ideal society are all grounded in the same principle and placed on the same plane. Sōka Gakkai's Toda Jōsei, while imprisoned during the war, is said to have undergone a mystical experience in which he realized that "Buddha is none other than life itself," an insight that underlaid his later explication of "life philosophy" (*seimei tetsugaku*).[36] In Sōka Gakkai literature, "life force" often replaces more classically Buddhist notions of emptiness or dependent origination as the ontological ground of reality. One sees this in Kōseikai publications as well. Interpreting the *Lotus Sūtra's* phrase "true aspect of the dharmas" (*shohō jissō*), Niwano Nikkyō not only equates "emptiness" with "life" but argues that realization of this "great life" is the source of world peace:

> Voidness [i.e., *śūnyatā*] is the only one, real existence that makes everything and every phenomenon of the universe. Scientifically speaking, it is the fundamental energy that is manifested in all phenomena, and religiously speaking it is the great life force that permeates everything that exists in the universe, namely the Eternal, Original Buddha... [I]f the real embodiment of all things is a single entity, ... when one can fully realize this, then fraternal love, the feeling that all human beings are brothers and sisters, will spring up in one's heart. One will be filled with a sense of harmony and cooperation. This sentiment of fraternity is the benevolence or compassion taught in Buddhism.[37]

The ethos of "Buddhism is daily life" taught by Sōka Gakkai and Risshō Kōseikai also has roots in what Yasumaro Yoshio has called the "conventional morality" (*tsūzoku dōtoku*) promoted by popular movements of self-cultivation that emerged among farmers and merchants during the Edo period (1603–1868) and stressed individual moral development through diligent efforts in one's given circumstances.[38] Self-cultivation was rooted in what Yasumaro terms a "philosophy of the mind (or heart)" (*kokoro no tetsugaku*), "mind" here indicating the universal ground of self, society, and the cosmos. In the rigidly stratified society of early modern Japan, this emphasis on personal cultivation, in Yasumaro's analysis, encouraged subjective formation of self and positive engagement with one's tasks, invested occupations such agriculture and trade with a profound moral, even religious, significance, and thus contributed to the process of modernization. While society is no longer divided into fixed status groups, the values of harmony, sincerity, and industry central to Yasumaro's "conventional morality," along with its assumptions about the limitless potential to be tapped through cultivating the mind, are still very much alive in what Helen Hardacre has described as "the world view of the New Religions."[39] Hardacre notes in particular the notion that "other people are mirrors" – meaning that other people's behavior is said to reflect aspects of one's own inner state. Harsh or inconsiderate treatment at the hands of others, even if the believer is not obviously at fault, is to be taken as a sign of one's own shortcomings or karmic hindrances and as an occasion for repentance and further effort – a point stressed repeatedly in the practical guidance of both Sōka Gakkai and Risshō Kōseikai.

Does this ethos effectively contribute to social betterment? On the one hand, there is much that may be said in its favor. First, it locates all agency in individuals, who are taught that – because they can tap the supreme life-force of the universe – there is no hardship that cannot be overcome. Such an outlook instills courage and cheerfulness in the face of adversity and the will to challenge limitations. It is also personally empowering, in that one's own efforts, however humble, are infused with immense significance as bodhisattva practice linked directly to the accomplishment of world peace. More than the actions of politicians, diplomats and world leaders, it is the daily acts of practitioners that are seen as laying the foundation for this goal. It may well be here, in this sense of individual empowerment and personal mission, that Sōka Gakkai and Risshō Kōseikai have exerted their greatest appeal.

By teaching that the individual is ultimately responsible for his or her circumstances, the ethos of these groups also works to undercut an egoistic sense of personal entitlement, litigiousness, and other unedifying tendencies to protect self at the expense of others. Jane Hurst, in her study of the Sōka Gakkai's movement in the United States, credits this ethos with the organization's remarkable level of racial harmony; belief that the individual is responsible for his or her own circumstances precludes racial or ethnic scapegoating as a way of blaming others for one's own problems.[40] At the same time, however, while personally empowering, the idea that external change is a function of inner cultivation tends to be politically conservative.[41] In particular, the notion that others' harsh or unfair treatment reflects some unresolved shortcoming in oneself undercuts even the concept of a structural problem, reducing everything to an issue of individual self-development. As Hardacre notes, "Placing blame and responsibility on the individual also denies the idea that 'society' can be blamed for one's problems; hence concepts of exploitation and discrimination are ruled out of consideration."[42] The continual injunction not to complain but to take even adversity and ill treatment as an occasion for spiritual growth may work to foster acquiescence to the status quo, rather than the critical spirit necessary to recognize social inequity and speak out against it. Some observers have also argued that excessive emphasis on personal cultivation is inadequate as a basis for achieving peace:

> [I]t tends to lose sight of the fact that wars occur as the result of a political process that cannot always be reduced to individual, or collective, greed, envy, hate, or whatever... until the concentric waves of morality have perfected every human being, arguably more will be done to avoid war – if not to establish true and lasting peace – by seeking to influence political processes.[43]

The conviction that social change, to be effective, must be accompanied by mental cultivation is probably shared by most forms of socially engaged Buddhism; this is, after all, what distinguishes it from purely secular programs of social melioration. One might ask, however, how far inner transformation can be emphasized before it becomes in effect an endorsement of the existing system, rather than a force for improving it.

Like the ethos expressed in the terms "human revolution" or "Buddhism is daily life," Sōka Gakkai's and Risshō Kōseikai's particular styles of social engagement, mobilizing broad-based volunteer efforts among their members, find parallels among contemporary Japanese religious organizations more generally, whether Shinto or Buddhist, New Religions or established denominations. The highly successful "donate one meal" campaign, for example, is conducted not only by Kōseikai but by the Shinto-based movement Shōroku Shintō Yamatoyama and other groups.[44] Kōseikai's Brighter Society Movement also has parallels among the social welfare and relief efforts initiated by established Buddhist sects, such as the Tendai sect's Light up Your Corner Movement.[45] These efforts reflect both the same virtues and the same limitations as the world-view supporting them. They enable large-scale participation and contributions of time and resources, raising members' awareness of the threat of nuclear weapons, food shortages, the environmental crisis, and other social problems, and also foster a desire to aid others. At the same time, this is a style of social engagement that tends to "work within the system"; it does not issue a direct challenge to existing social structures or attempt fundamentally to transform them.

Nipponzan Myōhōji: civil protest and absolute non-violence

In contrast to the two large lay movements introduced above, Nipponzan Myōhōji is a small Nichiren Buddhist order of about 1,500 persons, including both monastics and lay supporters. Its monks and nuns lead a life of utmost simplicity, fasting on designated days of the month and chanting the *daimoku* many hours daily. They are also committed to non-violent social protest and can be seen at marches and rallies, dressed in their saffron robes and chanting the *daimoku* to the beat of hand-held, fan-shaped drums (*uchiwa daiko*). "Peace walks" – one of Nipponzan Myōhōji's major activities – unite the "march" as a form of non-violent political demonstration with the traditional Nichiren Buddhist ascetic practice of chanting the *daimoku* while walking to the beat of a hand-held drum. Nipponzan Myōhōji is especially active in the anti-nuclear cause and first began to participate in civil protest around 1954, during the popular anti-atomic weapons movement touched off when crew members of the Japanese tuna trawler *Lucky Dragon Five* (*Daigo Fukuryūmaru*) were exposed to fallout from United States H-bomb testing on Bikini Atoll. Nipponzan Myōhōji members joined demonstrations at American army bases, where their courage, even in the face of police brutality, won them respect within the Japanese peace movement. In Japan, they have consistently opposed expansion of the US military presence, conducted peace walks to commemorate the Hiroshima and Nagasaki bombings and protest against nuclear weapons, and, during the Gulf War, staged a hunger strike in front of Shibuya Station in Tokyo. Nipponzan Myōhōji followers have also been active in Cambodia, Bosnia, Costa Rica, Nicaragua, and elsewhere. In the United States, beginning with their participation in the 1976 Continental Walk for Disarmament and Social Justice sponsored by the War Resisters League, their marches have criss-crossed the country; in a recent "prison walk" in California, Nipponzan Myōhōji members joined in calling for prison reform and protested against the death penalty.[46] The order has shown particular sympathy for peoples who have suffered Western aggression and colonization, and its members in the United States have been active on behalf of Native American rights. Nipponzan Myōhōji is unusual, perhaps even unique among Japanese Buddhist groups, for its commitment to civil protest. Its founder, Fujii Nichidatsu (1885–1985) at one point wrote:

> In the beginning I also thought that religion, as something concerned with the inner human spirit, should have no say about politics or concern itself with social problems, but should stick to giving spiritual guidance to each individual person. However, these days, the problems we need to be concerned with necessarily involve the large social structures of the state, or even further, the world. Until the world itself changes, even individual moral cultivation is impossible.[47]

In a survey designed to examine the attitudes toward peace of members of six different Japanese new religious movements, including the three under discussion here, Robert Kisala found that Nipponzan Myōhōji members differed substantially from those of other religious groups in deeming local civic action, rather than support for global organizations such as the United Nations, to be the most effective method for achieving peace.[48]

Fujii Nichidatsu began his religious career as a priest of Nichirenshū. From early on, he demonstrated an aptitude for the more ascetic side of the Nichiren tradition and undertook such austerities as fasting and self-mortification. From a young age, he adopted the life of an itinerant monk, and in 1916, inspired by Nichiren's example of "admonishing the state," took up a stand at Nijūbashi opposite the imperial palace, chanting the *daimoku* and beating the drum in an act of remonstration with the Taishō emperor to take faith in the *Lotus Sūtra*. Fujii was particularly struck by Nichiren's prophecy that Buddhism, which had spread eastward from western regions in the True and Semblance Dharma ages, would return from the east to the west in the Final Dharma age. Determined to do his part in realizing this prophecy, Fujii crossed in 1917 to Manchuria to disseminate Nichiren's teachings there. He founded a temple at Liaoyang in 1918, an event later regarded as the founding of Nipponzan Myōhōji and a break with Nichirenshū, though the nature of Fujii's differences with the parent sect remain a subject for further investigation. News of the Great Kantō Earthquake in 1923 brought him home; in light of Nichiren's *Risshō ankoku ron*, he saw the earthquake as an omen of disaster facing Japan and believed it his duty to return and pray for the country's welfare. But in 1930 he again turned his attention west and sailed for India to propagate the *daimoku* there. In 1933, he spent a month at Gandhi's Wardha Ashram, where he had two brief interviews with Gandhi.[49] He was yet to embrace Gandhi's *ahimsa* doctrine; rather, evidence suggests that Fujii at this time sympathized with Japanese military advances into Asia, which he construed as the holy task of liberating Asian peoples from Western imperialism.[50] More than a decade later, however, he would undergo a transformative experience that led him to condemn violence absolutely:

> What led me to assert non-resistance, disarmament and the abolition of war was not my encounter with Mr. Gandhi. When the atom bombs were dropped on Hiroshima and Nagasaki, and I saw hundred of thousands of innocent women and children die as though burned at the stake and poisoned, victims of a tragedy unprecedented in human history; when I saw Japan forced to accept unconditional surrender, then I understood the madness, folly, and barbarousness of modern war.[51]

Fujii's espousal of Gandhi may be said to have begun at this point, for the post-war Nipponzan Myōhoji sangha has embraced an uncompromisingly literal reading of the first precept and an absolute rejection of force, even to protect one's own life. The group is able to maintain this extreme stance by virtue of its monastic-centered orientation and its marginal position in Japanese society; as Robert Kisala has noted, members of large lay organizations such as Sōka Gakkai and Risshō Kōseikai, who are involved in the social mainstream, tend to embrace a more qualified pacifism that allows, say, for the right of self-defense. Yet, impracticable though it may be as a majority position, a commitment to absolute non-violence such as that of Nipponzan Myōhōji can nonetheless "remind us that there are values worth the ultimate sacrifice" and "act as brake on the tendency to resort to the use of force too easily."[52]

There seems little doubt that the primary influence shaping Nipponzan Myōhōji's post-war pacifism has been Gandhi's teaching of non-violence, rather than the *Lotus Sūtra* or the Nichiren Buddhist tradition. Nichiren himself, while sharing in the general Buddhist ethos that rejects killing as sinful, drew the major part of his following from among lower and middle-ranking samurai and their dependants. By virtue of their hereditary profession, killing was sometimes inevitable for these men, and the thrust of Nichiren's teaching – as of much of medieval Japanese Buddhism – was that sincere devotion (in this case, to the *Lotus Sūtra*) could save one from painful retribution for those sins that one cannot avoid committing.[53] Thus it is extremely difficult to derive a stance of absolute pacifism from Nichiren's writings. Fujii, however, did succeed in deriving a model for absolute nonviolence from the *Lotus Sūtra*, in his particular reading of the conduct of Bodhisattva Never Despising (*Sadāparibhūtā, Jōfukyō*), described in the sūtra's twentieth chapter. Bodhisattva Never Despising "practiced only obeisance," bowing to everyone he met in reverence for the someday-to-be realized Buddha potential within them. Though mocked by others, he never gave way to anger, even when abused and struck. Eventually, he was able to lead those who despised him to supreme Buddhahood.

In the context of the *Lotus*, Bodhisattva Never Despising illustrates forbearance, one of the six perfections or *pāramitās* that Mahāyāna bodhisattvas must cultivate. This refers especially (as in the case of Never Despising) to the forbearance of insult when mocked or criticized by adherents of the "lesser vehicle," who at the time constituted the mainstream Buddhist establishment. Thus, in its original historical context, the story of Never Despising is part of a Mahāyāna polemic against the so-called "Hīnayāna." In Fujii's reading, however, it becomes a model for absolute nonviolence.[54] The way of "practicing only obeisance," Fujii maintained, represents correct practice now in the Final Dharma age and is the sole path to realizing the Buddha land in the present world. Fujii interpreted "practicing only obeisance" in terms of the three categories of action: to bow reverently to others with one's body; to chant the *daimoku* with one's mouth; and to revere with one's mind the Buddha nature inherent in all. Such actions, he asserted, plant the seed of Buddhahood in the field of the *ālaya*-consciousness and will eventually sprout as the spiritual reconstruction of humanity.[55]

Another link that Fujii forged between his post-war pacifism and the *Lotus Sūtra* was Nipponzan Myōhōji's campaign of building "peace pagodas," in keeping with the eternal Buddha's words in the sūtra that he will appear wherever beings long to see him and "widely make offerings to my *śarira*." In 1933, during a pilgrimage to Sri Lanka, Fujii is said to have received Buddha relics from some Theravāda monks, who urged that they be enshrined in a stūpa. It was Fujii's abiding conviction that, wherever the stūpa cult had flourished after Śākyamuni Buddha's death, that society had enjoyed peace – though his own ideas about how peace would be realized differed strikingly before and after the end of the war. In 1938, following the Japanese invasion of China, Fujii presented some of his Buddha relics to the Japanese army and navy, whose victories, he wrote, would bring about the peace of Asia, the liberation of Asian peoples, and the reconstruction of Asian culture.[56] After Fujii's post-war conversion to pacifism, however, Nipponzan Myōhōji's Buddha relic veneration took the form of building peace pagodas. The first was erected in Kumamoto, Fujii's birthplace, in 1954. To date, more than eighty pagodas have been built worldwide, in Asia, Europe, and the United States, through the volunteer labor of Nipponzan Myōhōji sangha members and supporters.

Intensive *daimoku* practice and the building of peace pagodas represent the explicitly religious dimension of Nipponzan Myōhōji's contemporary social engagement, said to lead to the spiritual transformation of humanity. This dimension of spiritual transformation links Nipponzan Myōhōji to other forms of socially engaged Buddhism, including the lay movements Sōka Gakkai and Risshō Kōseikai. Nipponzan Myōhōji's outward forms of social engagement, however, are not primarily the efforts at building harmonious relations or the grassroots volunteerism seen in these Buddhist lay organizations, but nonviolent civil disobedience and a critical stance toward global structures of power and authority. This orientation can be traced to the influence of Gandhi; to Nipponzan Myōhōji's heritage, through Fujii, of the ascetic side of the Nichiren monastic tradition; and to its marginal status as a small, monastic-centered order. One senses in its current activities of social protest something similar to Nichiren's defiance of worldly authority, although such protest is framed – not in Nichiren's own terms, as a defense of the sole truth of the *Lotus Sūtra* – but as a commitment to absolute nonviolence and to a literal reading of the first precept.

The wartime legacy and the goal of "world peace"

The goal espoused by the three religious movements under discussion here is "world peace." Peacemaking, as Kenneth Kraft notes, is a characteristic concern of socially engaged Buddhists everywhere, a commitment to implementing the first precept on a global scale.[57] And yet "world peace" is a protean theme; like the "one vehicle" of the *Lotus Sūtra*, it has meant different things to different people. This contemporary goal of Sōka Gakkai, Risshō Kōseikai and Nipponzan Myōhōji, along with the modes of activism employed to achieve it, does not emerge fully formed from the *Lotus Sūtra* or from Nichiren's teachings but has been shaped by more recent historical circumstances. "World peace" is currently promoted as the goal of a number of Japanese religious bodies, including established Buddhist denominations as well as new religious movements, and often entails at least in part an attempt to define, *vis-à-vis* the world community, a unique role, perhaps even a sacred mission, for Japan – "Japan" here being represented by the particular religious group doing the defining. In religious rhetoric of the post-war decades, as in that of the peace movement more broadly, notions of a uniquely Japanese pacifist mission were formulated around three axes: (1) Japan must atone and make reparation for the sufferings inflicted on other Asian peoples during its period of militant imperialism; (2) only Japan has experienced the horrors of atomic warfare and is therefore both uniquely responsible and uniquely qualified to work for the abolition of nuclear weapons; and (3) only Japan has a Constitution expressly renouncing the right to wage war. The goal of "world peace," therefore, was not promoted solely as a global humanitarian concern – though it was undeniably that as well – but has also entailed a complex attempt to resolve guilt over wartime atrocities; to co-opt, in a manner restoring agency to Japan, the humiliation of national defeat and the imposition of the Occupation Constitution; and to define a particularistic Japanese identity within the context of global community.[58] For Nichiren Buddhists, the post-war project of defining Japan's special mission for world peace was complicated by two additional factors. First was a need to overcome lingering images, forged during the modern imperial period, of Nichiren Buddhism as a particularly nationalistic and militant religion, and the second, a need to reappropriate, in a manner suited to an international age, a Japan-centered element in Nichiren's own writings.

To take up these matters in reverse order: Nichiren, like other educated Buddhist monks of Japan's medieval period, participated in a discourse of what it meant, as a Buddhist, to be living in the degenerate Final Dharma age, long after the time of the historical Buddha. Temporal separation was mirrored by physical distance, for Japan was seen as a small country, far from the Buddha's birthplace, on the edge of the Buddhist cosmos. Buddhist thinkers labored to devise a positive Buddhist significance for the fact of having been born in the last age in this peripheral land. For example, some argued that Japan's local deities were the special "traces" or guises manifested by the Buddhas and bodhisattvas as a "skillful means" to lead the inhabitants to Buddhism; thus Japan, despite its remoteness from the land of Buddhism's origin, was nonetheless a place where particular signs of the Buddha's compassion had been displayed. Nichiren's own writings reflect a deep ambivalence about Japan.[59] On the one hand, he viewed it as an evil land, full of people who slandered the Dharma by placing other teachings above the *Lotus Sūtra* and who were therefore destined for great sufferings, such as attack by the Mongols. On the other hand, the Tendai tradition in which he was trained had long posited a particular karmic link between the *Lotus Sūtra* and Japan. Nichiren appropriated and reinterpreted the idea of this connection by defining Japan as the very place where – through his own efforts, as the Buddha's messenger – the Great Pure Dharma for the time of *mappō* had first appeared. Thus far, he wrote, the Buddha-Dharma of India had spread from west to east. But its light was feeble; it could never dispel the darkness of the degenerate Final Dharma age. In the time of *mappō*, the Buddha-Dharma of Japan would rise like the sun, returning from east to west, and illuminate the world.[60]

Nichiren's references to Japan do not, as some scholars have argued, constitute a form of proto-nationalism. Like much of medieval Buddhist discourse about Japan, his thinking on the subject was mythic, rather than geopolitical, and represents an attempt to construct a particularistic religious identity within the larger context of an imagined Buddhist world. Nor, in asserting that the Wonderful Dharma for the last age would "return to India," did Nichiren ever assert that the Japanese people as such were charged with a particular mission to spread it. This element in Nichiren's thought remained chiefly rhetorical and was not widely interpreted as a call to action until the late nineteenth century, when Japan, as a fledgling nation-state, had to negotiate a place in the world community.

Japan's leaders at that time were acutely aware of the need to gain economic and political parity with Western powers to avoid being exploited by them. Educators, opinion-makers and government spokesmen sought to rally citizens to the tasks of modernization and industrialization by instilling a strong sense of national identity. Growing nationalistic sentiment in turn placed a strain on Buddhist institutions. Ideologues with Shinto or Confucian leanings criticized Buddhism as institutionally corrupt, a superstitious relic of the past, a drain on public resources, and an alien import that had oppressed the indigenous Japanese spirit. The Meiji Restoration of 1868 also brought to an end the state patronage that Buddhist temples had enjoyed under the preceding Tokugawa regime (1603–1868). Buddhism was thus challenged to prove its relevance to an emerging modern nation. Throughout Japan's modern imperial period (1895–1945), virtually all Buddhist denominations – and other religions as well – supported nationalistic and militaristic aims, sending chaplains abroad to minister to Japanese troops, missionizing in subjugated territories, interpreting doctrine in light of national concerns and promoting patriotism among their followers.[61]

The various Nichiren Buddhist denominations were no more (and no less) committed to such endeavors than were other religious institutions. But Nichiren circles produced some extremely influential ideologues, able to construct nationalistic readings of their tradition that, at the time, proved powerfully compelling. A leading propagandist was Tanaka Chigaku (1861–1939), a former Nichirenshū priest who abandoned his robes to become a lay Buddhist leader, traveling throughout Japan on a lifelong career of writing and lecturing. Tanaka was the first to coin the term "Nichirenshugi" (Nichirenism), by which he meant, not the traditional Nichiren Buddhism of temples and priests, but a popular Nichiren doctrine reinterpreted in the light of modern national aspirations.[62] Tanaka founded a number of lay organizations to promote Nichirenshugi, most notably the Risshō Ankokukai, founded in 1885 and reorganized in 1914 as the Kokuchūkai (Pillar of the Nation Society).[63] Tanaka's hermeneutical innovation was to equate the truth of the *Lotus Sūtra* with the Japanese national essence or *kokutai*, the ideological foundation of the Japanese state, said by many nationalist thinkers to have been passed down in a direct line from the Sun Goddess to her divine grandson, Emperor Jinmu, the legendary founder of Japan. By identifying the Japanese national essence with the *Lotus Sūtra*, Tanaka raised the former to a position of universal significance and in effect equated the spread of faith in the *Lotus Sūtra* with the extension of Japanese imperial rule. Armed expansion into China and Manchuria was even described as "compassionate *shakubuku*." Where Nichiren himself had subordinated the ruler's authority to that of the *Lotus Sūtra*, Tanaka's Nichirenshugi placed Dharma and empire on the same plane. Militant Nichirenism did not remain confined to Tanaka's following but was adopted by other lay groups and by the more ardently nationalistic factions among Nichiren temple organizations. Another staunch advocate was Tanaka's colleague Honda Nisshō (1867–1931), leader of the Nichiren denomination Kenpon Hokkeshū, who founded a number of lay societies to combat socialism, discourage organized labor movements, rallied workers in support of government and promoted grassroots patriotism. While enjoying broad-based support among the urban working class, the lay movements of Nichirenshugi won approval from military officers, educators, scholars, writers, government bureaucrats and businessmen.

Repugnant as its rhetoric and goals may appear to many people today, one must nonetheless acknowledge that militant Nichirenshugi, like much of Japanese Buddhism during the modern imperial period, *was* socially engaged Buddhism. Its leaders were committed practitioners who called for action in society as an indispensable element of Buddhist practice. That action, as it happened, ultimately entailed brutal aggression against other Asian countries and exacted terrible sacrifices from ordinary Japanese citizens. Yet Nichirenshugi leaders appear genuinely to have believed that the worldwide extension of Japanese empire for which they strove – equated in their reading with the universal spread of the *Lotus Sūtra* – would liberate Asia from the tyranny of Western imperialism and usher in an era of peace and harmony for people everywhere. This is a disquieting example, indicating as it does that "social engagement" in and of itself is not necessarily beneficent, or even benign.

Full discussion of the wartime situation of the three movements treated in this chapter must await another opportunity and can only be touched upon here. In 1939, with the passing of the Religious Organizations Law, all religious bodies came under increasingly strict government surveillance, new religious movements in particular. Niwano Nikkyō was briefly imprisoned under the Public Security Preservation Law on charges that

Naganuma Myōkō's spirit revelations were "confusing the people" but was soon released. Prior to 1942, he had made a habit of donating small sums offered by Risshō Kōseikai members to the local police station in Nakano, Tokyo, for contribution to the armed forces – a circumstance that probably contributed to his lenient treatment. Moreover, as he wrote:

> Because of the militarists' mistaken belief that the teachings of Nichiren ... and those of the *Lotus Sūtra*, could be put to the service of ultranationalism, less pressure was applied to organizations – like Risshō Kōseikai – that professed faith in that sutra.[64]

The Sōka Gakkai (or Sōka Kyōiku Gakkai, as it was then known) did not escape so easily. Faithful to Nichiren's exclusive truth claim, and to Nichiren's example of defying worldly authority when it contravened devotion to the *Lotus Sūtra*, Makiguchi Tsunesaburō refused to allow his membership to enshrine the talismans of the Ise Shrine, as mandated by the wartime government. In 1943, he and twenty other leaders of the society were imprisoned on charges of *lèse-majesté*; Makiguchi died while still incarcerated the following year.[65] Nipponzan Myōhōji monks were active in occupied China and Manchuria, and while not present there in a official capacity, still seem to have supported the imperial enterprise and did not come under official scrutiny. Yet, whether as individuals they had enthusiastically or reluctantly supported militarism, publicly or privately opposed it, or simply tried to keep their heads down, for Nichiren Buddhists in the post-war era, militant Nichirenshugi, as a discredited ideology, would prove a burdensome legacy. The new movements in particular struggled simultaneously to reposition their teachings as embodying the mission of a new, pacifist Japan and to divest their own Nichiren Buddhist heritage of its ultranationalistic and militant associations forged during the modern imperial period.

Literature published by Sōka Gakkai, Risshō Kōseikai and Nipponzan Myōhōji in the post-war decades often addresses this challenge in terms that retain the conceptual theme of a unique Japanese mission – found so often in both Nichirenist and other wartime Buddhist rhetoric – but repudiate its militant content.[66] Sōka Gakkai's post-war publications, for example, frame Japan's special mission for peace in terms of the Gakkai's exclusivistic claim for sole validity of the *Lotus Sūtra* as explained by Nichiren. Japan was to lead the way to world peace as an act of repentance – not only for its role in World War II, but for "slander of the *Lotus Sūtra*," that fundamental evil on which Nichiren blamed the disasters of his own time. A Sōka Gakkai handbook maintains that:

> even though the most secret and correct of all Dharmas had been established in Japan, for seven hundred years [since Nichiren

revealed this Dharma], the people did not see nor hear it, were not moved by it, nor did they try to understand it. Therefore they received general punishment and the country was destroyed.[67]

This extremely deep evil karma, said to have been incurred by the Japanese for adhering to "heretical" forms of Buddhism, was, as noted earlier, blamed for all national sufferings, past and present:

> The Japanese are reportedly the first nation to have been baptized by gunpowder, when it was attacked by the Mongols seven hundred years ago. It was Japan again that first suffered from atomic warfare. Looking back on this unhappy history, it is hoped that the Japanese people will realize that they are destined to work more strenuously than any other country of the world for the achievement of world peace.[68]

Yet this burden of repentance was at the same time construed as a lofty mission. In Ikeda's words:

> Japan is the only nation in the world which has experienced the dread of nuclear weapons. Japan is also the first country in the world that that has adopted a Constitution of absolute pacifism ... We want to stress, therefore, that Japan is entirely qualified to be in the vanguard, to mobilize all the peace forces of the world, to assume their leadership, and to rouse world opinion through the United Nations.[69]

Risshō Kōseikai also invested Japan with a unique mission and responsibility in creating world peace. One reason often cited was the need to redress evils committed during the war, an issue that has been explored in study seminars by the Japanese Committee of the WCRP. Kōseikai's youth division has been especially active in developing ties with the Philippines, Singapore, Korea, and other places in East and South-east Asia where bitter memories of Japanese aggression still linger. Niwano Nikkyō stressed Japan's experience of the atomic bombings, and thus, unique knowledge, of the true horrors of modern warfare. He also placed great significance on the Peace Constitution, explicitly renouncing war, which he even credited with Japan's post-war economic success: "To the world's people, I say again that Japan is proof that any country at all can achieve prosperity if it renounces war and refuses to spend money on armaments."[70]

Assertion of Japan's sacred mission to bring peace to the world took a more confrontational form in the writings of Nipponzan Myōhōji's Fujii Nichidatsu. Fujii implacably opposed "Western civilization," which he saw not as civilization at all but as its opposite – rampant materialism, reliance on the rule of force, and science run amok. Humanity's hope lay in its displacement by the "civilization of the East," whose essence Fujii claimed was embodied in the precept "not to take life" and in the words of the *daimoku*.[71]

> The civilization of the East, which is to deliver the world from suffering, is to chant Nam-Mu-Myo-Ho-Ren-Ge-Kyo to the world... Their [adherents'] strength will become the strength to reverse the entire civilization of the West.[72]

Japan's specific role in this confrontation, as Fujii saw it, was to act as a moral exemplar of absolute non-violence. For him, the atomic bombings had in one sense been a case, in the *Lotus Sūtra*'s words, of "curses returning to their originators," but from another perspective represented a noble sacrifice offered by the Japanese people in order to demonstrate the tragedy of atomic weapons and thus prevent the extermination of humanity.[73] This role should be actively maintained in the future as well:

> What would we do if Japan were suddenly attacked from outside while we were unarmed and defenseless, having renounced war? In such an event, our leaders would stand in a line before the awesome weapons of the invaders, bow to them with their palms joined and undertake peaceful negotiations with them. We, men and women of Japan, would follow our leaders and do the same. Should Japan meet the invaders in this way, no soldiers, of whatever nationality, would shoot at our people and bomb our land, however great their hostility toward us might be... However, it is conceivable that the invaders would mercilessly attack the men and women of Japan as well as all our leaders, all of whom would be bowing with their hands joined, seeking peace. Should this happen, we would all lie side by side and meet our death. This holy sacrifice would bring about perpetual world peace. It would be the bodhisattva-practice of bodhisattvas who would deliver all humankind from its danger and suffering.[74]

In this way, all three organizations, in a manner consistent with their distinctive readings of the *Lotus Sūtra* and Nichiren, were able to refigure earlier, militaristic notions of Japan's sacred mission to unite the world, replacing their aggressive content with that of a unique mission for world peace. At the same time, they could reclaim Nichiren's prophecy that the Dharma for the last age would return to the West from Japan in a way that freed it from earlier imperialistic associations.

As noted above, however, "world peace" is a malleable concept, and its

Japanocentric orientation in the post-war teachings of Sōka Gakkai, Risshō Kōseikai and even Nipponzan Myōhōji has for some time been subject to erosion as the result of growing international ties. Risshō Kōseikai's and, more recently, Sōka Gakkai's involvement in interreligious dialogue and international peace efforts has drawn them increasingly into a web of multinational connections and global structures. Sōka Gakkai also has a substantial worldwide membership, estimated at one million outside Japan. As these groups expand their transnational ties, more globally oriented discourses of "world peace" seem to be emerging.

Conclusion

This chapter has attempted to identify some of the historical and social factors that have shaped the modes of social engagement seen in Sōka Gakkai, Risshō Kōseikai, and Nipponzan Myōhōji. It has suggested that, while inspired and legitimized by creative readings of passages from both the *Lotus Sūtra* and Nichiren's writings, their modes of social activism have heavily incorporated, and been influenced by, elements that have no particular connection to the *Lotus Sūtra*, Nichiren, or even Buddhism itself. In the cases of Sōka Gakkai and Risshō Kōseikai, such elements include the "vitalistic theory of salvation" of the New Religions and the "common morality" of modern Japanese religious culture more broadly, or, in the case of Nipponzan Myōhōji, the nonviolent resistance to colonial power advocated by Gandhi. All three have been additionally been shaped by the legacy of war, by struggles against the negative heritage of militant Nichirenism, and by the need to redefine Japanese identity in ways that have become increasingly linked to global community. To note that the followers of these groups have drawn selectively from the *Lotus Sūtra* and Nichiren's writings, highlighting or creatively re-reading some elements while passing over or muting others, is in no way to challenge their legitimacy as "Nichiren's heirs." Classic analogies of Dharma transmission, such as a flame passed from lamp to lamp or water poured from one vessel to another, suggest a pure, unchanging heritage and thus serve a self-legitimizing purpose. But what actually occurs is an ongoing exercise on the part of each era's practitioners in hermeneutical triangulation, as they work to reconcile their personal religious needs and aspirations; the external demands of their particular social context and historical moment; and the content of their received tradition. Nichiren drew selectively on his Tendai background in *Lotus Sūtra* studies as well as elements in the broader medieval Japanese religious culture to formulate an interpretation that he saw as answering the needs of his time. And his successors in later ages have done likewise. Exponents of the nationalistic Nichirenism of Japan's modern imperial period reinterpreted his teachings to legitimize their participation in nation-building, imperialism and war, while

Nichiren- and *Lotus Sūtra*-based engaged Buddhists in the contemporary period have similarly re-read these teachings in light of their own commitment to non-violence and world peace.

That religious communities reinterpret their received traditions is hardly an original observation, yet it has particular relevance to the study of socially engaged Buddhism, in underscoring the "constructed" nature of that enterprise. Received tradition, especially as expressed in scripture and doctrine, does not in and of itself determine contemporary forms of social activism. This point is forcefully illustrated by modern Buddhist movements devoted to the *Lotus Sūtra*, which in the twentieth century alone has been read both as a mandate for Japanese imperial conquest and as a blueprint for global peace. Specific programs of activism may be inspired by elements within a given tradition, which are read through the lens of contemporary needs, or such programs may be influenced by completely extraneous factors and then legitimized by reference to the tradition's history and sacred texts. What criteria determine the forms that "Buddhist social engagement" takes? What aspects of received tradition are retained as normative, which downplayed or set aside, and on what grounds are such choices made? These are questions that, although perhaps for different reasons, demand the attention of both the historian of religion and the socially engaged practitioner.

Notes

1   "Namu-Myōhō-renge-kyō" represents proper scholarly transliteration of the *daimoku*, but slight variations in pronunciation may occur according to the particular Nichiren Buddhist lineage. Sōka Gakkai, for example, following the practice of the Nichiren Shōshū sect with which it was formerly affiliated, elides the "u" of "Namu" in actual recitation.

2   "Introduction," George J. Tanabe, Jr. and Willa Jane Tanabe (eds.), *The Lotus Sutra in Japanese Culture* (Honolulu: University of Hawaii Press, 1989), pp. 2–3.

3   Traditional East Asian Buddhist eschatology divides the process of Buddhism's decline into three successive periods following the Buddha's final *nirvāna*: the True Dharma age (*shōbō*), the Semblance Dharma age (*zōhō*), and the Final Dharma age (*mappō*). According to the chronology most widely accepted in Japan, the True and Semblance Dharmas ages last for a thousand years each, and the Final Dharma age, for ten thousand years and more (Jan Nattier, *Once Upon a Future Time: Studies in a Buddhist Prophecy of Decline* [Berkeley, CA: Asian Humanities Press, 1991], pp. 65–118).

4   *Risshō ankoku ron, Shōwa teihon Nichiren Shōnin ibun* (hereafter STN), ed. Risshō Daigaku Nichiren Kyōgaku Kenkyūjo (Minobu-chō, Yamanashi Prefecture: Minobu-san Kuonji, 1952–1959; revised 1988) vol. 1, p. 226.

5   "Nyosetsu shugyō shō," STN 1:733.

6   Canonical sources contrast *shakubuku* (literally, "to break and subdue") with *shōju* ("to embrace and accept"), a milder method of leading others gradually without criticizing their position. Zhiyi (538–597), the great Chinese Tiantai master, explicitly connected *shakubuku* with the *Lotus Sūtra*.

7   Jacqueline Stone, "Rebuking the Enemies of the *Lotus*: Nichirenist Exclusivism in Historical Perspective," *Japanese Journal of Religious Studies* 21/2–3 (1994): 231–259.

8   Obtaining reliable figures for religious affiliation in Japan is notoriously difficult. The above figures are based on *Shin shūkyō jiten*, ed. Inoue Nobutaka *et al.* (Tokyo: Kōbundō, 1990), pp. 737, 785.

9   Names are given in Japanese order, with the surname first. In notes, I have followed whichever order is used in the source being cited.

10 On the break with Nichiren Shōshū, see for example Trevor Astley, "A Matter of Principles: A Note on the Recent Conflict between Nichiren Shōshū and Sōka Gakkai," *Japanese Religions* 17/2 (July 1992): 167–175; Jan Van Bragt, "An Uneven Battle: Sōka Gakkai vs. Nichiren Shōshū," *Bulletin of the Nanzan Institute for Religion and Culture* 17 (Spring 1993): 15–31; and Daniel A. Métraux, *The Soka Gakkai Revolution* (Lanham, MD: University Press of America, Inc., 1994), pp. 71–97.

11 On Kōmeitō, see, for example, Daniel A. Métraux, *The Soka Gakkai Revolution*, pp. 39–69; Robert Kisala, "Sōka Gakkai, Kōmeitō, and the Separation of Religion and State in Japan," *Bulletin of the Nanzan Institute for Religion and Culture* 18 (Spring 1994): 7–17; and Hiroshi Aruga, "Soka Gakkai and Japanese Politics," in David Machacek and Bryan Wilson (eds), *Global Citizens: The Soka Gakkai Buddhist Movement in the World* (New York: Oxford University Press, 2000), pp. 97–127.

12 "A Proposal for Lasting Peace," address to the thirty-fifth general meeting of the Sōka Gakkai (1972), in Daisaku Ikeda, *A Lasting Peace* (Tokyo: Weatherhill, 1981), pp. 21, 22.

13 Niwano Nikkyō, *Lifetime Beginner*, trans. Richard L. Gage (Tokyo: Kosei Publishing Co., 1978), pp. 85–88. See also Kyādanshi Hensan Iinkai (ed.), *Risshō Kōseikaishi* (Tokyo: Kōsei Shuppan, 1982–85), vol. 1, pp. 64–66.

14 Niwano Nikkyō, *Lifetime Beginner*, pp. 191–196.

15 Niwano Nikkyō, *A Buddhist Approach to Peace* (Tokyo: Kosei Publishing Co., 1977), p. 63. See especially Chapters 2 and 3.

16 Ibid., pp. 59–60.

17 Ibid., p. 65.

18 Considerable friction seems to have existed between the two groups in the post-war years, which, according to Risshō Kōseikai's official history, stemmed from the Sōka Gakkai's intemperate attacks (*Risshō Kōseikaishi*, vol. 1, pp. 743–780). On 16 December 1994, however, representatives of the two organizations met to initiate dialogue aimed at mutual understanding (*Asahi Shinbun* 28 February 1994, p. 3).

19 Sōka Gakkai Kyōgakubu, (ed.), *Shakubuku kyōten* (Tokyo: Sōka Gakkai, 1951; revised 1968), pp. 265–268.

20 Ibid., pp. 393–394.

21 <http://www.sgi.org/english/about_sgi/SGI_chrt.html>

22 *A Buddhist Approach to Peace*, pp. 71, 68–69.

23 *Buddhism for Today: A Modern Interpretation* (New York and Tokyo: Weatherhill/Kosei, 1976), p. 230.

24 Around 1950, Risshō Kōseikai participated for a time in a council of various Nichiren Buddhist organizations, and Niwano hoped eventually to unite all Nichiren-based groups under the leadership of Mt. Minobu, the head temple of Nichirenshū, the major traditional Nichiren denomination. His proposal was rebuffed, however, both by the council and by Mt. Minobu, whose officials accused Risshō Kōseikai of leading Nichirenshū followers to forsake their temple affiliation. After this episode, Niwano redirected his efforts toward

helping to establish the Union of the New Religious Organizations in Japan (*Risshō Kōseikaishi*, vol. 1, pp. 714–729).

25 Though its target of critique is not Risshō Kōseikai, a group of Japanese scholars espousing what they call "critical Buddhism" (*hihan Bukkyō*) has recently called attention to the negative ideological potential of religious *inclusivism* to erase difference and silent dissent via a hegemonic discourse of "harmony" or "oneness." See Jamie Hubbard and Paul L. Swanson (eds.), *Pruning the Bodhi Tree: The Storm over Critical Buddhism* (Honolulu: University of Hawaii Press, 1997).

26 "Epilogue: Religion and Progress in Modern Asia," in Robert N. Bellah (ed.), *Religion and Progress in Modern Asia* (New York: Free Press; London: Collier Macmillan, 1965), pp. 191–192. Sallie B. King draws attention to the potential problem of "overtolerance" with respect to socially engaged Buddhism in her discussion of "Buddhist Identity and Self-Negation" ("Conclusion: Buddhist Social Activism," in Christopher S. Queen and Sallie B. King (eds.), *Engaged Buddhism: Buddhist Liberation Movements in Asia* [Albany, NY: State University of New York Press, 1996], pp. 422–430).

27 Niwano Nikkyō, *Lifetime Beginner*, pp. 227–230.

28 For an overview of this controversy, see Jacqueline Stone, "Inclusive and Exclusive Perspectives on the One Vehicle," *Dharma World* 26 (Sept./Oct.1999): 20–25.

29 The current name is "Movement for a Brighter National Community." See http://www.kosei-kai.or.jp/english/activ/Movement.html and also Niwano Nikkyō, *Lifetime Beginner*, pp. 251–254.

30 On Sōka Gakkai's "peace education" movement, see Daniel Métraux, "The Sōka Gakkai's Search for the Realization of the World of *Risshō Ankokuron*," *Japanese Journal of Religious Studies* 31/1 (March 1986): 31–61, and *The Sōka Gakkai Revolution*, pp. 112–116.

31 http://www.sokagakkai.or.jp/html1/peace1/related_p1/Toda_Institute_profile1.html

32 http://www.sokagakkai.or.jp/html1/peace1/p_activities1/grassroots_jpn1.html

33 "Shohō jissō shō kōgi," *Daibyakurenge*, Nov. 1977 (*rinji zōkango*), p. 66.

34 For more on these connections, see,for example, Fujii Takeshi, "Seikatsu kiritsu to rinrikan," in *Shin shūkyō jiten*, pp. 236–243, and Robert Kisala, *Prophets of Peace: Pacifism and Cultural Identity in Japan's New Religions* (Honolulu: University of Hawaii Press, 1999).

35 Tsushima Michihito *et al.*, "The Vitalistic Conception of Salvation in Japanese New Religions: An Aspect of Modern Religious Consciousness," *Japanese Journal of Religious Studies* 6, 1–2 (March–June 1979): 139–161.

36 This experience is described in Ikeda Daisaku, *Ningen kakumei*, vol. 4, in *Shinpan Ikeda Kaichō zenshū* (Tokyo: Seikyō Shinbunsha, 1977–80), vol. 4, pp. 5–20. Toda's "life-philosophy" is outlined in his 1949 essay "Seimei ron," in *Toda Jōsei zenshū* (Tokyo: Seikyō Shinbunsha, 1981–), vol. 4, pp. 5–22. For an analysis of Toda's doctrinal innovations in terms of the vitalistic theory of salvation, see Shimazono Susumu, "Sōka Gakkai and the Modern Reformation of Buddhism," trans. Robert Kisala, ed. Takeuchi Yoshinori, in *Buddhist Spirituality: Later China, Korea, Japan, and the Modern World* (New York: Crossroad Publishing Co., 1999), pp. 435–454.

37 Niwano Nikkyō, *A Buddhist Approach to Peace*, p. 37.

38 Yasumaro Yoshio, *Nihon no kindaika to minshū shisō* (Tokyo: Aoki Shoten, 1974).

39 Helen Hardacre, *Kurozumikyō and the New Religions of Japan* (Princeton, NJ: Princeton University Press, 1986), pp. 3–36.

40 Jane Hurst, *Nichiren Shoshu Buddhism and the Soka Gakkai in America: The Ethos of a New Religious Movement* (New York and London: Garland Publishing, Inc., 1992), pp. 79, 156.

41 Gender definition is a case in point. Compared, say, to traditional Buddhist temple organizations, both Risshō Kōseikai and Sōka Gakkai give women immense scope to express their abilities through leadership roles, especially within the women's divisions. However, the ideal image of the female lay Buddhist espoused in these groups is largely limited to a traditional one of wife and mother, and few women appear in the higher echelons of organizational leadership. This has begun to change, however, in Sōka Gakkai International branch organizations outside Japan. On women in these groups, see, for example, Nakamura Kyōko, "The Religious Consciousness and Activities of Contemporary Japanese Women," *Japanese Journal of Religious Studies* 24, 1–2 (Spring 1997): 87–120, and Atsuko Usui, "The Role of Women," in *Global Citizens*, pp. 153–204.

42 *Kurozumikyō*, p. 23.

43 Robert Kisala, *Prophets of Peace*, pp. 156–157.

44 An article on Risshō Kōseikai's website traces the origins of this campaign to the Tempō era (1830–1844), when Inoue Masakane, founder of the religious movement Misogi-kyō, launched efforts to aid famine victims (http://www.kosei-kai.or.jp/english/activ/DonateOne.html).

45 See Stephen Covell, "Lighting Up Tendai: Strengthening Sect-Parishioner Bonds through the Light Up Your Corner Movement," *Asian Cultural Studies* 27 (March 2001).

46 http://walk.prisonwall.org.

47 *Tenku* (1992), cited in Robert Kisala, *Prophets of Peace*, p. 134.

48 *Prophets of Peace*, p. 135. Nonetheless, like Sōka Gakkai and Risshō Kōseikai, Nipponzan Myōhōji has NGO status in the United Nations.

49 This period is detailed in Fujii's "Wardha Diary," in *Buddhism for World Peace: Words of Nichidatsu Fujii*, trans. Yumiko Miyazaki (Tokyo: Japan-Bharat sarvodaya Mitrata Sangha, 1980), pp. 44–78.

50 On the issue of Fujii's endorsement of Japanese imperialism in Asia, see Tokoro Shigemoto, "Gendai ni okeru ronsō: Nichiren no heiwa shisō ni tsuite," in Tamura Yoshirō and Miyazaki Eishū (eds), *Nichiren shinkō no rekishi*, *Kōza Nichiren* 3 (Tokyo: Shunjūsha, 1972), pp. 225–28; Miyazaki Eishū, "Kinsei kyōdan no shintenkai," in Tamura Yoshirō and Miyazaki Eishū (eds), *Nihon kindai to Nichirenshugi*, *Kōza Nichiren* 4 (Tokyo: Shunjūsha, 1972), pp. 255–257; and Robert Kisala, *Prophets of Peace* , pp. 50–51.

51 *Dokku*, quoted in Tokoro Shigemoto, *Kindai Nihon no shūkyō to nashonar-izumu* (Tokyo: Fuzanbō, 1966), p. 228.

52 *Prophets of Peace*, p. 182.

53 E.g., "Whether or not evil persons (*akunin*) of the last age attain Buddhahood does not depend on whether their sins are light or heavy but rests solely on upon whether or not they have faith in this sūtra. You are a person of a warrior house, an evil man involved day and night in killing. Up until now you have not abandoned the household life [to become a monk], so by what means will you escape the three evil paths? You should consider this well. The heart of the *Lotus Sūtra* is that [all dharmas] in their present status are precisely the Wonderful [Dharma], without change of original status. Thus without abandoning sinful karma, one attains the Buddha Way" ("Hakii Saburō-dono gohenji," STN 1:749).

See also the "Kōnichi-bō gosho," in which Nichiren assures a devotee that her own faith in the *Lotus Sūtra* will expiate the sins of her son, a warrior who killed others and was himself killed in battle (*STN* 2:1158–1161; *The Writings of Nichiren Daishōnin*, ed. The Gosho Translation Committee [Tokyo: Soka Gakkai, 1999], pp. 659–666).

54 Nichiren's writings also frequently invoke the example of Bodhisattva Never Despising. For Nichiren, the bodhisattva represented proof that those who embrace the *Lotus Sūtra* in the last age will suffer persecution, and that, by persevering in faith, they will ultimately achieve Buddhahood, also leading to liberation those who have tormented them.

55 For more on Fujii's vision of this spiritual reconstruction, see for example his "Risshō ankoku" in Yoshida Kyūichi (ed.), *Gendai Nihon shisō taikei*, vol. 7 (Tokyo: Chikuma Shobō, 1965), pp. 355–376, and also Ha Poong Kim, "Fujii Nichidatsu's Tangyō-Raihai: Bodhisattva Practice for the Nuclear Age," *Cross Currents* 36, 2 (Summer 1986): 193–203.

56 "Kōkuyō shari," in *Fujii Nichidatsu zenshū* (Tokyo: Ryūbunkan, 1994-), vol. 3. See especially pp. 13, 160–164.

57 Kenneth Kraft, "New Voices in Engaged Buddhist Studies," in Christopher S. Queen (ed.), *Engaged Buddhism in the West* (Boston: Wisdom Publications, 2000), pp. 491–493.

58 On this theme, see Robert Kisala, *Prophets of Peace*, especially Chapters 1 and 6. Kisala argues that since peace theory in Japan was first formulated during the early modern period in response to the memory, not of conflict with foreign powers, but of prolonged and bloody internecine struggles in the late medieval period, it placed emphasis on internal social order and stability, which then became identified as particular markers of Japanese cultural superiority to be extended as part of the "civilizing" of foreign countries. This conceptual structure, Kisala suggests, underlies both the ideology of imperialist expansionism and the post-war peace theory of New Religions.

59 For an outline of Nichiren's ideas on Japan, see Jacqueline Stone, "Placing Nichiren in the 'Big Picture': Some Ongoing Issues in Scholarship," *Japanese Journal of Religious Studies* 26, 3–4 (Fall 1999): 411–417. A more detailed treatment of this topic is in progress.

60 *Kangyō Hachiman shō*, *STN* 2:1850.

61 On the construction of "modern" Buddhism in Japan, see James Edward Ketelaar, *Of Heretics and Martyrs in Meiji Japan: Buddhism and Its Persecution* (Princeton, 1990). On Buddhist ideological and institutional support for militarism, see, for example, Nakano Kyōtoku (ed.), *Senjika no Bukkyō* (Tokyo: Kokusho Kankōkai, 1977); Brian Victoria, *Zen at War* (New York: Weatherhill, 1997); and Christopher Ives, "The Mobilization of Doctrine: Buddhist Contributions to Imperial Ideology in Modern Japan," *Japanese Journal of Religious Studies* 26, 1–2 (Spring 1999): 83–106.

62 The term "Nichirenshugi" is sometimes used in a very broad sense to include all modern forms of Nichirenist interpretation, of any period or political persuasion. I use the term here in a narrower sense to indicate nationalistic readings of Nichiren of the modern imperial period.

63 From Nichiren's famous vow: "I will be the pillar of Japan, I will be the eyes of Japan, I will be the great ship of Japan" (*Kaimoku shō*, *STN* 1:601). On Tanaka in English, see Edwin B. Lee, "Nichiren and Nationalism: The Religious Patriotism of Tanaka Chigaku," *Monumenta Nipponica* 30 (1975): 19–35, and George J. Tanabe, Jr., "The *Lotus Sutra* and the Body Politic," in *The Lotus Sutra in Japanese Culture*, pp. 191–208.

64 Niwano Nikkyā, *Lifetime Beginner*, pp. 121, 128.

65 Post-war Sōka Gakkai has characterized Makiguchi's death as a sacrifice made to oppose not only government control of religion but also militarism and imperialism, a claim whose accuracy has recently emerged as the focus of some scholarly disagreement. For example, Koichi Miyata, "Tsunesaburo Makiguchi's Theory of the State," *The Journal of Oriental Studies* 10 (2000): 10–28, and Hiroo Sato, "Nichiren Thought in Modern Japan: Two Perspectives," ibid., pp. 46–61, both argue that Makiguchi was indeed critical of militarism and imperialism. For a contrasting view, see Brian Daizen Victoria, "Engaged Buddhism: A Skeleton in the Closet?," *Journal of Global Buddhism* 2 (2001): 75–80 http://jgb.la.psu.edu.

66 Jacqueline Stone, "Japanese *Lotus* Millenialism: From Militant Nationalism to Contemporary Peace Movements," in Catherine Wessinger (ed.), *Millenialism, Persecution, and Violence: Historical Cases* (Syracuse, NY: Syracuse University Press, 2000), pp. 261–280.

67 *Shakubuku kyōten*, p. 226.

68 Daisaku Ikeda, *The Human Revolution* (Tokyo: Seikyo Press, 1965), vol. 1, p. 70.

69 Daisaku Ikeda, "The Vision of the Komeito," in *Complete Works of Daisaku Ikeda* (Tokyo: Seikyo Shinbunsha), vol. 1, pp. 230–231.

70 *Heiwa e no watakushi no teishō* (Some Thoughts on Peace), bilingual pamphlet (Tokyo: Kōsei Shuppan, 1984), pp. 31–35.

71 *Buddhism for World Peace*, pp. 25, 27. For Fujii's critique of Western civilization, see also Ha Poong Kim, "Fujii Nichidatsu's *Tangyō-Raihai*." On reverse orientalism in Nipponzan Myōhōji, see Robert Kisala, *Prophets of Peace*, pp. 56–57, 159–162. Kisala argues that the group's sympathy for victims of Western aggression underlay Fujii's sole post-war departure from an absolute pacifist position, when he praised the actions of north Vietnamese nationalists during the Vietnam War as according with the spirit of the first precept.

72 Remarks delivered at the Kudan Dōjō in Tokyo on February 15, 1976, http://www.indiano.org/pagoda/fujii7.htm

73 "Risshō ankoku," p. 354; *Buddhism for World Peace*, p. 119.

74 *Dokku*, quoted in Ha Poong Kim, "Fujii Nichidatsu's *Tangyō-Raihai*," pp. 203–204.

II

ASIAN NARRATIVES

4

BUDDHISM AND DEVELOPMENT

The Ecology Monks of Thailand

Susan M. Darlington

In 1991, the Thai Buddhist monk Phrakhru Pitak Nanthakhun sponsored a tree ordination in Nan Province. The ritual, conducted by twenty northern Thai monks and attended by close to 200 villagers, district officials and journalists, formally established and sanctified a protected community forest for ten adjoining villages. The hour-long ceremony included chanting, sanctification of water, and wrapping a monk's orange robes around the largest remaining tree in the forest. The ten village headmen drank the holy water to seal their pledge to protect the forest. This ritual was one of numerous tree ordinations conducted by Buddhist monks in the 1990s in an effort to preserve the nation's rapidly depleting forest and protect people's livelihoods within it.

"Environmentalist monks" (*phra nak anuraksa* in Thai) form a small percentage of the total number of monks in Thailand. Nevertheless, their actions are visible in Thai society. They tackle urgent and controversial issues, such as deforestation and the construction of large dams, using modified Buddhist rituals and an ecological interpretation of Buddhist teachings.

The effectiveness of environmentalist monks' projects remains unclear. As these monks have only been active in Thailand over the past decade, not enough time has passed to assess projects aimed at stopping deforestation or cleaning polluted rivers. Their projects do not have sufficient scope to change what most environmentalists perceive as the destructive patterns of deforestation and growth-oriented economic and industrial development dominant in Thailand since the 1960s.

Despite their small numbers and limited effectiveness, this group represents a case of people within a specific cultural setting implementing their own environmental concepts. They reinvent human relationships with nature in the face of what Arturo Escobar criticizes as the capitalization of nature worldwide.[1] Their environmental seminars and their relations with local people illustrate the processes through which this small group of monks challenges the dominant trend of "ecological capital."[2] Despite a

96

historical link between the Buddhist *Sangha* (the community of monks) and the Siamese state, these monks reject the state's definition of development and how it is implemented.

A high degree of environmental degradation has accompanied the government's growth and export-oriented development policies. The Thai forest has been cut down at one of the fastest rates in Asia. According to official figures, forest cover in Thailand decreased from 72 percent of the total land in 1938 to 53 percent in 1961 and 29 percent in 1985.[3] Most environmental non-government organizations (NGOs) estimate that less than 15 percent of the country's total land area can be considered forest today. Activist monks join a growing, popular environmental movement that questions the government's priorities and policies.

The contemporary development concept was first formulated in the mid-1800s when King Mongkut brought his kingdom into the global economy and restructured the Buddhist *Sangha* to legitimize the central government. Changing Thai governments have continued to use Buddhism to support their development agendas, especially since the 1960s. This process resulted in the rise of independent "development monks" in the 1970s and "environmental monks" in the late 1980s who challenged the government's concept of development, Buddhism's legitimation of it, and the suffering they believed it caused the Thai people. Ironically, engaged Buddhism in Thailand emerged out of the same political-economic situation and close relationship with the state that it seeks to change. Engaged Buddhism and Buddhist environmentalism are significant less because of their use of Buddhist principles than because they incorporate people's culture, values and concerns for their livelihood and an understanding of the historical, social and political context into a creative approach to dealing with social problems.

Development in Thailand

Siam, as Thailand was formerly known, remained a small, relatively isolated kingdom until 1855 when the Bowring Treaty with Great Britain formally brought it into the emerging global economy. Even as the Siamese attempted to limit foreign access to their markets, the colonial economies being developed in neighboring countries forced them to rethink their relations with the international community and begin to modernize. Initiated by King Mongkut (Rama IV, reigned 1851–1868), Siam introduced modern scientific concepts, economic practices and education.

Mongkut also instituted religious reform in the 1830s and 1840s, and established the Thammayut Order of the *Sangha*. Similar to his modernization of other aspects of Thai society, Mongkut rationalized the religion, aiming to eliminate practices he felt were too ritualistic, metaphysical or overly influenced by local or regional culture:

Mongkut attempted to develop an interpretation of Buddhism consistent with Western science and learning and this attempt marked the beginning of a fundamental epistemological shift in doctrinal Thai Buddhism. The theoretical shift, which continues to have significant religious implications today, involved the rejection of the layered or hierarchical notion of truth which underlay traditional Buddhist teachings and its replacement with the notion of a single, universal, and all-encompassing truth.[4]

Mongkut linked the *Sangha* hierarchy with the absolute monarchy based in Bangkok, using it to legitimize the central government and weaken the influence of regional forms of religion and the power of regional political leaders. The legitimizing role the *Sangha* played toward the state was strengthened as Bangkok expanded its control to the peripheral regions, using wandering forest monks to forge relations with remote rural peoples.[5] During the modernization period, Siam – renamed Thailand in 1932 – established the three-fold concept of religion, monarchy, and nation, formalizing the connection between religion and state even further.

Three *Sangha* Acts enacted by the Thai government in 1902, 1941 and 1962 brought the *Sangha* formally under the government's control.[6] Each of these Acts created a state-imposed organizational structure for the *Sangha* that paralleled the current forms of government: in 1902, Siam was still a monarchy and the hierarchical, centralized *Sangha* was headed by a Supreme Patriarch; in 1941, a decentralized *Sangha* structure was established that paralleled the democratic, constitutional monarchy in place at the time; in 1962, a top-down structure was reintroduced to match the autocratic government of Field Marshall Sarit Thanarat. Underlying the Acts, especially that of 1962, was an effort to garner support not only for the current government, but to legitimize its development policies as well. The 1962 Act, in particular, aimed to use the *Sangha* to foster Prime Minister Sarit Thanarat's development agenda.

After coming to power through a coup in 1958, Sarit aggressively pushed Thailand into an intensive development policy. Based on a western model, Sarit promoted agricultural intensification and expansion toward an export-oriented and industrial economy. He encouraged a shift toward cash cropping, bringing more forest land under cultivation, thus "civilizing" the wild forest[7] and making it useful for humans. He also drew on traditional cultural values to promote his development agenda. Yoneo Ishii comments:

Sarit thought that national integration must be strengthened to realise national development. To attain this goal he planned to start with fostering the people's sentiment for national integration through the enhancement of traditional values as represented by the monarchy and Buddhism.[8]

Using the concept of a single, absolute truth and a centralized *Sangha* organization, Sarit incorporated Buddhism into his development campaign through community development and missionary programs involving monks.[9] These programs included *thammathud*, which sent monks as missionaries to politically sensitive and economically poor border provinces; *thammacarik*, through which monks worked with the Department of Public Welfare among minority hill peoples to convert them from animism and develop them; and community development programs sponsored by the two national Buddhist universities. Their aim was to strengthen the sense of national identity of peripheral peoples through Buddhism. These programs were – and are still today – supported and overseen by the government rather than the *Sangha*.[10]

Governments following Sarit's have continued his aggressive industrial and export-oriented development and agricultural intensification policies. The results have been mixed: Thailand's growth until the economic crisis of 1997 was phenomenal, but the rate of environmental degradation, especially forest loss and pollution levels, was among the highest in Asia. The gap between rich and poor widened, and consumerism spread, symbolized by the growth of malls and McDonald's restaurants. Rural people's quality of life deteriorated as they moved from subsistence to market farming, or left the countryside to seek work in urban factories. Through the use of a national, centralized concept of Buddhism, local culture and regional diversity were devalued.

"Development monks"

Not all members of the *Sangha* agreed with either the government's development agenda or the involvement of monks in it. Beginning in the early 1970s, a handful of monks began independent rural development projects based on their interpretations of Buddhist teachings and in opposition to the capitalism promoted by the government. Of particular concern was the impact of the government's rapid development program on rural people's lives and, because of the government's emphasis on Buddhism as a form of nationalism, the erosion of traditional local Buddhist values. These monks feared the effects of growing consumerism and the dependence of farmers on outside markets. Working in specific villages and addressing localized concerns and problems, these self-proclaimed "development monks" (*phra nak phatthana*) began conducting alternative development projects.[11]

One of the first development monks, Phra Dhammadilok, formed his own NGO, the Foundation for Education and Development of Rural Areas (FEDRA), in 1974 just outside of Chiang Mai city in Northern

Thailand.[12] He realized that if people are hungry, cold and sick, they will not and cannot devote their energy toward religious ends. Similarly, without spiritual development and commitment, they cannot overcome material suffering. FEDRA was established with the goal of developing spirituality and economics simultaneously. FEDRA's projects, located in over thirty-five villages today, include rice banks, buffalo banks (which provide buffaloes for poor farmers to plow their fields), credit unions, small revolving funds for agricultural development initiatives, integrated agriculture projects, and training for rural women in traditional handicrafts and sewing to enable them to supplement their agricultural incomes.

Unlike most government programs, the projects of Phra Dhammadilok and other development monks are aimed at local rather than national or regional development. They respond to immediate needs identified by the rural peoples themselves. Most of the development monks are from the areas in which they work, making them aware of the problems rapid economic change has brought to rural people. They initiate projects designed for a specific location and problem using local cultural concepts and beliefs rather than pulling people into a national agenda that often ignores their needs and wants.

The emergence and growth of development monks paralleled and accompanied the rise of NGOs engaged in alternative development. NGOs since the 1970s have become a major social opposition movement within Thai society. Both secular NGOs and development monks emerged because of concern over the negative impacts of government development policies toward Thai society, culture and environment. Together they have fostered the rise of a national environmental movement.

Rise of the environmental movement

While development monks worked on a local level, the environmental movement grew on a national level in response to the government's economic development agenda. Many of the NGOs engaged in a search for alternative forms of development moved into environmental activism because of their concerns about the rate of environmental destruction and degradation caused by the policies of the central government.

The causes for environmental degradation in Thailand are numerous, multifaceted and virtually impossible to verify, but the coincidence of the nation's rapid economic growth from the 1960s until the mid-1990s and its high rate of forest loss and environmental problems during the same period fuel fierce debate.[13] The government, supported by international organizations such as the World Bank, argues that environmental destruction is primarily due to poverty, making economic growth imperative to solving environmental problems. Environmentalists, on the other hand, point to the inequalities underlying the government's development agenda as the root of much of the country's poverty. The government's policies, they argue, further promote destruction of the forest through encouraging agricultural intensification and capital growth through the exploitation of natural resources. The arguments are complex and beyond the scope of this chapter, but it is critical to note the range of positions surrounding environmental issues, even within the environmental movement.

The case of forest reserves and national parks illustrates the complexity of environmentalism in Thailand. Forests represent a major natural resource for the nation. Thailand invested heavily in logging until a ban was passed in 1989 after 300 people died in floods caused by deforestation and erosion.[14] Debates still rage concerning the best way to manage the country's forests and the role of local people. The creation of national parks and forest reserves points to an environmental sensitivity on the part of the government. Few of the parks have been well managed, however.

No one agrees, even within the environmental movement, on the best way to manage the forest reserves and parks. On one side, local peoples living within the forests are blamed for destructive agricultural practices such as slash and burn. Advocates of this perspective argue that to preserve the remaining forest land these people should be moved out of the forest and trained in more environmentally friendly methods. Others argue that it is the local people who best look after the forest as their livelihoods depend on the natural resources they contain. Therefore, rather than moving them out and allowing illegal loggers, hunters and developers to take advantage of the changes, forest dwellers should be granted title to the land they have used for generations.

Environmentalist monks are also caught up in this debate. The majority takes the position that local forest dwellers will best protect the forest. A few others argue strongly that people must be removed from forests, especially watersheds, if there is to be any chance of protecting the remaining forested land.

Thai environmentalism cannot be simplified into a two-sided debate. It entails multiple perspectives, grounded, according to Philip Hirsch, in a variety of material and ideological bases.[15] As seen in the debate over forests, "environmentalism in Thailand needs to be seen as a multi-faceted discourse that deals with key social, economic and political issues, including questions of control over resources by empowered and disempowered groups."[16] The environmental movement is composed of both a growing middle class with the time, resources, and influence to engage in environmental debates and rural farmers whose livelihoods depend on a healthy environment. Many middle-class Thais were educated abroad and therefore tend to approach these issues informed by a Northern concept of environmentalism. They see the need to protect and preserve nature from human impact. Most farmers see themselves as caretakers intimately familiar with and dependent upon a natural environment which includes people as part of a whole ecological system.[17] Activist monks often use the latter argument as an example of the Buddhist concept of dependent origination, showing the interdependence of all things.

Even within the environmental movement, with its diverse interpretations supporting a wide range of economic and ideological interests, the influence of the concept of environmentalism in Thai society cannot be denied. NGOs carry significant weight within environmental discourse and influence government policy. Crucial environmental legislation was enacted due to NGO activism and its popular support. For example, environmentalists won a major case in 1988 when the government decided to shelve the Nam Choen Dam in Kanchanaburi Province in response to protests by a diverse "coalition of local groups, farmers, journalists, Buddhist monks, students and foreign environmentalists."[18] This event, early in the environmental movement, demonstrated its potential, even though several other controversial dams have since been built.

Emergence of environmentalist monks

It is within the context of debates over development and the rise of a diverse yet influential environmental movement that the self-proclaimed environmentalist monks emerged. Just as the environmental movement in Thailand grew out of the concerns of NGOs about the ecological impact of government development policies and global ecological capitalism, the work of environmentalist monks evolved from that of independent development monks with concerns about local people's lives and spirituality.

The first case in which Buddhist monks took an environmental position *as monks* involved the 1985 proposal to build a cable car up Doi Suthep mountain and through Doi Suthep-Pui National Park in Chiang Mai to promote tourism and economic development.[19] Chayant describes the importance of the site for Northern Thai Buddhists:

> Doi Suthep is a mountain lying at the outskirts of the town of Chiang Mai, named for a seventh-century Lawa chieftain who converted to Buddhism, became a monk, and retreated from the world to the mountain which now bears his name. It is the location of an important Buddhist monastery, Wat Pra That, which houses a relic of the Buddha. Local people revere the mountain temple as a destination of spiritual significance for Buddhists. Since the construction of the temple in the fourteenth century, Doi Suthep has been an important pilgrimage site.[20]

Reflecting the emerging environmental movement as a whole, opposition to the cable car project included students, people's organizations, social action groups, local media and the general public of the city. Buddhist monks joined the protests as the cause gained publicity and the full ecological and cultural impacts of building the cable car became apparent. Concerns were raised over the deforestation of the mountainside, especially through a national park that contained diverse plant, bird and animal species.

Arguments focused on environmental conservation versus economic development, but the motivation of the monks involved was mostly framed in terms of concepts of sanctity and the threat to a sacred Buddhist heritage site. One monk in particular, Phra Phothirangsi, district head of the *Sangha* for the city of Chiang Mai, took a leading role in the fight against the cable car. He articulated a link between Buddhism and preserving trees and the forest, beyond the immediate religious concern for a pilgrimage site.[21] He argued that Buddhism and the forest cannot be separated.

The cable car case was the first time Buddhist monks concerned about development incorporated environmental concerns in their actions. It is not typical of the kinds of actions in which environmentalist monks engage, however, as their fears involved the threat to a sacred Buddhist site as much as to Doi Suthep's ecosystem. Nevertheless, it was the first time Thai monks had articulated the relationship between Buddhism and the natural environment as a motivation for social and political activism. They responded to a local social and historical situation as much as to an ecological issue; the threat to the sacred sites of Doi Suthep and Wat Pra That should not be underestimated as a powerful motivation for monks to move into political activism. As a result of this initial action, the Thai public was less surprised by more explicit environmental actions by monks that followed.

Environmentalist monks cannot be described as forming a coherent social movement, although the potential for effecting social change clearly exists within their actions. Many of the monks engaged in environmental projects participate in an informal network that periodically brings them together to share their activities, concerns, obstacles and successes, and generate new ideas. It is through these Buddhist environmental seminars, sponsored by NGOs five to ten times a year and involving from twenty to 200 monk participants at a time, that a new concept of human relations with nature and human responsibility toward nature is being constructed.

Despite the importance of the dialogue and exchange of ideas that take place at these seminars, the real construction of knowledge occurs through the interaction between monks and villagers as they implement their ecological projects within local environments and informed by local histories. The new social relations forged between monks and villagers, local officials and businessmen are as important as the localized ecological conservation efforts enacted. The work of two monks in Nan Province,

northern Thailand, illustrates the process and the potential of the knowledge created by environmentalist monks.

The first monk is Phrakhru Pitak Nanthakhun. He was born and raised
in the village of Giew Muang, deep in the mountainous forest north of
Nan city. His introduction to both environmental concerns and Buddhism
arose out of an incident when he was a child. Phrakhru Pitak witnessed his
father shoot a mother monkey while hunting. Its baby clung to the
mother's body, allowing itself to be captured. For three days, it cried from
its cage, and when the boy finally released it, it went, still crying, straight
to the skin of its mother hanging out to dry. This experience contributed
not only to Phrakhru Pitak's later conservation work, but also was part of
the reason he ordained as a novice and has remained in the *Sangha* for
almost thirty years. He realized that the teachings of the Buddha could
help prevent such human-induced suffering.[22]

Growing out of his childhood experience with the baby monkey,
Phrakhru Pitak incorporated a message of the environmental responsibility
of humans into his teachings. The urgency of preaching an environmental
ethic became clearer to him as he witnessed the continual deforestation of
the mountainous province. This was caused by logging concessions, illegal
logging, slash-and-burn agriculture and overuse of the land by villagers,
and the introduction of cash cropping.

In the late 1980s, Phrakhru Pitak realized that preaching alone was not
enough, and that he needed to become actively engaged in conservation
work. He visited Phrakhru Manas of Phayao Province, the monk generally
credited with first performing tree ordinations to raise awareness of the
value of the forests.[23] Symbolically ordaining large trees in an endangered
forest by wrapping monks' orange robes around them serves several
purposes. First, the action draws attention to the threat of deforestation.
Second, the ritual provides the opportunity for the ecology monks and the
laity who work with them (predominantly non-government environmentalists and development agents) to teach about the impact of
environmental destruction and the value and means of conserving nature.
Finally, the monks use the ritual to teach the Dhamma and to stress its
relevance in a rapidly changing world.

After visiting Phrakhru Manas, Phrakhru Pitak returned to Nan and
began actively teaching villagers about environmental conservation,
presenting slide shows and holding discussions with people about the
problems they face due to deforestation. In 1990, he helped his home
village formally establish a community forest encompassing about 400
acres of land. The community forest was officially consecrated and the
villagers' commitment to preserving it marked by the ordination of the
largest remaining tree. Letters were sent to the surrounding villages
announcing the creation of the protected area, and that it was forbidden to
cut trees or hunt within it. The villagers also performed a ceremony

requesting the local tutelary spirit to help them protect the forest and its wildlife.[24]

Phrakhru Pitak's work is not limited to his home village but is constantly being expanded. Since 1990, he has sponsored several tree ordinations and *phaa paa* ceremonies, traditionally to give "forest robes" to monks but in these cases they include giving seedlings for reforestation. Lay people make religious merit through their donations and participation. In May 1993, an adapted traditional ceremony was held to preserve and lengthen the life of the Nan River in conjunction with a seminar to highlight the problems of desiccation and pollution the province faces. A fish sanctuary was established at the site of the ceremony as well. By 1999 over thirty-nine community forests and 100 fish sanctuaries have been established by Phrakhru Pitak's NGO, the Love Nan Province Foundation.

Phrakhru Pitak emphasizes basic Buddhist principles such as dependent origination and an interpretation of the Buddha's life that highlights a close relationship with the forest. His work is significantly less because it incorporates Buddhism with ecological conservation principles than because he works closely with local villagers to identify and develop ways of dealing with the problems they face. Phrakhru Pitak also encourages sustainable development practices such as integrated agriculture and growing food for subsistence rather than for sale. Villagers are willing to try his approaches because of their respect for him as a monk and their awareness of his concern for their well-being. He is outspoken in his criticism of government-sponsored economic development promoting cash crops and the use of chemical fertilizers. Although Phrakhru Pitak has become famous, and his NGO has grown to work in several villages and on multiple conservation projects, his work is still based in the specific environmental context of Nan Province. He has also inspired several other environmental projects, some sponsored by monks, others by lay people in their own villages.

The case of Phra Somkit represents the second example of an environmentalist monk engaged in the construction of new knowledge. Phra Somkit, unlike Phrakhru Pitak, only works in his home village. Similarly concerned with deforestation around his village, Phra Somkit began in the early 1990s to protect the village's forest. He went *bindabat* for forest, which is traditionally the practice of going on alms rounds offering lay people the opportunity to make merit through giving food to monks. Phra Somkit's innovation entailed offering villagers the opportunity to make merit through donating land to the village temple. His father was the first to make an offering, presenting approximately an acre of hilly land that had been denuded through intensive cultivation of corn as a cash crop.

As a means to protect the forest Phra Somkit began a model integrated agriculture farm on land belonging to his temple. With the help of his younger brother he maintains two fishponds, raises free-range chickens, and plants natural rice plots behind the temple. In the chaotic garden pigs feed among numerous varieties of fruit trees. Phra Somkit does not kill the fish, chickens or pigs, raising them only to show villagers integrated agricultural methods. He uses no chemical fertilizers, pesticides or herbicides to demonstrate to the villagers the benefits of natural farming. On the land donated by his father Phra Somkit has allowed the forest to regenerate naturally. In the almost ten years since the original gift, the forest has again grown dense. When I visited him in October 1999, Phra Somkit told me he counted close to one hundred separate species of plants in the area.

A steady train of visitors comes to see Phra Somkit's natural farm. In 1999 he received over a thousand people from both Thailand and abroad. In September ten British students spent one week volunteering on the farm to learn about integrated agriculture and sustainable development. Even more important is Phra Somkit's claim that all but about ten of the more than one hundred families in the village have begun to implement some form of integrated agriculture.

Phra Somkit strongly believes in the importance of education in the protection of the natural environment. Using the mountainous terrain surrounding the village, he regularly takes children on ecology meditation walks. He works with them to consider the value of the plants and wildlife with which they share their environment. His belief is that through teaching children about human responsibility toward nature, they will take their lessons home and teach their parents. Phra Somkit undertakes all this work as part of what he perceives as his own responsibility as a Buddhist monk.

Conclusion

Both Phra Somkit and Phrakhru Pitak illustrate ways in which environmentalist monks respond to changing national, regional and global agendas concerning development and the environment within local contexts. Their motivation comes from witnessing environmental degradation and the suffering it creates. Actively seeking out the causes of this suffering has led them to redefine the underlying concepts of development and progress. Their awareness has led them to reexamine Buddhist teachings to support their work, rather than following any inherent ecological principles within the scriptures. As Buddhists have done since the Buddha's time, they adapt their interpretations and practices of the religion to fit a changing socio-political – and natural – environment, in this case, a result of modernization. Their work is an example of the concept of environmental imaginary formulated by Peet and Watts, which they describe as follows:

[T]here is... an environmental imaginary, or rather whole complexes of imaginaries, with which people think, discuss, and contend threats to their livelihoods... Notions like "environmental imaginary," which draw on the Marxist conception of consciousness, poststructural ideas about imagination and discourse, and, dare we add, environmental determinism from early-modern geography, open political ecology to considerations so different that we propose a new term to describe them – liberation ecology. The intention is ... to raise the emancipatory potential of environmental ideas and to engage directly with the larger landscape of debates over modernity, its institutions, and its knowledges.[25]

While environmentalist monks do not form a united, coherent movement, the collective implication of their work illustrates the concept of liberation ecology described by Peet and Watts. Their emergence within a particular historical, political, economic and environmental context enables them to reassess Buddhism to fit that context and engage in debates over modernity and one of its primary institutions, development. They demonstrate a willingness to confront the traditional mutual support of the *Sangha* hierarchy and the state – a relationship that was itself a product of modernization. The impact of their individual projects may be impossible to assess, but the potential of their activism to challenge Thai Buddhists to rethink their religion, their society and their place in both the political and the natural world cannot be denied.

Acknowledgements

I would like to thank the following organizations for their support of my research: the National Endowment for the Humanities, the Social Science Research Council, Fulbright Foundation, the National Research Council of Thailand and Hampshire College. Thanks are also due to the monks, villagers and non-government organization workers in Thailand who gave their time, knowledge, experience and patience to me while I did field research, particularly Phra Dhammadilok, Phrakhru Pitak Nanthakhun and Phra Somkit. This chapter is based on research in Thailand in 1986–1988, 1991, 1992–1993, 1994, 1995 and 1999. Finally, I am grateful to Barbara Ito for helpful feedback and close editing of my chapter.

Notes

1   Arturo Escobar, "Constructing Nature: Elements for a Poststructural Political Ecology," in Richard Peet and Michael Watts (eds.), *Liberation Ecologies: Environment, Development, Social Movement* (London: Routledge, 1996), pp. 46–68.

2 Ibid.
3 Philippa England, "UNCED and the Implementation of Forest Policy in Thailand," in Philip Hirsch (ed.), *Seeing Forests for Trees: Environment and Environmentalism in Thailand* (Chiang Mai: Silkworm Books, 1996), pp. 53–71.
4 Peter A. Jackson, *Buddhism, Legitimation, and Conflict: The Political Functions of Urban Thai Buddhism* (Singapore: Institute of Southeast Asian Studies, 1989), p. 44.
5 See ibid.; Kamala Tiyavanich, *Forest Recollections: Wandering Monks in Twentieth-Century Thailand* (Honolulu: University of Hawai'i Press, 1997); Stanley J. Tambiah, *World Conqueror and World Renouncer: A Study of Buddhism and Polity in Thailand against a Historical Background* (Cambridge: Cambridge University Press, 1976); Stanley J. Tambiah, *The Buddhist Saints of the Forest and the Cult of Amulets* (Cambridge: Cambridge University Press, 1984); Jim Taylor, *Forest Monks and the Nation-State: An Anthropological and Historical Study in Northeastern Thailand* (Singapore: Institute for Southeast Asian Studies, 1993).
6 See Jackson, op. cit.; Tambiah, *World Conqueror*.
7 Philip Stott, "*Mu'ang* and *Pa*: Elite Views of Nature in a Changing Thailand," in Manas Chitakasem and Andrew Turton (eds.), *Thai Constructions of Knowledge* (London: School of Oriental and African Studies, University of London, 1991), pp. 142–154.
8 Yoneo Ishii, "Church and State in Thailand," *Asian Survey* VIII, 10 (1968): 869.
9 See Tambiah, *World Conqueror*, pp. 434–471.
10 See Somboon Suksamran, *Political Buddhism in Southeast Asia: The Role of the Sangha in the Modernization of Thailand* (London: C. Hurst and Co., 1977); Somboon Suksamran, *Political Patronage and Control Over the Sangha*, Research Notes and Discussions Papers No. 28 (Singapore: Institute of Southeast Asian Studies, 1981); Somboon Suksamran, *Buddhism and Politics in Thailand* (Singapore: Institute of Southeast Asian Studies, 1982).
11 See Susan M. Darlington, "Buddhism, Morality and Change: The Local Response to Development in Thailand" (Ph.D. dissertation, Ann Arbor, MI: University of Michigan, 1990); Somboon Suksamran, *Kaanphadthanaa Taam Naew Phuthasaasanaa: Karanii Phra Nak Phadthanaa* (A Buddhist Approach to Development: The Case of "Development Monks"), in Thai (Bangkok: Social Science Institute of Thailand, 1987); Somboon Suksamran, "A Buddhist Approach to Development: The case of 'Development Monks' in Thailand," in Lim Teck Ghee (ed.), *Reflections on Development in Southeast Asia* (Singapore: ASEAN Economic Research Unit, Institute of Southeast Asian Studies, 1988), pp. 26–48.
12 Darlington, "Buddhism and Morality".
13 See Philip Hirsch, "Environment and Environmentalism in Thailand: Material and Ideological Bases," in Philip Hirsch (ed.), *Seeing Forests for Trees: Environment and Environmentalism in Thailand* (Chiang Mai: Silkworm Books, 1996), p. 17; Jonathan Rigg (ed.), *Counting the Costs: Economic Grow and Environmental Change in Thailand* (Singapore: Institute of Southeast Asian Studies, 1995).
14 Pinkaew Leungaramsri and Noel Rajesh (eds.), *The Future of People and Forests in Thailand After the Logging Ban* (Bangkok: Project for Ecological Recovery, 1991).
15 Hirsch, "Environment and Environmentalism".
16 Ibid., pp. 15–16.

17 See Jonathan Rigg, "Counting the Costs: Economic Growth and Environmental Change in Thailand," in J. Rigg, (ed.), *Counting the Costs: Economic Grow and Environmental Change in Thailand* (Singapore: Institute of Southeast Asian Studies, 1995), p. 8.

18 Ibid., p. 13.

19 See Chayant Pholpoke, "The Chiang Mai Cable-Car Project: Local Controversy over Cultural and Eco-tourism," in Philip Hirsch and Carol Warren (eds.), *The Politics of Environment in Southeast Asia: Resources and Resistance* (London: Routledge, 1998), pp. 262–277.

20 Ibid., pp. 265–266.

21 Interview with Phra Phothirangsi, 5 Sept. 1992.

22 See Arawan Karitbunyarit (ed.), *Rak Nam Naan: Chiiwit lae Ngaan khaung Phrakhru Pitak Nanthakhun (Sanguan Jaaruwannoo)*, (Love the Nan River: The Life and Work of Phrakhru Pitak Nanthakhun [Sanguan Jaaruwannoo]), in Thai (Nan, Thailand: Sekiayatham, The Committee for Religion in Society, Communities Love the Forest Program, and The Committee to Work for Community Forests, Northern Region, 1993); Susan M. Darlington, "Not Only Preaching – The Work of the Ecology Monk Phrakhru Pitak Nanthakhun of Thailand," *Forest, Trees and People Newsletter*, vol. 34 (September 1997), pp. 17–20.

23 Susan M. Darlington, "The Ordination of a Tree: The Buddhist Ecology Movement in Thailand," *Ethnology* 37, 1 (1998): 1–15.

24 See ibid.

25 Richard Peet and Michael Watts, "Liberation Ecology: Development, sustainability, and environment in an age of market triumphalism," in Richard Peet and Michael Watts (eds.), *Liberation Ecologies: Environment, Development, Social Movement* (London: Routledge, 1996), p. 37.

5

MAHA GHOSANANDA AS A CONTEMPLATIVE SOCIAL ACTIVIST

Matthew Weiner

The twentieth century has been a period of severe testing for Buddhism. In nearly every Asian country where Buddhism has flourished in the past, civil wars, foreign invasion, or systemic poverty and tyranny have intervened. Meanwhile, Buddhist leaders have responded with unique forms of social engagement. The Dalai Lama's response to the crisis in Tibet, Thich Nhat Hanh's response to the war in Vietnam, and Aung San Suu Kyi's response to the Burmese dictatorship come immediately to mind. In the face of severe oppression, these leaders have acted with tremendous force and creativity in a manner that epitomizes the non-violent social action called engaged Buddhism.

One engaged Buddhist movement that has received less attention from scholars can be found in Cambodia, perhaps the most devastated Buddhist country in modern times. In the context of its twenty-year civil war, some two million Cambodians were killed during the Khmer Rouge period, when Buddhism was targeted for elimination. Buddhist monks were killed or forced back into lay life, and most temples were destroyed or desecrated.[1] The primary Buddhist response came in the person of a quiet meditation monk named Samdech Preah Maha Ghosananda, who emerged from a decade-long retreat to help the Cambodian survivors. Ghosananda's activism began with the rebuilding of Cambodian Buddhism, teaching peace through example, and being completely non-partisan, successfully offering his peace ministry even to members of the Khmer Rouge. His activism culminated in the famous *Dhammayietras*, peace walks through war-torn, landmine-infested regions of Cambodia. It is for this bold undertaking that Ghosananda has achieved international acclaim and received five nominations for the Nobel Peace Prize.

Engaged Buddhists call Ghosananda one of their own, in spite of criticism by some conservative Buddhists. However, the label "engaged Buddhist" is not without hermeneutical and categorial difficulties, and questions have been raised about the practical effectiveness of Ghosananda's work. Some critics have pointed to his failure to make a sustained critique of social and governmental structures at the center of

Cambodia's crisis. Moreover, Ghosananda's stance seems only to exacerbate these questions. He makes few attempts to justify his work or explain how it has been effective. He does not acknowledge a difference between traditional Buddhist practice and social action. For him, a meditation retreat, rebuilding the sangha, and leading a national peace walk are all activities for peace. He speaks almost exclusively about inner peace through self-transformation as the means to achieve social peace; in a sense, internal transformation is his form of social ethics. Finally, he and his followers agree that his service as an exemplar – a genuinely peaceful non-partisan presence in volatile settings – is his most valuable role as an activist.

Considering these issues and Maha Ghosananda's undisputed reputation as a model of engaged Buddhism, we shall need to review our definition of engaged Buddhism to include his unique approach to peacemaking. Because the Dhammayietra is the activity for which Ghosananda is widely known, and further because it exhibits the numerous and paradoxical elements of his work, we begin with its brief history. First, we describe the Dhammayietra itself and evaluate its intentions and effectiveness. Second, taking into account Ghosananda's frequent silence on the question of activism, we shall approach the Dhammayietra from the perspective of his associates and followers. In the process we shall come to see Ghosananda as a truly unique figure. It will be necessary to distinguish between the traditional understanding of activism and Ghosananda as a unique agent, so that we may weave what we learn from his character and life back into our understanding of engaged Buddhism.

The Dhammayietra

The Dhammayietra is an annual month-long peace walk comprised of monks and lay people who travel through politically unstable regions of Cambodia to promote peace.[2] It was conceived in 1992 as a one-time event in order to ease the fear of Cambodian civilians and begin the reconciliation process after the genocide of the twenty-year war. Years of propaganda had led to factionalism among Cambodians in the Thai border refugee communities, as well as those living in the country under Vietnamese rule.[3] As the United Nations brokered a peace agreement between warring parties, Maha Ghosananda and a group of aid workers, including Elizabeth Bernstein, the Jesuit brother Bob Maat, and Cambodian refugees, recognized the need for a non-partisan, spiritually-based event to begin the healing in Cambodia. While the UN planned the logistics to repatriate some 350,000 refugees, this group, loosely known as CPR (Coalition for Peace and Reconciliation), understood the need to address the fear and trauma in a new way.

Maha Ghosananda had approached these problems in the camps for many years through his re-establishment of Buddhism and meditation. But with repatriation, a new vehicle for these methods was necessary. A peace walk was collectively conceived as an effective non-violent approach. Maat, Bernstein, and Ghosananda were all students of Gandhian nonviolent activism. They met with Quaker activists and conducted educational programs with engaged Buddhist leaders that helped to foster and clarify their strategy of consensus-building and nonviolent action.[4] This involved developing group decision-making skills, nonviolent activism, and the application of Buddhist teachings to personal and social issues that the Cambodians faced.[5] Training and activism were necessary even for the walk's preparation; although one might assume that a peace walk which was intended to complement other peace efforts would have been welcome, the organizers faced opposition by all four Cambodian factions and the Thai government.[6]

The first Dhammayietra began in the refugee camps on the Thai border, traveled through Khmer Rouge territory and highly contested land, and ended in Phnom Phen. The first walkers were more than one hundred refugee Cambodians, but hundreds of local supporters joined as it proceeded through the countryside, initiating a pattern that continued and grew with subsequent walks. The large numbers of people who joined or assisted the walk is a testament to the Dhammayietra as a vehicle for overcoming fear, and an expression of the eagerness for peace. Both poor villagers and soldiers joined the march or received blessings from the monks. Soldiers commonly laid down their arms and explained to the walkers that they did not want to kill any more people. In perhaps the most remarkable response, villagers gathered spontaneously in the early mornings to receive a water blessing from the monks as a means of psychological purification.[7] Another unexpected outcome was that walkers began to meet relatives they had not seen for decades:

> Deep reconciliation and re-connection of the walkers on the personal level became such a regular occurrence that many walkers began calling the walk "Dhamma Teak Tong" or "Dharma Contact." Almost every walker from the border camp was re-united with family members... [They] would disappear into a house off the side of the road ... only to reappear hours later, beaming ... "I found my daughter! After twenty years! Now she has a daughter! And she told me my other daughter is still alive!"[8]

Through emotional healing, reduction of fear, and reunion with relatives, the Dhammayietra greatly facilitated the repatriation program.[9]

The success of the walk led to an annual event with year-round preparation and training.[10] Each year the walkers overcame tremendous difficulties, demonstrating their commitment. There was extreme heat, insufficient food and water, the danger of landmines, and the danger of encountering warring factions along the route. The walkers often heard gun battles, and the one time that they allowed an armed escort, the escort itself drew an attack that ended tragically with the deaths of two walkers.

The Dhammayietras developed through the years as needs changed and the activists focused on new issues, such as deforestation,[11] democratic elections and a democratic constitution,[12] domestic violence and women's issues,[13] landmine awareness and a national campaign to support the International Campaign to Ban Landmines.[14] However, the basic format and intention remained the same: a group of people, led by Maha Ghosananda, took vows of nonviolence, received instruction in Buddhist meditation, and walked peacefully through parts of Cambodia that had not experienced peace for several decades.

The Dhammayietra organizers hoped to bring peace to the walkers themselves, to those who helped or encountered the walk, and others who were touched by it. This took place through workshops, literature on nonviolence, and Ghosananda's daily Dharma talks, explaining how Buddhist practice leads to peace. Furthermore, Ghosananda himself served as the primary role model for individual, social, and organizational behavior. An overarching objective of the Dhammayietra was for the activity itself to be peaceful. For Ghosananda, the act of walking peacefully is essential for an ethically consistent and effective peace walk; thus meditation was the first mandatory training. Following Ghosananda's posture for action, the intention of the walk is to create activists who will peacefully and positively affect those that they encounter:

> The Dhammayietra movement believes that no other skill is as important as the development of compassion in personal preparation for the walk or social action, because only compassion gives staying power in a protracted nonviolent struggle... [W]ithout clarity of mind ... one is not truly capable of peace in action.[15]

In leading the Dhammayietras, Ghosananda is explicit in the need for an ethically conditioned mental state that will bring social peace: "Peace [will] triumph over war" he has said, "when people can walk down the street with peace in their minds. That's the only step-by-step process that will bring an end to the great suffering of the Cambodian people."[16]

Maha Ghosananda's story

There is consensus that Ghosananda was the visionary who provided moral and spiritual leadership for the Dhammayietra, and that his presence was essential for the development and the success of the walks. Yet everyone also agrees that he played no conventional management or organizational role whatsoever, and would not have organized the Dhammayietra or a peace movement on his own initiative, as this would be entirely out of character. It was rather aid-workers-turned-activists such as Maat, Bernstein, and others who, with remarkable sensitivity and vision, helped to mobilize activism alongside Ghosananda's approach to peacemaking.

Not surprisingly, the Dhammayietra's effectiveness and Ghosananda's approach to action and leadership have been called into question by those who perceive an incongruity between the extreme levels of destruction and the quiet Buddhist response, raising a question about the lack of tangible results. The reply of those sympathetic to the Dhammayietra is that critics misunderstand both the context and Ghosananda's objective. To better understand the Dhammayietra, we must look more closely at Ghosananda's approach towards peacemaking, as exhibited in his biography, teachings, and personality.

Maha Ghosananda's biography is known only in the most rudimentary form. This is because of his extreme reticence to reflect on his past, and a lack of documentation and testimony from his early years. Almost everyone he knew was killed during the Khmer Rouge regime. For these reasons Ghosananda remains a mysterious figure.

Ghosananda was born in Takeo Province, Cambodia in 1924.[17] Even as a child he was known for his generosity: a story goes that one day his parents left him to watch their shop and he gave everything away to passers-by. He began serving as a temple boy at a young age, and at nineteen was ordained as a novice monk, studying under the Supreme Patriarch, Somdech Prah Sangha Raja Chuon Noth at Wat Unallom. As a favorite student of the Patriarch, he was sent to study Buddhist philosophy at Nalanda College in India, where he received a doctoral degree in 1957.[18] While this was a period of rigorous academic study, he also learned Gandhian methods of engagement from Nichidatsu Fujii, founder of the Japanese Buddhist sect Nipponzan Myohoji. It was here that Ghosananda's early instincts for social service developed through a form of activism that complemented Buddhist teachings.

In 1965 he went to Thailand and studied with the famous Buddhist reformer Bhikkhu Buddhadasa, known for connecting meditation practice with his radical social philosophy. He then began a nine-year meditation retreat under the master Achaan Dhammadaro. Ghosananda was already well-versed in Buddhist ritual and morality (from his early years in Cambodia), and Buddhist philosophy (primarily from his time in India), and he was familiar with sophisticated social philosophy (from Buddhadasa). What Dhammadaro taught him was the experiential value of meditation. Ghosananda recalls Dhammadaro as a strict teacher who accused Ghosananda and other scholar monks of being "parrots" because of their superficial, memorized knowledge. This anti-intellectual focus on meditation for understanding and personal transformation had a great impact on Ghosananda's social teachings.

It was during Maha Ghosananda's meditation retreat in 1975 that the Khmer Rouge gained power. As news of the genocide spread, Ghosananda was grief-stricken. Like all Cambodian survivors, he suffered great losses – his entire family, including sixteen siblings, were killed. But Dhammadaro, fiercely insistent on mental control, incorporated the tragic situation into his instructions, exhorting his student "not to let the suffering of Cambodia imprint on your mind."[19] Ghosananda wanted to help his people but knew his efforts would be futile. So he remained in the forest to prepare spiritually for the right opportunity to be of service.

That opportunity came in 1979 when Vietnam invaded Cambodia, forcing the Khmer Rouge to the northern jungle. Refugees flowed into factional Thai-border camps. Within days of their arrival Ghosanada emerged from his retreat to greet them. Because of his retreat, he was one of the few surviving senior monks, and was received as a saint-like figure by the refugees. Known for selfless service, traditional knowledge, and now an accomplished mediator, he began his active peace-work in the form of Buddhist ministry and restoration. He established simple shack-temples in all of the refugee camps and taught meditation and the need for inner peace. Because of this, Ghosananda was not welcomed by the authorities of any faction-run camp, especially the Khmer Rouge. But he insisted on non-partisanship and non-violence, keeping a "no weapons" rule in his temples, thus establishing the only respected "neutral space" that refugees had for moral and spiritual sustenance. This powerful stance was later implemented in the Dhammayietras.[20]

In addition to rebuilding the Buddhist community, he sought out remaining monks and began to ordain novices. Most monks had been killed or disrobed, and the spiritual and moral needs of the people were unmet. Ghosanada, legitimized through his discipleship under the previous patriarch, had the authority to begin this process as no one else could. Yet it was his focus on peacemaking and non-partisanship that established a tone of Buddhist moral authority and created an acceptable working model for the Dhammayietras and other engaged Buddhist activities. For Ghosananda, Buddhist restoration in the form of temple building, ordaining monks and providing education is peace work because it functions as a vehicle for transformation, which leads to inner peace, and finally social change.

During this time, large numbers of refugees moved to North America and Europe. In 1981 Ghosananda came to the USA and began opening temples, which also served as community centers. To date, Ghosananda has founded some fifty temples, perhaps 90 per cent of all Cambodian temples outside of Cambodia. During these years he co-founded the Inter-religious Mission for Peace, became the Cambodian nation-in-exile's consultant to the UN Economic and Social Council, and dedicated himself to fostering international awareness of Cambodia's plight. In 1988 he was elected Supreme Patriarch, a title later reconfirmed by King Sihanouk,[21] and led a contingent of monks to the UN-sponsored peace talks between the four warring Cambodian factions. Here Maha Ghosananda asserted that there was a fifth force that he called "an army of peace," comprised of monks and other peacemakers. It would use "courage" and "bullets of loving-kindness (*metta*) for ammunition" in its struggle for reconciliation.[22] It was soon after this that his decade-long peace advocacy culminated in the organization of the Dhammayietra.

Reviewing the history of Ghosananda's career reveals evolving phases of education and experience that create the framework for a model of social teachings. His traditional Buddhist education likely provided his focus on nonviolence and internal transformation. His meditation training as a forest monk reinforced this, and also taught him the central value of inner peace as a basis for social peace-work.[23] His training with social thinkers led him to an effective form of social work in the camps and activities such as the Dhammayietra. Similarly his traditional training as a monk revealed the complementarity of Buddhist practice and social harmony. Buddhist narratives familiar to Cambodians provide a model for Buddhism to serve as a healing force for individuals and society at large.[24] Ghosananda's approach was relevant to Cambodians by virtue of being both immediate and long term, accessible to all, and totally inclusive. As we consider the various facets of his approach we can see how the strategies contained in the Dhammayietra draw upon these influences.

Ghosananda's social teachings

Maha Ghosananda's social teachings are preplexingly simple: he asserts the need for inner peace to create social peace and suggests the use of Buddhist meditation to reach this goal. Personal transformation is teh master key for social transformation. For Ghosananda, Cambodians are one family,[25] and therefore human-level reconciliation cannot be avoided. Citing the Buddhist narrative of the killer-turned-saint Angulimala, he asserts that even the worst criminals can be transformed and re-integrated into society.[26] Society will only be healed when everyone, both perpetrators and victims, are transformed through inner peace. Therefore a gathering in which people walk peacefully and encounter others who are transformed by this peace is a natural outgrowth of his notion of social engagement.

For Ghosananda, consciousness is the starting point for social ethics because one's mental state generates all verbal and physical activity.[27] All involved are personally responsible for the health of society. Therefore

Ghosananda unfailingly starts and returns to one's mental state when discussing social action. For example, when discussing the landmine crisis, he asserts that to remove landmines, the metaphorical landmines in one's heart (greed, anger and delusion) must first be removed.[28] Furthermore, by gocusing on internal peace he instists on the continuity of thought, speech, and action. Such consistency is necessary because all behavior has ethical implications. Nevertheless, mental activity is the forerunner and therefore central. This is a simple applicationof the Buddhist law of karma as it applies to ethics, and it takes the focus on menatl activity and the need for radical internal transformation at face value. It assumes that mental purification is primary both for Buddhist soteriology and Buddhist peacemaking. In this way, Ghosananda answers questions about social justice with straightforward discussion about the Buddhist teachings of no-justice with straightforward discussion about the Buddhist teachings of no-self (*anattā*) and karmic causality (*paticcasamuppada*).

Therefore while Ghosananda is correctly classified as an advocate of traditional nonviolent strategies towards peacemaking, his all-encompassing form of nonviolence is often overlooked.[29] For Ghosananda, nonviolent action means first eliminating violent thoughts, thus maifesting a consistently nonviolent ethic. In traditional fashion Ghosananda posits that the mental activity of anger is unethical and something that can and must be actively avoided.

Q   How do you stop from being angry?
A   If you come to my door I say, "Yes, please come in." But I can also say, "I am busy right now." You can do this to anger.[30]

While meditation is commonly seen in contrast to social action, or at best a comlementary tool, for Ghosananda it is the prerequisite for internal and external peace. Ghosananda's personal history demonstrates how meditation was a necessary preparation for his effective ministry. As seen in the description of teh Dhammayietra, complementary methods of meditation, such as *metta (lovingkindness), samadhi (*concentration*)*, and *vipassana* (insight) are applied by Ghosanada for the purpose of internal peacemaking and effecdtive nonviolent action, and are inherently understood as ethical activity that leads to social harmony. Through his example, Ghosananda guides his followers to see meditation as part of their collective peace work. It is an activity, though mental, which is seamlessly part of social action.

The idea that inner peace is inherent to social peace can be seen in Ghosananda's explanations of how to bring peace to Cambodia. While he uses narrative and philosophical examples, these tend to be simple, such as comparing peace to water that flows everywhere. His famous poem illustrates this idea:

Cambodia has suffered deeply.
From deep compassion comes a peaceful heart.
From a peaceful heart comes a peaceful person.
From a peaceful person comes a peaceful family and community.
From peaceful communities comes a peaceful nation.
From peaceful nations come a peaceful world.[31]

One way to understand Ghosananda's notion of how this process can happen is to see self-generated peace as a gift that is offered to those in need. The ethical activities of giving and selfless service are well developed within the Theravada tradition as synergistic roots for both personal spiritual development and social action.[32] One common framework is the reciprocal relationship of giving that exists between lay and monastic communities, a pattern that the organizers have attempted to replicate in the Dhammayietra.[33] For Ghosananda, giving (*dana*) is the primary perfection (*parami*). While he is known for spontaneously giving away priceless belongings, and even running into difficulties as the abbot of a temple for giving money to poor refugees, all agree that the most important thing he has to offer is his peaceful mental state. When asked what he did in the refugee camps in his shack-temple when there was "nothing to do," his response was characteristically simple: "I was seeking peace so I would have something to give to others."[34]

Ghosananda lived as a forest monk for years, and the contemplative way of being which he has maintained since then is directly expressed in his posture for activism. The apparently paradoxical life styles of activist and contemplative merge seamlessly in Ghosananda because it is his contemplative state that he is actively offering. His peace-giving can take the form of meditating (personal), having tea with refugees (ministerial), being a peaceful presence during negotiations (social), and establishing a temple or leading a 1,000-person peace walk (organizational). In all cases Ghosananda understands it as action and indeed social action; the line between activism and other activities is erased when the appropriate mental state is established. There is no sense in which his peace-giving differs for him from the moment-to-moment or that it is contingent upon a certain situation. Nor does Ghosananda lead us to believe that he has an over-arching strategy towards social action other than developing an internal posture of mental peace (as a contemplative) leading to a response of selfless service (as an activist).

Maha Ghosananda has produced nothing in the way of doctrinal commentaries or strategic overviews that might serve other engaged Buddhist leaders and remain as his literary legacy. Rather, his internal posture leads him to respond reflexively to particular crises in a consistently nonviolent manner. His responses are straightforward. Consider the following examples:

1   Understanding that a return to Cambodia during the genocide would be both suicidal and ineffective, he remained meditating to prepare himself to be of service.

2   When Cambodians fled to the camps he arrived within days and provided effective ministry, something he was capable of because of his retreat.

3   The re-establishment of Buddhism was also desperately needed, and Ghosananada, legitimized as a surviving senior monk, began this work.

4   During UN peace negotiations, Ghosananda provided a much-needed non-partisan peaceful presence.

5   Finally, when government factions declared a peace agreement, a peace movement among the people themselves was needed; Ghosananda provided an appropriate posture and vehicle for this with the Dhammayietra.

In each case it can be seen that Ghosananda provided something essential for the Cambodian people in that moment. In no case does he attempt to justify his work other than to reiterate the necessity for peace within individuals for societal peace, implying that his consistent posture is intended for this outcome. Ghosananda is not a conventional activist. While he has a distinct personality, he is also a Buddhist monk in the most ordinary sense. His response to situations is in some cases complemented by those who organize his work into what is traditionally thought of as activism. Perhaps it is the ordinariness of Ghosananda's responses within a Buddhist context, and the lack of apparent activism that allow a wide range of Cambodians and all polarized factions to take part in his work.

Personality as pedagogy

Ghosananda teaches primarily by example. This is especially evident in his focus on personal transformation and peacemaking, exemplified in his own internal posture which has led to remarkable instances of social activism. It is in fact his personality – described as radiant, peaceful, gentle, and prone to quizzical Zen-like answers – that is remembered and remarked upon. Though scholarly accounts ignore this, articles and interviews with co-workers focus on his state of consciousness or his character.[35] This is most poignantly exemplified both by his remarkably consistent peaceful state, which is in sharp contrast to the experience which he and his people have been through, and by his transformative presence. Thus while respected for what he has said and done, he is primarily respected for how he is.

Because understanding his character is essential for understanding his work and teachings, several of Ghosananda's personality traits are noteworthy. *First*, he seems to live in the moment. He is fond of saying, "Here. This. Now," as a way of focusing attention on the present. His teachings are spontaneous and often humorous, and yet relentless in their consistent return to first principles.

Q   In your life you must have had several very special moments.
A   Yes.
Q   Could you tell us about a few of them?
A   All of the moments.[36]

Complementing this, he has little interest in the past or the future:

Q   What is the future of Cambodia?
A   I don't know the future. We take care of the present moment. The future will take care of itself.[37]

Second, he does not appear goal-oriented other than to be peaceful in the present moment. Replying to questions of how peace can come to Cambodia he often replies, "Step by step. Each step is a meditation ... each step builds a bridge."[38] Another typical example that also demonstrates his non-partisanship comes from an interview with Ghosananda conducted during a walk for peaceful elections:

Q   Why are you walking?
A   We walk for peace so there will be a peaceful election.
Q   Who do you hope wins?
A   Peace wins.
Q   Can you elaborate?
A   No.[39]

Even quantifying a situation can extend beyond his realm of evaluation:

Q   It seems that Cambodia has good luck now.
A   Good luck, bad luck, who knows?[40]

Nevertheless, as explained above, being a peacemaker in the present moment is taken with extreme seriousness – to such a degree that it can appear absurd to those skeptical of merely having a peaceful presence during peace negotiations:

Q   You were involved with the UN peace negotiations?
A   Yes.
Q   What precisely was your role? What did you contribute?
A   We were there.[41]

Third, he manages to be both non-confrontational and unwavering in his approach

Q   I am confused by bad people (the Khmer Rouge).
A   Yes, they can change.
Q   People seem to kill here in Cambodia very easily.
A   (laughs) Yes, but we try to have them take care.
Q   How do you feel about corruption?
A   Yes, everything, we try to correct it.
Q: A lot of corruption?
A: Yes, therefore we say about the five precepts
Q: In Cambodia I see a lot of sexual misconduct
A: Yes, so we tell them, "Take care."
Q: Do you think Cambodia is getting closer to peace?
A: Every step we have to take care.[42]

Another example goes as follows:
"Wherever there is conflict we will walk ... it's like breathing. If we stop
  we die."[43]
He is also often criticized for being an activist (by conservative monks) or for being too passive (by activists):

Q: You have been criticized by some as an activist.
A: Yes. We walk for peace and plant trees.[44]

Fourth, while a Supreme Patriarch, he lives an itinerant life style and has no official staff. Though he established some fifty temples he has no official or legal relationship with any of them. This is also the case with the peace movement he leads. He does not have a school or disciples in the traditional sense. He travels unaccompanied, arrives unannounced, and his whereabouts are often unknown even to his closest associates.[45] *Fifth*, he is known for giving things away. He hands people books, food, his wool cap, and gifts that people have given him. He as easily gives away precious items to random people without a moment's hesitation, such as a valuable Buddha statue that the Dalai Lama gave him. It see alsoms he owns nothing but his robes and passport. *Sixth*, while he is the quintessential senior monk, he is also known as an eccentric. Other Cambodian monks remark on his odd practice of bowing back to those who bow to him. In another example, once when in his mid-seventies he was asked during a dharma talk at Harvard Divinity School about the relationship between wisdom and compassion, he stood up and began hopping on one leg saying, "Wisdom and compassion are like two legs. If you only have one, you will fall down!"[46] Though he often gives one word or single sentence answers throughout an interview, he is reported to speak sixteen languages and often gives dharma talks in four languages simultaneously.[47]

In addition to the peaceful nature that some misconstrue as inaction, and his eccentricity which others dismiss as unnecessary, there are examples of true heroics. Besides working amongst the Khmer Rouge who killed his family, one story goes that he smuggled orphans out of a camp under his robes. Another incident confirms his consistent and fearless nature: when caught in crossfire on one of the walks, Ghosananda and others took refuge in a temple. Moments later a grenade came through the window and landed on the floor. Everyone scrambled, but Ghosananda sat peacefully as in any other situation. The grenade did not detonate, and Ghosananda quietly asserted that the Buddha had saved them all.[48]

Through Ghosananda's personality and history we can see that he holds a great deal of authority as a peacemaker for several reasons. First, he is seen as a link to Cambodia's past because of his discipleship under the previous patriarch and his advanced Buddhist education. While Cambodians struggle to rebuild their society, they look to Buddhism and their Buddhist history as a means by which to return to a happier more stable time; Ghosananda provides this as few can.[49] Second, his authority comes from the noticeable degree to which he demonstrates what he teaches: mindfulness and peace in the present moment. Third, his authority is increased many-fold from his complete lack of interest in authority or in wielding power, as shown above. In this way he is subversive to the power structures that may wish to oppose him, such as the Cambodian government and various political factions, and the power structures that he supposedly controls. Whether this is intended as part of his teachings is open to speculation – predictably, he does not reflect upon such questions.

Conclusion

Maha Ghosananda's simple and direct approach to peacemaking creates a complicated task for those attempting to describe him and his work. The undertaking is more difficult still when moving beyond description to classification and evaluation of his effectiveness. In terms of classification, several seemingly opposing categories are bridged. Ghosananda is a social activist who sees restoring Buddhism as peacemaking. He is a meditation monk who understands internal transformation through Buddhist practice to be the primary aspect of social action. At times he upsets both activists and traditionalists because he not only sees no contradiction between bringing peace to Cambodia and striving towards internal peace, but instead implies a necessary co-dependence of the two.

To conclude, we are best served to return to Ghosananda's simplicity. For Ghosananda, the most important action for a peacemaker is to be peaceful, because without this all other actions are inconsistent, unethical, and therefore cannot lead to real peace. An angry peacemaker is not a peacemaker at all. In contrast, a peaceful person is inherently a peacemaker, because their being peaceful has a positive effect on others. Because these teachings are simple, they remain immediate and accessible to everyone; under the circumstances of a holocaust in which the population is left powerless and without resources, individual peace can be found, a semblance of order installed, and social peace cultivated.

While some aspects of Ghosananda's work are case-specific, others can serve as models for replication or adaptation. For Cambodians and non-Cambodians alike, Ghosananda's example calls for self-reflection amongst individuals and nonviolent social activists in particular. It reveals an intimacy between the activist's motivation and work, and implies a need to incorporate one's own ethical development, which must include consciousness, into both daily life and activism. It asks us to examine this relationship in hopes of moving towards a more ethically sound and consistent approach to social action.

Acknowledgement

The following individuals were essential in various aspects of my understanding of Maha Ghossandra's work, and the conception, design and editing of this chapter: Elizabeth Bernstein, Sitopa Dasgupta, Lindsay French, Maha Ghosananda, Erin Hasinoff, Melissa Kerin, Sallie B. King, David Little, Bob Maat, Kevin Malone, Jane Mahoney, Yeshua Moser, David Mumper and Christopher Queen.

Notes

1 Charles Keys, "Communist Revolution and the Buddhist Past in Cambodia" in Charles F. Keyes, Laurel Kendall, Helen Hardacre (eds.), *Asian Visions of Authority* (Honolulu: University of Hawaii Press, 1994).
2 The routes were as follows: Dhammayietra 1, 1992: Tapraya, Thailand to Phnom Penh, Cambodia; Dhammayietra 2, 1993: Siem Reap to Phnom Penh; Dhammayietra 3, 1994: Battambang to Siem Reap; Dhammayietra 4, 1995: Thai-Cambodian border to Cambodian-Vietnam border; Dhammayietra 5, 1996: Phnom Penh-Kampot-Phnom Penh.
3 The four factions who claimed the right to leadership and were involved in the armed struggle were: The State of Cambodia (SOC), created under Vietnamese occupation in 1980; the Khmer Rouge; the Royalist faction, known as FUNCINPEC; the KPNLF, a non-Communist group that received US aid.
4 This process of consultation continued throughout the history of the walks, beginning with discussions with the Quaker activists Lillian and George Willabee, and followed by consultations from INEB (the International Network of Engaged Buddhists) and Non-Violence International. The following unpublished funding reports document trainings that took place in conjunction with INEB, CPR; and the Thai Inter-Religious Commission for

Development: "Meditation for a Peaceful Future in Cambodia: Buddhism for Reconciliation and Reconstruction in Cambodia", and "Buddhist Conflict Resolution: SA Training Seminar for Cambodians". Consultations continued after the third walk, which encountered violence. George Lakey, a well-known Quaker activist was invited to organize role-playing training sessions for the walkers (unpublished report: "Cambodian Training in Nonviolent Social Change Curriculum", 1996 by George Lakey and Karen Ridd, Training for Change).

5   For example, while the trainings focused on factional violence among Cambodians they also addressed issues such as domestic violence in Cambodian family life.

6   Yeshua Moser-Puangsuwan, "The Buddha in the Battlefield: Maha Ghosananda Bhikkhu and the Dhammayietra Army of Peace," in Simon Harak, S.J. (ed.), *Nonviolence for the Third Millennium* (Macan, GA: Mercer University Press, 2000) p. 127; see also, "Even Genocidal Khmer Rouge Regime Failed to Kill Buddhists' Faith," *The Cambodian Daily*, May 1998. Many of these parties were later supporters of the walk (or attempted co-opters as the case may be).

7   For a description and interpretation of this traditional ritual and its significance, see Monique Skidmore, "The Politics of Space and Form: Cultural Idioms of Resistance and Re-Membering in Cambodia," *Sante Culture Health.* 10, 2 (1993–1994): 35–59.

8   Yeshua Moser-Puangsuawan and Elizabeth Bernstein, "Washing Away the Blood," *Nonviolence Today* 29 Nov.–Dec. 1992.

9   *One Million Kilometers for Peace*, http//www.igc.apc.org/nonviolence/ niseasia/ dymwalk/dy2.htm.

10 Basic training consisted of a mandatory three-day training program that included an explanation of the walk's philosophy; a five-point pledge: (1) commitment to pre-walk training; (2) commitment to nonviolence and neutrality; (3) commitment to not drinking alcohol or riding on vehicles; (4) commitment to not carrying weapons; (5) walkers who do not follow these guidelines will be asked to leave the walk; first aid; and landmine awareness training. See "Report on Dhammayietra" (Dhammayietra Center, unpublished), Rolien Sasse, *Evaluation of the Dhammayietra Center for Peace and Nonviolence*, Feb./Mar., 1999 (produced by the Khane Khane Foundation) and *One Million Kilometers for Peace*, http://www.igc.apc.org/nonviolence/niseasia/dymwalk/dy2.htm.

11 Dhammayietra 5 focused on this issue. Despite opposition by the authorities almost 2,000 trees were planted along the walk. See *One Million Kilometers for Peace*, http//www.igc.apc.org/nonviolence/niseasia/dymwalk/dy2.html. See also "Shante Sena in the Forest", and "We Must Walk" (The Dhammayietra Center, unpublished). See also "Long Dusty Road Takes Marchers to Nation's Heart," *The Cambodian Daily*, May 1998 p. 16. In 1994 Ghosananda was appointed special representative for the protection of the environment by King Sianook; see Ian Harris, "Buddhism in Extremis: The Case of Cambodia," in Ian Harris (ed.), *Buddhism and Politics in Twentieth Century Asia* (London and New York: Pinter, 1999), pp. 1–25.

12 Dhammayietra 2 was dedicated to safe elections, and organizers assert that the walk helped to bring this about. See "Summary of the Focus, Political Highlights, and Important Results of the Dhammayietras 1992–1996" in *One Million Kilometers for Peace*,http://www.igc.apc. org/nonviolence/niseasia/dymwalk/dy2.htm. Furthermore in 1993, during the opening of the newly elected Constituent Assembly, Ghosananda led

monks and nuns to"congratulate the new members and also meditate for a 'just constitution'. The group also requested seats as observers ... to press their demands for an independent judiciary, Bill of Rights, and safeguard for women and children to be included in the charter"(Chris Burslem, "Maha Ghosananda's Peace Revolution," *Phnom Phen Post*, July 16–29, 1993).

13 As noted above, working against domestic violence was a formative theme of the early non-violence training for the Dhammayietra. Furthermore, a women's rights group, run by Nou Smbo, part of a coalition of human rights groups, was formed around Ghosananda (Burslem, op. cit.). Gender equality was also addressed early on by CPR through training women into leadership roles for the Dhammayietra. Furthermore the "Take Back the Night" walks conducted in Phnom Phen used the Dhammayietra as their working model (author's interview with Kevin Malone, July 15, 2000).

14 Specifically on Dhammayietra 4.

15 *One Million Kilometers for Peace*: "Training for Nonviolence" and "Developing Compassion," http://www.igc.apc.org/nonviolence/niseasia/dymwalk/dy2.htm.

16 Patric Cusick, "Maha Ghosananda, a true peacemaker," *Bangkok Post* May 30, 1993.

17 Some mystery surrounds the year and date of Maha Ghosananda's birth. His birthday is celebrated on at least two different days. Ghosananda himself does not seem interested in rectifying the situation, attending birthday parties for him whenever they are held.

18 Maha Ghosananda's dissertation has apparently been lost.

19 Maha Ghosananda, *Step by Step*, Editor's Introduction (Berkeley, CA: Parallax Press, 1992) p. 16.

20 William Collins has noted that Buddhist temples serve as a refuge from political influences, where the ideology of Buddhist morality can prevail. Such a space was also created by the Dhammayietra itself. See William Collins, *UNDP/CARE Local Planning Process: Reinforcing Civil Society: Case Studies from Battambang May 1999*: Center of Advanced Study Phnom Penh, Kingdom of Cambodia. I am indebted to Lindsay French for this important insight.

21 His election took place in France in a democratic vote of Cambodian monks in exile. Such an election, and the need for one, was unprecedented. "Cambodian Buddhists Elect Patriarch," *Rhode Island Journal-Bulletin* July 30, 1988. Ghosananda succeeded Somdech Hout Tatch, who died in 1975 under the Khmer Rouge regime.

22 Yeshua Moser-Puangsuawan, "The Buddha in the Battlefield: Maha Ghosananda Bhikkhu and the Dhammayietra Army of Peace," in G. Simon Harak, S.J. (ed.), *Nonviolence for the Third Millennium* (Macan, GA: Mercer University Press, 2000), pp. 126–127.

23 The notion of the forest monk who practices wandering and meditation (*todong*) appears to imply a non-systematic approach to life that would disallow social action. However, being dramatically focused on one's state of consciousness is an essential aspect of Ghosananda's activist approach. See Susan Green, "Calm in Chaos: Monk Keeps His Peace Through Terrors of Cambodia," *The Burlington Free Press*, p. 1D, October 18, 1981.

24 See Charles Hallisey and Anne Hansen, "Narrative, Sub-Ethics, and the Moral Life," *The Journal of Religious Ethics*, 1996, pp. 305–327, for an account of how Buddhist narrative prefigures, configures, and refigures the moral life. This article uses the case of Cambodia and the use of narrative in a manner applicable to our discussion.

25 The notion of treating everyone with dignity because all people belong to the same family comes up often in Ghosananda's thought. See "Monk Tells of Lifelong Commitment to Peace Through Compassion," *The Cambodia Daily, World Buddhism Supplement*, May 1998, p. 4.

26 Chris Burslem, "Maha Ghosananda's Peace Revolution," *Phnom Phen Post* July 16–29, 1993; See also Thaitawat Nusara, "Eminent Cambodian Monk Stresses Path of Forgiveness," *Inside Indochina, Bangkok Post*, Tuesday, Feb. 27, 1996. In Nusara's article Ghosananda suggests that members of the Khmer Rouge shave their heads and ordain as a middle way between punishment and exemption. Perhaps this is an allusion to the way in which Angulimala was ordained by the Buddha. See also: "Monk Tells of Lifelong Commitment to Peace Through Compassion," p.4, *The Cambodian Daily, World Buddhism Supplement*, May 1998.

27 *The Dhammapada* Chapter 1, Verse. 1, trans. Ven. Narada Thera, (Colombo, 1971).

28 "Speech by Samdech Preah Maha Ghosananda on the Occasion of International Peace Day, 19 September 1995 and Cambodian Festival 'Ptchum Ben,'" *The Dhammayietra Center for Peace and Non Violence*.

29 Both Scott Appleby, in "Militants for Peace," *The Ambivalence of the Sacred: Religion, Violence, and Reconciliation* (Lanham, MD: Rowman & Littlefield) and David Little in "Coming to Terms with Religious Militancy" (The Dermot Dunphy Lecture, delivered at Harvard Divinity School Dec. 1, 1999) use the case of Ghosananda to exemplify nonviolent action. While their work creates an effective typology, perhaps further clarification would be useful to describe the differences between various forms of nonviolent activism. Louis Gomez's chapter "Nonviolence and the Self in Early Buddhism," in Kenneth Kraft (ed.), *Inner Peace, World Peace* (Albany, NY: State University of New York Press, 1992), shows how one might approach this. To quote Gomez: "What distinguished (or should distinguish) advocates of nonviolence who identify themselves with Buddhist teachings is a recognition of the indispensable link between nonviolence and self-cultivation."

30 Author's interview with Maha Ghosananda during the INEB conference in Thailand, July, 1997.

31 Maha Ghosananda, *Step by Step*, p. 28.

32 The role of giving as a means for spiritual perfection has been effectively presented by Donald Swearer in "Buddhist Virtue, Voluntary Poverty, Extensive Benevolence," *The Journal of Religious Ethics* 26, 1 (Spring 1998): 71–103. Swearer offers examples of narrative accounts. Traditional sources do not propose the giving of a mental state in this context, however, Ghosananda seems to be employing the traditional ideas of giving with traditional notions of internal peace as a means for creating such a transaction.

33 Skidmore, op. cit., pp. 35–59.

34 The question was asked by the Zen monk Eishin Nishimura during the Gethsemini Encounter, a Buddhist–Catholic dialogue. See Leo D. Lefebure, "Monks in Conversation," *The Christian Century*, October 16, 1996.

35 Examples of this are almost an inherent aspect of articles about Maha Ghosananda. A poignant example can be found in the press release of the American Friends Service Committee for their nomination of Ghosananda for the Nobel Peace Prize, *"Gandhi of Cambodia" Nominated for 1996 Nobel Peace Prize By 1947 Recipient*, Feb. 2, 1996.

36 Interview with Jane Mahoney for *Step by Step*, Sept. 1990.

37 Ibid.

38 There are numerous variations on this theme, both in Ghosananda's common conversation, and in *Step by Step*, pp. 35, 44, 76, 81.

39 Interview with Jane Mahoney for *Step by Step*.

40 Interview with Robin Garthwait, October 1998, *Garthwait and Griffin Productions*.

41 Dharma talk at Harvard Divinity School, hosted by the Harvard Buddhist Community, November 8, 1999.

42 Interview with Maha Ghosananda by Elizabeth Wright, April 7, 1998 for *The Cambodian Daily*. Ghosananda often uses the expression "Take care," as a way of expressing the need for mindfulness and ethical behavior.

43 Burslem, op. cit.

44 Dharma talk at Harvard Divinity School, hosted by the Harvard Buddhist Community, November 8, 1999.

45 In recent months, because of his advanced age, Maha Ghosananda is usually accompanied by an attendant.

46 Dharma talk at Harvard Divinity School, hosted by the Harvard Buddhist Community, November 8, 1999. A similar story is told about Ghosananda meeting with King Sianook and the other two Supreme Patriarchs. At the end of the meeting Sihinook bestowed on him the title of Supreme Patriarch (author's interview with Yeshua Moser-Puangsuan, 8/25/00 and Fall 1997).

47 Maha Ghosananda, *Step by Step*, p. 16.

48 "Walking for Peace in Cambodia," an interview with Bob Maat, *America Magazine*, January 28, 1995.

49 This is a common explanation by Cambodians for Ghosananda's importance. See Burslem, op. cit.

6

SARVODAYA SHRAMADANA'S
QUEST FOR PEACE

George D. Bond

The Sarvodaya Shramadana Movement has been one of the major voices for peace during the long-running conflict in Sri Lanka. Sarvodaya has organized peace marches and peace meditations since 1983 with the most recent one being held in March, 2002. This chapter examines Sarvodaya's peace campaign and peace discourse to trace its evolution and to compare and contrast Sarvodaya's views on peace with those of other movements. In its analysis of the problem, Sarvodaya has reflected the discourse of diverse voices such as the Janatha Vimukthi Peramuna (JVP) and some nationalistic Sinhala Buddhists, but in its proposed solution, Sarvodaya's peace plan blends Buddhist elements with elements of Gandhian idealism and New Age or Victorian spirituality to call for a total, non-violent revolution. Sarvodaya's peace plan forms an integral part of its distinctive vision of a non-violent, socially engaged Buddhism.

Sarvodaya's peace movement

In July 1983, the ethnic conflict that had been simmering in Sri Lanka for many years erupted into fiery riots between the Sinhalese and the Tamils. Reacting to atrocities by Tamil militants in the north, Sinhalese militants in the South rioted, burning the homes and businesses of Tamil residents in a number of towns and cities in the southern and central parts of the island. Hundreds of Tamils were killed and thousands left homeless by the rioting, which went on for several days, leaving the country paralyzed and in shock. The Sarvodaya Movement's response to these terrible riots came straight from its Gandhian heritage of non-violence and peace. Within twenty-four hours after the first riots in Colombo, Sarvodaya began to organize camps for the refugees and aid for the victims. Sarvodaya also began working with the government and with other NGOs to plan a major peace conference to try to find a solution to the problem. On October 1, 1983, Sarvodaya convened a major conference to discuss the causes of the conflict and the path to peace. Some two thousand people representing all segments of Sri Lankan society came together in the Bandananaike

Memorial International Conference Hall, the largest venue in the country. Representatives came from all of the major political parties, from all of the religious groups, from the Sinhala, Tamil, and Muslim communities, and from all strata of society. At the end of the two-day conference the delegates unanimously adopted a "People's Declaration for National Peace and Harmony."[1]

Reflecting the views of Dr. A. T. Ariyaratne and his Sarvodaya colleagues, this declaration analyzed the causes of the conflict and put forward recommendations for restoring peace. Chief among the causes that it identified was the "destruction of the value system ... built upon the ancient Hindu-Buddhist codes which accepted the postulates of respect for life."[2] It noted that this value system and the spiritual culture that it nourished broke down with the invasion of the "Western imperialists," the destruction of the agricultural economy and the colonial emphasis on a "commercial culture." The Declaration proposed several steps to try to re-establish national peace and cooperation, including strengthening those institutions that can restore the value system, revising the current educational system and implementing the laws of the state in an equitable manner. What is needed, according to the Declaration, is to reject "the empty Western economic pattern" and to replace it with "an appropriate economic lifestyle weighted in favour of a ... simple, plain and affordable life-style."[3]

Following this conference, Ariyaratne sought to implement the aim of the conference "to create a spiritual, mental, social and intellectual environment" for peace in the nation, by planning a Gandhian peace march or "peace walk" from the southern tip of the island to Jaffna and Nagadeepa in the north. The march was set to begin on December 6, 1983, and as the date approached, thousands of people began assembling at Kataragama to take part. The march by representatives from all ethnic groups was to last one hundred days and to pass through some of the most troubled areas of the country. The plans for this dramatic march put Sarvodaya in the national and international spotlight. Ultimately, however, the march was not to be. Led by Ariyaratne, some ten thousand marchers had gone only a few miles when the President of Sri Lanka, J. R. Jayawardene, came to the site and requested them to stop. Jayawardene's stated reason for stopping the march was that he feared it would disrupt the work of the government's negotiations at the impending All Party Conference. Jayawardene also said privately that the government had information that terrorists were plotting to assassinate Ariyaratne during the march in order to cause further rioting by the Sinhalese. The march was therefore halted in order to prevent further violence.[4]

After the first peace march was cancelled, however, Ariyaratne and Sarvodaya continued to pursue the path of peace in the following months and years. The movement continued to organize other major and minor peace marches, including two massive peace marches to Sri Pada in 1985 and 1986. On both of these marches, over 30,000 people representing all the religious and ethnic communities of Sri Lanka walked through the hill country and hiked up the sacred mountain. A few years later in 1990, an even larger march from Kandy to Sri Pada was held. These peace marches had great symbolic value at a time when most people in the country longed for peace but felt helpless in the face of the increasing violence. Through the peace marches, Ariyaratne and his supporters stood up to the terrorists in protest. During one march Ariyaratne said, "Let it be known to those who bear arms that there are about two million members in Sarvodaya who are prepared to brave death anywhere and any time."[5] From the Sarvodaya perspective, the peace marches served the purpose of healing the spirit and restoring unity among the people. The marches always included a time for meditation when the participants were guided in the meditation on loving kindness for all beings.[6]

In 1987, during the time that the conflict in Sri Lanka was made even more complex by the intrusion of a large Indian Army "Peace Keeping Force," Sarvodaya launched a program that it called the People's Peace Offensive (PPO). The PPO was intended to do more than just stage peace marches, it was conceived as a third option to the political and military attempts at a solution to the conflict. Ariyaratne described this as "an active intervention by organized groups of peace loving people ... confronting violence with non-violence."[7] This offensive aimed to organize dialogue between all sides and to set the stage for an effective ceasefire to be monitored by PPO committees.

Some of the other peace activities that Sarvodaya has carried out include the following:

1   Ariyaratne and other Sarvodaya officials made two widely publicized trips to Jaffna to meet with the LTTE (Liberation Tigers for Tamil Eelam) leadership to try to start a peace process. Although these trips did not result in any dramatic breakthroughs, they represented important contacts with the LTTE that kept the door open for peace. The LTTE requested these meetings with Ariyaratne because they felt that he was one of the few Sinhala leaders whom they could trust.
2   As a result of his work for peace, Ariyaratne received several major international awards during this period. In 1992 he was awarded the Niwano Peace Prize, by the Niwano Foundation of Japan. The Niwano Foundation recognized Ariyaratne for his dedication to peace as demonstrated by his thirty years of service to the villagers and his relief and reconciliation work during the conflict. In 1996 he received India's Gandhi Peace Prize from the Government of India. India established this award on the 125th anniversary of Mahatma Gandhi's birth and it is awarded annually for "social, economic and political trans-

formation through non-violence and other Gandhian methods."[8] Ariyaratne was the second person to receive this award.

3   In 1998, Sarvodaya established the Vishva Niketan Peace Center near its headquarters in Moratuwa. This center was designed as place for study, negotiation and meditation on peace.

Continuing this campaign for peace, Sarvodaya has mobilized its supporters to hold some major peace meditations and demonstrations in recent years. In 1999 Sarvodaya launched a new peace campaign, the People's Peace Initiative: a program of peace marches and peace meditations that had the aim of "creating peace within the 'psychosphere' through meditational practices." The People's Peace Initiative began with a peace march and meditation in August 1999 that saw some 170,000 people from across the Island come together in Vihara Maha Devi Park in central Colombo. At that march, Dr. Ariyaratne led the ecumenical group in a meditation on non-violence and unity. Following that initial event, the Sarvodaya Peace Secretariat organized eight other regional peace meditations, so that altogether over 215,000 people participated in this campaign for a people's peace. In January 2002, Sarvodaya announced plans for an even larger gathering for peace to be held in Anuradhapura in March. Accordingly, on March 15, 2002, Sarvodaya's "Peace Samadhi Day" in the sacred city of Anuradhapura attracted 650,000 people from 15,000 Sinhala, Tamil and Muslim villages to meditate for peace. Joanna Macy, who participated in the event, described it thus:

> Sitting on the grass as far as I could see, 650,000 people made the biggest silence I have ever heard. As the silence deepened, I thought: This is the sound of bombs and landmines not exploding, of rockets not launched, and machine guns laid aside.[9]

Sarvodaya's philosophy of peace

The philosophy behind Sarvodaya's peace campaign was first articulated in two key documents in the 1980s: the "People's Declaration for National Peace and Harmony" (1983) and A. T. Ariyaratne's book, *The Power Pyramid and the Dharmic Cycle* (1988). Ariyaratne explains that the People's Declaration was drafted using "the Buddha's approach to problems, namely the Four Noble Truths."[10] Following this structure the Declaration equates the conflict with the first truth or *dukkha*, and then goes on to examine the causes of the problem and the possible solutions.

In its analysis of the causes of the problems in the 1980s, Sarvodaya shared the views of some of the critics of the government. Two of the most vocal critics of the government at that time were members of the Sangha and the JVP. Leading monks such as Venerable M. Sobhita criticized the government's response to the "terrorists" and demanded that President Jayawardene "eradicate terrorism militarily."[11] Particularly after the LTTE staged two vicious attacks on Buddhists in 1985 and 1986, leading monks labeled Jayawardene a traitor and insisted that he resign. Venerable M. Sobhita blamed the government for "the river of blood" that had flowed in Anuradhapura and demanded that "the government must resign without destroying the country and the nation."[12]

The JVP's discourse also blamed the government for failing to curb the "terrorism" that threatened both the Dhamma and the unity of the nation. When President Jayawardene signed the Indo-Sri Lanka Peace Accord in July 1987, the JVP accused him of being a "traitor," and newspaper articles declared that the Peace Accord represented "the biggest treason the government has committed against Buddhism."[13]

Sarvodaya echoed this discourse and entered into a debate with Jayawardene's successor, President Premadasa, challenging his authority to rule. Sarvodaya's criticism focused on the conflict but also on what it regarded as the structural violence caused by the government's programs such as the open economy. Ariyaratne contended that the context that permitted violence arose as a result of the colonial period in Sri Lanka. After independence, Sri Lanka's post-colonial governments, for the most part, had continued the same approach as their colonial mentors, pursuing social, political and economic programs that ran counter to the Buddhist spirituality that had traditionally guaranteed peace. Ariyaratne wrote:

> When Sri Lanka was Buddhist, both in precept and practice, there was no need to talk of peace-making because there was no fundamental value crisis in Sri Lankan society in spite of internally or externally caused strife and power struggles ... Peace prevailed in the minds of the general public and their communities because the generally accepted value system remained unattacked by contending groups.

He went on to say that now, however, "legalized structural violence prevails and extra legal violent methods are used as well to resolve conflicts."[14]

In *The Power Pyramid and the Dharmic Cycle*, Ariyaratne noted that President Jayawardene's government "has reached a helpless stage where the law of force is in operation instead of the force of law." He wrote that the youth in the North and the youth in South (i.e., the LTTE and the JVP), were reacting to the failed policies of the government and those "who have made themselves out to be Sinhala Buddhists."[15]

But although Sarvodaya echoed the contemporary discourse about the cause of the problem lying with the government's policies, Sarvodaya differed from that discourse in its view of the solution to the problem.

Where the JVP and others called for a violent response, Sarvodaya called for a non-violent revolution. The remedy for violence, Ariyaratne said, is not more violence, but non-violence and truth. "It is only by the turn of the wheel of righteousness consisting of justice and non-violence that the vicious circles of violence and injustice can be broken."[16]

Consistently calling for a nonviolent solution, Sarvodaya's Peace movement has expressed the two central goals of the Sarvodaya movement: liberation and power. These two goals fit together in Sarvodaya's program: spiritual liberation as the base for people's power. Spiritual liberation creates a context in which people are able to awaken to their true potential and work for peace by countering the structures that have created the conflict. Sarvodaya's understanding of the two-fold nature of the quest for peace distinguishes their approach from that of secular and political efforts to find peace. Sarvodaya's peace movement focuses on the need to restore the human spirit and work for peace from the bottom up rather than attempting to impose it from above. The kind of peace that Sarvodaya seeks represents not merely a return to a form of *status quo* but rather a total social revolution that reforms the values and the structures that created the conflict. By building a spiritual infrastructure, they seek to "promote an alternative and parallel series of processes within the law leading to a social order which manifests Buddhist values and objectives."[17]

The three sources of Sarvodaya's peace campaign

Sarvodaya's campaign for peace and non-violence reflects the three influences that have shaped the movement: Gandhian ideals, Buddhist teachings and a belief in an ecumenical spirituality. From the Gandhian side, Sarvodaya's vision of peace draws on Gandhi's commitment to non-violence (*ahimsa*) and self-realization (*swaraj*). Gandhi understood clearly that these values could not exist without changing the violent and oppressive structures of society. His "Constructive Programme" sought to address these structures and re-establish traditional values in society. As Kantowsky has noted, Gandhi believed that, "Only when an equal share has been given 'unto this last,' is a non-violent social order (*ahimsa*) possible; only in such a society can Truth (*satya*) and Self-Realization (*swaraj*) grow."[18]

From the Buddhist side, Sarvodaya's vision of peace finds a rich resource in the classical Theravada teachings, which Ariyaratne regards as cognates of the Gandhian ideals and also in the ideology of Sinhala Buddhism. For Buddhism, the central datum for peace is the mind, and the definitive statement about the centrality of the mind is found in the first two verses of the *Dhammapada*.[19] These verses have been viewed as answers to the questions: "What is the source of suffering or happiness?" or "What is the source of violence or peace?"

A third factor in Sarvodaya's peace efforts is Ariyaratne's basic belief that there is an underlying spiritual unity to all religions and that the achievement of peace depends on being able to actualize this unity. He speaks about "universally just spiritual laws" that transcend the historic religions.[20] Ariyaratne also describes all religions as "intrinsically messages of peace and brotherhood."[21] This kind of ecumenical spirituality in the Sarvodaya movement actually represents another link to the Gandhian heritage, for both Gandhi and Vinoba Bhave regarded all religions as equal paths to God and liberation.[22]

Adherents of the various religions might disagree with Ariyaratne (and with Gandhi and Vinoba Bhave, as well) about the degree of spiritual unity between religions and whether this emphasis on unity obscures significant differences. Nevertheless, ecumenical spirituality and spiritual consciousness constitute basic premises of Sarvodaya's peace movement as well as of Ariyaratne's personal faith. The goal of Sarvodaya's peace marches and of the meditations that Ariyaratne has led during them has always been, as he says, "to create a critical mass of spiritual consciousness and then to create conditions to sustain that level."[23] Sarvodaya employs the peace meditations to move the hearts and minds of people toward nonviolence and compassion. Recognizing that two decades of conflict in the country have created a culture of war that allows people to accept the violence and view it as normal, Sarvodaya seeks to create a culture of peace that makes the violence unacceptable and unthinkable.

Sarvodaya's peace movement seeks to awaken the people's spiritual consciousness and restore what it regards as Buddhist and ecumenical spiritual values in order to counter the dominant material values that have led to the violent structures and the oppression of the people. From Sarvodaya's Gandhian-Buddhist perspective, the transformation of consciousness facilitates all of the other transformations: transformations of the social, political and economic structures that lie at the root of the suffering and the violence. Sarvodaya holds that lasting peace and justice depend on this kind of people's revolution in society, economy and politics and it draws on its three sources – Gandhian, Buddhist and spiritual – to envision this revolution.

Notes

1 The full text of this document is given in A.T. Ariyaratne, *Collected Works*, vol. III (Moratuwa, Sri Lanka: Sarvodaya Vishva Lekha, 1985), pp. 184–204.
2 A.T. Ariyaratne, *The Power Pyramid and the Dharmic Cycle* (Moratuwa: :Sarvodaya Vishva Lekha, 1988), p. 147.
3 Ibid., p. 153.

4 Most people that I interviewed seemed to understand why Ariyaratne had to stop the peace march. But I spoke with some who were critical of his capitulation to the president. (Interview, Colombo, June 27, 1985).

5 Speech delivered on 26 September, 1986. See "Peace Walk Ceremony in Vavuniya on Behalf of Mr. K. Kadiramalai," *Dana* xi, 10–11: 26.

6 See *Power Pyramid*, pp. 163f. for an example of this kind of peace meditation.

7 A.T. Ariyaratne, *Peace Making in Sri Lanka in the Buddhist Context* (Moratuwa: Sarvodaya Vishva Lekha, 1987), p. 16.

8 Gandhi Peace Prize presentation booklet, p. 2.

9 Joanna Macy, "The Sound of Bombs *not* Exploding," *Yes* (Summer 2002): 53.

10 "Peace Making in Sri Lanka in the Buddhist Context," (Sarvodaya Press,1987), p. 11.

11 *Atta*, January 30, 1984. Cited in Ananda Abeysekera, "The Saffron Army, Violence, Terror(ism): Buddhism, Identity and Difference in Sri Lanka," *Numen* 48: 16.

12 *Dinarasa*, May 15, 1986. Cited in Abeysekara, "The Saffron Army", pp. 18, 24.

13 *Dinarasa*, September 9, 1987. Cited in "The Saffron Army," p. 24.

14 "Peace Making in Sri Lanka in the Buddhist Context," p. 1.

15 *The Power Pyramid*, p. 3.

16 Ibid.

17 "Peace Making in Sri Lanka in the Buddhist Context", p. 6.

18 Detlef Kantowsky, *Sarvodaya the Other Development* (New Delhi: Vikas Publishing House Pvt Ltd, 1980), p. 10.

19 *Dhammapada*, 1&2:

> "Mind is the forerunner of all realities. Mind is supreme and all are mind-made.
> If one speaks or acts with an impure mind, suffering follows as the wheel follows the foot of the ox.
> Mind is the forerunner of all realities ...
> If one speaks or acts with a pure mind, contentment/peace (sukha) follows as the wheel follows the foot of the ox".

20 *Power Pyramid*, p. 177. See also p. 108 where he says that "By the term 'religion' I do not mean a particular religion or religions. I would analyse the term 'religion' to mean any spiritual nature that is prevalent at any stage among the people."

21 "Peace Making in Sri Lanka in the Buddhist Context," p. 14.

22 Hans Wismeijer, *Diversity in Harmony: A Study of the Leaders of the Sarvodaya Shramadana Movement in Sri Lanka* (1981), p. 41.

23 *People's Peace Initiative* (Sarvodaya Vishva Lekha Press, 2000), p. 31.

7

THE BUDDHIST TZU-CHI
FOUNDATION OF TAIWAN

C. Julia Huang

Legend has it that on a late spring day in the 1960s, amid the quiet back-water of the poor eastern Taiwan, thirty housewives knelt at a young Buddhist nun's feet and tearfully asked her not to leave them for another town. Moved, the nun granted the women's solemn wish, yet agreed to stay under one condition: they would have to devote themselves to the charitable mission she and her five monastic disciples had been endeavoring to create. That was the birth of the Buddhist Compassionate-Relief Merit Society (*Fuojiao Ciji Gongde Hui*; presently formally registered in English as the "Buddhist Compassion Relief Tzu Chi Foundation," here-after, Tzu-Chi),[1] a lay Buddhist movement under monastic leadership, whose goal was to defray medical costs for the poor. The housewives donated NT $0.50 (buying power about US $0.025 at current exchange rate) every day from their grocery money and drew their friends and fami-lies in. The nuns made handicrafts whose sale supported the monastic order and added to the relief funds. The monthly charity funds in the first year came to less than US $30.

Tzu-chi survived its initial hardship, growing slowly in its first decade and then rapidly across the island in the late 1980s – the time when Taiwan was moving into a wealthier economy and more democratic polity. Thirty-five years after it was founded, Tzu-chi is now the largest formal nongovernmental organization in Taiwan and a growing transnational association among overseas Chinese. By 2000, it claimed to have five million members worldwide,[2] with branches in twenty-eight countries. It runs two state-of-the-art 900-bed Western hospitals, a university, a high school, and a TV channel in Taiwan. Tzu-chi controls over NT $18.6 billion (approximately US $0.6 billion) in funds[3]; US $300 million was raised in 1999.[4] Over the past decade, it has delivered relief to over thirty countries around the world. These accomplishments won its founder and leader, the Dharma Master Cheng-yen, the 1991 Philippine Magsaysay Award, the so-called Asian Nobel Peace Prize, and the 1993 nomination for the Nobel Peace Prize, among other international honors.[5] In 2000, a textbook for high school students in Canada devoted one chapter to Tzu-chi and Cheng-yen as an exemplary religious influence;[6] and *Business Week* reported Cheng-yen as the only Taiwanese and the only religious leader among the fourteen political and business "stars of Asia."[7]

I have argued elsewhere that Tzu-chi manifests itself not only as an example of engaged Buddhism, but also as a case of engaged Buddhism's response to globalization: that it adapts its efforts to globalization and hence brings Buddhist symbols to the global arena; and, at the same time, as Tzu-chi becomes an international religious organization, it suppresses the territorial boundaries of the increasingly ambiguous international status of Taiwan, where Tzu-chi headquarters are based.[8] Based on my multiple-site fieldwork and a compilation of Tzu-chi primary literature, in this chapter, I intend to analyze, albeit in a preliminary manner, the border-crossing flows in Tzu-chi's worldwide growth by asking the question of "what travels?" in engaged Buddhism's response to globalization. This study consists of two parts. The first part is a brief introduction to Tzu-chi by summarizing the three dimensions – leadership, doctrine, and public symbols – in which Tzu-chi demonstrates engaged Buddhism. The second part is an illustration of the two sides of Tzu-chi's worldwide growth: global engagement, that is, Tzu-chi's projects of international outreach; and religious transnationalism, namely, Tzu-chi's overseas branches and its emerging transnational system.

Tzu-chi as engaged Buddhism

This section will briefly introduce the phenomenon of Tzu-chi in terms of the three dimensions of Christopher Queen's scheme for identifying examples of engaged Buddhism.[9] These three dimensions are: (1) the leaders as a reformer with recognized Buddhist identity; (2) the doctrine as a modern reinterpretation of ancient Buddhism; (3) and the institution as a manifestation of Buddhist symbols in the public sphere.

Leadership

The Venerable Cheng-yen is the founder and the leader of Tzu-chi. She is an ordained *bhikshuni* whose identity is clearly Buddhist and whose vocation abides by the maxim given by her tonsure master as well as mentor, the Venerable Yinshun, "At all times do everything for Buddhism, everything for all living beings! (*shishikeke wei fojiao, wei zhongsheng*)."[10] Cheng-yen is short and frail, and always appears in traditional Buddhist sangha attire. Although she has little education and certainly no western college degree (in comparison to such engaged Buddhists as Ambedkar), her biography, as described in Tzu-chi literature, and her leadership of the Tzu-chi organization clearly align her with other engaged Buddhist reformers, "high-profile personalities whose careers straddled and sometimes blended East and West."[11] More specifically, Japanese Buddhism and Catholicism have both played significant roles in her creation of Tzu-chi in the following two respects.

First, according to Tzu-chi literature, prior to her transformation from lay to ordained life, Cheng-yen was deeply influenced by a Buddhist nun in her hometown in central western Taiwan. After studying in Japan, this nun opposed the common practice of Chinese Buddhist priests who rely for their livelihood on chanting sutras for fees. This nun's view inspired Cheng-yen to seek autonomy, both in her individual pursuit of Buddhist priesthood and in her creation of a monastic order.

Second, one of the two events that prompted Cheng-yen to form Tzu-chi was the visit of three Catholic nuns to Hualian in eastern Taiwan, where she was studying the Lotus Sutra on her own after ordination.[12] Although they originally intended to convert her to Christianity, the three missionizing nuns were eventually convinced by Cheng-yen that Buddha's compassion was as great as the universal love of the Christian God. But the Catholic nuns then asked why Buddhists, with their concept of universal love, tended to concentrate only on improving themselves and did not build schools or hospitals as the Christians did.[13]

In addition to blending elements of East and West by acting as a modern CEO with international influence, Cheng-yen fits Queen's second description of engaged Buddhist reformers, who are "dauntless activists for cultural renewal, social change, and an ecumenical World Buddhism ... [often] honored by their followers as saints and bodhisattvas."[14] Cheng-yen's heart disease limits her travel abroad but not her dauntless activism. Every day at the headquarters, she gives sermons to hospital volunteers who come from different parts of Taiwan and of abroad; oversees and directs Tzu-chi's domestic and international missions; and grants audience to international journalists and foreign dignitaries. At least once a month, she travels around Taiwan preaching at Tzu-chi branches and public stadiums; she meets as a grass-roots fund-raiser and negotiator with state officials; and, as the roving CEO of a modern organization, she examines local mission developments and recruits new professional staff.[15] She is reverently seen by her followers as a living bodhisattva with great personal appeal. Followers respectfully call her *shangren* ("supreme person"), prostrate themselves at her feet, and tearfully deliver testimonials and vow to carry out Tzu-chi missions to walk on the Buddha's path.

Doctrine

Like other engaged Buddhist movements surveyed by Queen, Tzu-chi manifests a "new reliance on the authority of *scripture* – indeed a propensity to create new scriptures, that is, authoritative and prescriptive texts."[16] Cheng-yen's book, *Still Thoughts*, was first published in 1989 and its success has since been enormous. As of 1992, it had been through one hundred printings. By year 2001, approximately 1,000,000 copies have been sold. It is now available in English and German, and a Japanese translation is forthcoming. The increasing number of teachers who use it to supplement the school curriculum has led to the development of pedagogical tools and the 1999 publication of *Still Thoughts* textbooks, complete with instructor's manuals for elementary schools.

Still Thoughts is a collection of quotes from Cheng-yen's teaching and sermons given at various times throughout her career.[17] It consists of brief paragraphs and concise sentences of Buddhist teaching, written in plain words and set in the context of modern life. It guides various aspects of ordinary life, from etiquette (gentle manners) to moral conduct (such as filial piety); it encourages the practice of Dharma in each moment, discerning "the precious now between the defiled past and the deluded future," and revealing the inevitability of death: "One only lives as long as one is breathing," "At every second, compete for goodness." It explains how the very experience of practicing Buddhism through social action among people (be it serving others or cooperating with fellow practitioners) is itself a form of meditation. These insights are often expressed in memorable aphorisms: "Just do it," "Cultivate the mind through engagement," "Enlarge others, shrink oneself," "Right or wrong? It's a matter of perspective," and Cheng-yen's usual closing advice, "Be mindful" (*duo yong sin*). *Still Thoughts* has inspired numerous readers to join on Tzu-chi's Buddhist path and has become a manual of maxims for lay followers to practice Tzu-chi as "a highly rationalized and moralistic Buddhism"; for many it is the holy scripture of engaged Buddhism.

Cheng-yen has further interpreted the processes of becoming a Tzu-chi devotee in light of the traditional Six Perfections.[18] These are summarized as follows:

1   Charity (*bushi*): One begins as a general checkbook member who donates money, participates as a volunteer who donates time to relieve others' suffering, and shares his/her Buddhist reflections with those who are suffering.
2   Morality (*chijie*): One enters the Tzu-chi path as an intern devotee and observes the Tzu-chi Ten Precepts.[19]
3   Patience (*renru*): One is certified as a commissioner,[20] and by wearing the Tzu-chi "gentle forbearance robe," pledges always to embody gentleness and forbearance.[21]
4   Effort (*jingjin*): One then continuously encourages oneself and the fellow practitioners to relentlessly pursue enlightenment, bearing the unbearable and overcoming obstacles.
5   Meditation (*chanding*): One becomes committed to the spirit of "the Buddha's mind is my mind, the master's resolve is my resolve"[22] (*yi*

foxin wei jixin, yi shezhi wei jizhi) and to the mission of "always for Buddhism and for all living beings."

6 Wisdom (*zhihui*): One then vows to follow Buddha and Dharma in every life, practice the bodhisattva path for all living beings, transcend life and death with the sentiment of compassion and relief, and treat all living beings with "Great compassion for those who are known and unknown, boundless mercy for all beings" (*wuyuan daci, tongti dabei*).

Thus the process of becoming a Tzu-chi follower actualizes the qualities that characterize engaged Buddhism, according to Queen, although Tzu-chi particularly emphasizes action itself as a form of meditation; it is "action dharma," if you will. One sees in the process a repetitive reinforcement back and forth between further action and further identification. What links action to further identification is the emphasis on experience – the experience of feeling another's suffering, leading to the "deep identification" between the self and the sufferings of the world. In Tzu-chi, this deep identification is embodied in the practitioners' spontaneous sobbing, common in the midst of volunteer practice.[23] In so identifying, one gradually experiences expanded awareness, until one reaches an awareness of universal interconnectedness among beings and across lives. One develops "universal compassion," the commitment to relieve the sufferings of all living beings throughout many life cycles.

Institution

In addition to its reformist leadership and its doctrine of universal compassion, Tzu-chi further manifests engaged Buddhism as a nongovernmental organization (NGO) with elaborate Buddhist symbols. Over three decades since it was first founded, Tzu-Chi's mission has expanded from uplifting the poor and caring for the needy in the 1960s and 1970s to building the Tzu-Chi hospital in the 1980s. Today the organization sees its future in terms of "Four Great Missions" (*si da zhiye*) and "Four Footprints" (*jiaoyen*).[24] The Four Great Missions are *charity* (on-site investigation, evaluation, and long-term care); *medical care* (Tzu-Chi hospitals); *education* (Tzu-Chi university, high schools, teachers' assocation and youth corps); and *culture* (Tzu-Chi publications and TV). The Footprints are *international disaster relief, bone marrow drives* (collecting samples for its international database and transplantation), *environmentalism* (recycling programs), and *community volunteerism* (cooperating with public social workers to provide long-term care for local seniors).

Cheng-yen has recently interpreted the Four Great Missions as the "four immeasurable minds," the traditional Buddhist *Brahma Viharas: ci* ("kindness," Sanskrit: *maitri*) is the mission of charity; *bei* ("mercy," *karuna*), the medical mission; *xi* ("sympathetic joy," *mudita*), the cultural mission; and, *she* ("impartiality," *upeksha*), the mission of education. As its followers build the enormous "hardware" of edifices and organizations, Tzu-chi, as the first legally registered nationwide Buddhist nongovernmental organization in post-war Taiwan, "materializes" the four immeasurable minds as collective institutions and public symbols.[25]

As in the examples of engaged Buddhism analyzed by Queen,[26] Tzu-chi names the various levels of its modern establishments in Buddhist terms, and clearly presents its institutional Buddhist identity in public symbols: The Tzu-chi symbol is a ferry circled by a blossoming lotus of eight petals. The ferry stands for Dharma and universal salvation, the eight petals symbolize the eight correct paths of practice that blossom into wisdom. This symbol of universal salvation is printed on the flags in front of all its mission buildings, is worn on the clothing of its thousands of commissioners and volunteers, and, above all, is conspicuously present on the packaging of relief goods sent to the many parts of the world. In bringing its public symbols into a global context, Tzu-chi distinctively manifests engaged Buddhism.

Global engagement through outreach projects

By 1990 Tzu-chi had begun to, in their terms, "envelope the world" as an immense "field of merit" through its international relief projects, free clinics, and bone marrow donation drives.[27] The overarching motif, as described in its pamphlets, reflects the Buddhist notion of the universal connection with and empathy for all living beings, regardless of categories such as race, ethnicity, and nationality. In Tzu-chi's words: "Great compassion for those who are known and unknown, boundless mercy for all beings" (*wuyuan daci, tongti dabei*).

International relief

The first international relief Tzu-chi delivered was to flood victims in the People's Republic of China in the summer of 1991. In line with her conviction – "When others are hurt, I feel their pain; when others suffer, I feel their sorrow" (*renshang wotong, renku wobei*) – the Venerable Cheng-yen appealed to her followers to help the victims across the Taiwan Strait. In four months, Tzu-chi had raised more than US$13 million.[28]

By 1998, Tzu-chi had delivered relief to the PRC at least once a year and had benefited people in more than sixteen provinces. This so impressed people in the PRC that one of Professor Robert Weller's informants in China called Cheng-yen "the Lei Feng of Taiwan." (Lei Feng is a savior and hero acclaimed in the Chinese Communist propaganda.)

Since 1992 Tzu-chi has also provided aid to the victims of natural disasters and of war and other man-made disasters in over thirty countries.[29] Yet despite that record, Tzu-chi is not an NGO (nongovernmental organization) represented at the United Nations, unlike the famous Japanese organization, Soka Gakkai.[30] This, perhaps, is due to the location of Tzu-chi headquarters: Taiwan. According to Huang Sixian,[31] the head of the Religion Department and the highest lay leader in the Tzu-chi volunteer organization, the UN told him in 1998 that while they recognize Tzu-chi as an active international NGO, they cannot register it at the UN, due to the UN's one-China policy of recognizing Beijing but not Taipei.

Nevertheless, Tzu-ch's teams of nuns, lay volunteers, and medical professionals continue their international activism in foreign countries.[32] Sometimes they work through other international NGOs.[33] Other long-term and urgent projects are initiated through Tzu-chi local branches.[34]

Bone marrow donations

In addition to the delivery of relief goods, Tzu-chi charity embodies the bodhisattva ideal of "giving one's head, eyes, marrow, and brain to others," through its international bone marrow drives. Tzu-chi founded its bone marrow registry in 1993. In five years, it collected data on over 163,932 volunteer donors. The registry is the largest databank in Asia and the third largest in the world. Tzu-chi has helped to carry out 164 non-relative transplants,[35] including over thirty international donations to countries such as the United States, Australia, Japan, and Germany.[36]

Overseas branches further collaborate in the mission. The Tzu-chi USA Bone Marrow Donor Registry, founded in March of 1996 in Los Angeles, has recruited over 6,240 donors over 100 drives in twenty-seven cities across the United States.[37] Almost every overseas branch has held donation drives in its local community to enlarge the databank and hence the probability of matching donors with recipients.

International free clinics

Although it has been providing free clinics regularly since before the opening of its first hospital in 1986, Tzu-chi formally established its International Medical Association (TIMA) in 1996. Along with Tzu-chi's recent overseas development, by the year 2000, TIMA has formed seventeen branches in nine countries (including Taiwan).[38] The Southern California branch has a free clinic center in Los Angeles which provides regular clinics and home visits to low-income patients of different ethnicities. Other branches conduct regular free clinics at fixed sites, or rotate their services throughout different places. Large-scale events often involve branches from more than one country (such as among Malaysia,

Indonesia, and the Philippines). The TIMA has also been active in recent years in areas where Tzu-chi delivers its international disaster relief.

Religious transnationalism

What travels in Tzu-chi's global engagement is the concept of Buddhist universal compassion, embodied in goods, service, money, and physical contributions. In these programs, Tzu-chi directs primary resources from Taiwan throughout the world. As the dispenser of international relief, a former US Aid recipient in the older version of global order reverses the flow. At the same time, the pivotal role of Tzu-chi headquarters and the fact that its projects of international outreach are ends in themselves and do not involve active local proselytization, bring us to the issue of localization.

Overseas branches

Tzu-chi's overseas congregations are the local carriers of the Ven. Cheng-yen's global mission. The first overseas branch, Tzu-chi USA, obtained legal status in California in 1985, and was formally founded in 1990 in conjunction with the opening of its chapter house, Still Thoughts Hall, named after the Ven. Cheng-yen's monastery, Still Thoughts Pure Abode, in Hualian, Taiwan. In the ensuing ten years, Tzu-chi devotees in other countries have opened their own branches. Of the 114 countries with Tzu-chi members, twenty-eight have formed local chapters (see Table 7.1).

Most countries have only one chapter, but the scale of local congregations varies considerably. Total local membership ranges from less than 100 (in the newly founded Netherlands chapter) to tens of thousands. Tzu-chi USA is the largest branch, with forty-five chapters. It has 50,000 of the 90,000 overseas members, and nearly 400 commissioners of the overseas total of 552.

In contrast to Christian missionization, which often begins with rural or remote areas, all Tzu-chi branches are located in the major cities or capital of their host countries. City-based congregations seem to overlap with the constituent immigrant communities. According to Huang Sixian, participants are primarily overseas Taiwanese, and secondarily Chinese. The Penang branch of Malaysia consists of only Malaysian Chinese. Participants in the Malacca branch are mainly Malaysian Chinese, although their leaders are a Taiwanese couple. In the USA, only San Francisco and Boston have overseas Chinese participants who are not from Taiwan. Ninety percent of the Tzu-chi USA participants are overseas Taiwanese; the remainder are Chinese emigrants from Vietnam,

Table 7.1 Tzu-chi overseas branches

Number of new branches founded this year	Africa	Asia	Oceania	Europe	Middle East	Latin America	North America
1990 2				UK			USA (45)
1991 2		Japan; Singapore					
1992 7	South Africa (6)		Australia (5); New Zealand (2)	Austria		Argentina; Brazil	Canada (4)
1993 2		Hong Kong; Malaysia (15)					
1994 2		Indonesia; Philippines					
1995 1	Lesotho						
1996 1						Paraguay	
1997 5		Thailand (2); Vietnam		Germany; Spain		Mexico	
1998 2				Netherlands	Jordan		
1999 3		Brunei		France		Dominican Republic	
2000 1					Turkey		
Total 28[47]	2[a]	9	2	6	2	5	2

Source: This table is based upon the directory of Tzu-chi branches in Tzu-chi Monthly (December 2001), the Tzu-chi Foundation. In cases where there is more than one location in a country, the total number of congregations is indicated in the parenthesis.

According to Huang Sixian, as of January 2000, there are thirty-four branches. However, the source of this table, the Tzu-Chi Monthly (December 2001), shows a total of twenty-eight branches. Both are authorized Tzu-Chi sources.

Cambodia, Laos, Hong Kong, PRC, Indonesia, and Korea. There are hardly any non-Chinese among Tzu-chi overseas devotees.[39]

Chinese ethnicity seems to parallel, to some degree, the practice of overseas branches. All overseas branches follow the social service and proselytization model established by the headquarters. The extent to which they cross Chinese ethnic boundaries varies, with the larger ones generally being more successful than the smaller ones. Practice at the least active level consists of the initiates' proselytizing efforts, volunteering at local social service institutions, and providing emergency help to Taiwanese and Chinese immigrants and travelers. As the level of activism increases, branches establish secondary socialization institutions that preserve Chinese cultural heritage and spread Tzu-chi teachings, such as Chinese language schools for second-generation immigrants and the Youth Corps for Taiwanese college students.[40] Large branches take a further step, transcending ethnic boundaries; they not only establish medical institutions and charity systems for the local poor of all ethnicities, but also initiate the delivery of disaster relief to neighboring countries.[41]

The Youth Corps is a feature of Tzu-chi's religious education mission, which brings students outside Tzu-chi institutions into contact with the Venerable Cheng-yen's teachings. The Tzu-chi Youth Corps of some chapters in the USA not only have their separate pages on the Tzu-chi web site, but also organize activities and function as a distinct group cooperating with local Tzu-chi followers.[42] In comparison, the Tzu-chi Youth Corps of Malacca, consisting of local-born Chinese rather than Taiwanese college students, has become the branch's most dynamic means of mobilizing local devotees for volunteer work.

An emerging transnational system

While its overseas followers so far remain within Chinese communities, Tzu-chi has developed its system of transnationalism, a system that both maintains its salience among overseas branches and contributes to the cross-cultural proselytization.

The importance of the Chinese schools and youth corps lies in the potential for multi-ethnic ties among Tzu-chi overseas members. When asked whether Tzu-chi has a plan to draw non-Chinese in, Huang replied immediately, "Tzu-chi youth are our future, because they study [abroad] and have their cross-ethnic social connections. When they are out of school and start working, they may draw in their classmates, colleagues, and friends." Although he pins his hope for crossing Chinese ethnic boundaries on the youth, my preliminary observation shows that these college students are still basically socializing only with other Taiwanese and local born Chinese youth.

Recently Tzu-chi significantly increased the use of a variety of languages and of the media. In addition to holding special meetings in English for local non-Chinese,[43] Tzu-chi has been distributing its English quarterly since 1993, along with a series of English translations of the Ven. Cheng-yen's teachings and their children's books, and a Tzu-chi monthly journal in Japanese (since 1997). The comprehensive Tzu-chi Web page in both Chinese and English not only reports its daily news and each branch's profile around the world, but also airs the programs of its Taiwan-based TV channel via the Internet. Programming on the TV, however, still uses only Chinese. Since 2001, all televised Cheng-yen's sermons have been subtitled in both Chinese and English.

While extending communication beyond the Chinese language and excelling in the use of global media, Tzu-chi has been steering its dispersed congregations toward a transnational system since 1995. Every January, core members of all US locals and branches in South America and Southeast Asia participate in the "Tzu-chi Spirit" retreat in Houston, Texas. In addition to horizontal ties between branches, the headquarters maintains direct ties to overseas branches. Huang Sixian, sometimes accompanied by one or two of the Ven. Cheng-yen's disciples, represents the headquarters and presides at all important ceremonies of each branch, such as the end-of-the-year Thanksgiving convocation. More important to the maintenance of salience among overseas followers is the "home-coming" to the headquarters in Taiwan. Overseas followers take individual trips to the headquarters in the name of *xungen* ("root finding") and often obtain a special audience with the Ven. Cheng-yen and priority in the long queue for volunteer opportunities at the Tzu-chi hospital. In addition, every year representatives of each branch join in a retreat in conjunction with the anniversary ceremony at the headquarters; the head-quarters runs vacation camps exclusively for overseas youth and the school-age children of followers.

The image of transnational "homecoming" and the future of Tzu-chi globalization is well symbolized in the ceremony of Tzu-chi's thirty-third anniversary, which was held in the Still Thoughts Memorial Hall at Tzu Chi headquarters in Hualian, Taiwan in May 1999. Over a thousand representatives of different overseas branches, all dressed in the "blue-sky-white-cloud" uniform of blue polo shirt and white pants, sat in lines, with the branch leaders holding the national flag of their host country. Opposite the sea of blue and white was the stage backdrop of a six-story-high portrait of Shakyamuni Buddha compassionately looking at, and laying his hand on, the globe. A ten-foot-high panel of the world map stood in front of the backdrop.

The ceremony climaxed in Ven. Cheng-yen's sermon. With lights out, representatives (mostly women) of each branch slowly entered the stage, each holding a candle and their respective national flag. They formed a row and knelt at the Ven. Cheng-yen's feet. Cheng-yen lit each one's candle. One by one, the representatives approached the world map panel, placed the candle and the flag below the map in a row, turned on one sparkling light on the map to indicate the location of the branch's host country, saluted the Ven. Cheng-yen, and left the stage. One followed another until the world map shone with the sparkling lights of Tzu-chi overseas branches.

The recent anniversary ceremony symbolizes the globalization of Buddhism as Tzu-chi's perceived future. Buddha is shown as having an impact on the globe; the ritual of candlelight and lights on the world map embodies how this vision will be realized: the lay followers who approach the Ven. Cheng-yen for enlightenment will carry her teachings to the world.

New York, Boston, Tokyo, and Malacca

As symbolized in the anniversary ceremony, overseas followers are the seeds and driving force for localizing the Tzu-chi globalization. To answer the question of "what travels," one of the first things we need to do is to see how Tzu-chi appeals to these overseas followers.

The four branches – New York, Boston, Tokyo, and Malacca – where I conducted field research were founded relatively recently in the 1990s and consisted of ethnic Chinese, but have always extended their charity beyond ethnic Chinese.[44] At the same time, these four branches show that Tzu-chi's overseas development was not a result of missionaries sent by headquarters but stemmed from individual responses and the support of people in different countries. Moreover, the founders were already pious Buddhists before taking up Tzu-chi practice; and all four chapters began with women's efforts. Women continue to play a crucial role in overseas Tzu-chi.

Many core members of the four branches traced their commitment to Tzu-chi to the Ven. Cheng-yen's personal appeal, either in their first audience or conveyed to them through tapes of Cheng-yen's sermons. That appeal was different for different people. Some found an element of Chinese identity resonated with Tzu-chi's humanitarian mission. For example, one of the founders of the Boston Tzu-chi, who is originally a Chinese Vietnamese, recounted her reaction to a videotape in which the Ven. Cheng-yen spoke about Tzu-chi's relief to flood victims in south China:

> [The Ven. Cheng-yen] built so many houses, one school, and a nursing home [for the victims]. I found myself crying while watching the tape. Although I was born in Vietnam, I always see myself as Chinese. My heart is always with China. I always care about China. So, what the Ven. Cheng-yen has done in China

really touched me. Although she is a master in Taiwan, she helps
China.

Still others – in fact, the majority of those of Taiwanese origin – spoke of
Tzu-chi's emphasis on secular action, as opposed to more traditional
Mahayana Buddhist practices. For example, the founder of the New York
Tzu-chi described why she chose Tzu-chi as her path:

> You know, temples are always separated from home, where you
> and your family actually live, and where your life really is. You
> may drop everything that bothers you for the time being while you
> are cultivating yourself at a temple. You feel peace of mind for
> that moment. But the problems come right back as soon as you
> return home, or step out of the temple and back into real life...
> One day I got some tapes of the Ven. Cheng-yen's speeches. I was
> so touched by listening to her compassionate voice that I found
> myself crying in the kitchen. I finally found the master with whom
> I really wanted to work.

As the current coordinator of the Boston Tzu-chi said: "The most important thing in Tzu-chi is the process." Only in the process of working on
suffering is one able to "cultivate the mind." Tzu-chi's appeal to overseas
followers does not lie mainly in its partial function of ethnic association, as
in the host societies there are a variety of secular and religious options for
one to claim Chinese or even Taiwanese identity. Rather, the core of Tzu-
chi's appeal is a Buddhist notion of engaged compassion. It is not just
about giving or doing goods. It emphasizes experience – the experience in
which one feels one is involved and capable of feeling other's suffering.
This is so that crying is a common and important experience among Tzu-
chi devotees throughout their practice. In other words, in contrast to the
American idea of well-being, Tzu-chi followers are people who look for
misery. Devotees' tirelessly endeavor to carry out their mission across
ethnic boundaries, for example, by working among the Christian missionaries for the homeless, caring for the elders at nursing homes, and serving
the local poor and non-Chinese refugees. Behind this engaged Buddhism
lies the emotion of charity and compassion – an emotional commitment
triggered by the personal appeal of their charismatic leader, and rooted in
Bodhisattva's compassion for all living things.

What travels?

Clearly, people travel. Tzu-chi's relief activities and bone marrow donations flow across national borders. More important, Tzu-chi's world-wide
growth builds largely on the wide dispersion of overseas Chinese and

particularly Taiwanese. Indeed, the 1990s – the period of Tzu-chi overseas development – saw a boom in Taiwanese emigration.[45] However, a population with roots in Taiwan, or a common cultural heritage alone, is not sufficient for a new religious movement from Taiwan to thrive. Two other ingredients are necessary. One is a catalyst. In the case of Tzu-chi, the personal appeal of its charismatic leader travels. Although she has never stepped outside Taiwan, the Ven. Cheng-yen's message of engaged compassion reaches across space to Chinese women and men in other societies. The second ingredient is a world-view universal enough to move across national boundaries and ethnic differences among societies. In Tzu-chi's case, it is the Buddhist notion of compassion for all living things and a sense of mission to relieve suffering. In the realm of universal compassion, the army of Tzu-chi volunteers embodies the collectivity of bodhisattvas that project the vision of the Buddha impacting on the globe.

Acknowledgements

I am grateful to the Venerable Cheng-yen, and all the Tzu-chi followers and staff, especially Mr Huang Sixian and the coordinators and core members of the four branches where I conducted field research – New York, Boston, Japan, and Malaysia. An early version of this article was presented at American Academy of Arts and Sciences, as the Third Lecture Event: "The revival of religious activism and the global order – the responses of Hindu nationalism and engaged Buddhism to the challenges of globalization", in the Fall 2000 Lecture Series of "Doing globalization justice – a view from the world's religions", the Center for the Study of World Religions, Harvard University, on December 6, 2000.

I am also grateful to the lecture series organizer, the late Vittorrio Falsina, for enlightening me to the topic of religion and globalization, and the lecture discussant, William Fisher, for his illuminating comments. I thank Merry I. White, Thomas Barfield, Charles Lindholm, and Linda Learman for their helpful comments.

I also benefited from the lively discussion – especially Janos Kovac's and Galia Valtchinova's – on my presentation of the preliminary version of this chapter at Institute for Human Sciences (Institut für die Wissenschaften vom Menschen), Vienna, Austria, on April 18, 2001. Christopher S. Queen has read different versions of this chapter and commented in detail. I thank him for his insightful suggestions, editorial help, and encouragement. All shortcomings are mine.

Notes

1 "Tzu-Chi (or Tzu Chi)" and "Cheng-yen (or Cheng Yen)" are the transliterations used by the group. It is loosely based upon the Wade-Gile system of Chinese transliteration, commonly used in Taiwan – loosely because its name

in correct Wade-Gile should be "Tzu Ch'i." Elsewhere I have been using the Pingyin transliteration, "Ciji," which is used in the People's Republic of China and in the last decade or so, has almost replaced the Wade-Gile in the English literatures on – especially contemporary – Chinese studies. In this article, I use their original transliterations to refer to the group, Tzu-Chi, and their leader, Cheng-yen. All other Chinese transliterations are in Pingyin.

2 Panel abstract for "Mission of the Global Citizen, A Case Study – Taiwan 921 Earthquake," BITSA Conference, November 11, 2000 in Cambridge, MA. Posted by Katherine J. Ma in Boston Tzu Chi Youth (BTCY) email newsgroup, November 7, 2000.

3 Himalaya Foundation (1997) *Foundations in Taiwan* (Taipei: Zhonghua Zhengxin She), p. 10.

4 *Business Week* (July 24, 2000): 72.

5 These include the 2000 Noel Foundation "Life" Award, which previously honored Margaret Thatcher and Mother Teresa, and recognition in the Heroes from Around the World Exhibit at the National Liberty Museum in Philadelphia along with Nelson Mandela, Mahatma Gandhi, and others.

6 Barry Corbin, John Trites, and James Taylor, "Master Cheng Yen," *Global Connections: Geography for the 21st Century* (Canada: Oxford University Press, 1999), p. 408.

7 *Business Week* (July 24, 2000): 72.

8 C. Julia Huang, "A Case Study of Global Engaged Buddhism in Taiwan: The Buddhist Tzu-Chi (ciji) Foundation," in Vittorio Falsina (ed.), *Doing Globalization Justice* (Cambridge, MA: Harvard University Press, in press).

9 Christopher S. Queen, "Introduction: The Shapes and Sources of Engaged Buddhism," in Christopher S. Queen and Sallie B. King (eds), *Engaged Buddhism: Buddhist Liberation Movements in Asia* (Albany, NY: State University of New York Press, 1996), pp. 1–44.

10 Jones's translation, see Charles Brewer Jones, *Buddhism in Taiwan: Religion and the State 1660–1990* (Honolulu: University of Hawai'i Press 1999), p. 202.

11 Queen, op. cit., p. 23.

12 The first triggering event in 1966 occurred when Cheng-yen paid a visit to one of her monastic disciple's father at a clinic in Fengling of Hualian, where she saw a pool of blood in the hallway and inquired about it. She was told that the blood was from an aboriginal woman who had a miscarriage. Although her family walked for eight hours to carry her to the hospital, the hospital refused to treat her because she could not afford the NT$ 8,000 (about US$ 200 at that time) deposit. The unfortunate woman had died because of her family's poverty; Peter Faun, *The Miracle World of Compassion* (Taipei, Taiwan: Tzu-Chi Cultural Mission Co. Ltd., 1991), p. 10. Cheng-yen nearly fainted upon learning such a tragedy. "How could humans be so cruel to each other?" she asked herself. See Huijian Chen, *Zhengyan fashi de ciji shijie* (The Venerable Cheng-yen's World of Tzu-Chi) (Taipei, Taiwan: Tzu-Chi Culture, 1998 [1983]), p. 28.

13 Chen, op. cit., p. 29.

14 Queen, op. cit., p. 24.

15 For ethnography and analysis of the Ven. Cheng-yen's monthly tour, see Chapter 4: "Circulation," in C. Julia Huang, "Recapturing Charisma: Emotion and Rationalization in a Globalizing Buddhist Movement from Taiwan," PhD dissertation in Anthropology, Boston University, 2001.

16 Queen, op. cit. p. 25.

17 In fact, Cheng-yen's sermons and teachings at various times and occasions have been the primary source of her prolific publications in a variety of forms – audiotapes, videotapes, and on the World-Wide Web. All Cheng-yen's sermons are filmed and recorded, and then broadcast daily through private radio stations and Tzu-Chi TV channel. One of her monastic disciples transcribes her sermons verbatim to provide the scripts for further publications.

18 For description and analysis of the processes toward a titled devotee in Tzu-Chi, see Chapter 3, "Organization," Huang, op. cit. 2001. Also see Jones's description of Cheng-yen's interpretation of the six perfections in Jones, op. cit. pp. 214–5. Jones's description is mainly based upon Huixin Lu, "Taiwn Fojiao 'Ciji Gongde Hui' de Daode Yiyi" (The Moral Significance of Taiwanese Buddhism's "Buddhist Compassion Relief Tzu Chi Association"), paper delivered at the Shanxi University International Symposium on Chinese Buddhism Thought and Culture, July 12–18, 1992, Taiyuan City. Jones, however, does not focus on the overlap between Cheng-yen's interpretation of the six perfections and the process of becoming a Tzu-chi commissioner.

19 The ten precepts consist of two parts: The first five are the five basic lay Buddhist precepts – no killing, no stealing, no adultery, no lying, no alcohol. Cheng-yen added another five: no smoking, no drugs, no betel nuts; no gambling, no opportunistic investments [especially in stock market]; must show filial piety, be soft spoken, have a gentle expression; must abide by traffic regulations; and not participate in political activities, protests or demonstrations.

20 Tzu-chi literature uses "commissioner" as the English translation for the title of certified core member (*weiyuan*).

21 *Roherenru yi*, the dark blue traditional Chinese dress (*quipao*). Among the great varieties of Tzu-Chi uniforms, the dark blue *quipao* is exclusively to be worn by certified (female) commissioners.

22 Jones's translation, see Jones, op. cit. p. 210.

23 For an ethnographic analysis of crying and emotion in Tzu-Chi, see Chapter 5, "Crying and Silent Melody – The Structure of Emotions in Tzu-Chi," in Huang, op. cit. 2001.

24 Tzu-chi uses "mission" in their English literature to refer to their work, *zhiye*.

25 Tzu-Chi applied to register with the central government of Taiwan as soon as it began to branch out from Hualian in its early years. However, its application could not be approved because Taiwan was still under martial law, which banned the formation of religious organizations at the national level. Cheng-yen refused to remove the term "Buddhist" from its applied name, and therefore Tzu-Chi has retained its legal identity on the level of the Provincial Government despite its nationwide development prior to the lifting of martial law. Tzu-Chi became the first religious organization to obtain national legal status as soon as martial law was lifted in 1987.

26 Queen, op. cit. pp. 27–28.

27 Tzu-Chi lists these three programs in its authorized English literature of international programs, *Enveloping the World with Great Love: Tzu Chi International Relief Effort 1991–2000*, http://taipei.tzuchi.org.tw/tzquart/book/book2/10.htm (accessed June 29, 2001).

28 Duanzheng Wang (ed.), *Zainan, wuyian de dengdai: Tzu-Chi Jijinghui daly jiuyuan jianjie* (Disasters, Waiting in Silence: Introduction to Relief to China, the Tzu-Chi Foundation) (Taipei, Taiwan: The Tzu-Chi Foundation, 1998), p. 6.

29 These include, in chronological order, Mongolia, Nepal, the refugee camps in Northern Thailand, Cambodia, Azerbaijan, Ethiopia, Rwanda, Chechnya, Ivory Coast, Afghanistan, Lesotho, Swaziland, South Africa, North Korea,

Liberia, Gambia, the Philippines, Vietnam, Peru, Papua New Guinea, Senegal, the Dominican Republic, Haiti, Honduras, El Salvador, Nicaragua, Guatemala, Colombia, the Kosovo refugees in Albania, earthquake victims in Turkey, and the current relief to Venezuela. See Duanzheng Wang, *Da'ai wu gupjie: Tzu-Chi jijinghui guoji jiuyuan jianjie* (Boundless Great Love: Introduction to International Relief, the Tzu-Chi Foundation) (Taipei, Taiwan: The Tzu-Chi Foundation, 1998); and the Tzu-Chi Foundation, *Buddhist Compassion Relief Tzu-Chi [Tzu Chi] Foundation* (Taipei, Taiwan: The Tzu-Chi Foundation, 1999).

30 Daniel A. Métraux, "The Soka Gakkai: Buddhism and the Creation of a Harmonious and Peaceful Society," in Christopher S. Queen and Sallie B. King (eds.), *Engaged Buddhism: Buddhist Liberation Movements in Asia* (Albany, NY: SUNY Press, 1996), p. 380.

31 All references to Huang Sixian in this article are based on our interview on January 21, 2000.

32 Such as building 1,800 houses for flood victims in Nepal.

33 For example, Tzu-Chi donated US $773,000 to the France-based Médecins du Monde (M.D.M.) to provide medical care to Ethiopia.

34 For example, in addition to being the first group delivering relief to the tidal wave victims in 1994, the Tzu-Chi Philippine branch has provided thirteen large-scale free clinic tours between 1995 and 1998. See Duanzheng Wang, *Da'ai wuyuan fojie: Tzu-Chi jijinghui jiuyuan jianjie.*

35 <http//www.tzuchi.org.tw/news/n_focus/n_focus.html> (accessed February 28, 2000).

36 Duanzheng Wang, *Tzu-Chi Yearbook 1998* (Taipei, Taiwan: Tzu-Chi Culture, 1999), p. 510.

37 Cixi Cai, *et al.*, *Tzu Chi USA 10th Anniversary: Annual Report* (Los Angeles, CA: The Tzu-Chi Southern California Branch, 1999).

38 These include Taiwan (north, central, and south), the United States (Northern California, Southern California, New York, New Jersey, Phoenix City, and Hawaii), Brazil (Sao Paulo), Dominican Republic (Santo Domingo), Indonesia (Jakarta), Vietnam (Ho Chi Minh City), Singapore, the Philippines (Manila), and Malaysia (Penang). Tzu-Chi Foundation (2000), "Tzu Chi Free Clinics," in *Enveloping the World with Great Love: The Tzu Chi International Relief Effort 1991–2000.* <http//taipei.tzuchi.org.tw/tzquart/book/book2/10.htm> (accessed June 29, 2001).

39 Huang Sixian listed the three exceptions. The current coordinator of the Orlando chapter is a Caucasian. Yet his wife is Taiwanese and he himself also speaks Chinese. One of the volunteer doctors in the Phoenix chapter is a Caucasian, but this does not necessarily mean that he is a Buddhist or a Tzu-Chi follower. A Caucasian volunteer in the Hawaii chapter, who is a hospital administrator by profession, has been a Tzu-Chi devotee to the extent that he has been proselytizing for Tzu-Chi and will receive his Tzu-Chi commissioner title this year.

40 Large branches in western societies – the United States, Canada, and the United Kingdom – have founded seventeen "Tzu-Chi Humanities Schools" (*Tzu-Chi renwen xuexiao*, the term itself highlights its curriculum of Tzu-Chi teaching as solely language-learning institutes) and currently have a total of over 2,000 pupils, whose parents do not necessarily participate in Tzu-Chi. Every weekend, youngsters up to twelfth grade learn Chinese characters through the official textbooks of the Taiwan-based Committee for Overseas Chinese Affairs as well as the Venerable Cheng-yen's "Still Thoughts" teachings through the

pedagogical methods formulated by the Tzu-Chi Teachers' Association in Taiwan.

41 For example, the Tzu-Chi USA runs a free clinic in Alhambra, California, which provides most of its services to local Hispanic speakers. At the same time, Tzu-Chi USA provides substantial support to relief to Mexico and other countries in Latin America, whereas Tzu-Chi Australia and Malaysia play leading roles in relief to countries in Southeast Asia.

42 For example, Berkeley and Boston.

43 For example, in December 1998 the Canada branch held a meeting to introduce Tzu-Chi in the English language. Audiences were staff of the institutions where Tzu-Chi followers regularly volunteer (e.g., children's hospital, AIDS association, and seniors' houses). See Duanzheng Wang (ed.), *Tzu-Chi Yearbook 1998*.

44 I participated in the New York branch in spring 1993, and conducted major fieldwork in the Boston branch between 1996 and 1997, and follow-up research from 1999 to the present. I visited the Japan branch during December 1997 and the two Malaysia branches in April 1999.

45 According to the Ministry of the Interior, Taiwan, from 1990 to 1996, the number of emigrants from Taiwan increased more than four times, from 25,500 to 119,100, quoted in Wang, Hong-luen, *In Want of a Nation: State, Institutions and Globalization in Taiwan*, PhD dissertation in Sociology, University of Chicago, 1999.

8

SOCIAL ENGAGEMENT IN SOUTH KOREAN BUDDHISM

Frank M. Tedesco

It is difficult to do justice to the variety and scope of the many Buddhist socially engaged activities in modern South Korea in a single chapter. I will attempt a broad overview of what is happening in Korea in general from our experience in the capital of Seoul where about a quarter of South Korea's population resides and where many organizations have their head-quarters. I will introduce a few of the more dynamic Buddhist organizations and leaders in Korea today. Very little has been available about Korean Buddhist activism in English until now, and I hope this chapter will at least partially fill a gap in the international understanding of the more pressing issues and challenges facing Korean Buddhism as a social force and Korean Buddhists as leaders of social transformation in their nation at the start of the twenty-first century.

What is the social and cultural context of Buddhist action in Korea? What issues do socially engaged Buddhists in Korea consider important and how are they addressing them? What challenges do Korean Buddhist activists confront to implement their visions and goals "on the ground"? A few Korean Buddhist groups and individuals, including representatives of the "new religion" of Won Buddhism,[1] have begun to respond to needs outside of Korea by serving communities abroad. What are they doing and why? How have the new forms of Buddhist social activism been received in more traditional and conservative Buddhist circles? What are the prospects for a socially engaged or pro-active Korean Buddhism in the future? We will attempt to answer these questions as we proceed.

Most of what I report in this chapter is based on my experience as a resident of Korea for more than fourteen years in the 1980s and throughout the 1990s. I have a number of personal associations and working relationships with many socially engaged Buddhist leaders in Korea as a consequence of my role as a foreign researcher of modern Korean lay Buddhism and a social activist during most of that time.[2] To describe Buddhist social engagement in Korea, I have tried to be as fair as possible by focusing on individual efforts and collective activities I partici-pated in, relying on first-hand accounts and direct interviews with the actors themselves. My contacts with busy leaders were frequently facilitated by my wife and research assistant, Jinsuk Lim Tedesco, an experienced interpreter and former administrator with the Korean National Commission for UNESCO. I alone am responsible for errors or omissions in this account, however.

It is inevitable that some Buddhist leaders or organizations in Korea may feel I have not done them justice. I wish to offer a heartfelt apology to them in advance. I beg their patience, forbearance and humor with this foreigner's brief and impertinent venture into their turf! I am confident they will eventually receive long overdue recognition for their efforts and greater support for their ongoing projects and plans for the future. As Buddhists know, the law of karma is inexorable. Korean people in general are renowned for their remarkable energy, single-minded determination and ability to survive and thrive in difficult circumstances. The engaged Buddhist activists I have met in Korea are exemplary religious activist-pioneers. They put their "open and true heart and mind" and dharma practice into action with great energy.

The Korean Buddhists who are succeeding against great odds to apply a dharma-inspired perspective to the social problems of Korea receive little assistance, and sometimes strong resistance, from conservative elements within the robed sangha, accompanied by general indifference and occasional disbelief and animosity from the non-Buddhist public. Many older or more conservative Buddhist citizens will openly criticize any monk or nun who dares to involve himself or herself in "worldly affairs" outside of the mountains or temple confines. These critics are purists who adhere to the belief that renunciants should only pursue enlightenment, as that is their one true and noble goal. In contrast, rigid, old Confucian or Christian critics blast Buddhist clerics as social leeches who delude the ignorant for alms. Such is the pervasive anti-Buddhist feeling that many children are taught to fear monks as devils! Some adults remember being afraid to pass by or enter temples when they were growing up! Many conservative Korean Christians living overseas carry these beliefs with them, and it is usually not difficult to elicit their negative opinions about Buddhism. Constructive Interfaith dialogue among Koreans is hard to find.[3]

Social and cultural context

It is important for the international community to understand the great efforts Korean Buddhist activists are making with the conscious intention of transforming Korean society into one that is more receptive to the teachings of the Buddha and the Mahayana goal of extending compassion to others. The new wave of "socially engaged Buddhism" in Korea's long history that I will describe is no more than ten to fifteen years old and is surging with great enthusiasm and organizational activities in many directions. The active Korean Buddhists we have met do not view what they are doing as a "new Buddhism" or "new yana," however, but rather as a re-empowerment or revitalization of Korea's ancient Buddhist heritage after centuries of demoralization and social impotence. The rebirth or re-emergence of Korea's Buddhist heritage is seen as an important component of Korea's unique, national identity and cultural distinctiveness.

Buddhism's low status in Korea was engendered by the ascendancy of an anti-Buddhist Confucian royal court during the Yi Dynasty (1392–1910) and the foreign intrusion of colonialist state Shinto Japan (1910–45). After the fall of Japan in August 1945, between the anti-religious and Marxist USSR and the capitalist and Christian United States led to the national division of the Korean peninsula that has not yet healed. In general, Korean Buddhist clergy throughout Korea and abroad (along with Christians), pray for the peaceful unification of their nation, but this sentiment rarely leads to any sort of tangible, political change.[4] The importance of Koreans' sense of national integrity and cohesiveness as a people should not be underestimated when trying to understand recent developments in Buddhist history. Continuity with the past glories of Korean Buddhism is a source of confidence in the face of obstacles and great pride.

Of South Korea's total population of nearly 47 million, about one-quarter considered themselves Buddhist at the time of government census and Gallup poll surveys in 2000. Among these, approximately 11–12 million Buddhists (Buddhist leaders like to claim 20 million believers!), only less than 40,000 are ordained and affiliated with about eighty sects. The Korean Buddhist Chogye Order is by far the wealthiest, most visible and most influential, with more than 16,000 bhiksus and bhiksunis.[5] The Chogye Order is the face of Korean Buddhism that most foreigners see in the little information about Korean Buddhism that is available outside of Korea in other languages. Most of the historically important temples are under the Chogye umbrella and represent what I call the "Korean Zen monastic stereotype" that is best known overseas. But there are actually about 19,000 temples of all sects or persuasions in the country. Their practice is eclectic – Pure Land, shamanist and Zen (Korean Seon) but predominantly oriented to achieving worldly success and happiness (kipok pulgyo, "Buddhism of good fortune") rather than "enlightenment." The great majority of their supporters are women, usually middle-aged and elderly (chima pulgyo, "skirt Buddhism"). Some of these ladies are dedicated environmentalists, hospital and prison volunteers and aides to the elderly, among other roles. The total number of Buddhist temples is swollen by very small, family-style temples or shrines, usually owned by married clergy or devout lay women (posallim).[6] There are only a few dozen ordained foreign monks and nuns in Korea, if that many, and fewer foreign lay Buddhist practitioners.[7] Their social engagement has been negligible so far.

This said, when foreign visitors land in Seoul for the first time today they are often struck by the absence of any signs or symbols of Buddhist culture, unless they happen to arrive in spring around Buddha's Birthday, an official national holiday (8th day of the 4th lunar month). Although Buddhism was first introduced to Korean territory in the fourth century CE during Koguryo times and has been practiced along with shamanism and other indigenous beliefs on the peninsula ever since, the modern lifestyle of the great majority of Koreans, even those avowedly Buddhist, betrays that history.

Unlike most Asian countries with a long Buddhist heritage, Korea has hidden its Buddhist practice, forcing the visitor to actively seek it out. There are no Buddhist shrines in shops and homes and virtually no Buddhist monuments on the thoroughfares. The fragrance of incense is confined to temples or Confucian family rituals. Not only are the great majority of temples located in the countryside or tucked into distant mountain valleys, but free-standing traditional, Buddhist architecture in the cities and suburbs is uncommon or isolated. A few urban branch temples of major monasteries in business complexes compete with dozens, if not hundreds, of Protestant "storefront churches." The most obvious structures in most countryside farming villages are churches, too.

Large or small, rural or urban, Korean Protestant (mostly Presbyterian) ministers almost invariably erect red neon crosses on top of their steeples or electrical towers. These symbols punctuate the South Korean skyline from the DMZ in the north to the seaport of Pusan on the southeast tip of the country, a sure reminder that Christianity has arrived in force on the peninsula. According to the latest Korean government survey in 2000, there are about 62,600 registered Protestant churches with 120,000 ordained ministers in 161 denominations. Christians also happen to dominate the modern fields of Western medicine, law and social welfare among others. Buddhists are poorly represented in these professions in Korea.

While Buddhist monks and monasteries were renowned in the distant past for disaster relief during famine and flood, and temples were refuges for the disenfranchised, orphans, the homeless, elderly and the disabled,[8] the state has absorbed the traditional role of temples and today's Buddhist social service institutions are small, few and far between. You will not find Buddhist hospitals (as in Taiwan) or many clinics except for traditional Chinese medicine.

As for Korean Buddhist educational facilities, there are very few Buddhist K-12 schools and only one full-scale Buddhist-founded university (Dongguk University). The nation's first medical school and Western-style medical hospital are only now under construction. For sake of comparison, although its population is triple that of Korea, Japan has

approximately seventy established Buddhist institutions of higher education and about 3,000 scholars pursuing Buddhist studies while Korea has
only about twenty such scholars. Temple-based daycare centers in Korea
are becoming more numerous, however, with bhiksunis and lay women
(*posallim*) operating them with varying degrees of profitability. The
majority of women have always worked hard at home in Korea, but today
many are obliged to work outside of home, and with the new, small
nuclear family there are no grandparents and siblings to function as built-
in baby sitters.

To get a better idea of the cultural uniqueness of Korea, I will briefly
describe the ethnic landscape from my perspective as a practicing
American Buddhist. It must be noted that the Western expatriate community in Korea is very small compared to those communities in Japan,
Thailand or Taiwan. Most of the long-term residents are associated with
the US military (about 37,000 troops), the US civil service, multinational
corporations, and the various religious denominations, including the
ubiqutous Mormons. Needless to say, very few resident aliens are Buddhist
except for staff and businessmen from Buddhist countries.

There is no cultural or ethnic heterogeneity in Korea, such as the ethnic
or indigenous minorities like the Ainu of Japan. There is not even a
Chinatown at present though there are plans to create one in Seoul by the
city government. Foreign laborers, both legal and illegal, from developing
nations congregate near where they work but they hardly constitute ethnic
enclaves as we know them in most parts of the world. In Korea in 2001,
except for certain quarters of Seoul or Pusan, foreigners remain rarities.
They are treated as objects of curiosity, cheap labor, or with suspicion by
many citizens, even though they may have relatives who have emigrated to
North America and even though they follow "Americans" everyday on TV
and in films.[9] Most Korean Christians will feel sympathy or camaraderie if
you are also Christian or Jewish. To be a Western Buddhist in Korea,
however, is to be ignored, ostracized or treated as a rather odd duck by the
general Christian populace – or to the contrary, flattered and even lionized
by Korean Buddhists who are still amazed that any Westerner could care
about their faith, let alone practice meditation regularly. Foreign interest
and overt belief in Buddhism are very heartening to them.

In general, Korean Buddhists do not view themselves as an influential or
prestigious force in Korean society and they have little political clout
compared to well-organized, wealthy Protestant and Catholic factions.
Those who have the courage and determination to struggle to change
Korean society as engaged Buddhists are a select and precious minority.
The sad truth is that Buddhism has low status in contemporary Korea and
engaged Buddhists who work in public often feel self-conscious and sometimes react with defiance or timidity when ostracized.

To underscore the Korean people's difficult past and Buddhism's place in it, it is important to remember that the Korean people have been trau-matized by a series of historical crises in the last hundred years that would defeat all but the strongest cultures. As mentioned earlier, the twentieth century began with the unsettling demise of the five-century-old Neo-Confucian Yi Dynasty (1392–1910) and thirty-five years of oppressive colonization by Japan. This was followed by ideological polarization and national division at the end of World War II (1945), followed by a destruc-tive civil war (Korean War 1950–53) and a series of ruthless, authoritarian regimes until the first democratically elected civilian president Kim Young Sam (1992–97). The dictatorial regimes (Rhee, Park, Chun, Noh) placed rapid industrialization over human rights, development over the environ-ment and so-called materialist science, technology and manufacturing over traditional cultural values. Korea changed from a rural and agricultural nation at the turn of the century to one that is more than 85–90 percent urban and industrial in the 1990s. Most of this population shift occurred from the 1970s onwards beginning with General Park Chung Hee's indus-trial development obsession to compete with Japan.

Ironically, Japanese pressure at the end of the nineteenth century freed Korean monks from isolation in mountain temples where they had been officially exiled during the anti-Buddhist Yi Dynasty. During the latter half of this period, Buddhist monks were ranked no higher than butchers, pros-titutes or shamanist sorcerers. The majority were soon coerced or tempted to forsake their traditional vows of celibacy and marry as Japanese monks had been forced to do in Meiji Japan. The Korean sangha today is still divided between the celibate (Chogye Order) and married priesthood (T'aego Order and many other smaller sangha organizations). Tensions and litigation over temple property ownership deriving from colonial times still continues but is disappearing as the older generation dies off. The chaos within Korean society after the Korean War was exemplified in the sangha as those elements who wanted to root out every vestige of Japanese influence in Korean culture won ascendancy with the support of the arch-nationalist, Princeton-educated, Christian autocrat, President Syngman Rhee.

In contrast to the Buddhists, Korean Christians have established many successful private universities, hospitals and schools of theology in the past fifty years. They have quickly dominated the highly visible and influential professions of medicine, nursing, law and the military. Christians, who account for about one quarter of the Korean population (approximately 12 million), matching the Buddhists, are overwhelmingly Protestant, outnumbering Catholics four to one. Korea is lauded as a phenomenal success story by Western evangelists because they consider it one of the world's fastest-growing Christian countries. Seoul boasts the largest single Protestant church in the world, the Yoido Full Gospel Church that purportedly has 700,000 members and over 10,000 per service, many times per Sunday.

In terms of numbers, Korean Christians have just exceeded Korean Buddhists within 100 years of missionary efforts in Korea. They are also training and sponsoring large numbers of their own Korean-born missionaries to win converts of different faiths in less economically developed countries like Mongolia, Sri Lanka, India, Indonesia, Russia, the former Soviet republics, China and others.

Buddhist leaders in poorer, distressed countries often do not have the experience or means to counter ambitious missionaries who can seduce local youth with material goods, medical care, and dreams of education. Korean Christians confidently claim that old, dysfunctional Korea was a clear example of the failure of Buddhism. To them, there is no refuge or salvation in Buddha, but only evasion of family and wider social duties (anathema to Confucian ideals) and a subterfuge to disguise selfish decadence by means of archaic Chinese mumbo-jumbo and idol worship. They assert or imply that all good things that have happened to Korea, materially and spiritually, have been associated with the Christian faith of their advanced Western (mostly American) liberators and the early Korean Christian converts who led the country. "Christian America 'under God' is the leader of the world" (and rich Korea, too!) Korean missionaries preach to struggling "Third World" neighbors who seek a better life for their children. Thus, Korea can be seen as a model of extraordinary economic development, thanks to American military protection (Christian soldiers) and the "amazing grace" of the missionaries.[10]

While the presence of US troops in South Korea is reassuring to older generations of Koreans, who saw their country leveled by war with the North and Maoist China, their continued presence on the peninsula after fifty years is a profound issue of national self-determination for many born and educated after the war. Student protesters and political activists consider the American military stationed in Korea as an overt symbol of American neo-colonialism, supported by Korea's tawdry history of obeisance and collaboration with stronger powers, in the form of corrupt military dictators and greedy family corporations (*chaebol*). They assert that for Korea to be reunified and truly independent, it must cast off the shackles of the American military and join with the people of the North as one Korean family (*tongil minjok*). They feel that the so-called American "liberation" in 1945 with the fall of Korea's Japanese colonial rulers was only the start of another geopolitical game with the United States dividing the Korean peninsula to get some strategic leverage over the Soviet Union, China and Japan.

Christian evangelical fervor represents an obvious implantation of American values into the Korean peninsula, according to many detached observers and North Korean (DPRK) propagandists, too.[11] Protestantism was a foreign religion with less than 400,000 followers in Korea in 1945 but it grew phenomenally after the Korean War (1950–53) when crusading missionaries of many American denominations became associated with massive humanitarian aid to the war-torn country. It is not surprising that older Koreans who benefited from this assistance feel deep gratitude and filial loyalty to their Christian brothers and sisters from *miguk*, the "beautiful country" that saved them.

Many younger Koreans who do not sense this degree of gratitude to Uncle Sam became protesters who angrily demonstrated against US-supported dictators (Rhee, Park, Chun, Noh) in battles against battalions of Darth Vader-like security police on campuses and city streets across the country. Red bandannas, truncheons and tear gas were the symbols and tools of social protest during the decades of the dictators. Chanting, meditation, prostration and selfless community action have replaced violence for those who have discovered their national identity in their ancient Korean Buddhist heritage. Some are now leaders of relatively small but growing Buddhist non-governmental organizations (NGO) dedicated to transforming Korean society by more peaceful and culturally familiar means.

Struggling as they have for the people's democratic rights in the face of the authoritarian force and the dreaded National Security Law,[12] many young idealists who eventually embraced Buddhism were able to hone their social and organizational skills "on the barricades and streets." They were personally chastened by the deaths, suicides and broken careers of their colleagues through torture, prison sentences, years in hiding and finally disillusionment with revolution and Marxist ideology at the fall of the Soviet Union. They experienced a period of wrenching suffering early in their lives that drove many to deeper levels of self-reflection and spiritual questioning than their less idealistic, materialistic brothers and sisters.

Engaged Buddhism

A socially responsive Korean Buddhism is still young and growing in many directions, but I do not see it as a major mass movement in Korea yet. It attracts a small number of very committed idealists whose influence extends far beyond their actual numbers. Modern, active Korean Buddhism is experiencing a variety of challenges and it is hard to predict what the seedling associations will become. Associations rise, thrive and transmute rapidly into different forms in response to different types of social, economic and environmental crises as they suddenly bloom in Korea's hyper-charged, roller-coaster economy and the tricky political landscape. Korean Buddhist activists deserve extra encouragement and support, too, as they struggle to overcome centuries of cultural stigmatization.

When you visit the many ancient temples ensconced in the mountains and valleys, you can easily imagine Buddhism as the national religion and predominant social and political force it was in Korea for a thousand years. The past six hundred years, however, were years of travail as many monastic communities were torn asunder. Repressive Confucian legislation designed to Confucianize the nation from the top down succeeded in effacing much of Buddhist thought and practice from the population. Later, thirty-five years of totalitarian colonial Japanese rule smashed the long, celibate tradition of Korean monasticism in the first half of the twentieth century. The intense competitiveness of Christianity instigated religious discontent and confusion among the masses and defensiveness and imitation among many Buddhists. Pressures to conform for success, coupled with a legacy of decadence, exacerbated by sensationalist media coverage of violent disputes among Chogye monks, have led many urban Korean youth (especially Seoulites) to ignore Buddhism as a viable religious alternative.

Among the various engaged Buddhist associations that are active in Korea today, I have selected four in particular that are attracting considerable notice and growing in influence as exemplary models of Buddhist social and moral commitment. Each of these associations contains independent and very active working groups that focus on specific social problems within Korea and overseas. Some focus on matters with significant international ramifications that transcend religious boundaries, such as the invitation to Korea of His Holiness the Dalai Lama of Tibet, and the reunification of the Korean peninsula. The Buddhist Coalition for Economic Justice (*Kyeongbullyon*) or "BCEJ"; the JungTo Society (*Cheongt'ohoe*) also known as "JTS" or the "Join Together Society" in English; the Buddhist Solidarity for Reform (*Ch'amyeopulgyo chaega yeundae*) or "BSR"; and the Indranet Life Community (*Indramang saengmyeong kongdongch'e*) are deeply committed to the renewal of Buddhist values in Korean society by reforming or innovating relations among divisions of the lay and ordained Buddhist community (the traditional fourfold sangha of male and female clergy and laity) and extending compassion to all others regardless of class or religion in the spirit of the Mahayana bodhisattva ideal. By describing the activities of these organizations in detail we can get a better grasp of the particular issues and problems Korean Buddhists face and the multifaceted character of their socially responsive Buddhism.

The Buddhist Coalition for Economic Justice

The Buddhist Coalition for Economic Justice (*Kyeongbullyon*) was founded in July 1991 by a group of lay Buddhists who were members of the influential national NGO, Citizen's Coalition for Economic Justice, founded in July 1989. The Buddhist Coalition for Economic Justice (BCEJ), the first Buddhist civil movement organization, purports to establish a democratic civil society where all people can prosper equitably regardless of their nationality, race, religion and social status. BCEJ members are involved in a wide spectrum of activities such as fair election campaigns, campaigns to prevent sexual violence, protection of human rights for foreign, migrant workers, aid to North Korean famine refugees and ethnic Koreans in China, aid for the impoverished in Third World countries, environmental protection and a consumer frugality movement.

BCEJ's various sub-committees (such as policy-making, women, environment and international cooperation) work closely together in order to raise social awareness among Buddhists throughout Korea and they join in solidarity with other civic organizations in order to enhance the development and social recognition of Buddhism in Korea as an autonomous social force. The Buddhist Coalition for Economic Justice sees itself as a non-violent, peace movement based on "the teaching of the middle path" and a movement to rescue humankind and nature from suffering based on the Buddhist teaching of interdependence. It seeks to bring Buddhism into the daily life of the general populace (not only in the mountains) and to bring about systemic and structural reform in order to realize social and economic justice for everyone. The BCEJ also wishes to raise the awareness of the need for the reform of social inequities in order to heighten "the spirit of all citizens as one community."

Various interdependent organizations within the BCEJ are the House of Compassion (*Chabi-ui jip*), the Migrant Workers' Human Rights and Culture Center, Helping Our Neighbors (*Yiwooseul tomneun saramdeul*), the Nepal Bihani Basti (*Ach'im-eul yeoneun chag'eun ma-eul*), the House of the Morning (*Ach'im-eul yeoneun chip*), Open Schools of Hope (*Huimang mandeulgi yeollin hakkyo*) and My Little Green Friend (*Nae ch'ingu ch'orogi*).

The House of Compassion of BCEJ is located in a poorer, working-class section of Seoul which is undergoing rapid redevelopment and consequent forced resettlement of many disadvantaged households. It provides free lunch for approximately 150 poor, elderly people without families along with various social service activities and programs to help poor families headed by children (without parents) and other neighbors in need. It is sustained by donations from about 1,600 supporting members and 200 committed volunteers.

The Migrant Workers' Human Rights and Culture Center of BCEJ was established in immediate response to needs of foreign workers in Korea. According to Jung Jin-Woo, a BCEJ leader at the above MWHR Culture Center:

it is estimated that more than 250,000 workers from foreign countries are employed in Korea at "3D" companies where Koreans are reluctant to work. Though they are doing essential labor in the service of Korea, nevertheless they are treated as "strange aliens." The cold treatment is aggravated by the discriminatory attitude toward persons whose skin is a darker color or who come from poorer countries...

Foreign workers are human beings just like Koreans. It is unacceptable for Koreans, who are known for our kindness and generosity, to discriminate against and mistreat foreign workers merely because they look different and speak different languages. We must act immediately to stop the cruel and deadly mistreatment, and to guarantee their equal status as workers and as human beings. Citizens and civil organizations should pay close attention to the proposed Employment Permit System for foreign migrants, now under discussion by the government, and make efforts to have it enacted as soon as possible.[13]

In early January 1994, some foreign workers began a sit-in at the offices of the Citizens' Coalition for Economic Justice (CCEJ). They had lost fingers and suffered other serious injuries in Korean factories where they worked for minimum pay, but they had been denied overdue wages and other compensation. They protested this unfairness and asked for CCEJ's help.[14] The Buddhists responded and eventually formally established the Community Center for Foreign Workers in April 1995. The Center not only provides counseling and other assistance but also helps foreign workers (many of whom are illegally overstaying visa permits), to understand Korean culture better by teaching them the Korean language and guiding them on cultural excursions.

The Nepal Buddhist Family was organized in January 1996 to help Nepalese workers in Korea and to organize the annual celebration of Nepalese lunar new year (Losar). Members of the Family also assist the Nepal Bihani Basti, a Vocational Center in Nepal. The Community Center for Foreign Workers was reorganized and renamed the Migrant Workers' Human Rights and Culture Center in November 2000. The main activities of Migrant Workers' Human Rights and Culture Center are assistance in labor disputes, medical assistance, legal counseling, education and cultural activities, monthly dharma meetings, temporary shelter, and activities in solidarity with other related organizations.

Helping Our Neighbors of the BCEJ was established in June 1996 in order to support families and children suffering from famine and disease around the world. Its main activities include the Nepal Bihani Basti (*Ach'im-ul yeoneun chag'eun ma-eul*) that is located in Kathmandu. This center provides free medical service, vocational training, Nepalese language and math education as well as Korean language education. The 1994 protest by foreign workers at CCEJ made Korean Buddhists abruptly realize the need to help foreign workers in their midst for the first time. Koreans began to understand why foreigners are forced to seek work abroad just as Korean migrants did in Hawaii and Germany and other places in the past. In an effort to ameliorate conditions of potential foreign exile workers in Korea, BCEJ organized the Nepal Bauddha Sewa Kendra' (Nepal Buddha Service Center) which was officially incorporated by the Royal Nepalese government in January 1997. BCEJ purchased a plot of land in Kathmandu in July 1997 and completed the Nepal Bihani Basti Building in May 1999.

On the domestic front, the House of the Morning of BCEJ opened in May 1998 at a park near the main Seoul railroad station. Seoul station became a meeting point for despairing homeless men and families who would sleep in corrugated cardboard boxes throughout the station's complex hallway system. The House of the Morning provided free meals, employment counseling, and medical care for those who were made homeless and without jobs due to the so-called "Korean IMF (International Monetary Fund) debt crisis" at the end of 1997. The House served dinners for more than 600 people and helped 700 people to find work as paid volunteers at welfare facilities every day until it closed down on May 1999. Another House of the Morning opened in a poor section of the city in January 1999 in order to continue to provide various rehabilitation and self-support programs for about twenty homeless and unemployed people.

The BCEJ Open Schools of Hope provide free dinner and after-school programs for elementary school age children of the unemployed. My Little Green Friend (*Nae ch'ingu ch'orogi*) is a store specializing in used goods, the proceeds of which are used for welfare activities.

The JungTo Society

The innovative and multidimensional JungTo Society (*Cheongt'o hoe*, "Pure Land Society") is cooperatively led by the founder Venerable Pomnyun (aged 48) and a committed group of about ninety full-time activists and supporters (about sixty in Seoul and thirty in other cities) and many temporary staff and short-term volunteer workers in Korea, India, China, the United States, Thailand and other parts of the world. The central office, dharma hall, lecture rooms and communal living center of this organization have recently been established in a newly constructed building in the trendy Kangnam area of Seoul, south of the Han River.

A complete, detailed picture of the background, history and many activities of the JungTo Society (JTS) since its inception a little more than a decade ago would require a number of graduate theses. A chronology of JTS's growth in Korea can be found in English on the JungTo Society web site.[15] The experienced and energetic leadership of former social protester, activist and dharma teacher, Venerable Pomnyun, has attracted many competent and dedicated associates who are ambitiously trying to bring about positive change in Korea and other parts of the world with very little personal aggrandizement and remarkable self-sacrifice.

An instructive vignette is worth retelling for the insight it provides about the nature and background of socially engaged Buddhism in Korea. In 1984, Venerable Pomnyun went to Seorim Seonwon (a Buddhist temple meditation center) with four activist students and started a community. In 1985, he was driven out from the temple because of his people's Buddhist (*minjungbulgyo*) activities. He reflects on what happened thus:

> What I asserted at the time was that democratization without national consciousness is problematic. In order to change our society, we have to understand our own national identity. We have to look into ourselves with our own eyes and understand exactly what the problems are. But all they did was examine us through Western eyes. I did not like that. They accepted foreign religion and foreign philosophy. I'm not saying that foreign things are wrong. But we have to study our own tradition to firmly establish our roots. Another thing that I pointed out was that our movement should not be used for personal success and fame. Spiritual practice is a must in a social movement. One has to devote his whole life to it without expecting personal gains.
>
> (Keongangdan, June, 2000)

The motto by which JTS members live by is rather simple: "There are pure minds. There are good friends beside you. Here and now we are creating a land of bliss." We will see that the rigorous pledge JTS members take to uphold their ideals distinguish them from conventional lay Buddhists in Korea and most of the clergy, too.

Venerable Pomnyun himself is not recognized as a bona fide monk by the Chogye Order Central Headquarters since he did not undergo training in a *kangwon* (monastic scriptural training hall) nor Dongguk University, and he did not receive formal ordination established by the Order.[16] Venerable Pomnyun's freedom from the constraints and questionable aura of the Chogye Order does not seem to have inhibited the success of the many projects JTS has initiated, and may even have helped the group garner more support from the general populace beyond the boundaries of religion and denomination. He is also able to maintain more egalitarian relationships with his colleagues and followers and not be subordinated to the customary age hierarchy and lineage fealties of mainstream monks.

As socially engaged Buddhists, members of the JungTo Society in Korea have been dedicated to practical action in environmental preservation and ecological education inspired by Buddhist Pure Land thought and frugal, communitarian idealism.

According to JTS literature, the JungTo Society is "a community established to realize *JungTo* or Sukhavati, a Land of Bliss in the world, here and now. This is a place where every individual is happy in a peaceful society surrounded by beautiful nature."

> By understanding that myself, society and nature are parts of one existence interrelated with another (Non-ego) and the law of cause and effect, we can discard the concept of "Mine"(Non-possession) and "My thought" (Non-self-assertion). Then, we set ourselves free from any adherence keeping our minds peaceful consuming the least amount of materials and sharing with others, therefore we are able to form a peaceful community with good relations among people and create a world with harmony and balance between human beings and nature.[17]

JTS teaches a kind of Buddhist-inspired eco-idealism that has popular appeal to many Korean youth without the burden of scriptural study and exegesis of classical Chinese texts of the mainstream establishment. JTS literature and dharma study are written in simple, pure Korean for the most part and it is not burdensome to follow for younger people who have not been schooled in Chinese characters. Literature produced by the Academy of Ecological Awakening, a unit of JTS, is similar in style yet incorporates the most up-to-date thinking on environmental issues and intentional communities from around the globe, while making basic Buddhist values and guidelines central to its orientation.[18] JTS as an organization attempts to live by the following slogan:

To Strive for Pure Minds, Good Friends and Clean Lands

Pure minds are thoroughly controlled minds, which are delightful, peaceful, and unfettered in any situation.

Good friends are those who, with a full understanding of interdependency, offer respect and are grateful to others and work together cooperatively, not competitively, for a peaceful society.

Clean lands refer to a world where balance and harmony with nature are well established and the Earth is no longer something to be conquered but to be preserved by observing the following three precepts.

1   To abandon lust and desire in order to develop a pure mind in our liveli hood.

2   To work together in harmony in order to make good friends with others.

3   To reject consumerism in order to keep the Earth a sustain able, peaceful and clean environment.[19]

Individuals who commit themselves to the values and goals of JTS take vows that are both indicative of a modern perspective on the problems of the world yet deeply integrated with fundamental Mahayana Buddhist teaching. Extracts from their extensive vows will illustrate their "progressive yet traditional" commitments:

Today we are faced with a decline of humanity, the breakdown of our communities, and the destruction of the natural environment. To overcome these crises we look to the fundamental teachings of Buddhism for solutions.

First, *we accept the law of Dependent Origination as our worldview*.

Existence of this is dependent on the existence of that. Without that, this will not exist. This mutual interdependence of existence is the true nature of all things. If you die I too will die and if you live I too will live. If you are unhappy, I am unhappy and if you are happy I am also happy. Hence, based on the worldview of Dependent Origination, we pursuit a path of coexistence and mutual happiness.

As variety of flowers make up a flower bed, a variety of unique people come together to attain harmony and balance in order to create a new culture, where jealousy and envy are surpassed to form love, antagonism and competition are surpassed to form harmony, conflict and war are overcome to form peace.

Second, *we take Buddha and the Bodhisattva as paragons of life*.

Taking the exemplary life of Buddha, having only a begging bowl and a robe, as an example to follow, we also live as seekers of truth. Eating less, having less clothes, and sleeping less, we become free from any attachment.

Considering the pain and suffering of sentient beings as our own, we throw ourselves into samsara and hell, take on the role of Avalokitesvara, the bodhisattva of compassion, and Ksitigarbha, the bodhisattva of the great vow, and vow to be bodhisattvas in order to liberate all sentient beings.

Third, *we take non-self, non-possession, and non-attachment to my own ideas as objectives of our cultivation.*

To build a Pure land (*JungTo*) I vow to let go of self, possessions, and attachment to my own views, and strive to become a bodhisattva who is compassionate towards all sentient beings. Reflecting on my mind and becoming free from attachments, I vow to become a liberated person who is free from suffering and hindrances.

Overcoming this crisis of humanity, we vow to build a peaceful and happy world, a Pure Land, by cultivating a happy life (a pure mind), a peaceful society (good friends), and a beautiful environment (clean land).

("Vows of JTS Members," paraphrased translation)

Part of the discipline of full-time JTS volunteer-members entails the following:

When we have an injured finger, our nerves, hands and feet instantly cooperate to cure the finger without any expectation of award. As such, it is natural that we don't expect any award from others when we have worked for others. Understanding the realization of *JungTo* is our duty, we voluntarily work for pleasure without expectation of any award ... In order to strengthen our oath for *JungTo*, the members of JTS began 10,000 days of prayer for thirty years commencing in March 1993. The 10,000 days are divided into ten 1,000-day periods, and every 1,000 days are divided again into ten 100 days. JTS members congregate every 100 days to evaluate the achievement of the goals in three fields – self-discipline, charity and voluntary service – then renew our oath and commitment. Through prayer, all members solidify their will to become awakened persons who are free and happy, to make a society free from competition and conflict and a world of where humans and nature are harmony.[20]

The Join Together Society is the international branch of JungTo that began in early 1991 when Venerable Pomnyun witnessed extreme poverty first-hand in India.[21]Since then, JTS has grown into a small but effective international assistance organization that has fostered educational and medical programs in the poorest villages of the Bihar province in India near Bodhgaya, and community development work in the same area in cooperation with the Sarvodaya Shramadana Movement of A. T.

Ariyaratne in Sri Lanka. JTS also began food relief efforts to feed starving children in North Korea in 1997 with the operation of a nutrient factory in the Rajin-Sonbong Economic and Trade Zone and a successful agricultural assistance project (1998–9). JTS has also provided financial support for the elderly and poor ethnic Korean families in China (1995), finances for the education of refugee children in the Chittagong Hill Tracts of Bangladesh (1999–2000), educational opportunities for Burmese refugee children in Thailand (1999–2000), a field survey for relief work in African countries (May 2000) and food and clothing assistance to Mongolia (summer 2000). There are long-term plans to continue these activities. The ultimate aim of these projects is "to help people to be independent and to create self-sufficient and sustainable societies" where people can "balance the spiritual and material aspects of life and live in harmony with the natural environment."

JTS has a unique and dedicated character among Buddhist groups in Korea because its leadership is comprised of former rugged, student activists who fought against political violence with systematic resistance and clandestine struggle for years. Venerable Pomnyun and JTS members seek to transcend both violent and non-violent resistance, however, and are actively pursuing positive alternatives for action. Environmental education at the grassroots that leads to care and concern for nature through mindful conservation, rather than demanding prohibitions against dumping waste, will bring about slower but lasting change. Pomnyun and other leaders in JTS understand that social change does not come easily and they have the battle scars of torture and prison records to prove it. The bodhisattva-activists of JTS demand real commitment from new members. Based on years of experience dealing with people, they are concerned that a member should have a strong will to live by JTS vows and so a requirement of 10,000 prostrations (deep bows with knees, elbows and forehead touching the floor) for anyone who wants to work with JTS was decided by the General Meeting of its members.[22] Those who complete this assignment usually last at least three months.

Buddhist Solidarity for Reform

The Buddhist Solidarity for Reform (*Ch'amyeopulgyo chaega yeondae*) is an association of lay Buddhists comprising over forty Korean Buddhist civil organizations. The main focus of the BSR is to bring about fundamental and lasting reforms within the Chogye Order. The organization was formed two years ago as a kind of emergency social response to the violent clashes and evidence of corruption and malfeasance at Chogye Order Headquarters at the time of the order's General Assembly elections. Televised scenes on CNN of monks fighting among themselves in the streets and with police shamed Korean Buddhists within the nation and shocked people around the world. Deeply distressed by the ordained sangha's inability to control their emotions and administer peaceful transitions of monastic authority during their elections, concerned lay Buddhist men and women began to protest against the troublemakers (some very senior monks) and demand that the guilty parties withdraw or face temple boycotts or excommunication from the order. Rallies and parades of lay people were held in the streets in the vicinity of the headquarters to muster public attention and support for reform. Lay leaders of concerned Buddhist organizations quickly organized to form the Buddhist Solidarity for Reform in order to articulate an agenda of action to reform the order and strengthen the morale of all Buddhists in the country.

Located in offices near Chogyesa Temple and Chogye Headquarters in downtown Seoul, the BSR has been closely monitoring the activities and dealings of monk-officials in the headquarters in order to expose serious abuses of power and encourage the Buddhist laity who wish to restore the honor of Buddhism within Korea. Unlike the JungTo Society, that functions independently of the restraints and power of the Chogye Buddhist authority, BSR is striving to reform the inherited tradition within the establishment by applying heretofore untested pressure from the laity.

Until now, monks have had almost total control of temple finances and decision-making and have not shared power with the lay people who support them. Buddhist Solidarity is trying to break the monastic monopoly on temple finances by dedicating itself to bring about transparency in temple bookkeeping and a responsible accounting of revenues and expenditures. Famous, large and historically important temples in Korea earn huge amounts of income very easily from a variety of sources, including admissions fees, if they are located in national parks, from national tax support for the preservation of traditional cultural assets and from anonymous donations from believers. The size and allocation of this money have not been open to the public. Priests have had all the authority to make decisions arbitrarily with only negligible or unsavory consultation with the laity. Often the clergy is totally wrapped up with the expansion and support of their monastic family or lineage (*munjung*), and with huge building projects rather than being of service to society. It is common knowledge that rancorous disputes over the corrupt selection of abbots of cash-flush regional temples and headquarters officials repeatedly break out at the time of Chogye Order elections. Dharma centers (*p'ogyodang*) located in the cities where the lay public has more input in temple affairs have better financial management. Lay people are often better trained and more experienced than Buddhist clergy in complicated worldly affairs, and "it is high time for both clergy and lay people to seriously explore ways to share responsibilities" according to Dr. Gwang-seo Park, a US-educated professor of physics who is chairperson of the BSR.[23] The exclusive and closed hierarchical patriarchy that has monopolized authority within major monasteries and temples in previous centuries is being challenged by a sophisticated lay public. Monks can no longer expect unquestioning support by a passive and subordinate laity as in the past.[24]

The Buddhist Solidarity for Reform recently exhibited in growing strength to bring about change within the bastions of the Chogye hierarchy by successfully forcing the resignation of a newly appointed Director of Planning for the Order.[25] Although this monk was a convicted and fined habitual gambler who had been in the news, the headquarters refused to remove him on grounds that gambling was not a disqualification under the constitution and regulations of the Chogye Order. The General Assembly had in fact approved his appointment without dissent. Buddhist Solidarity welcomed his resignation at a news conference the day after the event and pointed out that the Buddhist tradition accepts suggestions and recommendations of lay members of the four-fold sangha if they are good and desirable. BSR hopes that this case will lead to the revival of a tradition that will be adopted by the administration of the Chogye Order. The present Chief Executive Venerable Chongdae opined that it was desirable for lay people to participate in the management of the order, but we have yet to see how this will be implemented.[26]

According to a Buddhist Solidarity for Reform manifesto, BSR plans to continually investigate the ignominious activities of sangha members in order to purify society and

> reestablish true Korean Buddhism through a reform of consciousness. Lay Buddhists in particular should review and reform their lives and devotional activities in order to become "true Buddhists" who, in turn, can uphold Korean Buddhism. Lay Buddhists should commit themselves to take the lead in restoring the social status and capabilities of Buddhism in Korea. This is the turning point of Korean Buddhism. Buddhist Solidarity shall make efforts to realize the teachings of the Buddha in this society truthfully, thus enabling Korean Buddhism to play a leading role in directing the spirit of the times.
>
> Buddhist Solidarity will lead a repentance movement focusing on the issue of violence that surfaced during the Chogye Order conflict in 1998. We would like to clarify our position that no violence shall be tolerated. Other urgent tasks are "transparent management of temple finances" and "decision-making by the four-fold sangha." We will create a "pure & clean sangha" that can be trusted by the laity as well as the general public through the eradication of violence and drastic reform in the questionable management of temple finances.
>
> Confident that the teachings of the Buddha is the best way to cure problems of modern society, the Buddhist Solidarity will

propagate the Dharma to the general public addicted to materialism and individualism. The Solidarity will make efforts to create an honest society through alternative social, civic, and solidarity movements which protect democratic values and the spirit of the community.

BSR will be an open, democratic institution and act to provide external protection of Buddhism and to actively address the oppression and desecration of Buddhism in Korea and elsewhere.

We will promote a "simple life movement" for the fourfold sangha that urges the sangha to avoid riding in deluxe cars and frequenting five-star hotels as well as other unnecessary displays of material wealth.

We will encourage a "merit transfer movement" through engagement in the society by initiating a universal community and peace movement entailing public culture of repentance and self-reflection, the peaceful reunification of Korea and a restoration of human rights movement and a recognition of religious conflict and need for inter-religious dialogue

We will also initiate a "together with our neighbors" movement on a regional basis according to local interest. We must promote an ecologically friendly culture in our daily lives and campaign to restore ethics for life and the environment. Our local "Centers for Merit Building through Social Engagement" will develop programs to demonstrate the potentiality of Buddhism to create a better society.[27]

There is no doubt that we will hear much about this Korean lay organization as it confronts generations of vested interests in the established monasteries of South Korea. BSR accepts the need to reform the Chogye Order and raise lay Buddhist consciousness about the purpose of the faith as imperative for the long term future of traditional Buddhism in Korea.

Indra Net Life Community

In September 1999, an important Buddhist community movement called the Indra Net Life Community (*Indramang saengmyong godongch'e*) was launched under the leadership of the highly respected senior monk Venerable Tobop, the abbot of Shilsangsa Temple, as its chairperson. Twenty-three socially active temples and Buddhist NGOs such as Chogyesa, Pongeunsa, Shilsangsa, Neung-in Seonwon, Hwagyesa, Toseonsa, Shinheungsa, Together for Good (*Urinun Seonwoo*), the Buddhist Academy for Ecological Awakening (BAEA) and others have participated in the network from its inception. Its major activities include "back to the farm" education, a cooperative livelihood movement, alternative education, the creation of local communities, and a movement to cement solidarity among groups working for the environment. These activities had been independently run by member organizations before consolidation in the Indra Net Life Community. This union has created a new and stronger social presence that can facilitate more effective social action programs that can resist government and corporate pressures to destroy what is left of Korea's pristine mountains like Chirisan. The Indra Net Life Community is expected to play a major role in virtually identifying Buddhism with the growing community spirit in Korea that reveres life and the environment of the peninsula. The Buddhist Academy for Ecological Awakening (BAEA) that is affiliated with the JungTo Society has a particularly strong role in the post-IMF period "back to the farm" movement for the unemployed as well as the Korean environmental action network. Experienced Korean Buddhist social activists with an environmental background like Mr Yoo Chong-gil are still relatively few and they are bound to wear many hats and frequently hold positions with multiple organizations around the country to achieve their collective, organizational goals.

According to a recent opinion poll of respondents working at Buddhist institutions and organizations, Venerable Tobop (b. 1949) was voted the most revered monk living in Korea, in the same class as Master Songch'ol, Master So-ong, and the immortal Wonhyo of Unified Shilla period. It is too soon to speculate about this monk's place in history but it is certain that he presents a very positive counter-image to the degrading stereotype of gangsterish, gambling and pot-smoking monks in which Korean media revels.

Venerable Tobop began to attract wide public attention to Buddhism in 1990 when he organized a Buddhist practice community called the "Good Friends Community" (*Seonwoo doryang*) with a group of young monks at Shilsangsa. They advocated the purification and reform of Buddhist practice within the Chogye Order in order to improve the public image of monks. During the Chogye Order election dispute of 1994, Tobop served as executive chairman of the Reform Council (*Kaehyokhoe-ui*). When the situation was resolved along with a new system of administration, he quietly went back to his mountain temple.

In 1995 Venerable Tobop established the Forest Retreat for Avatamsaka Studies (*Hwaomhangnim*) that provides an intensive two-year course on the *Avatamsaka Sutra* (K. *Hwaomgyeong*). Right behind the temple, a research institution named the Hwaom Forest Center (*Hwarimwon*) was opened in 1998 in order to diagnose modern society and suggest alternative remedies based on the Buddhist understanding of the world.

Venerable Tobop found himself in the public eye again in 1998 at the next unfortunate re-occurrence of Chogye Order election conflict. This time he was appointed acting Secretary-General (Chief Executive) of the

Chogye Order. After the resolution of the conflict, he again retreated to Shilsangsa Temple in the Chirisan Mountains.[28] He now runs the Buddhist Back to the Farm School (*Pulgyo guinong hakkyo*) that opened in 1998 and strongly promotes the national Buddhist environmental and ecological education movement.

Those who study agricultural techniques at the Back to the Farm School apply their knowledge in practice on the Shilsangsa Temple organic farm (approx. 24.5 acres, a substantial area in mountainous Korea). The Back to the Farm School offers three-month-long courses twice a year. So far, about one hundred people have completed the program. A farm community (founded in 1996) consisting of six families has formed.

Another of Venerable Tobop's innovations worthy of note is the "Small School," the first alternative Buddhist middle school in Korea. It is another inspiration to connect the Buddhadharma to society and it is receiving a lot of attention in religious circles. Readers may be aware that the Korean K-12 educational system is an intensely competitive pressure cooker-like environment that is specifically designed to passing college entrance exams. Classes are very large (40–60 in Seoul) and conformity and discipline rule the day. Non-conformity and creativity are almost squashed because parents and teachers fear disadvantaging their children's chances of success in standard exams. Most children attend "cram schools" and also receive expensive home tutoring by university students who passed the entrance exams of the school of choice. Parents make great financial and personal sacrifices to give their children a competitive edge. There is no time or space for questioning and freedom of thought and expression. It is truly "exam hell" for years. Non-acceptance of this mode of life presages failure and/or foreign boarding schools for the well-to-do.

The Small School at Shilsangsa is quite a courageous alternative. Only fifteen Korean students are enrolled so far. Classes are held in the temple compound and taught by eight teachers. Two to three students live with a teacher in a nearby village and share household chores. Students take the usual subjects like Korean, math, English, social science and natural sciences but learning is integrated with guided work and instruction in agricultural principles, special assignments to develop personal interests and meditation in the morning. National teacher certification is not required and it is no surprise that Small School is not accredited by the government yet.[29] Small though it may be, the appearance of the Small School is an indication that certain Korean Buddhists are committed to changing Korean society at its deepest roots – in the character and education of its children. The faith and values expressed by this experiment in education are bound to have repercussions throughout Korea and attract interest in people who have little experience with Buddhist ideas and practice but who long for a better life for their descendants.

Reflecting the past, projecting the future

The formidable energy and enthusiasm that Korean Buddhists have displayed in the last decade or so will continue as many different groups of socially committed Buddhists continue to implement their ideal to transform Korea and the wider world into an ideal Pure Land on earth. The organizations we have described above have been succeeding in practical ways to alleviate the immediate suffering of others both in Korea and abroad and also to address fundamental inequities and distorted values in modern society. Their optimism and the deeply held vows of their members are remarkable when we consider the context of Korean history. The past six hundred years have not favored Buddhism in Korea. Korean Buddhists have witnessed their prestige and influence fall from being the established national religion of over a thousand years to a pariah faith driven into distant mountains during the Yi. They experienced a brief and confusing resurgence during the Japanese colonial period, then were virtually overshadowed by Christianity since the Korean War. From this murky swamp of karmic effects has risen a revitalized social commitment, like a lotus flower that promises to bring enlightenment into the daily life of Korean citizens.[30]

Besides the admirable activities of the four larger umbrella organizations mentioned here, there are strong urban-based temples such as Neung-in Seonwon, led by the capable former *Korea Times* journalist Venerable Gi Gwang, that apply the new wealth of the Korean middle and upper classes to develop Buddhist social welfare and educational programs. These more progressive lay sanghas are ready to muster support for causes that strengthen Korea's nascent democratization, like protesting government resistance to the invitation of His Holiness the Dalai Lama to Korea for the first time and exposing corrupt political practices in forthcoming elections.[31]

Quietly but effectively working for changes in social values in Korea, are other associations, like the Buddhist Volunteer Association (*Pulgyo chawonbongsa yeonhaphoe*), run by the Buddhist nun Venerable Seongdeok, who apply their spirit of compassion at a grassroots level. The BVA has reinforced the presence of Buddhist sensibilities in Korea by initiating free hospice volunteer and funeral ritual education courses, home caretaker training programs, soup kitchens, clothes distribution drives for the poor and elderly and wild animal feeding and reforestation projects during times of extreme weather and forest fires.

Venerable Seongdeok has also pioneered a Buddhist Fetal Life Protection campaign that honors the millions of human spirits whose human corporal lives are abruptly cut short by abortion. In Korea's impatient drive to limit family size for economic reasons, abortion has become a convenient "final solution" (and often the only solution) in family planning. Korea's unwanted pregnancy rate is very high due to the failure of effective birth control implementation and cultural inhibitions to deal with issues of sexuality and "female matters" directly. Many Korean women, regardless of religion, have experienced multiple abortions (2–15 or more). Among these, numerous Buddhist women have begged Seongdeok and other clergy to perform "auspicious rebirth ceremonies" (*nakt'ae-a cheon-doje*) to transfer merit to the babies they have sacrificed and assuage their conscience.[32] Seongdeok has used their concern to publicly educate Buddhist women and men about the first precept against killing and to sensitize them to the value of life and our rare opportunity as humans to attain enlightenment and to render compassionate service to others.

The revered bhiksuni Seongdeok and dedicated lay women like Ahn Ch'onjonghaeng,[33] are the unsung bodhisattva heroines who have kept the wise and compassionate spirit of Korean Buddhism alive at the deepest level, beyond attachment to empty formalities, male lineage struggles and the obscure Zen dialogues of patriarchs that are meaningless and irrelevant to sentient beings in suffering.

A frequent spiritual practice among socially engaged Buddhists in Korea today is the remembrance of Kwanumbosal (Avalokitesvara), the bodhisattva of the *Lotus Sutra* with a thousand hands and eyes who sees and helps all beings in the world,[34] and the bodhisattva of action, Samantabhadra (*Pohyeon*) of the *Avatamsaka Sutra* (*Hwaomgyeong*), who takes rigorous vows to employ all skillful means possible to practice good.[35] Paintings and sculptures of these extraordinary ideal models of active service can be found in every Korean Buddhist temple and shrine. What is happening among socially active Korean Buddhists today is a revitalization and reformulation of the spirit of their inherited tradition which is adapting to the rapidly changing conditions of their tense and dynamic nation.

Notes

1 The humanitarian work of the Won Buddhist Reverend Park Chung Soo, or "Mother Park" has extended from the poor countryside and inner cities of Korea to over thirty-four countries around the world, including Africa, India (Ladakh), Sri Lanka, Cambodia, Mongolia, Russia and North Korea. She is a prolific poet and essayist as well as a sensitive vocalist. Most books by and about her are in Korean. *The Lonely Struggle*, a TV documentary about her life (subtitled in English), is available from the Won Buddhist Kangnam Temple in Seoul. See the web site <www.motherpark.org> for an outline of her life and activities in Korean and English. Won Buddhist representatives are also actively working for inter-religious harmony and world peace at the United Nations in New York.

2 I first ventured to Korea in July, 1980 a few months after the infamous Kwangju citizens' protest and massacre by Korean paratroopers. Alleged US military direction or acquiescence in this event, where hundreds if not thousands of civilians died, is still a sore point with many Koreans. I worked as a US Peace Corps volunteer and public health worker (leprosy control) at a rural

county health clinic. I returned to Korea in 1988 just before the Summer Olympics, sponsored by a successful Philadelphia-based Korean businessman with the purpose of studying Korean Buddhism and its relevance to modern life in America. I eventually finished a doctoral degree in Buddhist Studies at Dongguk University in 1998. I wore "many hats" during my Korea sojourn from 1988 to 2001 – short-term "wannabe" monk, student, consulting editor of the *Korea Journal*, member of Korean National Commission for UNESCO, researcher in bioethics, lecturer in Korean Buddhism for the University of Maryland Asian Division at Yongsan Army Base in Seoul, international symposium organizer, English language professor, radio host of my own program with my wife Jinsuk Lim, and, my greatest joy, husband and father. I also took frequent trips to other parts of Buddhist Asia during this time.

3   See Frank M. Tedesco, "Questions for Buddhist and Christian Cooperation in Korea," in *Buddhist-Christian Studies* 17, pp. 179-195 (1997). Also see the International Association for Religious Freedom web site www.iarf-religious-freedom.net under "Advocacy." Venerable Jinwol (Lee Young Ho) has recently initiated a Korea branch of the United Religions Initiative to enhance active interfaith dialogue and activities.

4   One Korean Buddhist leader of South Korea devoted to the issue of unification and actual communication with North Korea, including meetings with North Korean Buddhist leaders, is Venerable Shin Bop Ta and his small One Korea Buddhist Movement (*Pyeongbulhyop*). He has written about his travels in the North and photographed temple sites and reconstructed buildings. He is also setting up an organization of South Korean Buddhist leaders for the restoration of famous temple sites in the Diamond Mountains. Venerable Bop Ta's commitment to unification has earned him constant surveillance by South Korean authorities and months of incarceration for possession of Buddhist literature printed in the North.

5   After over 1,600 years of Buddhist presence on the Korean peninsula, however, it is difficult to deny that aspects of Buddhist thought and culture have not permeated every area of Korean life even if it is denied by converts to Western sects or is not apparent on the surface. For an interesting discussion of contemporary Korean religious beliefs, see C. Fred Alford, *Think No Evil: Korean Values in the Age of Globalization* (Ithaca, NY: Cornell University Press, 1999).

6   Various compendia of statistics are available, compiled by different groups, and mostly of questionable accuracy.

7   The Korean monasteries best known for foreign ordained practitioners are Songgwangsa, especially when the famous master Kusan was alive, Hwagyesa in Seoul, Musangsa near Taejon, affiliated with the Kwanum Zen School of Master Seung Sahn, and the Kanghwa Island meditation retreat of the Lotus Lantern International Buddhist Center. There are a few other temples where foreign monks and nuns reside for unspecified lengths of time. Guryongsa in Seoul has been the home for a few monks from north India and Ladakh. One young Tibetan monk lived at the great Buddha Jewel monastic complex of T'ongdosa for two or three years before being given his own temple in Pusan. To the best of my knowledge to date, Western and non-Korean Asian monks are not known for any "socially engaged Buddhist activities" in Korea except for occasional counseling related to personal dharma practice or English instruction.

As for lay practitioners, there are very few temples in Korea where instruction or dharma talks are given in English or any other language other than Korean on a regular basis. Accordingly, foreign lay Buddhists have little chance of forming a strong community for fellowship or practice. At this time of writing I have very little personal contact with Soka Gakkai (SGI-Korea) members, the Japanese Nichiren sect. Their literature claims a million followers in Korea but they do not appear to associate with traditional Korean Buddhists at all, so they will not be discussed further in this chapter.

8 The informal roles of temples as places of solace, sanctuary and recuperation are still greatly appreciated by a minority, and romanticized in movies and novels as refuges for the heartbroken and martyred. For a very interesting discussion of healing and the role Buddhist clergy, see Don Baker, "Monks, Medicine, and Miracles: Health and Healing in the History of Korean Buddhism," in *Korean Studies* 18 (1994): 50–75.

9 Foreign workers are known to perform the three "D's" – work that is dirty, difficult and dangerous. Native Korean workers aspire to easier, safer and more lucrative ways of earning a living.

10 To repeat, 37,000 US troops are always resident on guard in South Korea, mostly on the Demilitarized Zone (DMZ). North Korean troops would confront them head-on at the start of any invasion, assuring US involvement and massive "defensive counter-assaults" by the US Air Force Pacific Command. Not even the People's Republic of China would want to challenge the USA by air for years to come.

11 See Shin Bup Ta (Shin, Kwangsu), *A Study of Buddhism in North Korea in the Late Twentieth Century: An Investigation of Juche Ideology and Traditional Buddhist Thought in Korea* (Minjoksa, Seoul, Korea, 2000).

12 This statute could be used against anyone who even faintly appeared to be sympathetic to North Korea, and by extension, the policies of the prevailing ROK government. It was used to check all opposition against authoritarian rule and any private or collective attempts to communicate with North Korean relatives. The government continues to try to uphold a complete monopoly on all communications with the North and has mirrored the totalitarian Kim Il Sung regime accordingly. Unlike other divided nations, there has been a complete prohibition of visits, mail, telephone, radio or TV interchange between North and South Korea until very recently. The National Security Law has been given different names at different times but it is still in force during the tenure of Nobel Peace Laureate President Kim Dae Jung. His refusal to abolish the law after promising to do so before election and receiving the Peace Prize is a sore point among social reformers in Korea, as is his lack of support for a visit to Korea by His Holiness the Dalai Lama. International human rights associations have not overlooked the shortfall of the Kim DJ administration.

13 From CCEJ web site <www.ccej.or.kr>.

14 The plight of foreign workers in Korea is relatively unknown or abstract at best to most readers. The following cases described by Mr Jung will illustrate the suffering of the workers that BCEJ members are responding to:

1)Friyanta and Nilmini (not their real names), a couple from Sri Lanka, were employed as unregistered foreign workers at a farm in Kaypong, Kyonggi Province since last April. Together they earned 1.3 million won a month at the price of a 14-hour day. Unable to endure the miserable working conditions, they notified the employer that they would resign. He demanded that they find their own replacements, and said he would not pay their wages till they did so.

They managed to find two replacements on Sept. 29, and prepared to leave the farm, but the two newly hired workers then refused the work. The employer reacted by preventing the couple's departure, forcing them to resume work and confiscated their pay. He threatened, in the presence of several local police officers, that he would expel them to Sri Lanka if they left without securing replacements. The policemen cooperated with the intimidation, brandishing handcuffs.

2)A Zambian man was found killed in an alley in front of Suwon railway station last October 7, and four Indonesian workers were arrested as murder suspects. The police officers took them to a small locker room in a nearby police station, where they made Mr Irawan (24) kneel, kicked him in the head with their boots, and banged his head against a chair. Even after he collapsed and lay bleeding, they continued kicking his head, which suffered a 7-centimeter-long cut, according to his statement to the lawyer of a human rights organization on Oct. 16. Mr Lahmann and the two other Indonesian workers testified that they had been treated the same way, being hit and kicked repeatedly.

At around 8.00 p.m. on Oct. 8, the police officers took them to Handok Hospital, where they were given simple treatment by a nurse who collected their blood samples for evidence. At 6 p.m. the next day, they were finally given proper treatment at the same hospital. Then they were delivered to the Mokdong Immigration Office, which is moving to expel them without due investigation of the incident.

3)Ms Riya, a Vietnamese citizen working at a factory in Taejon, was brutally attacked by a Korean co-worker at 12.30 a.m. on Oct. 20, and was hospitalized, unconscious, at 4.10 a.m. the same day. She never awoke from a coma, and died at 9.30 a.m. on Oct. 26. At the time of her admission to the hospital in critical condition, she was suffering hemorrhaging and acute edema of the brain, bleeding in the eyes, and multiple face and scalp contusions. A photo taken after the attack showed many red bruises on her wrists, and her face and head were swollen like a balloon. The police did not investigate the facts, but only listened to the testimony of the Korean attacker and closed the case quickly. The company claims that it has no responsibility whatever, either moral or legal.

> The above cases did not occur over a period of some years, but during a single month. Such miserable infringements of the human rights of foreign migrant workers are repeated again and again in Korea, yet – to our shame – we do not yet have a law or system to protect the foreign workers.

15 See <www.jungto.org> for information in Korean, Japanese and English.
16 Venerable Pomnyun was privately ordained as a sramanera (novitiate vows) in 1969 when he was 16 and an "ordained" shaven head monk thirty years later in 1989 by his teacher, the senior monk Venerable Tomun. It was and is still not uncommon for Buddhist teachers in Korea to establish their own lineages in this way without the recognition of the Chogye Order hierarchical establishment.
17 See <www.jungto.org> web site.
18 We have been associated with the Academy of Ecological Awakening since its inception and have cooperated with its head, Mr Yoo Chong-gil, in networking with other international engaged Buddhist leaders such as Sulak Sivaraksa, A. T. Ariyaratne, Gary Snyder et al.
19 See <www.jungto.org> web site.

20 Ibid.
21 Ven. Pomnyun, the chairperson of JTS, explains the motivation of establishing of JTS:"I first went to India in 1991. There I witnessed eye-opening poverty and suffering. In Calcutta, where beggars are visible everywhere, I was approached by a woman with a baby in her arms. She pulled me by the sleeve into a small shop and pointed at something with an appealing gesture. It was a can of dried milk. However, the price of 60 rupees surprised me enough that I ran away from her. It was because I was very frugal during my trip and ate meals worth only 5 rupees at the food vendors on the streets. Later, during my trip I saw many people, particularly children who were malnourished, and I began to feel compassion for the people's suffering. I regretted having ignored the woman at the shop because of measly 60 rupees (US$1.5). I made an oath then to compensate for my behavior by working for a greater number of unfortunate people who suffered from hunger, diseases and illiteracy."
22 There are three types of people who are working for JTS: (1)those who are spiritually prepared and committed to social action. Most of them have given up personal life such as marriage. They are the main force of JTS and know what they have to do. They make decisions on major projects through bi-annual meetings and accept their job as part of the organizational activity rather than Pumnyun's work; (2) those who work with JTS because of their love of the work but still have some conflict within themselves; and (3) those who come to live at the center and help work with JTS in an attempt to avoid their personal difficulties. They do not stay long. The center is open to these people. They can come and live there if they want and they are free to leave when they want to.
23 Hankyoreh 21, #342, January 18, 2001. While most of the news about disputes and issues within the Chogye Order is only available in Korean, some news articles are available in English in the print and electronic archives of *The Korea Times* and *The Korea Herald* published in Seoul as well as popular Asian news magazines such as the *Far Eastern Economic Review* and *Asiaweek*.
24 See the earlier references to "skirt Buddhism" of elderly women (*posallim*) and "good luck" practices.
25 "Concrete action" was taken to protest Ven. Songhye's appointment in the form of the submission of a formal letter of protest by the BSR, a signature collection drive for his dismissal, picketing in front of the Headquarters Building and an Internet survey coupled with media releases.
26 Hyundae Bulkyo news, Feb. 12, 2001 and personal communication.
27 Translation of excerpts of a working manuscript, December 2000.
28 Shilsangsa is located in the southern basin (valley) of Chirisan Mountain in Namwon-gun, Chollabuk-to. The temple was founded at the end of the Unified Shilla period (828 CE) as one of the Nine Mountain Zen School (Kusan seonmun).
29 The Small School website is http//silsang.edufree.co.kr.
30 Those interested in knowing more details about Korean Buddhism's complex modern history may wish to read the special issue of *The Korea Journal* I edited entitled "Vitality in Korean Buddhist Tradition," 33, 3, Autumn 1993. See especially "Buddhism in Modern Korea," by Mok Jeong-bae.
31 To learn about the efforts by Koreans to invite the Dalai Lama to Korea, see <www.tibetfriends.org>.
32 See Frank M. Tedesco, Chapter 7, "Abortion in Korea," in Damien Keown (ed.), *Buddhism and Abortion* (Honolulu: University of Hawaii Press, 1999).

33 Ahn Ch'onjonghaeng Posallim (b. 1920) has single-handedly pursued a Buddhist prison mission and Dharma teaching program throughout the Korean penal system, including death rows, for over thirty years. She has met great resistance from Christian ministers who tried to stop her work. She received very little support from Buddhists until a few years ago. She was recognized as "Volunteer of the Year" by Korean president Kim Youngsam in the mid-1990s. Her *hwadu* or focus of spiritual query like a repetitive mantra is "serving others" (*pongsa*). *"How can I be of service?"* Personal communication.

34 Read about Korean Avalokitesvara devotion in "The Activities of the Korean Buddhist Chontae Order Toward World Peace" by Venerable Jeon Chong-yoon in David W. Chappell (ed.), *Buddhist Peacework: Creating Cultures of Peace* (Boston: Wisdom, 1999), pp. 103–111.

35 A brief and general exposition of the bodhisattva Samantabhadra ideal as expressed by a former troubled Chogye Order administration under Chief Executive Venerable Song Weolju is Ven. Jinwol Sunim, "A Mahayana Vision of Dharmic Society in Korea: Through 'the Enlightenment of Society Movement,'" in Jonathan Watts, Alan Senauke and Santikaro Bhikkhu (eds.), *Entering the Realm of Reality: Towards Dhammic Societies* (INEB, 1997), pp. 182–217. Available through the Buddhist Peace Fellowship in Berkeley, CA.

9

BUDDHISM AND THE *BURAKUMIN*

Oppression or liberation?

Leslie D. Alldritt

In James Clavell's celebrated novel *Shogun*, the following description appears: "Jan Roper interrupted, 'Wait a minute, Vinck! What's wrong, Pilot? What about *eters*?' 'It is just that the Japanese think of them as different. They're the executioners, and work the hides and handle corpses.'"[1] Elsewhere in the book the term *eta* ["*eters*"] appears, yet an explanation of these people is never provided.

The *eta*, or now more appropriately called *burakumin* – literally, "village people" – are an oppressed class within Japan. As noted by DeVos,[2] the *burakumin* are Japan's "invisible race." Emiko Ohnuki-Tierney states that the *burakumin* are "invisible" due to the fact that there are no physical characteristics that distinguish them from other Japanese.[3] However, there have been and continue to be arguments that the *burakumin* are racially distinct from the majority of the Japanese people.[4]

The *burakumin* have also been referred to as the *eta-hinin*, a term that is still in use today. The word *eta* can be translated as "much or very polluted/unclean"[5] and the word *hinin* simply means "non-person." Thus, this group within Japan has been determined to have no identity by the majority Japanese, no genuine personhood (another derogatory term used against the *burakumin* is *yotsu*, which refers to a four-legged animal), and therefore, not surprisingly, oppression and mistreatment have historically been their lot. Despite a general betterment of their situation in the last three decades – primarily due to legislation[6] – the *burakumin* continue to be considered disparagingly in the Japanese public consciousness and subjected to discrimination.[7]

This chapter will briefly examine three dimensions of the *burakumin* situation: first, the current state of the *burakumin* will be elucidated; second, the historical genesis of their oppression; and third, the primary focus of my discussion seeks to answer the questions, "How have Japanese religions contributed to the oppression of the *burakumin* in Japan?" And consequently, "How can Japanese religions contribute to the greater liberation of the *burakumin* of Japan?" This section will include selected narrative accounts obtained from interviews of religious reformers working in Japan today. The chapter will conclude with a section offering initial thoughts on additional roles that Japanese religion might play in contributing to *buraku* liberation.

The *burakumin* today

Ohnuki-Tierney states that the *burakumin* are said to number approximately three million people (in a Japanese population of about 126 million). There is, however, much dispute concerning the number of *burakumin* in Japan. Jean-François Sabouret writes in his book, *L'autre Japon, les Burakumin,*[8] "According to official estimates, the *burakumin* population (in 1978) was 1,841,958, distributed in 4,374 ghettos, and disseminated in 1,041 towns and villages in thirty-four prefectures."[9] However, Sabouret cites the BKD (League for Liberation of *Buraku*) [Japanese: *Buraku Kaiho Domei*] as arguing that the government figures are inaccurate:

> According to the BKD (League for Liberation of *Buraku*), the government figures are inexact for two reasons: the first is that not all of the *burakumin* are in poverty, and not being poor, they do not solicit government subsidies [apparently one of the devices the Japanese government uses to determine numbers]. The others prefer to remain in [financial] difficulty so as to not publicly declare that they are *burakumin, better to be equal to a poor Japanese than to an assisted burakumin.* The second reason is similar to the first, in effect, the sum allowed for the resolution of the *buraku* problem is not proportional to the amount of demand, and the BKD accuses the government of not wanting to hold to the genuine figure for the sake of the economy.[10]

Interestingly, Sabouret states the BKD advances the three million people number based on a projection dating back to the Meiji Period (1867–1912), that as 3 percent of the population was made of *burakumin*, and as the population was approximately thirty million, then as the population of Japan has quadrupled, so then too has the *burakumin* population increased four times to its approximate three million figure:

> According to the Management and Coordination Agency of the government, as of March 1987 there are 4,603 *Buraku* districts with a total population of 1,166,733. These figures, however, only represent those areas classified as Dowa districts. Actual figures

may amount to as many as 6,000 *Buraku* districts with over 3 million *Burakumin*.[11]

The *Buraku Liberation News* (March 1998), stated that, according to a survey conducted by the Japanese government, "there are 4,442 communities with 298,385 households and a population of 892,751 throughout the country where Dowa projects have been implemented."[12] This number, however, does not take into account other communities not covered by the Dōwa legislation and the numbers of *Buraku* people who live in non-*Buraku* areas. In the same article cited above, Shigeyuki Kumisaka, the Director of the IMADR (International Movement against All Forms of Discrimination and Racism), goes on to support the 6,000 community number:

> The *burakumin* tend, as do the Dalits of India,[13] to be found in selected occupations. Many *burakumin* are employed in small factories connected with their traditional occupations, such as butchering and leather and fur processing. Others are farmers, fishermen, and unskilled laborers. Although many individuals have become economically or socially prominent, the average standard of living is far below that of the non-*burakumin*.[14]

A prominent theory that is put forward to account for *buraku* discrimination is precisely that they historically did those tasks (butchering, leather-work, etc.) no one else wanted to do and, as a result, were classified as lower class and so began a tradition of societal discrimination.[15] In regard to marriage, the *burakumin* have historically been endogamous[16] – bias being perpetuated primarily by the non-*burakumin* and certainly in part by the *burakumin* themselves. As Ian Neary comments, "Many *burakumin* themselves accepted this [prejudice and discrimination], regarded themselves as different and their separate and unequal treatment as justified."[17] The genesis of this "separate and unequal treatment" has both a political and religious aspect.

Origins of *burakumin* oppression[18]

Japan, from its earliest history, has had groups of people which were discriminated against socially. The discriminated group that seemingly evolved over time into the *burakumin*, however, has differed in membership such that it can be reasonably claimed that *buraku* discrimination, as such, did not exist before the Tokugawa period. Kitaguchi agrees with this assumption and makes the point that modern-day *burakumin* may not be traced back to the *Edo* (Tokugawa) period.

As a great majority of them [modern-day *Buraku* people] can in fact be traced back to this group, it is only natural that the *Buraku* story could start with the Edo period. However, if we are tracing the lineage of modern-day victims of *Buraku* discrimination, on the assumption that every single one of them is a blood descendant of the *eta* caste, we could not be further from the truth.[19]

Notwithstanding the difficulty in tracing *buraku* lineage, a closer examination of the historical pattern of discrimination against the oppressed group in Japan that foreshadows the *buraku* is instructive toward elucidating the current, justificatory claims for discrimination in that the source of current discrimination stems from traditional practices and stereotypes.

Interestingly, in ancient Japan, lower-class groups may have had some privileges. Jinsaburo Oe, in *Fukaisareta Fukashokumin Kannen*[20] ["The Juxtaposition of the Untouchables Idea"] asserts that, "In ancient times, *hinin* discrimination did not exist. Rather, due to their ability to associate with the *Kami*, they were feared and respected."[21]

Further, these people were additionally respected for their involvement in the arts, notably as dancers and Noh musicians. Ohnuki-Tierney describes the case for substantial contributions by these people in *kabuki, noh*, and *kyogen*:

> Biographies of many of the artists and artisans during this period recorded their "humble origin," that is, their belonging to the special status group. Examples include Zen-ami (1393–1490?), who designed the Fushimi Castle for Hideyoshi; Kan-ami (?–1384) and Zeami (?–1443), the father–son pair who developed the *sarugaku* (the forerunner of the noh play); and Noami (1397–1471) and other masters of the tea ceremony.[22]

At this time in Japanese history there did, however, exist discrimination toward certain occupations such as "leather workers, grave keepers, people who cleaned, and horse handlers"[23] This occupational discrimination certainly has survived to the modern period.[24]

With the coming of Buddhism to Japan in the middle of the sixth century (ce) came opprobrium against eating meat that was extrapolated to concerns about the impurity in handling meat. As in India, this injunction came to be associated with handling dead humans as well. Consequently, anyone who engaged in related activities was, by definition, impure and to be avoided.[25] This emphasis on purity and impurity had a long history in Japan associated with Shinto, yet the Buddhist doctrines invigorated and dogmatized this proclivity within Japanese society:

As Buddhism permeated Japanese society, the notion of pollution came to include the idea that it could be caused by contact with the bodies of dead animals, and thus came to be associated with leather work and even the eating of meat. Gradually the Shinto concepts of *imi* (taboo) and *kegare* (pollution), which were associated with human death, became linked to the Buddhist prohibition on taking any life. The first government proclamations which outlawed the eating of flesh of certain domestic animals occurred in ad 676.[26]

This gap between the pure and impure was exacerbated during the Heian Period (794–1185) where the lowest in society were termed *senmin* (as opposed to the *ryomin*, "the good"). These *senmin*, during the tumultuous *Sengoku jidai* ("Warring period" of the fifteenth and sixteenth century) came to be the leather workers that assisted the *daimyos* (warlords) in supplying them with leather "armor" and other battle equipment. The *senmin*, for their contribution, were generally provided with some tax relief, poor land, and expected to be the first line of defense in case of attack by other *daimyos* or any peasant revolt.

It was during the Tokugawa Period (1603–1867) that specific discriminatory policies arose toward the *burakumin* and it is here that it is generally argued that the *burakumin* became established as a discriminated group. As Shigeyuki Kumisaku describes:

> In the period of the 16th and the 17th centuries, the ruling class placed these groups at the bottom of the social hierarchy. Feudal lords assigned them some duties as petty officers, while forcing them to contribute leather goods as tax.[27]

There were other occupations that the *Buraku* people developed proficiency in during this period including shoemaking, making bamboo articles, and ceremonial drum (*taiko*) construction.[28]

Atsutane Hirata (1776–1842), the Shinto reformer, in his writing *Shinteki Nishuron* argued that the inherent baseness or impurity of the *burakumin* necessitated their separateness.[29] The *burakumin*, who once served important functions in Shinto shrines, were now barred from shrine visitations (1774).

Specifically between 1715 and 1730, a reform entitled the *Kyoko Kaikaku* came into effect and began to deliberately separate the *burakumin* from other members of Japanese society:

> In Tokyo, from the mid 1720s, *hinin* were regarded as being of lower status than the *eta*, they were all (apart from their chiefs) forbidden to wear any kind of headgear even when it was raining,

the men were to keep their hair cut short, the women were not to shave their eyebrows or blacken their teeth.[30]

This discriminatory marking of the oppressed classes soon spread to the rest of Japan. This marking was particularly effected through the use of registries:

> In Kyoto (1715) and Tokyo (1719) surveys of the *eta:hinin* population were carried out and the registers drawn up were ordered to be kept separate from the other registers... At the same time, the authorities introduced a taxation system which placed burdens on the *eta* who were under direct control of the *Tokugawa* and placed restrictions on the type of clothes the *hinin* were permitted to wear.[31]

This use of registries is critically important if we are to understand the history of oppression against the *burakumin*. If one was a handler of meat, dead bodies, or engaged in other polluting activity, then one would be ritually impure for a time. After a period of time, the impurity would or could, through certain ritual activity, be expunged and no longer relevant. Yet, with the use of the registries, the incidence of pollution within certain occupations became stigmatized and permanent in that not only was an individual deemed as inherently impure but so too his or her entire family name.

The first half of the nineteenth century brought about yet another extension of separateness. Included in the Tempo Reforms (1830–44), in an obvious movement to draw more acutely the differences between commoners and the *burakumin*, there was a restriction on *burakumin* entering the homes of peasants. In addition, a further stratification developed, separating out, somehow, what had previously been conceived as one group into two – the *eta* and the *hinin*. This confusion of ranking, exacerbated by differing, regional stratifications, only perpetuated the cycle of government-sanctioned discrimination, which perhaps was its intent. That is, to provide for competing groups to be influenced against another by the *Tokugawa* as need be. It was not that all discriminated groups and individuals followed these rules, and certainly many were successful in working around them; however, there was a systematic effort to politically institutionalize discrimination through enacting policy.

The Meiji Period ostensibly should have brought a better situation for the *burakumin* as Japan ended its period of relative isolation from the international community. In 1871, with the "Meiji Emancipation Edict" (Ordinance no. 61), the Japanese government did take steps to discontinue the lowest social ranks and removed their official status by renaming the *eta* as *shin heimin* (New Common People); however, no real financial or educational support was provided to make this emancipation a reality and, similarly, no change had been effected in the Shinto-Buddhist views of the now "new common people." Furthermore, the period ensconced a new hierarchy with the Emperor at its head that continued to promote separateness.[32]

> Thus they [*burakumin*] were forced to live as tenant farmers in rural areas, and in urban areas as laborers, continuously falling into the ranks of the unemployed or semi-employed, or as the proprietors of small businesses. Discrimination, far from being eliminated, became even worse.[33]

It was not until the twentieth-century that a *buraku* liberation movement began in earnest. Influenced by other international liberation movements such as the Hyonpyonsha movement in Korea, the Russian revolution, and the Rice Riots (*Kome-Sodo*), the National Levelers Association (*Zenkoku Suiheisha*) was founded in March 1922. Some social advances were initially obtained, but the World War II suppressed the movement.

In 1946, the movement re-instituted itself as the National Committee for *Buraku* Liberation.[34] The war devastated all of Japan and the *burakumin* – already in dire conditions prior to the war – experienced an intensification of penury and disease. Through sustained political activism, the *burakumin*, in conjunction with concerned others have passed legislation since the war that has dramatically bettered conditions for themselves. These improvements have come primarily in such issues as better housing and education – inexpensive housing has increased dramatically in *dōwa* areas and where twenty-five years ago, only 30 per cent of *burakumin* students matriculated to high school, currently over 80 per cent do.[35] There have been both corporations and religious bodies involved in the struggle for greater opportunities for the *burakumin*. This is not to say that the problems do not persist for the *burakumin* as they continue to suffer from, in comparison to the majority Japanese, higher illness rates, higher unemployment, lower wages for the same jobs, illegal lists that corporations buy and use to avoid hiring *buraku* people, discrimination in marriage, and myriad abusive, discriminatory attacks on their person and position.

The religiosity of the *burakumin*

John Donoghue, in his study of the *burakumin* entitled, *Pariah Persistence in Changing Japan*,[36] includes a section that describes the religious views of the inhabitants of a *buraku* section of the city of Toyoda in Northern Japan. Within *Shin-machi* ("New City"), the name of the *buraku* section in which he was working, Donoghue noted that:

The more educated and socially sophisticated persons in Shin-machi stressed the fact that the *Buraku* people were very religious. They pointed out that everyone in the community belonged to a Buddhist sect. They also indicated that their Shinto beliefs, rituals, and ceremonies were the same as those found in communities throughout Japan.[37]

No student of Japanese religions would find this particularly significant as this is a normal occurrence among the greater Japanese population as well; however, when one examines the role of Japanese Buddhism in casting the *burakumin* down, it is surprising that they tended not to blame Buddhism. Rather, as Donoghue further observed, "They [*burakumin*] were convinced that religion was wholly *unrelated* to their lowly position in society."[38]

Donoghue goes on that say that most *burakumin* in the community follow Pure Land Buddhism (*Jodo-shu*) and that this sect had, in the past, supported *burakumin* rights.[39] The members of the community seemed, in Donoghue's estimation, to practice religion much like their fellow citizens in regard to attending *matsuri* (festival).[40] There were some differences in their religious views; for example, the *burakumin* in Shin-machi did tend to be less "superstitious" than the majority Japanese population.[41] Additionally, the community did exact monies on a voluntary basis – the amount determined by town meetings and adjusted by income level – for supporting the upkeep of the local shrine and cemetery,[42] which is a some-what unusual practice in Japan. One critical difference though between the majority Japanese observation of *matsuri* and the *burakumin* observance was the foci of their orations:

> In every speech and every prayer, there were references either directly or indirectly to the community in its relation to the world outside. Some were pleas for greater cleanliness in the village, or the advisability of curtailing dog killing, others centered around the *Burakumin's* lowly position in Japanese society, or the cruelty of the world expressed in one or another particular instance of discrimination against them. Other orations invoked the aid of the gods for the attainment of economic success, for the marriage of daughters and for less discrimination against them by outsiders.[43]

From Donoghue's account, despite some notable differences, it seems the *burakumin* do not differ greatly from their countrymen in their under-standing or practice of religion.

In an issue of the *Buraku Liberation News*, an English-language, bimonthly publication of the *Buraku Liberation and Human Rights Research Institute*,[44] the question of Buddhism and discrimination was taken up in the section entitled, "*Buraku* Problem Q & A." The question was, "Is Buddhism free from *Buraku* discrimination?" What follows is part of the response to the question:

> There is a tradition that people carve a religious name for the dead on the face of a tomb as a sign of worship. That is a practice for many Buddhist religious organizations. The name for the dead is *Kaimyo*. Posthumous *Kaimyo* is given by a Buddhist priest and is recorded in a post-memorial-notebook at the temple the dead belonged to. Of late, it was discovered that discriminatory names and characters in the notebooks and on the faces of the tombs exist.
>
> These were given by Buddhist priests to the dead who were of *Buraku* origin. The names include the characters for beast, humble, ignoble, servant and many other kinds of derogatory expressions. Upon the disclosure, Buddhist organizations started to widely investigate notebooks and tombs in response to the requests of the BLL [*Buraku* Liberation League]. They found discriminatory *Kaimyo*, at many Buddhist sects in most parts of Japan. While the majority seems to have given a long time ago, there are some names given even since the 1940s.[45]

Such discriminatory practice is an indication that Buddhism has historically contributed to *burakumin* oppression. As the Japanese people inescapably employ Buddhist death rituals, it is not surprising that it is here that Buddhism can make its own contribution to *burakumin* discrimination. Buddhist temples that were located in *Buraku* communities "were called 'impure temples' [*eta-dera*] and were not allowed to communicate with temples in non-*Buraku* areas."[46] Further, as the Dalits were told from the Hindu perspective, the *burakumin* were taught that it was their karma that placed them in this unsavory life and that forbearance was necessary if the next life was to be favorable.[47]

In a recent treatment of Japanese Buddhism and the *burakumin*, William Bodiford has examined the role of Zen Buddhism and its efforts to reform its tradition of discrimination (*sabetsu*) against the *Buraku* people.[48] Bodiford outlines the recent developments of Soto Zen from its reaction to the Machida controversy to the establishment of a Central Division for the Protection and Promotion of Human Rights (*Jinken Yogo Suishin Honbu*). This concern by the *Soto-shu* manifests in several dimensions. In the past, the sect, following the pattern mentioned previously, has created problems for *buraku* (and other marginalized groups in Japan) by utilizing the temple registration (*tera-uke*) system to provide the Tokugawa government with information that was used to further discrimination; the use of necrologies (*kakocho*) as a device of discrimination of marginalized groups, including use of discriminatory names in the register and alternate registers that would be "off the books"; the use of kaimyo; and discriminatory rituals – particularly death rituals – that were prescribed for Soto priests to use with the *burakumin*.[49]

Another area of Japanese Buddhism that has generated discussion has been the presence of discriminatory passages in Buddhist texts, including sūtras. One critical issue here surrounds the Japanese term *issendai* (Sanskrit: *icchantika*) and its implications for the doctrine of Buddha-nature (*Bussho*). According to Buswell, the meaning of icchantika is multivocal:

> It is generally presumed to be some variation on the present participle "*icchant*" (desiring), a view supported by the translations of the term in Chinese and Tibetan. In addition to Chinese transcriptions, which render the term as *i-ch'an-t'i* or the abbreviated *ch'an-t'i*, the Chinese also translated it as (*ta-*)*shen-yü*, "greatly hedonistic (or dissipated)," a rendering suggestive of the Tibetan equivalent *hdon chen* (*po*), "subject to great desire."[50]

Buswell further notes that the term is not in the Pali *Nikāyas* or the Chinese *Āgamas*, yet we do find it in the Mahāyāna texts along with its synonym, *samucchinnakuśalamūla*.[51] In the Mahāyāna text, *Yang-chueh-mo-lo ching (Aṅgulimāla-sūtra)*, Buswell finds icchantikas represented as "perverse determined," said to "be the most vile of beings, and to engage in all the ten evil types of conduct in the same way that the bodhisattvas perfect all the ten *pārāmitas*." ."[52]

The *Mahāparinirvāṇa-sūtra (Nehangyo)* is additionally cited in its use of the *icchantika* (Japanese: *issendai*) doctrine.[53] Ishikawa Rekizen in an article entitled, "Karma, Chandala, and Buddhist Scriptures"[54] looks at the *Nehangyo* as providing support for discriminatory practices. Ishikawa asserts that in the literary works (*chojutsu*) of every Japanese sect founder, one can finds the use of the term *chandala* (*sendara* in Japanese[55]), including work of such luminaries as Kukai and Dogen. However, he singles out the *Nehangyo* as a "representative" Mahāyāna *sūtra* and posits that this *sūtra* provides a theoretical foundation for other *sūtras* that develop the idea of the *chandala* (which he associates with the idea of the *icchantika*) Ishikawa argues that this *icchantika/issendai* concept (that some sentient creatures are unable to realize the Buddha-nature) contravenes the Buddhist notion of *issai-shujo shitsu aru bussho*, that is, that all sentient creatures have Buddha-nature.[56]

What perhaps is most confusing in surveying the *Nehangyo* is that it is difficult, despite the number of passages in which the *issendai* concept is invoked, to gain much clarity on what exactly is being asserted regarding the possibility of salvation of this group. Further, exactly who should be included in this category of the "non-savable" is a question. In regard to the issue of the text being used to justify discrimination, these ambiguities alone should be enough to forestall exegetical free play by those interested in using this *sūtra* to support discrimination. The citation of a few passages from the *Nehangyo* may prove insightful toward demonstrating these difficulties. In Chapter 16 "On Bodhisattva," the text states:

> The same is the case of the *icchantika*. No bud of *bodhi* comes forth even if they give ears to this all-wonderful great *Nirvāṇa-sūtra*. It is never that such a case happens. Why? Because such a one has totally annihilated the root of good. As in the case of the burnt seed, no root or bud of the *bodhi* mind will shoot forth.[57]

Other passages in the *Nehangyo* present a similar message:

> Also, I [Gautama] was, in Jambudvīpa, an *icchantika*. People all see me as an *icchantika*. But truth to say, I was no *icchantika*. If I am an icchantika, how could I gain the unsurpassed *bodhi?*[58]
>
> What is the *icchantika*? The *icchantika* cuts off all roots of good deeds and the mind does not call forth any association of good. Not even a bit of thought of good comes about. Anything like this never comes about in true emancipation.[59]

Yet, some additional passages seem to argue that why *icchantikas* remain beyond saving is not due to birth or class, but rather from their attitude toward the Dharma – an attitude that can be rectified:

> So, I, always say that beings all possess the Buddha Nature. Even, I say that the *icchantika* possesses the Buddha Nature. The *icchantika* has no good law. The Buddha Nature too is a good law. As there are the days to come, there is also a possibility for the *icchantika* to possess the Buddha Nature. Why? Because all *icchantika* can definitely attain the unsurpassed *bodhi*.[60]

This passage seems clear: the *icchantika* not only can possess Buddha Nature, but he or she can also "attain" it. Therefore, to argue that the *icchantika* precept can be consistently advanced from the *Nehangyo* to support discriminatory Buddhist attitudes or practices seems ill-founded. Buswell also asseverates the same conclusion in his reading of the *Nehangyo*:

> There is some contradiction, however, in this *sūtra's* attitude toward the *icchantikas*; earlier portions state that they are utterly incapable of attaining *nirvāna*, whereas later sections allow that they still possess the innate buddha-nature (*Buddhadhātu*,

fohsing), and thus have not lost irrevocably all capacity for enlightenment.[61]

It seems important that the relevant Buddhist sūtras that have been used selectively to provide "doctrinal cover" should be more fully explored and, if discriminatory, rebutted on the basis of the clearer, unambiguous Buddhist ethic that is informed by the precepts and the eightfold path (sīla). That is, the Great Compassion (*Mahākaruṇā*) that Buddhism espouses as its resolution should be more referenced in articulating the content of the appropriate Buddhist ethical view toward marginalized groups.

There are notable efforts of reform and assistance of the *buraku* problem from the Japanese religious community today and it is critically important to allow the voices of people active in the *buraku* liberation movement to be heard. Two groups that are currently involved in the human rights concerns of the *buraku* are the Japanese religious sects of Tenrikyo and Shin Buddhism. The selection of these two particular groups for discussion is threefold. First, Tenrikyo is a "new" religious tradition that has reached out to the *burakumin*. Its efforts in support of this oppressed group may presage a positive direction for Japanese religiosity. Second, the Shin tradition is an ancient one in Japan and has been involved in the *burakumin* issue since first coming to the Japanese shores. *Shin-shu* is additionally interesting in that it has been historically most egregious in discriminating against the *buraku* people and yet currently, in certain ways, is at the forefront of Japanese religious groups promoting greater *buraku* liberation. The third reason is that, for the purposes of interviewing, two of the more articulate, active members of the *Dōshuren* (Osaka Conference for the Dōwa issue) are local leaders in these sects. What follows then are narrative accounts of recent interviews with representative from these sects concerned with the *burakumondai* (Buraku problem).

Religious reform in Japan today

Tenrikyo

Tenrikyo is generally regarded as a "new religion" in Japan although it traces its founding to the nineteenth century. This movement argues that all human persons have a common parent, God the Parent (*Oyasama*). Due to our self-centered nature, however, we fail to realize our true kinship with others. Through individual effort as well as the workings of God the Parent, human beings can achieve salvation. By focusing on self-less action (*hinokishi*) and the healing power of faith, we can save ourselves by acting to save others. Tenrikyo has spread outside of Japan and has a significant presence in the American religious scene.

In May 1998, the author had the opportunity to visit and speak with Takashi Ikenishi, the leader of the Niwadani temple of Tenrikyo in Sakai City, Osaka. Mr. Ikenishi, besides being a Tenrikyo official for many years, had also previously been in a position of leadership in the Osaka Conference for the *Dōwa* issue (*Dōshōren*). In response to a question regarding the Tenrikyo position on discrimination, Ikenishi replied that, "All people on the earth are brothers and sisters. As siblings, we are all the same regardless of social status. We are all children of Oyasama."

Mr. Ikenishi went on to argue that while Buddhism also has this view of equality, in the past, Buddhism has discriminated against the *buraku* people through such devices as discriminatory *kaimyo* and improper use of ancestor registries. He continued that one of the reasons that *buraku* people are attracted to "newer" religions in Japan is that they do not have the history of such practices. As to the Buddhist idea of karma and its use to support discrimination – that is that unequal treatment of certain people is appropriate due to karmic impurities – Ikenishi stated that as Tenrikyo does not have *kaimyo*, it also does not accept the idea of karma. Instead the religion has the concept of *innen*, which means that all souls go back to the present. As new clothes are put on, a new life is begun with no effect on the next life. One strives in Tenrikyo, according to Ikenishi, to be a better person by taking personal responsibility for one's improvement. It is not other people, but oneself that one needs to improve. Consequently, Tenrikyo does not adhere to the concept of *akunin* (inherently bad people) – rather, everyone is on the same line.

In reply to the question about *burakumin* in his church, Mr. Ikenishi replied that no unequal treatment happens in their worship. All members, consistent with their theology, are treated equally. A persistent problem, Ikenishi noted, was the idea of *kiyome* or *kegare* (pollution). Toward initiating change in the idea of pollution, he has argued in several forums against the continuation of using salt as an agent of purification after funerals. If death were seen as non-polluting of others, then some of the medieval stigma against those who dealt with dead bodies, both human and animal, would be removed. There is resistance to removing salt from such usage, particularly from Shinto sources who historically have emphasized salt in this way, however, Ikenishi feels very strongly that this would be a positive step.[62]

The author accompanied Mr. Ikenishi to the apartment of a member of his congregation. It was a matsuri day for the family and, accordingly, he visited the home to participate in certain rituals. This family had an apartment in a *dōwa* area and had become Tenrikyo members following several family problems, most notably a son who had developed mental problems. The mother, in particular, was an ardent follower of Tenrikyo and had presented her conversion story and beliefs in schools and other meetings.

Mr. Ikenishi, the parents, and intermittently the son, performed a ritual dance (*Teodori*) before the Tenrikyo altar, chanting and utilizing accompanying *mūdras* (hand positions) and turnings of the body. At the conclusion of this ritual, Ikenishi laid hands on the boy and lightly pounded his shoulders while speaking very softly to him. It seemed clear that Tenrikyo, through the good offices of Mr. Ikenishi, had a profound impact on this *burakumin* family.

Shin Buddhism[63]

Shin Buddhism is the largest Buddhist sect in Japan and, correspondingly, the one that most *burakumin* have belonged to historically. Shin Buddhism, shaped in Japan by Honen (1133–1212) and Shinran (1173–1262), is a devotional Buddhist sect with prayers, rituals, and chanting offered by the penitent toward deliverance into the Pure Land upon death. The attitudes and actions of Japanese Shin Buddhism are thereby important in gauging the overall Japanese religious community's view on the *burakumondai*.

Mr. Uemoto is of the Shinshu Ohtani sect in Osaka City. His temple is a post-war structure placed in the heart of the business district in downtown Osaka. Uemoto had started teaching Buddhism at the age of nineteen at the sect headquarters. At that time, he discovered that he too had discriminatory thinking. He met an old woman from the *Buraku* who told him that she had been discriminated against and never had been supported by Buddhist priests or monks. At this encounter, Uemoto did not quite understand her position, but also realized that he could not deny her charge. Although a young priest who initially could not believe priests would engage in discriminatory practices, in time he came to learn that priests had done such things.

At the age of thirty-three, he became director of Human Rights for the temple and committed himself to being honest and to talking to people about this issue. Uemoto feels very strongly about sharing one's real self with the people that he talks to and, when asked to speak, depends about 80 per cent on his prepared remarks and 20 per cent on his heart. Initially, he feared being misunderstood or criticized, but has opted for the open approach.

In the past, Shin Buddhism had been one of the major offenders of *burakumin* human rights and had compounded their discriminatory policies and actions with more recent discriminatory public remarks. According to Mr. Uemoto, the structure of discrimination has still not changed sufficiently. When asked what sort of action the Shin sect was taking to change this structure, he replied that education of members was a central concern. Twice a month the temple sponsored a workshop to educate members, and four times a year there were public meetings to educate the larger public. The temple is well placed, Uemoto noted, to reach the public due to its central location, and everyone is invited to attend these informational meetings. There are approximately 650 temples in the Osaka *kyoku* and 200–300 households in his temple, so many people can be reached through this educational effort.

In regard to questions on Buddhism and its discriminatory practices, Uemoto stated that not only Buddhism should be focused on, but all Japanese religious bodies. In Osaka prefecture, 6,200 religious organizations are registered as official. To try and unite these disparate groups to fight discrimination the *Dōshuren* was established fifteen years ago. The *Dōshuren*, he explained, is an organization, representing 680 of these groups, dedicated to concerted dialogue and action to fight discrimination. This group was established in part due to the impetus of the initial Machida remarks.

Certainly Buddhism has been involved in discrimination, noted Uemoto. *Kaimyo* was a problem and its extent is still being discovered. As to the doctrine of karma, Uemoto believes that people have misused it. Some priests have used it to gain believers and extend teachings, but that is not its actual meaning. Some Buddhist priests became arrogant and distorted the idea of karma for the sake of reputation and appearance. Such arrogance, though often unintended, can easily beset anyone, he argued, so we must learn from the *Buraku* Liberation movement and be able to say, "Yes, I have discriminatory feelings."

Uemoto has found that if he speaks, writes, and teaches at a level that people can easily understand, then people will come to believe without having to delude them through complicated language or misrepresentation of Buddhist ideas. Even the seemingly insignificant use of *furigana* with *kanji* on letters or signs is important in order to reach all people. Shinshu's model for this, Uemoto believes, should be Shinran, the sect's founder.[64] Shinran too talked in plain language to small groups of people rather than large groups. We need to return, Uemoto averred, to such a procedure of imparting simple teachings to ensure better understanding. As Secretary of *Dōshuren*, Uemoto worked to make these changes and opened the meetings to the public. Since the meetings have become public, Uemoto believes the meetings have been more dynamic and the exchange has been more cooperative. Also, the dialogue has extended beyond the religious representatives to included people from various corporations. Although representing their respective groups, Uemoto suggested that people need to look at the *Burakumondai* (*Buraku* problem) from the viewpoint of an individual person who can personally connect with the pain of discrimination, then stand, as a representative, within the larger dialogue. Including the corporations where discriminatory practices have manifested, has truly been beneficial. Such exchanges have helped the *Dōshuren* become more visible to the outside community and show the organization to be open to scrutiny and criticism. *Dōshuren*, he stated, is not an organization of elites, but one of the people.

As Shinran had been mentioned, the author asked Uemoto how perhaps having a strong religious faith may help one bear and fight discrimination. In response to this question, Uemoto suggested that it is easy to discriminate and that people always want to target the weak. Religion though helps us to see what one really is. Faith will support us, help us. Religion has much to do, Uemoto agreed, with the *buraku* problem. It is very important, he added, as Shinran advocated, to continue educating people. Buddhism has changed a lot from an academic, elite tradition. Uemoto believes that it is time to come back to the people and create an education movement that will address the *buraku* issue. Some people are already campaigning and involved in such a movement.

Uemoto discussed what he saw as the future of the fight against *buraku* discrimination. He stated that the twenty-first century will be the century of human rights. In the future, we should look beyond our particular interests; human rights means being more transparent, learning from one another. All liberation movements are united around the goal of living harmoniously, he noted. In addition, working with the *Buraku* Liberation League to address the present discrimination was important.

Toward *Burakumin* Liberation

It is evident that the liberation of the burakumin has made great strides, yet what seems to be lacking is a coherent philosophy of liberation that can inform and sustain the *burakumin* liberation movement. There is merit though in considering Alastair McLauchlan's practical suggestion that:

> The successful formula is a combination of sound legislation, balanced but firm enforcement, and increased levels of education and awareness programmes, especially targeting young people before they are able to be influenced by family and friends who themselves do not have the correct information.[65]

While a strong case can be made for Christian liberation theology[66] and perhaps in particular African-American liberation movements, to provide considerable material for Asian emancipatory movements to study, the operant model of political liberation for the *burakumin* may be the model of civil rights activism as employed by African-Americans in the United States.[67] This movement for human rights was begun and nourished in the Black Churches of the United States and benefited greatly from a spiritual basis for its activism, though it was largely secular. This is a model that certainly resonates with portions of the Dalit community in South India, and – with adaptations appropriate for a Japanese societal context –

perhaps it is one the *burakumin* of Japan should explore more thoroughly.[68]

A further source for potential guidance, particularly in the area of integration education in Japan (Japanese: *Dōwa kyoiku*), may be critical pedagogy.[69] According to the *Buraku Kaiho Shimbun* (July 1997) only 1 per cent of Dōwa finances are used for educational purposes. The critical pedagogic emphases on the ontological treatment of the limited nature of all personal, dialogical relationships have direct relevance to the problem of oppression. A continuing development of improved emancipatory educational models for use in *dōwa kyoiku* – instituted and operated in the entire country of Japan, not just certain areas – that includes a discussion of the Japanese religious perspective on the burakumin and how that perspective is undergoing revision would also be an important step. It may help make a place and case for Japanese religions as part of the long-term solution to the *burakumondai*. From the Japanese Buddhist perspective, as engaged Buddhism may suggest, the deployment of a more faithful reading of the sūtras and an expanded use of *upāya* (skillful means) in education and communication regarding *buraku* discrimination is essential. It is demonstrably true that, as has been asserted by the *Buraku* Liberation and Human Rights Institute, "liberation begins and ends in education."[70]

It seems evident that any political or economic solutions to the problem of oppression – whether in the Indian context of the Dalits or the Japanese context of the *burakumin* – that neglect the spiritual nexus of the problem will not be sufficient. Through an increase in the development of close, spiritualized communities the *burakumin* may be aided by Japanese religiosity in their search for increased freedom from discrimination. Such communities would allow the creation and fruition of personal spirituality that would support the claim for genuine individuality and self-esteem as the believer sought his/her personal salvation while, at the same time, sanctioning the communal, continuing demand for social justice. This is precisely what engaged Buddhism argues for – a Buddhism that supports the *Buddha, Dharma,* and *Saṅgha* in such a fashion that the physical, emotional, and spiritual well-being of all human persons is enriched.

While one may concur with Sulak Sivaraksa's call upon Japan to "recall her rich spiritual tradition,"[71] and so meliorate the negative effects of its rampant materialism, it seems at best naive to expect this to occur (although perhaps with the 1990s' downturn in the Japanese economy, there may be an opportunity for such a recollection). The popularity of newer religions notwithstanding, the question whether the engaged Buddhist premise cited above can garner the support (and the power) to substantially effect pervasive, attitudinal change in Japan is a critical one to raise. What the *buraku* liberation movement lacks is a religiously inspired person who comes to symbolize the movement, such as Aung San Suu Kyi (Myanmar), B.R. Ambedkar (India), Sulak Sivaraksa (Thailand), or Thich Nhat Hahn (Vietnam). There are such inspired individuals working for buraku liberation in Japan, but no one has yet stepped forth into prominence.

The larger, related issue of linking human rights and religiosity may be argued more persuasively if, as Sivaraksa contends, Japan better realizes its responsibility as a world power and understands that as a "civil society" it cannot evade the question of the civil rights of its citizenry. The problem though, as noted by B.J. McVeigh in a recent book, is that Japan's version of civil society is "premised on a moral authority that is top down and state ordained rather than bottom up and popularly advocated."[72] This problem, if validly drawn, creates a structure that makes it difficult for populist, liberation movements such as the *Buraku* effort to gain widespread support – this same dilemma may also be an issue for other Asian liberation movements as one could arguably posit the same claim of "top-down direction of moral authority" for most Asian countries.

In a very real sense, from a Buddhist perspective, until we can uproot this discriminating consciousness – as in a Buddhist Awakening – then genuine relating, genuine dialogue is impossible. Thus, in terms of the debate within Critical Buddhism as to whether Original Awakening (*hongaku*) or the idea of *icchantika* is the operative nexus of Japanese Buddhism, it seems evident that, in practice, the classism of Japanese society and religion has historically and to today extolled the latter position. It is crucial to recall however that at the core of Buddhist philosophy stands a non-obstructionist, non-objectifiable, and thus non-discriminatory resolution that cannot – ontically or axiologically – support such oppressive classism any more than it can rightly support sexism, racism, or ageism. As is stated in the *Nehangyo* itself, "Emancipation is Ônot being oppressed."[73]

We certainly need to be cautiously optimistic about the opportunities for greater successes in the individual and communal lives of the *burakumin*. It is critical that their plight is better known and supported throughout the world, along with that of the other oppressed peoples in Asia. It is time, as the Buraku Liberation effort puts it, "to wake the sleeping child" and not to presume that burakumin oppression, or any oppressive regime, will resolve itself as humankind socially evolves. My hope in presenting this research is that more scholars and activists will become interested in studying and teaching others about the *burakumin* so as to aid the Japanese people in "waking the sleeping child."

Notes

1   James Clavell, *Shogun* (New York: Dell Publishing, 1976), p. 870.
2   George DeVos; Hiroshi Wagatsumo, *Japan's Invisible Race: Caste in Culture and Personality* (Berkeley, CA: University of California Press, 1966). A helpful, recent treatment on Japanese minorities groups, including a chapter by Ian

Neary on the *burakumin*, is Michael Weiner (ed.), *Japan's Minorities: The Illusion of Homogeneity* (London: Routledge, 1997).

3 Emiko Ohniki-Tierney, *The Monkey as Mirror: Symbolic Transformations in Japanese History and Ritual* (Princeton, NJ: Princeton University Press, 1987), p. 98.

4 Ninomiya lists three main theories for the origin of the *burakumin* – these include the "etori" theory, the "aborigines theory", and the "foreign-immigrant theory". The dominant theory is the "etori" theory which is the one taken in this chapter. The "aborigines" theory argues *burakumin* descent from the Orokko tribe or a Hebrew tribe. The "foreign-immigrant" theory tries to argue that the *burakumin* were Korean or perhaps Filipino immigrants. (Shigeaki Ninomiya, "An Inquiry Concerning the Origin, Development, and Present Situation of the Eta in Relation to the History of Social Classes in Japan", *Transactions of the Asiatic Society of Japan* 10: 47–154.)

5 Connecting the eta of the Tokugawa period and the eta of the medieval period is highly problematical. Apparently, the term existed in earlier periods (Kamakura, Muromachi) but there was a differing population in the Edo *eta* than the previously group. See Suehiro Kitaguchi's description of these differences in his *An Introduction to the Buraku Issue: Questions and Answers*, translated, with introduction by Alastair McLauchlan, (Richmond, Surrey: Curzon, 1999), pp. 80ff.

6 The foremost contributor to the betterment of the *buraku* situation has been the Law on Special Measures for *Buraku* Improvement Project (Dōwa Taisaku Jigyō Tokubetsu Sōchihō). "Between 1969 and 1994, under the terms of the LSM, almost 14 billion yen was spent on 'target areas', with responsibility shared between state administration and the smaller, sub-prefectural authorities of city, town, and village authorities" (Kitaguchi, op. cit., p. 4).

7 This discrimination continues, in part at least, due to the sparsity of media coverage and educational mention (not in Japanese textbooks until 1972) of the *burakumin* situation, in Japanese as well as English. Ignorance continues to be the primary source of the *burakumondai* (buraku problem). What further complicates obtaining and distributing reliable information about the burakumin is that the literature lends itself to polemics – that is, one tends to discover tracts either written by *buraku* sympathists who sometimes rely on severe examples or apologist's material which query why the *burakumin* continue to complain. (Cf. Kitaguchi's, *An Introduction to the Buraku Issue: Questions and Answers,* pp. 1ff.)

8 Jean-François Sabouret, L'autre Japon, les Burakumin (Paris: La Descouverte/Maspers, 1983) [quotes from this book are my translations].

9 Ibid., p. 15.

10 Ibid., p. 15 (original emphasis). Along with an acquiescence to inequality by some *burakumin*, there has been a continued effort by others within the community to conceal their identities and going to great lengths to do so. This is not uncommon in oppressed communities, and we see this in India as well. The toll this deception exacts on an individual, his or her family, and the burakumin community is often quite high.

11 *The Reality of Buraku Discrimination in Japan* (Osaka: *Buraku* Liberation Research Institute Publications, 1994), p. 2.

12 Shigeyuki Kumisaka, "The Current Condition of Minorities in Japan and Challenge – The *Buraku* Issue," *Buraku Liberation News* 101 (1998): 3, 5.

13 The Dalits of India are commonly referred to, in the West, as the Untouchables (in Japanese, they are referred to as the *Fukashokumin*). The Dalit Liberation organizations and the *Buraku* Liberation movements have become increasingly

linked in their efforts to uproot their respective oppressions. This aligning of human rights groups in Asia is continuing to expand and is a very positive development. The respective situations of the Dalits and the burakumin seem very similar in the extent and specific types of discriminatory practices. The Dalits were also forbidden to enter temples and were required to conform to certain dress and demeanor.

14 Ohnuki-Tierney, op. cit., p. 98.

15 This "employment difference" theory is further explained by Kitaguchi, op. cit., pp. 85ff.

16 Marriage discrimination was and continues to be a ubiquitous form of bias shown toward the burakumin.

17 Ian Neary, *Political Protest and Social Control in Pre-War Japan: The Origins of Buraku Liberation* (Atlantic Highland, NJ: Humanities Press International, 1989), p. 12. Neary further supports this lack of "self-esteem" as, at least in part, a product of "the development of a set of religious beliefs which supported the regulations systematically imposed from the eighteenth century" (ibid., p. 26).

18 The term *burakumin* is being used here as a generic term for the historical groups that have been similarly oppressed. The term though does not really gain currency until the nineteenth century. Neary reports that, "it was only in the early eighteenth century that policies were pursued which insisted on making legal distinctions between these groups [eta,hinin] and other commoners." (Neary, *Political Protest and Social Control in Pre-War Japan,* p. 12.)

19 Kitaguchi, op. cit., p. 79.

20 Jinmiro Oe, ed., *Dawa Bunken: Sabetsu Kozo Keukyu* [Dawa Literature: Discrimination Research Organization] (Tokyo: Jinmiro Oe, 1991), pp.61-63.

21 Ibid., p. 61 [my translation, with the assistance of Ms. Miho Marui]. Their duties were primarily in cleaning the shrine.

22 Ohnuki-Tierney, op. cit., p. 89. She is referencing Michihiko Noguchi, "Chusei no shomin seikatsu to hisabetsumin no doko (The Life of the Common People and Movements of Discriminated People during the Medieval Period), in Buraku Kaiho Kenkyusho (ed.), *Buraku Mondai Gaisetsu* (Introduction to Buraku Problems) (Osaka: Kaiho Shuppansha, 1978), pp. 86–99.

23 Oe, op. cit., p. 61.

24 See Edward Norbeck's article, "Pollution and Taboo in Contemporary Japan," Southwestern Journal of Anthropology 8, 3 (1952): 269–285.

25 In time, the burakumin became associated with these unclean occupations. "Their work consisted of disposing of dead cattle and horses, tanning hides, sweeping the shrines, and crafting bamboo." (The Reality of Buraku Discrimination in Japan, Osaka: Buraku Kaiho Kenkyusho, 1994, p.2.).

26 Neary, op. cit., p. 13. Interestingly, one of the practical reasons for this prohibition may have been to prevent peasants from killing useful work animals such as horses and cattle.

27 Shigeyuki Kumisaka, "The Current Condition of Minorities" in *Japan and Challenge – The Buraku Issue,* p. 5.

28 The making of drums by burakumin is perhaps not very well known. In a visit to the Osaka Human Rights Museum, the author saw a display presenting this information. The Director of the Museum told me that the *Buraku* artisans would put their names inside the large taiko before strapping the leather heads on the drums.

29 Oe, op. cit., p. 61.

30 Shigeaki Ninomiya, "An Inquiry Concerning the Origin, Development, and Present Situation of the Eta in relation to the History of Social Classes in Japan", *Transactions of the Asiatic Society of Japan* 10, p.47-154.

31 Ibid., p. 17.

32 The current President of the *Buraku* Research Institute, Sueo Murakoshi, told the author in an interview conducted in May, 1998 that he believed the Emperor system was largely responsible for the stratification of people and the low placement of the burakumin in the nineteenth century. He believes that more attention should be paid to the historic role of this system in buraku discrimination.

33 *The Reality of Buraku Discrimination,* p. 4. Interestingly, the numbers of *buraku* increased during this period (early eighteenth century) perhaps in part, as Neary writes, "In some areas eta:hinin were more reluctant to practice abortion or *mabiki* [infanticide] to control the size of their families because of their pious devotion to Buddhism" (op. cit., p. 23).

34 In 1981, the Joint Conference of Religions coping with the Dōwa Problem was created consisting of representatives from fifty-nine sects. (*The Reality of Buraku Discrimination in Japan*, p. 8).

35 According to the Ministry of Education, the enrollment in Colleges or Universities are 39 percent for all Japanese compared to 26.5 percent for *burakumin*, a 12.5 percent difference. (1996 statistics) A very important source of improvement for the buraku people, as with other oppressed peoples elsewhere, lies with the number of buraku that can receive a college education. This is particularly so in Japan where status is closely tied to one's occupation. It is useful to note, however, that the burakumin movement still struggles with the issue of illiteracy, particularly in the older people who were not able to pursue education due to work, illness, or other obstacles brought on by poverty and discrimination.

36 John Donoghue, *Pariah Persistence in Changing Japan* (Washington, DC: University Press of America, 1978).

37 Ibid., p. 65.

38 Ibid., p. 66.

39 In his book, *Interpreting Amida: History and Orientalism in the Study of Pure Land Buddhism* (Albany, NY: SUNY Press, 1997), Galen Amstutz corroborates this view in stating, "Postwar Shin remained involved in the services which it developed in the early part of the century, especially education (two universities, many high schools, and various institutes) and lobbying for *burakumin* rights" (p. 37).

40 Involvement in "outside" *matsuri* by *burakumin* had, before the War, been a recipe for violence as other people had tried to exclude them from the festivities. The "inner" *matsuri* was useful for the *burakumin* as it served to unify the village around common ancestry and sentiments (Donoghue, op. cit., p. 70, 71).

41 The *burakumin* did not follow the popular superstitions and it was explained to Donoghue that this was because. "We kill and eat many kinds of animals [animals are often a focus of superstition in Japan] and therefore, we have developed realistic attitudes ... thus superstitions are minimized" (op. cit., p. 66). This indicates the pragmatism that their lives and traditional occupations have demanded of the *burakumin*.

42 Ibid., p. 67

43 Ibid., p. 70.

44 The *Buraku* Liberation Research Institute is located in Osaka, Japan. It changed its name to the *Buraku* Liberation and Human Rights Research Institute in July 1998.
45 *Buraku Liberation News*, September 1996 (no. 92), p. 10. This discriminatory practice was originally uncovered in the early 1980s. A *Buraku Liberation News*, dated October 1981, has a story and a picture of a tombstone with the Chinese characters for *caṇḍāla*, which, according to a definition in Soothill's, *A Dictionary of Chinese Buddhist Terms* (Dehli: Motilal Banarsidass, 1937) means " derived from violent, and interpreted as a butcher, bad man" (p. 326).
46 *Buraku Liberation News*, p. 10.
47 Ibid., p. 10.
48 William Bodiford, "Zen and the Art of Religious Prejudice: Efforts to Reform A Tradition of Social Discrimination," *Japanese Journal of Religious Studies* 23, 1–2 (1996): 1–27.
49 The interested reader should reference Bodiford's excellent article for more details on each of these examples.
50 Robert E. Buswell, Jr.'s chapter entitled, "The Path to Perdition: The Wholesome Roots and Their Eradication," in Robert E. Buswell, Jr. and Robert Gimello (eds.), *Paths to Liberation: The Marga and Its Transformation in Buddhist Thought* (Honolulu: University of Hawai'i Press, 1992), p. 119.
51 Buswell, op. cit., pp. 118, 119.
52 Ibid., p. 119.
53 The translation used herein is Yamamoto Kosho, *The Mahayana Mahaparinirvana-sutra*, three volumes (Ube, Japan: Karinbunko, 1973–1975). It is acknowledged to be a problematic translation, yet it is (at this writing) the only complete translation of this *Daihatsu-nehangyo* (the Nanpon-Nehan, so-called "Southern edition"). The "Northern edition" (Hokuhon-Nehan) awaits English translation.
54 Rekizan Ishikawa, "Karma, Chandala, and Buddhist Scriptures," *The Bulletin of Buraku Liberation* 90, 2 (1993): 1–13.
55 *Chandala* (Japanese: sendara) refers to the so-called "untouchables" or, more preferably, the Dalits (see note 45 above for more on the etymology of this term). Ishikawa points out in his article that in the Jodoshu text, Kanmuryojukyo, there is a story of Bimbashara (Sanskrit: Biṃbiśāra), the fifth king of the Saisunaga Dynasty in Magadha and a follower of Buddhism. Bimbashara and his wife were imprisoned and the king was subsequently murdered by his son, Ajase (Sanskrit: Ajātaśatru; Japanese: Mijoon). This act, which Ajase later repented, was considered a *chandala* act, a polluting act (*shogyo*). As Ishikawa notes:

> This tragic story was believed by Shinran to be representative of the entire text. This negative connotation of *chandala* was perpetuated throughout the Jodoshu tradition. However, what is important to note, is that Shinran himself understood the importance of the story to be that even evil people, such as Ajase, are "still within the embrace of Amida's compassion.
>
> ("Karma, Chandala, and Buddhist Scriptures," p. 5)

56 I concede the difference at this point that one may make between being bestowed with Buddha-nature and realizing Buddha-nature. A good discussion of this problem is found in the discussion between Sallie King and Matsumoto Shiro in Jamie Hubbard and Paul Swanson (eds), *Pruning the Bodhi Tree: The Storm Over Critical Buddhism* (Honolulu: University of Hawai'i Press, 1997), pp. 165ff.

57 Yamamoto (trans.), *Nehangyo*, p. 225.
58 Ibid., p. 114.
59 Ibid., p. 120.
60 Ibid., p. 658.
61 Buswell, op. cit., p. 121. Buswell suggests this tension between the notion of *icchantika* and the primary message of the *Nirvana Sutra* which is buddha-nature of all beings is one that has "consistently plagued the traditional Buddhist commentators."
62 McLauchlan voices the opposing view on the import of *kegare* when he states, "it is no secret that Japanese people are regarded as pragmatic about religious and spiritual matters, and it is highly unlikely that spiritual adherence plays a major role in modern-day anti-*Buraku* sentiment, especially among Japanese youth" (Kitaguchi, op. cit., p. 32, 33). Certainly, as McLauchlan states, the average Japanese person does not trouble herself with whether meat or leather is unclean nor whether the person next to her on the train is a *burakumin*. Yet, while not questioning the presence of pragmatism in Japanese religious views, Reader and Tanabe in their *Practically Religious* (Honolulu: University of Hawai'i Press, 1998), argue this practicality is wed to supernatural belief and practice that does include *kegare* as an element. As for Japanese youth, perhaps they subscribe to other reasons for continuing the discriminatory views of their elders by depicting the *burakumin* as "violent, gang-related, or frightening" or possessing "strange eating/work habits" (the two most popular, current negative impressions of the *Burakumin*, according to a recent poll (Kitaguchi, op. cit., p. 67)).
63 Kitaguchi forwards an interesting theory regarding a possible formation of the Tokugawa *burakumin*. He argues that, "As we now know, there is a very close connection between the *Ikkō ikki* uprising and the creation of the Buraku" (op. cit., p. 95). The *Ikkō ikki* was a popularist rebellion of the fifteenth and sixteenth centuries that was abetted by the Jodo Shinshu sect.
64 In his introduction to Kitaguchi's, *An Introduction to the Buraku Issue*, p. 7.
65 A good example of the Christian liberation theological perspective on this is the work of Kuribayashi Teruo, such as his *Keikan no Shingaku* (A Theology of the Crown of Thorns), (Tokyo: Shinkyo Shuppansha, 1991). Christian liberation theology and its often stated claim to "preference the poor" may seem odd to apply to a developed country like Japan, but it is relevant to the *buraku* situation.
66 There does seem to be interest among the *burakumin* to explore the connection between the respective plights of African-Americans and themselves. The *Buraku* Liberation League has sponsored programs that included representatives from the NAACP and Reverend Jesse Jackson. The League was also strongly anti-apartheid.
67 There are several obstacles to the suggestion that African-American liberation theories or Christian liberation theology can contribute significantly to the *buraku* liberation effort – such as the relative small percentage of Christians in Japan (1 percent) and the enduring prejudice that exists in Japan toward African-Americans. Yet, it can be contended that there are fertile ideas in these movements that can be adapted to the Japanese buraku context without falling prey to the obscurantist climate Japan sometimes displays. There has been, as well, some movement of conversion by the *buraku* toward Christianity.
68 Works by critical pedagogues such as Paulo Freire, Ira Shor, bell hooks, etc. should be referenced and utilized in shaping dōwa kyoiku. The Japanese educators likewise working in this area should be used as consultants.
69 Kitaguchi, op. cit., p. 11.

70 Sulak Sivaraksa, *Seeds of Peace: A Buddhist Vision for Renewing Society* (Berkeley, CA.: Parallax Press, 1992), p. 22. See also Christopher Queen and Sallie King (eds), *Engaged Buddhism: Buddhist Liberation Movements in Asia* (Albany, NY: SUNY Press, 1996). This excellent text outlines prominent liberation movements in Asia, including the Soka Gakkai in Japan.

71 Brian J. McVeigh, *The Nature of the Japanese State: Rationality and Rituality* (London: Nissan Institute/Routledge, 1988), p. 188.

72 Kosho, trans., *Nehangyo*, p. 119.

III

WESTERN FRONTIERS

10

ENGAGED AND MEDITATING

Vipassana Hawaii's Burmese connection

Harriet Kirkley

Christopher Queen's argument that intention is the *sine qua non* of any definition of engaged Buddhism is at once pragmatic and substantial. That is to say, we can regard as authentically Buddhist social action in which principles and techniques are practiced in the name of the Awakened One, in accord with the teachings of wisdom and compassion, and in the spirit of an unbroken community working in harmony with the Three Refuges. Ajarn Buddhadasa's suggestion that what quenches *dukkha* is Buddhist similarly directs us to both intention and its manifestations in consequence. In these forms, nomenclature does not separate the life of action from that of the spiritual path. Rather, they are seen as complementary.[1]

The aim of this chapter is to describe a model now in the process of implementation by Vipassana Hawaii, an organization based in Honolulu and founded in 1984 by Steven Smith and Michelle McDonald-Smith. The model has evolved as part of and in response to the founders' more than twenty years of experience in the Insight Meditation Society.[2] In addition, the model reflects their work with the environmental movement in North America, and their active engagement with an ongoing series of developmental projects located in the Sagaing Hills of Central Burma, which has long been a center of Burmese Theravādin practice.

With respect to Theravāda communities and practices in the West, Paul Numrich's "parallel worlds thesis" offers a suggestive approach that complements the pragmatic definitions offered by Queen and Buddhadasa Bhikkhu. Inhabited by immigrant Theravādins, on the one hand, and what Gil Fronsdal dubbed the Vipassana Community – a largely European American contingent – on the other, Numrich's image of a Thai temple invites a study of changing processes of interaction between the communities he describes, those of immigrant and convert, which in his thesis coexist amiably and interact to a limited degree, but with little sustained contact.[3]

The unique structure of the model being implemented by Vipassana Hawaii, I shall argue, offers us a significant possibility of situating

Numrich's parallel worlds on the same plain, not within a Thai immigrant temple, but by bringing a Burmese monastery and a Hawai'ian American retreat center together in common endeavors. These involve training in *sīla* and *dāna* (morality and generosity), as well as cross-cultural experiences for Burmese and North Americans. The North American preoccupation with the teaching and practice of meditation thus functions in conjunction with MettaDana, ("Kindness-giving") a well-established organization devoted to socially engaged Buddhist development aid, carried out with the direct involvement of an innovative monk, Sayadaw U Lakkhana, Abbot of Kyaswa Monastery in central Burma.

The twin foundations of the model, which integrate engaged social action with the teaching and practice of meditation, were present at its inception. Steven Smith, in conjunction with his teacher Sayadaw U Pandita, developed it during a sabbatical devoted to returning to his Buddhist roots in the Burmese monastic reform tradition. Eventually it led him to the Sagaing Hills, where Smith recognized a possibility for his Western students to express the practice of loving-kindness through a concrete practice of generosity, carried out by, given, and received reciprocally by peoples who live half a world away. That insight, as well as the hard work that it entailed to bring MettaDana into being, has borne rich fruit.

The MettaDana Project

Because the topic on this occasion is that of engaged Buddhism, I shall begin with that pillar of the foundation. The link between Vipassana Hawaii and the Kyaswa Monastery began, when Mr Smith returned from sabbatical in Burma to found the MettaDana Project, a development aid project designed to bring medical, educational, and developmental assistance to a particular monastic community and its surrounding villages. Its overall goal is to "help the people of the Sagaing Hills face the challenges and opportunities of the twenty-first century, while maintaining its role as an ancient center of wisdom and nurturing the relationship between lay community, monasteries, and nunneries that has been its strength for centuries." To that end, the project's mandates focus on public health; education, especially primary school; improving local infrastructure, especially roads and the water supply; and preserving Buddhist monuments.[4]

Kyaswa Monastery itself already had an innovative Abbot, Sayadaw U Lakkhana, who had founded the Wachet Hospital in 1984, as well as a tradition of providing services for the villagers who supported them. MettaDana has thus entered upon and helped to extend that existing tradition both with funding and the transfer of expertise. At present, the officers of MettaDana include Steven Smith, president; Susan Usitalo, vice-president; Alan Jassby, vice-president; and Roy Awakuni, treasurer. The board of advisors includes Sayadaw U Pandita Bhivamsa, Mirabai Bush, Michelle McDonald-Smith, Bruce Lockhart (MD), and Kathryn L. Braun (University of Hawai'i). Aung San Suu Kyi, leader of the democracy movement in Burma and Nobel laureate, also serves as a friend and adviser to this project. Donations to it are channeled through the Kyaswa Monastery directly to health, education, and related activities in the immediate vicinity of the monastery. No government agencies are involved, and the operating expenses of MettaDana are met by volunteer staff.

Primary education is a central goal for MettaDana. Its projects to date have included improving the facility of the Wachet Primary School in a village nearby the Monastery, initially by putting up bamboo walls and a roof. In 1998, MettaDana began to provide all supplies, texts, and fees for all students who wish to attend school. The number of students has since increased from about 250 to 300 students. With this increase, the school has reached capacity, although the number of children eligible to attend it is 450. Because the school, in the past, has often been closed because of flooding in the rainy season, MettaDana has this year funded the construction of one of two planned new school buildings on a higher site. In addition to participating in its construction, the villagers themselves have insisted on funding the second building as circumstances permit. Immediate MettaDana plans include building a teachers' residence to save the teachers from making long commutes on bicycle. The estimated cost for the school program, including the residence, is $15,000.

MettaDana's efforts in health care focus on the Wachet Jivitadana Sangha Hospital. Founded in 1984 by Sayadaw U Lakkhana, the fifty-bed hospital functions mainly as an outpatient clinic for monks, nuns, and villagers, although in the rainy season, many require hospitalization for acute gastrointestinal and other illnesses. To support the resident staff of the hospital, MettaDana has provided a dental x-ray machine, medicines, bandages, and other supplies. In addition, the project funded a program in which senior nurses from Rangoon trained fifteen local students to act as nurses aides. One of the surprise successes that MettaDana has brought to the hospital, now a branch of the Institute for Traditional Medicine in Mandalay, is acupuncture. When the presence of American acupuncturist Michael Zucker at the hospital was announced, he experienced an endless flow of patients from eight o'clock in the morning until five in the evening, seeing a total of ninety patients in five days. Future plans call for training local practitioners to deliver acupuncture.

A longer-term undertaking is the Wachet TB Control Project. The prevalence of HIV-AIDS in the area is as yet unknown, but tuberculosis remains a major cause of morbidity and mortality. The TB Control Project will target the 3,000 villagers and 7,000 monks and nuns in the area. The estimated cost for the first phase of this program – which will focus on strategies for controlling and preventing TB – is $20,000. A public health education specialist and a physician with experience in Asia and with TB care have volunteered to work in this phase.

MettaDana's initial effort to improve local living conditions, the improvement of a road along the river, has been followed up by the construction of a water purification system. In 1998, a Burmese Buddhist association contributed a water purification system to the monastery that links up with a system put in place by MettaDana. In 1998, at the invitation of MettaDana, water-engineering expert, Susan Murcott of the Massachusetts Institute of Technology (MIT), worked with a retired local physician, U Pe Thoe, to establish a water-testing laboratory at the hospital and tested samples of water from the river, storage reservoirs, and village wells. Armed with a much clearer understanding of the water contamination problems, MettaDana is now seeking public health professionals with expertise in surveying hygiene behavior to begin formulating the next phases of the water purification project.

The fourth item in the mandate of MettaDana is helping to preserve some of the many beautiful Buddhist monuments and buildings in the area. A recent project was restoration of the tomb of Mekin, a famous nun from the nineteenth century who taught meditation and scripture to thousands of students. Another project has been to restore access to the Lokamakaik pagoda, whose access was denied when a road was built that destroyed the steps necessary to reach the pagoda.

Viewed as a whole, the organizational structure and mandate of the MettaDana Project, as well as its careful approach to development aid, show a commendable emphasis both on low budget sustainable development undertaken by a dedicated group of individuals and the active participation of the Burmese community that it serves. The project thus combines local input with both Burmese and Western expertise in what amounts to a collaborative endeavor. From a Buddhist perspective, the model has an added attraction of engaging ordinary individuals, Burmese, North American, and European, in a context where each stands to learn from the others. Nor should we underestimate the ramifications of the dialogues that a common experience will initiate and enhance as it continues. To be sure, they often require a translator fluent in Burmese, English, and Pāli, but as a metaphor for this shared enterprise, that of translation has much to offer when compared with adaptation, acculturation, and baggage.

Hawaii Insight Meditation Center

If, as I have suggested, MettaDana functions as both an expression and a mirror of loving-kindness, the construction of the Hawaii Insight Meditation Center (HIMC), now underway, will complement this by teaching the practices of mindfulness and loving-kindness. The Hawaiian center, which will be located on the big island, Hawaii, is still in the planning stages. As stated in its mission statement, when completed:

> [HIMC] will be an international retreat center bridging East and West, tradition and innovation. The great forest monastery tradition of Southeast Asia merged with the spiritual geography of the Hawaiian Islands will provide a unique environment in which to offer these accessible contemplative practices of Mindfulness and Loving-Kindness.

In addition to serving those in North America who have traditionally sought out Buddhist teachings, the center plans to offer retreats tailored for young adults and families, and environmental, medical, educational, and corporate leaders. The latter goal is a result of the HIMC teachers' experience with the Center for Contemplative Mind in Society.[5]

The broad model that the Smiths and their associates are currently working to bring to fruition thus rests on complementary foundations, both fundamental to the teaching and practice of Buddhism. In it the teaching and practice of meditation take place in conjunction with socially engaged Buddhism in the form of MettaDana, an ongoing aid project in which Burmese and North Americans work together. Fronsdal's article on the Vipassana Community accurately linked the teaching of generosity, as it exists in that community, to the IMS-IMW effort to continue the tradition of offering the teachings freely, and hence depending on voluntary donations by students to sustain the teachers. As he reported, the verdict on the success of that effort is still out.

Like its sister institutions, Vipassana Hawaii will depend on *dāna* in this form. The innovation in its model, however, is to give the practice of generosity a clear and direct focus outside the immediate needs of sustaining the organization itself. MettaDana and its work in Burma with a Burmese monastic community and its lay supporters provide a basic foundation of the model, which is an integral part of the teaching of Buddhist practice as it will be given at HIMC.

Smith's model also actively involves Asian and Western teachers who offer retreats jointly; these retreats are now given annually both in Hawaii and at the Kyaswa monastery in the Sagaing Hills on the western bank of the Ayeyarwady River in central Burma, opposite the city of Mandalay. Here, in hills that have been a center of Buddhist practice for 2,000 years, Western yogis practice alongside Asians who themselves experience the teachings as given by Western teachers. These retreats are already oversubscribed, with far more applicants than places. A retreat for older students is planned for January 2000.

To this point, I have emphasized the international and collaborative dimensions of the Vipassana Hawaii model, but the organization also acts locally, primarily in community-building and the teaching of meditation. Its guiding teachers, Steven Smith and Michelle McDonald-Smith, sponsor weekly sittings and give day-long, as well as residential, retreats at the Palolo Zen Center. The organization publishes a newsletter and reports on the MettaDana project, and maintains a web site. Furthermore, as their focus shifts to the plans for constructing HIMC, the guiding teachers continue to maintain teaching schedules on the mainland. Steven Smith is a guiding teacher of the Blue Mountains Meditation Center in Australia, and his work with the Center for Contemplative Mind in Society involves him in developing programs for those who attend CMIS functions. He is thus actively involved internationally in extending the reach of *Dhamma* teaching in America to those active in environmental causes, business, journalism, and philanthropy. Despite all this, both guiding teachers find time to consult planners, architects, and other professionals who are helping to formulate and design the HIMC.

These plans, as they have developed so far, have a distinct Hawaiian as well as Buddhist flavor. The site purchased, on Hapu'u Bay, consists of 180 acres. Extending from an elevation of 300 feet to the sea shore, the land was chosen with an eye to the traditional Hawaiian concept of *ahupua'a*, a place of nurture and refuge, "rich in cultural history & ancient Hawaiian sites... a place of mana (spiritual power)."[6] As the vision statement says:

> Extending between ocean and mountain, and inclusive of diverse bioregions of flora and fauna, streams and valley, the ahupua'a models an intimate interrelatedness between people and their surround... Our planned mini ahupua'a includes projects such as preservation and protection of the land, reforestation of rare and endangered native species and restoration of traditional agriculture. In all of our activities we are guided by the traditional Hawaiian values: *malama* – to care for and preserve (resources, values); to serve, honor (what is worthy of honor); and *pono* – the sum total of all human virtues and the foundation of moral leadership in goodness ... Incorporating sustainable tropical design elements, our retreat facility will reflect both Eastern and Western influences while resting gently on the land.[7]

Plans call, in due course, for the usual facilities of a Western retreat center: meditation hall; residence building for sixty participants; kitchen and dining hall; multi-purpose building for administration; library; interview rooms for students and teachers; and individual cottages for long-term retreatants and teachers in residence. In addition to weekend and somewhat longer brief retreats, plans include offering two- and three-month retreats for experienced students as well as a "hermitage-like setting" for more extended individual retreats.

Central to the concept of HIMC, moreover, is the principle of retreats taught and sat jointly by Asian and Western teachers and students. Sayadaw U Pandita and Sayadaw U Lakkhana, both renowned Burmese masters, have offered to teach in the center. In the summer of 1999 each of the two Burmese Sayadaws taught a retreat jointly with Stephen Smith in Hawaii. Michelle McDonald-Smith has taught three retreats with Sayadaw U Lakkhana – the first at IMS in Barre and two subsequent retreats in Burma. Together, they will teach a retreat for older students in January 2000. Senior Western teachers will also be invited to teach at HIMC from time to time. Insofar as the model of Vipassana Hawaii combines socially engaged Buddhism with a unique model of the Western retreat center, it represents a departure from existing models in the Vipassanaa Community. Because the model also implies an altered version of this form of American Buddhist identity, its ramifications for the processes of defining that identity warrant brief consideration.

Parallel worlds

Queen's pragmatic approach to defining the term "engaged Buddhism" as it applies to post-Victorian liberation movements in Asia finds an echo in Thomas Tweed's recent essay on convert or "new" Buddhists in the United States. Tweed's similarly pragmatic approach to questions about scholarly definitions of religious identity as they apply to the amorphous category that has come to be called American Buddhism is useful. For some, his proposed term, "sympathizer," comes with unhappy associations, but Tweed's definition is capacious and flexible enough to be useful: "Sympathizers are those who have some sympathy for a religion but do not embrace it exclusively or fully."[8] Abandoning an essentialist/normative route to include self-identification as a Buddhist (or as a member of any tradition) need not, as Martin Baumann fears, necessarily entail its opposite, mere nominalism. An epistemological and methodological stance that allows for give and take, in which an author is aware of both normative and nominalist issues but is bound wholly to neither, is arguably a valuable perspective from which to view protean diversity, that rich tapestry called "American Buddhism."

Vipassana Hawaii describes its American affiliation as "IMS"; it will also belong to the world-wide network of teaching institutions that derive from and continue the lineage of Mahasi Sayadaw. I need not tell scholars of Buddhism how rare it is for a Western Buddhist organization to seek active affiliation with an Asian parent.

It would be premature to speculate what the effects of the Vipassana Hawaii model will have in the years to come as its vision becomes reality. I would argue, however, that the model represents an important opportunity for the "parallel worlds" posited in Numrich's thesis to become a synergy in which Tweed's "night-stand Buddhists" begin to know more directly and respect ancient traditions, even perhaps to add classical Buddhist texts to the books piled on the night-stand, and begin to ground their practice not only in texts about Buddhism written by Western writers, but also in Buddhist texts, perhaps even the *Suttapitaka* and the *Visuddhimagga*.

Nor will the synergy work in only one direction. As actively engaged Buddhists know too well, Western ideology and social visions have no corner on the issues of modernity that face the entire planet. Still less does Western ideology have solutions to problems that we, in large measure, have created. The attempt to respond to modernity in all its protean forms affects us all, West and East alike. Indeed, socially engaged Buddhism as it exists in the West at present seeks either to act locally (somewhere on the planet) within a Buddhist framework and/or to bring Buddhist perspectives to bear on the problems created by a predominantly Western ideology of technology and secularism. Seen from this perspective, Vipassana Hawaii is addressing both sets of issues in interdependent and creative ways.

To my mind, the Vipassana Hawaii model has the potential to help prepare a ground in which processes of mutual education and exchange can flourish between and across cultures. The MettaDana projects in the Sagaing Hills of Burma speak for themselves. The understanding and respect for Asian traditions that the project has engendered in Western students is less quantifiable, but equally important. Even those who have not been to Burma know about the steps to the pagoda; a young woman who became a weaver; the x-ray machine; and suitcases filled to overflowing with chalk, crayons, and textbooks for the Wachet Primary School.

Some evidence, however slender, exists that indicates other small ways in which the parallel worlds of Asian traditions and Western converts may be converging, however nascent that process is to date. As many North American Buddhist organizations reassess their traditionally restricted focus on meditation, Buddhist leaders in Asia meet publicly to consider new directions for Buddhism in Asia as they struggle to adapt and respond to pressures of modernity as well as militant forms of Christian evangelism. Both, in different ways, threaten to undermine the cultures that traditionally supported Asian monasticism.

At a recent meeting in Sri Lanka attended by senior Asian monastic leaders of many traditions and lineages, the Dalai Lama reported on his experience of Western ways. He mentioned particularly that Western teachers teach what he called "the basics" more widely than is done currently in Asia, a practice that, if adopted, would presumably make these teachings more directly accessible beyond traditional monastic communities and enrich the devotional and ritual practices of Buddhist lay people. The BBC World Service, which reported on the meeting, did not report responses to the Dalai Lama's observation. Its importance, however, may well be that the topic was broached at all in a strategic meeting of key Asian Buddhist leaders.

The model of Vipassana Hawaii bears watching. Its uniqueness lies partly in its willingness to mandate the development of *sila* as part of the ongoing practice of meditation that involves both meditation and acting in the world. Its model actively incorporates the practices of *dāna* and *sila* with that of *sati* and the *brahmavihāras* and strives to integrate Asian values with American ones in a context that also respects Hawai'ian traditions. It integrates an international socially engaged Buddhist project with the teaching and practice of meditation as it has evolved in Western retreat centers. This international perspective provides a much-needed counterbalance to unrecognized forms of parochialism in what threatens to become a long series of self-conscious attempts to define an American Buddhism.

That these attempts so often occur solely within, and are *de facto* limited to, what Tweed calls the convert community is, in my opinion, short-sighted. These internal discussions are not irrelevant. They need to occur, if only because the convert community itself is so diverse, and includes Theravāda, Zen, and Vajrayāna antecedents, to cite the most obvious. The danger is that defining "American Buddhism" in this context alone can only impoverish the exercise.

An equally serious difficulty exists for the "creatures" whom Tweed describes and for the scholars who try to study them: the books on the night-stand are mostly depictions of Buddhism seen through Western eyes and are usually tailored to fit an author's vision and goals, to say nothing of the book-buying public. I do not say this dismissively; it helps to explain the proliferation of both confused "creatures" who meditate and the confusions that trying to study them in a scholarly context can entail. It is no small wonder that the scholar trying to contend with it all may throw up her hands in despair or that paradigms of nomenclature and taxonomy proposed to bring order to the study of this population now multiply annually.

Conclusion

My aim in this chapter has been to describe a new, and I believe, constructive model in the broad continuum that includes socially engaged Buddhism as well as the conundrums of defining Buddhist identity in its protean Western forms. My hope is that the model will bring us closer to a day when *Buddhism* is the key word, when Westerners and immigrant Buddhists alike perceive themselves as participants with distinctive roles to play in dialogues that are cross-cultural as well as ethnic, parts of an national community as well as a local one. To one who has sat retreats, as

I have – organized by a Mexican-Canadian in which participants included Thais, Thai-Canadians, Indo-Canadians, and Euro-Canadians, all of whom heard the same teaching from Mahāthera Henepola Gunaratana, a Sri Lankan teacher who has long worked with immigrant Buddhist communities in the United States and Canada – the vision of parallel worlds converging, or at least interacting constructively, does not seem wholly removed: difficult certainly, but not impossible.

Charles Prebish's decision to examine closely a range of particular communities in his chapter on Buddhist communities in the United States is telling.[9] Whatever the forms "American Buddhism" takes, they will surely be pluralistic, as indeed that partly fictional monolith "traditional Asian Buddhism" is, and always has been. Scholars know, and have always known, that such phrases are misnomers. Yet many Western converts do not recognize the pluralism, especially perhaps those in Fronsdal's "Vipassana Community." The pervasive syncretism that Paul Numrich and others justifiably lament is at times a consequence of Western teachers' own diverse experiences and/or whatever private synthesis is useful to them. As often, however, the night-stand sympathizer goes to a bookstore or library, chooses a title that appeals, and reads and interprets what she reads as "Buddhist" with little sense that the term alone is probably insufficient to describe the teachings as presented in the book that she chose.

Hence the importance, in the context of Western forms of Theravāda Buddhism, that Vipassana Hawaii has decided to affiliate itself with the strong lineage that primarily shaped its guiding teachers. That decision in itself will give its Western students a framework and degree of coherence often lacking in teachings that mix and mingle bits of one tradition and another, a recipe known perhaps to the teacher, but not so clear to those who receive the teaching. My enthusiasm for the model being implemented by Vipassana Hawaii is thus partly that the model affirms a lineage. Its programs are designed to give Western students and their Burmese counterparts in the Sagaing Hills, many of whom are monks and nuns, a shared experience of working directly and together as well as sitting together in meditation retreats taught jointly by Western and Burmese teachers. It is hard to imagine an American state better placed – geographically and demographically – to carry forward a vision of Theravādin teachings at once socially engaged and cross-cultural. Hawaii's long history of multiculturalism can only enhance the project as modeled.

I conclude with an apology. What seems American and parochial in many discussions of the future of Buddhism in the United States may, in my perceptions, take on exaggerated and distorted significance, out of proportion to the whole. My view is that of a Westerner who has a night-stand piled high with books, who happens also to be an academic, and who lives 50 kilometers north of the 49th parallel. From this vantage point, it can seem that academics and non-academics alike emphasize "American" in the phrase "American Buddhism" and pay lip service – if they do not tacitly exclude – ethnic and other communities. Yet both congregations in Numrich's metaphorical temple struggle with problems of self-identification, whether as American, as Buddhist, or as an Other that the term "American" necessarily constructs.

It is hard to overestimate the positive possibilities implicit in a model like that taking form in the ongoing association between HIMC and Kyaswa Monastery, combining the MettaDana Project and retreats taught by Asian masters and Western teachers with Asian and Western students sitting side by side. The Western convert community, or at least Theravādin strands in it, stand to gain much from a teaching community that, although not narrowly sectarian, nevertheless is committed to remaining firmly grounded in a strong lineage, takes its lineage seriously, and thus stands at some distance from what has been called, rightly, the "*Dharma* shopping mall approach." To end where I began, when the sympathizer's pile of books on the night-stand includes at least some parts of the *Suttapitaka*, we will have achieved – if not some form of consensus – at least a body of teachings that the various relevant communities recognize in common.

Notes

1 Christopher S. Queen, "Introduction," in Christopher S. Queen and Sallie B. King (eds.), *Engaged Buddhism: Buddhist Liberation Movements in Asia* (Albany, NY: SUNY Press, 1996), *passim*, esp. pp. 28–33; Santikaro Bhikkhu, "Buddhadasa Bhikkhu: Life and Society Through the Natural Eyes of Voidness," in Queen and King, *Engaged Buddhism*, pp. 156–157.

2 For a fuller account of IMS, see Charles Prebish, *Luminous Passage: The Practice and Study of Buddhism in America* (Berkeley, CA: University of California Press, 1999), Chapter 3.

3 See Paul David Numrich, "Local Inter-Buddhist Associations in North America" Duncan Ryūken Williams and Christopher S. Queen, (eds.) *American Buddhism: Methods and Findings in Recent Scholarship* (Surrey: Curzon Press, 1999), pp. 117–142; *Old Wisdom in the New World: Americanization in Two Immigrant Theravada Buddhist Temples* (Knoxville: University of Tennessee Press, 1996), and Gil Fronsdal, "Insight Meditation in the United States: Life, Liberty and the Pursuit of Happiness," in Charles S. Prebish and Kenneth K. Tanaka (eds.), *The Faces of Buddhism in America* (Berkeley, CA: University of California Press, 1998), pp. 163–180.

4 *The MettaDana Project Update*, May, 1999, "Guiding Principles."

5 Both IMS and IMW, within this movement, offer retreats for young adults. The founders of Vipassana Hawaii currently teach the Young Adults Retreats at IMS. IMW is in the process of developing a strong family program as well.

6 "Hapu'u Bay Refuge," in *Insight: A Joint Newsletter of the Insight Meditation Society and the Barre Center for Buddhist Studies* Fall (1999): 8.

7 "Our Vision"; <http//www.geocities.com/~viphawaii/>

8 Thomas A. Tweed, "Night-Stand Buddhists and Other Creatures: Sympathizers, Adherents, and the Study of Religion," in Duncan Ryuuken

Williams and Christopher S. Queen (eds.), op. cit., pp. 71–90; reviewed by Martin Baumann, *Journal of Buddhist Ethics* (1999): 200–204.

9   Charles Prebish's Chapter 2, "Shaping the *Sangha*," in *Luminous Passage* offers a very helpful survey and analysis of the Herculean efforts required to fashion a working terminology that is consistent and comprehensible within the vocabulary of the academic study of religions; he also makes the points about the tacit exclusion of ethnic Buddhists well, and with tact (ibid., pp. 51–93).

11

WIDENING THE CIRCLE

Communities of color and Western Buddhist convert *sanghas*

Sharon Smith

Buddhism is now one of the fastest growing religions in the West, though so far, people of African, Caribbean, and Asian descent form only a small minority of those who have chosen to convert to Buddhism. This has significant implications for Western Buddhists, both as individual practitioners and for their faith communities. Many practitioners are now based in increasingly diverse communities that face both the promises of multiculturalism and challenges from racial discrimination and social exclusion. However, although there has been an increasing amount of work on Buddhist *sanghas* in the West, little has explored the extent to which these reflect the diversity of the population from which they are drawn.

This chapter considers possible causes for the present lack of diversity within the Western *sangha* of convert Buddhists. Its suggestions arise from comparing the processes through which Western Buddhism has been transmitted into the West, particularly the United States and the United Kingdom, with the social and religious histories of black diaspora communities in these countries. It then outlines some strategies being deployed by faith communities of those who have converted to Buddhism (Western Buddhist convert *sanghas*) to encourage wider ethnic and cultural diversity.

Modes of Buddhist transmission to the West

Buddhism in the West is generally described as falling under two categories. The first is that practiced by Asian immigrants to the West and is generally described as "ethnic Buddhism." The other is that of people indigenous to the West, predominantly white European, who have converted to Buddhism. They are generally referred to as Western Buddhists, European Buddhists, or "white Buddhists."[1]

However, this two-fold model is difficult to apply to the issue under consideration because of its assumption of two distinct and internally homogeneous groups – one largely Asian, the other predominantly white

European. Because of this tacit presumption, it is difficult to use this model to explore any differential impact of Buddhism on the wide range of ethnic communities within the West, particularly its long-standing diaspora communities from Africa, the Caribbean and Asia.[2] This model has also been questioned for other reasons, leading to discussions about possible alternatives.[3]

An alternative three-fold model has been suggested by Nattier,[4] based on her understanding of how religions come to new locations and communities. She categorizes modes of transmission of new religious traditions as "import," "export" and "baggage."

The "import" mode is more "demand-driven." Here an individual actively seeks the new tradition, initially encountering it through travel abroad, reading, or visits from an indigenous teacher. In the "export" mode, individuals initially encounter the tradition through missionary activities of the new group. Faith communities in the export mode therefore develop through proselytizing by the new tradition. The "baggage" mode of transmission applies where groups of immigrants carry their religious traditions to the new location. Here religion is seen as a means of support and of maintaining identity, with little, if any, missionary activity taking place, although outsiders may come to be part of the community through, for example, intermarriage.

Nattier argues that "import" Buddhism in the West requires sufficient money and leisure time to operate as a mode of transmission, and describes it as "a Buddhism of the privileged, attracting those who have the time, the inclination, and the economic opportunity to devote themselves to strenuous (and sometimes expensive) meditation training." On this basis, she refers to it as "elite Buddhism" because "the primary common feature of this group is not its ethnicity or sectarian affiliation, but its class background." She observes that "in North America Buddhist groups of this type have a variety of sectarian connections, but most are affiliated with a form of Tibetan Buddhism, Vipassana or Zen."[5]

Sōka Gakkai is seen as the group that best falls under the category of "export Buddhism" and to have achieved a more diverse range of membership through proselytizing activity. Nattier therefore terms it and other such groups as "evangelical Buddhism." Where others have come to the United States as immigrants, but unlike "evangelical Buddhists" not primarily for religious reasons, faith communities developed through the "baggage" traditions that they bring with them are referred to as "ethnic Buddhism."

According to Nattier's model, Western Buddhist convert *sanghas* would largely consist of elite and evangelical Buddhist groups, and her observations, particularly those on elite Buddhism, may in part account for the low level of representation of black diaspora communities in these faith communities. However, there may also be utility in using the model further to consider the historical and social circumstances that may have affected the impact of Buddhism on black diaspora communities. These may give a greater sense of the situation from the perspective of diaspora communities of the accessibility and the relevance of Buddhism for them.

Western sanghas and minority communities

During the nineteenth century, Buddhism was carried west as a result of colonization and the imposition of spheres of influence in Asia.[6] Interest in Buddhism developed mainly in the upper and middle classes, who had access to Asian literature in translations. From the early nineteenth century to the 1880s, no Asian Buddhist missionaries are reported, so Buddhism in its early days was very much an "import religion" in America.[7]

Buddhist sympathizers from Christian backgrounds were accustomed to liberal, nonconformist traditions. Of those ethnic minorities in the West who were Christian, the majority had come to be involved in Christianity through evangelical sections of the church that tended to be more critical of Buddhism than sympathetic to it. Interaction between people of color, particularly African Americans, and Buddhist sympathizers would also have been limited by the social conditions of racism at the time. In the United States, the initial promise of the Civil War and the period of Reconstruction was followed by a bleaker period of decreasing prospects for racial harmony and justice. As Timothy Fulop observes:

> The last twenty-five years of the nineteenth-century have appro-
> priately gone down in African-American history as "the Nadir."
> Disenfranchisement and Jim Crow laws clouded out any rays of
> hope that Reconstruction had bestowed in the American South.
> Darwinism and phrenology passed on new "scientific" theories of
> black inferiority, and the old racial stereotypes of blacks as beasts
> abounded in American society. The civil, political, and educational
> rights of black Americans were greatly curtailed, and lynching
> reached all-time highs in the 1890s.[8]

The practice of segregation extended even to religious institutions. The prevailing attitude toward race relations in the United States was described by Fannie Barrier Williams, the only woman in the small African-American delegation invited to the World's Parliament of Religions in 1893 in these terms:

> At present there seems to be no ethical attitude in public opinion
> toward our colored citizens. White men and women are careless
> and meanly indifferent about the merits and rights of colored men

and women. The white man who swears and the white man who prays are alike contemptuous about the claims of colored men.[9]

In the United Kingdom during that period – although there was no legalized segregation of black people from white people – an informal, yet significant, color bar did operate. This was also a period of significant racial tensions, with organized attacks on black communities in Cardiff and Liverpool.[10]

People of color would likewise have been underrepresented in the the forums where interest in Buddhism initially developed. Although some Buddhist sympathizers took a progressive stance on many social issues, issues of anti-black racism in the United States and United Kingdom were not generally a focus of their attention. Thomas Tweed suggests that in America, "although Euro-American Buddhists challenged the dominant social, political, and economic patterns in various ways, their dissent was most fundamentally cultural."[11]

Similar factors were to come into play during the next significant wave of interest in Buddhism in the West during the 1960s and 1970s. The 1960s saw a new wave of interest in Eastern religions as part of the counter-cultures of that period[12] following the activities of the "Beats" in the 1950s.[13] However, those attracted to Eastern spirituality were but one of a myriad of groups among the counter-cultures of the 1960s period. Some of these groupings were antipathetic to one another, having significant differences in their views about the strategies to be deployed in order to achieve social change. Paul Heelas suggests that:

> one can think of the counter-culture in terms of three main orientations: that directed at changing the mainstream (for example, the political activists engaged in civil rights or anti-Vietnam demonstrations); that directed at rejecting mainstream disciplines to live the hedonistic life (the "decadent" world of "sex, drugs and rock-and-roll"); and that directed at finding ways of life which serve to nurture the authentic self (for example, by taking "a journey to the East").[14]

Each of these parts of the 1960s' counter-cultures had different appeal for different ethnic groups, with black people forming only a small minority of those "rejecting mainstream disciplines" and "looking to the East for Enlightenment." Hence once again, because of their location within society, black people formed a minority of those who were attracted to Buddhism. Furthermore, given that one of the principal ways that new religious movements spread is through word of mouth,[15] this would have been another factor working against the introduction of Buddhism to black communities. The effect observed for Buddhism can also be seen in other "Eastern" traditions, such as Hinduism, that were also gaining greater profile during the 1960s and 1970s. As in Buddhism, most of those converting have been white, middle-class individuals.

The issue of racial discrimination also gained significant prominence in the 1960s with the civil rights movement and the emergence of Black Power in the United States. Post-war black immigrants to the United Kingdom also found themselves at the receiving end of intense racial discrimination, particularly in employment, education, and housing.[16] Black people in the United Kingdom found themselves inspired by the anti-racist movements in the United States and sought to form similar organizations there. In both the United States and the United Kingdom, black-led faith communities continued to play a key role in supporting anti-racist activity, as well as giving black people a sense of identity and social support.

Religious traditions of communities of color

In the late nineteenth and early twentieth centuries, minority Christians tended to belong to denominations different from those in which a critique of Christianity was leading whites to embrace Buddhism.[17] Black communities developed their own "creole" traditions that permitted expression of their original culture and their perspective on their particular historical and social situations.[18] Such creole traditions were, and continue to be, significantly different from conventional Christianity.[19]

For black people of African descent another key factor in these creole traditions is what Long refers to as "the meaning of the image and historical reality of Africa."[20] Long mentions how, during slavery:

one was isolated from any self-determined legitimacy in the society of which one was a part and was recognized by one's physiological characteristics. This constituted a complexity of experience revolving around the relationship between one's physical being and one's origins. So even if he had no conscious memory of Africa, the image of Africa played an enormous part in the religion of the black man. ... Even among religious groups not strongly nationalistic the image of Africa and Ethiopia still has relevance.[21]

The significance of Africa suggests that, whereas some in the 1960s' counter-culture would have sought out Asian religions, many blacks would have been more likely to look to Africa for a sense of meaning. We can see this, for example, in the influence of Rastafarianism in the United Kingdom during the 1970s.[22]

The final key difference that may impact on "pushes" and "pulls" would be differences related to the level of religious commitment of ethnic minorities compared to that of whites. Findings from the *Fourth National Survey of Ethnic Minorities* in the United Kingdom[23] suggest that this is a key area where "minority groups manifest a cultural dynamic which is at least partly at odds with native British trends." Though the number of regular churchgoers in Britain is decreasing, Modood *et al.* found in their survey that nearly 20 percent of Caribbean people, a third of Indians and African-Asians, and two-thirds of Pakistani and Bangladeshi respondents – compared to 5 per cent of white people – aged 16 to 34 reported that religion was very important to the way in which they live their lives. The survey reported that "non-white Anglicans are three times more likely than white Anglicans to attend church weekly, and well over half of the members of black-led churches do so"; furthermore, "black-led churches are a rare growth point in contemporary Christianity." This suggests that a significant proportion of black people of African and Asian descent are already firmly ensconced in a religious tradition.

However, the survey also observed that as many Caribbean people as white people do not have any religion and that "the general trend down the generations within every ethnic group is for younger people to be less connected to a religion than their elders (though perhaps to become more like their elders as they age)."[24] This would suggest that Buddhism is more likely to appeal to the younger generation of black people than to people in the older generation. But what current "pushes" and "pulls," arising from the way that Buddhism has developed, would there be for members of these communities?

Issues of cultural and social relevance

Buddhism in the West has largely developed as an "import" tradition, and it is useful to consider its aspects as a religious tradition in this respect. Key influences on the development of Buddhism in the West have been the notions of individualism, autonomy, and self-reliance[25] that Tweed describes as:

> that call for mature self-regulation that echoed in the writings of Protestant reformers like Martin Luther, Enlightenment thinkers like Immanuel Kant, and Romantic writers like Emerson. It found expression in various areas of American life. It has been associated with life on the frontier. It was evident in the economic sphere ... [and] the religious sphere... This individualism ... became associ-

ated with Buddhism and affirmed by a number of American promoters of the religion.[26]

Such notions of individualism continue to have a strong influence on the way Buddhism is approached by Westerners yet contrast with the ways in which people from black communities are more likely to perceive themselves.[27] Victor Hori, in considering the differences between "Western Buddhists" and "ethnic Buddhists," suggests that notions of the person differ radically for "Westerners" (presumably European people) and non-Westerners, with Westerners being more likely to see the person as an autonomous individual, and non-Westerners viewing the person as a "nexus of social relation."[28] This leads to non-Westerners' – and, I would argue, black and minority ethnic people – seeing themselves in terms of their family and community relationships compared to majority ethnic people.

Such cultural differences may not be identified by those seeking to promote Buddhism in the West, meaning that their implications are often not realized. For example, in the development of a Buddhist approach to Western psychotherapy, the considerable body of work on black and minority ethnic people and mental health is often not taken into account.[29] This reflects a larger problem with the new scholarship on Buddhism in the West. Only recently have scholars begun to consider issues of multiculturalism and ethnicity in treating varieties of western Buddhism with eastern Buddhism.[30]

The development of "engaged Buddhism" offers new opportunities to address issues of ethnicity and race, especially as many of those involved in Buddhism in America were also active in the civil rights movement of the 1960s. However, apart from the efforts of the Sōka Gakkai, race and cultural issues have not figured prominently in engaged Buddhism.[31] In contrast, Christian churches have decades of experience addressing issues of racial disadvantage and discrimination, which has given rise to a considerable body of theological work and reflection.

Furthermore, many of the issues that socially engaged Buddhism has embraced, such as human rights, ecology, and peace have been less pressing to communities of color than criminal justice, community safety, education, and access to quality healthcare and employment. Hence, socially engaged Buddhists and members of black communities are generally unlikely to be working in the same arenas.

Communities of color and engaged Buddhists are also more likely to approach similar issues from different vantage points. For example, with respect to the environment, black communities have been less involved than engaged Buddhists in ecology campaigns that emphasize the need for conservation.[32] On the other hand, communities of color have been more involved in campaigns against environmental racism, such as cases of dumping of toxic waste in poorer localities with a high population of black residents. Responses to racial diversity issues by Western Buddhists have tended to be the exception rather than the rule, even within the engaged Buddhist tradition.

Sōka Gakkai and diversity

The Sōka Gakkai movement has a considerably broader band of member-ship than other Buddhist traditions.[33] In the first study to examine racial diversity within Sōka Gakkai International (SGI) – or any other Western Buddhist group – David Chappell estimates that the overall proportion of people of color in Sōka Gakkai was almost three times that for the United States population as a whole (12.7 percent in the general US population; 34.6 percent in the sample).[34] From his survey of Sōka Gakkai district leaders in major cities, Chappell concludes that "[g]iven the failure of other Buddhist groups to attract black membership, the most striking achievement of SGI-USA is its success in breaking down the color barrier."

Chappell suggests that SGI-USA has attracted this diversity by various means. In some cities, personal example had led to racial diversity in groups' leadership and membership. Many members were attracted to the movement by the social support that they had received from SGI members; "they found a practice that enabled them to improve their attitude and circumstances, that gave them a purpose that was larger than themselves, and that involved them in working with and helping others." The diversity is also seen to result from the "aggressive evangelism" that took place during the 1960s and 1970s.

Jane Hurst suggests other causes of Sōka Gakkai's appeal to minority groups:

> Sōka Gakkai's teaching of Nichiren Buddhism offers hope for individuals through accessing the power of the Gohonzon by chanting *Nam-myōhō-renge-kyō*. Thus minority Sōka Gakkai members can experience its ethos of individual power, the freedom to change one's life no matter what one's circumstances, and the support of the mission for world peace. Nichiren Buddhism's ethos is enlightened self-interest. As a practitioner improves his or her own karma and creates positive cause for positive effects, the world itself can become more peaceful and "a better place." These are very American values experienced by minority Nichiren Buddhists in a nontraditional way. It makes sense that Nichiren Buddhism's unusual approach to these values should be embraced

by minority groups often ignored or rejected by mainstream American society.[35]

This finding of the impact of chanting is also echoed in the studies of Chappell[36] and Wilson and Dobbelaere of SGI-UK.[37]

Chappell also observes the strong, high-profile stance that SGI's President Daisaku Ikeda has taken on issues of diversity. Though Ikeda has stated that the concept of race is "pernicious," "false," and an "artificially constructed idea," at the same time he has stated that "the most pressing problem facing the United States on the home front is that of racial discrimination." Ikeda has championed key figures working for the civil rights of black people, notably Nelson Mandela and Rosa Parks. This two-fold strategy of regarding race as primarily having no significance while recognizing aspects of racial discrimination and their impact in society is similar to that taken by many black churches.[38] For example, in her ethnographic study of a largely African-Caribbean Pentecostal church in Birmingham, England, Nicole Toulis found that members regarded themselves more as Christians than as black.[39] The predominantly black nature of the church was seen by participants to signify the need for greater evangelism within the community. Toulis suggests that the primacy given to religious identity by the Pentecostalists enabled them to address racial discrimination from the wider society. In a similar vein, Chappell found that:

> Several Sōka Gakkai members refused to give any ethnic or racial identification on the questionnaire I distributed in 1997. Others asserted that one reason they were members was because SGI-USA ignored issues of race, but affirmed the solidarity of humans as equally bodhisattvas of the earth, each with a buddha-nature. For example, one district leader who had practiced since 1972 identified her race as the "human race," but her culture as "Black, Native American, Japanese," and her social role as "bodhisattva," which she claimed as central in her life. When asked for another factor important in her identity, she listed "character."[40]

This suggests that black members find benefits from their membership in Sōka Gakkai similar to those obtained by members of "black churches."

As part of its high-profile stance on diversity issues in the United States, Sōka Gakkai has developed diversity committees that function at both national and local levels to consider minority issues and ensure that minorities have a voice within the broader movement.[41] Workshops to address diversity issues from a Buddhist perspective are also conducted as part of a process of "sustained compassionate dialogue".[42]

The situation with Sōka Gakkai in the United Kingdom, however, is significantly different. Though Sōka Gakkai is observed to be considerably more diverse than other Buddhist groups, there is no formal structure to consider diversity issues as such. There are, however, heritage groups for South Asians, Africans, and Caribbeans, which are organized to help new members of different ethnic backgrounds become integrated into the movement.[43] This approach to diversity echoes the general approach taken by Western Buddhists in the United Kingdom where, despite a significant level of engaged Buddhism and a generally sympathetic stance toward diversity, work is not taking place on a similar scale to that in the United States.[44]

Four approaches to diversity

Work on the links between Western Buddhism and ethnic diversity within other *sanghas* is very much in its infancy, mostly occurring during the last five years. So far, *ad hoc*, practitioner-driven initiatives have predominated, but few groups have addressed the challenge. The initiatives fall under four main categories, with examples given below. Because many of these initiatives are in their early stages, only a preliminary assessment can be made.

Raising awareness

Education on issues of diversity in Buddhism has been spearheaded by public talks, articles in Buddhist publications, and groups that seek to raise practitioners' awareness and to encourage debate. One example was the special issue in the American Buddhist magazine *Tricycle* on "Dharma, Diversity and Race" in 1994, which included contributions on Buddhists of color practicing in the *sangha* and articles on the differences between ethnic Buddhism and western Buddhism by bell hooks, Victor Hori and Rick Fields.[45] The Buddhist Peace Fellowship (BPF) magazine *Turning Wheel* also recently had a special issue on this topic.[46]

So far, the level of debate has been general, with discussions of practitioners' attitudes and personal awareness, but little theoretical discussion of the larger issue of Buddhism and race. In a recent issue of *Tricycle*, an African-American *Dzogchen* practitioner, Charles Johnson reflects on how Martin Luther King's vision of "beloved community" was "a sangha by another name."[47] He suggests that Buddhist practices could enable African-Americans to transcend "the internalized racial conflict" that W. E. B. DuBois termed "double consciousness," arising from discrimination against black people in American society. Johnson also suggests that Buddhist practices can enable blacks to let go of "fabricated, false sense of self positions" arising from "samsaric illusions" around race and "all the essentialist conceptions of difference that have caused so much human suffering and mischief since the eighteenth century."

Another way that awareness is being raised is through diversity work-shops. Sala Steinbach, a black Vipassana leader in California points out that groups may often think that one workshop is sufficient.[48] "It's just the beginning," she warns; "It's so important to follow through." She also notes the risk of burnout on account of being one of the few black leaders in a predominantly white *sangha* and being seen as "the authority" on diversity issues. But she also acknowledges the difficulties of remaining silent. Dharmacharini Muditasri, a black woman member of the Friends of the Western Buddhist Order (FWBO), based in Britain, observes that some *sanghas* act as though "colour doesn't matter" and imply that whiteness as an invisible norm. She makes a similar observation of the dilemmas involved for black people entering the *sangha*:

> Confronted with differences or conflict, a black woman is likely to have one of two responses. She can remain silent, seeming to concur with the 'colour-blind' approach, and avoid standing out. Fear of acknowledging her difference, or weariness of the role of educator, is often at the bottom of this silence... Another equally unhelpful response is the exact opposite. Here, one becomes the centre of attention by highlighting every cultural disparity, thus becoming the group's educator on issues connected with black people... Ideally a middle way needs to be found between these two extremes.[49]

Finding such a middle way is facilitated when all *sangha* members take ownership of diversity issues rather than seeing them solely as the respon-sibilities of black people who want to become involved. One example of such good practice is the "Healing Racism in our *Sanghas*" group that was started in 1998 by BPF. It operates on an ongoing basis and was formed after it was found that:

> many People of Color do not feel comfortable in our Western *sanghas*. Too often People of Color feel isolated, exoticized and disillusioned when they find that Western Buddhist *sanghas* suffer from the same unconscious, institutionalized racism that American society at large suffers from." The group states, "We proceed from the understanding that there are already People of Color who are interested in Buddhism. Our goal is not to recruit People of Color, but to make our *sanghas* more open and welcoming for people of all racial and ethnic groups who are seeking a place to practice."[50]

The BPF is sponsoring a year-long training and curriculum-development course on "Buddhists Unlearning Racism." In their guidelines for BASE programs for organizing social action placements, BPF recommends that groups discuss racism and other forms of discrimination. Although the developing debate is welcome, it tends currently to focus on instances of racism at the micro- and small-group level. It appears that issues of institutionalized racism from larger organizations within society that have such significant impact on black people's education, employment opportunities, social welfare, and access to criminal justice are yet to receive more detailed or thorough examination and analysis by socially engaged Buddhists.

Peer support and practice groups

Some Buddhist organizations offer forums where people of color can explore issues of ethnic diversity, discrimination, and disadvantage, and their impact as Buddhist practitioners. In addition to those organized by Sōka Gakkai, BPF has established a peer-support group for racial minorities called the "People of Color *Sangha*."[51] One participant described its monthly meetings as a "watering hole," a place where "your shoulders can come down a little bit, because you're not the only one. This gives tremendous support for my dharma practice."[52] This would seem to echo the point made by American Vipassana teacher Lewis Woods when he suggested the creation of "a predominantly African American meditative community, where black folks can go to study and practice the dharma without having to deal with racism and Eurocentric assumptions, attitudes and behaviours."[53] There are similar groups meeting in other parts of the United States, including cyber-*sanghas* such as the e-mail groups for black Buddhists and Buddhists of color.[54]

Targeted outreach initiatives

Some programs are targeted at black communities to encourage their participation and involvement in Western Buddhist convert *sanghas*. For example, for several years, the Friends of the Western Buddhist Order's main center in London has organized specific events for black people who are newcomers to meditation. Like its program of specialized events for gay and lesbian newcomers, the FWBO's outreach to racial minorities different groups has had a good response. So far the majority of those attracted have been African-Caribbean women and South Asian men. The center has now started to organize specific events for black men in order to redress the balance. It also organized a day event as a refresher for black newcomers to celebrate the African-American festival Kwanzaa at Christmas. Events for black people are generally organized at the beginner's level in order to assist the eventual participation of those choosing to take things further in the mainstream *sangha*. This would appear to echo the approach taken by Sōka Gakkai in its 'heritage groups' mentioned earlier. In the United States, specific retreats for people of color are organized by the Spirit Rock meditation center in California; scholarships are provided to those who cannot afford to attend. According to Sala Steinbach, these appear to have increased the number of people of color attending Spirit Rock events.[55]

Social action programs

Some Buddhist Peace Fellowship programs are oriented to minority communities. For example, its Buddhist Alliance for Social Engagement (BASE) placements have included a doctor's service at a clinic for low-income patients; support counseling to marginalized Latina women in a community center and in a group home for severely emotionally-disturbed pregnant and mothering teenage girls; support to public schools seeking to develop initiatives around equity, diversity, and powerful learning; and the foundation of an urban community garden project. So far BPF reports a moderate level of success in this area, but it reports continuing difficulty in getting more diverse participation because of the low level of ethnic diversity in its membership and the lack of links between ethnic and convert *sanghas*.[56]

Conclusion

Several factors have been suggested as contributing towards the low representation of ethnic and racial minorities in Western Buddhist convert *sanghas*, and these require further exploration. These include the lack of contact and awareness between people of color and Buddhist institutions and the activities that they sponsor. Communities of color and those attracted to Buddhism are not part of the same social networks due to class, religious affiliation, and, in some cases, racial segregation. This means that people of color have not had the same level of access to information about Buddhism as other groups.

Meanwhile members of ethnic and racial minority groups are affiliated with a wide range of prior religious traditions that provide them with social and cultural support. Interest in Buddhism among black communities may therefore be reduced even in cases such as those in which information becomes more readily available; members of black communities may be less likely to participate in Buddhist activities because of prior religious commitments. Age may also be a factor here, with younger people more likely to become involved than their elders.

More research is needed to identify other factors that have an impact on minority participation in Western Buddhist convert *sanghas*. Examples of such factors are economic security and the availability of leisure time, and the effects of social pressures from racism. A black person may wish to visit a Buddhist institution, for example, but feel unable to do so because of fear of racial attack. Black people may also be deterred on account of reasonable concern that they will experience discrimination, whether direct or in the form of "residual insensitivity" from a largely white *sangha*.[57]

Western Buddhists are increasingly practicing in multiracial and multicultural environments. Issues of racial discrimination against black people are also of critical importance, as the debates around the Rodney King and Amadou Diallo cases in the United States and the deaths of Stephen Lawrence and Ricky Reel in the United Kingdom indicate. The Buddhist response developed to these issues, in terms of encouraging more diverse *sanghas* and developing *sanghas*' capacity to respond more fully to issues of diversity and institutionalized racism in the wider community, promises to have growing significance for Buddhism in the West and society at large.

Acknowledgements

I would like to thank Dr. Damien Keown for his helpful comments and encouragement. However, any errors are mine.

Notes

1 Rick Fields, "Confessions of a White Buddhist." *Tricycle: The Buddhist Review* 4, 1 (1994): 24–26 and "Divided Dharma: White Buddhists, Ethnic Buddhists and Racism" in Charles S. Prebish and Kenneth K. Tanaka (eds.), *The Faces of Buddhism in America* (Berkeley, CA: University of California Press 1998), 198–206. Also Kenneth K. Tanaka, "Epilogue: The Colors and Contours of American Buddhism," in Prebish and Tanaka (eds.), op. cit., pp. 287–298.

2 See, for example, Peter Fryer, *Staying Power: The History of Black People in Britain* (London: Pluto Press, 1984) for a history of British black communities since the fifteenth century; Edward W. Said, *Culture and Imperialism*. (London: Vintage, 1994) for a discussion of the interaction and resulting hybridity of Western and Eastern cultures following colonialism; and Mike Phillips and Trevor Phillips, *Windrush: The Irresistible Rise of Rise of Multi-Racial Britain* (London: HarperCollins, 1998) for a discussion of the history of a developing black British identity.

3 Charles S.Prebish, *Luminous Passage: The Practice and Study of Buddhism in America* (Berkeley, Ca: University of California Press, 1999), pp. 57–63.

4 Jan Nattier, "Who is a Buddhist? Charting the Landscape of Buddhist America," in Prebish and Tanaka, op. cit., pp. 183–195.

5 Ibid. p. 189.

6 J. J. Clarke, *Oriental Enlightenment: The Encounter Between Asian and Western Thought* (London: Routledge, 1997), p. 71.

7 Martin Baumann, "Buddhism in the West: Phases, Orders and the Creation of an Integrative Buddhism," *Internationales Asienforum* 27, 3–4 (1996): 345–362.

8 Timothy E. Fulop, "The Future Golden Day of the Race: Millennialism and Black Americans in the Nadir, 1877–1901," in Timothy E. Fulop and Albert J.

Raboteau (eds.), *African-American Religion: Interpretive Essays in History and Culture* (London: Routledge, 1997), p. 230.

9 Fannie Barrier Williams, "What Can Religion Do to Advance the Condition of the American Negro?," in Richard Hughes Seager (ed.), *The Dawn of Religious Pluralism: Voices from the World's Parliament of Religions, 1893* (La Salle, IL: Open Court, 1993), p. 149.

10 Peter Fryer (1994) op. cit., pp. 298–316.

11 Thomas A. Tweed, *The American Encounter with Buddhism 1844–1912: Victorian Culture and the Limits of Dissent* (Bloomington and Indianapolis: Indiana University Press, 1992), p. 88.

12 Martin Baumann (1996), op. cit.

13 Paul Heelas, *The New Age Movement: The Celebration of the Self and the Sacralization of Modernity* (Oxford: Blackwell Publishers, 1996), pp. 49–50.

14 Ibid., p. 51.

15 Lorne Dawson. "Who Joins New Religious Movements and Why: Twenty Years of Research and What We Have Learned," *Studies in Religion/Sciences Religieuses* 25 (1996): 141–161.

16 Mike Phillips and Trevor Phillips, (1998) op. cit. and Peter Fryer (1984), op. cit., pp. 372–386.

17 Thomas Tweed, (1992) op. cit., pp. 92–94.

18 Thomas Tweed, "Night-Stand Buddhists and Other Creatures: Sympathizers, Adherents, and the Study of Religion," in Duncan Ryuuken Williams and Christopher S. Queen (eds.), *American Buddhism: Methods and Findings in Recent Scholarship* (London: Curzon, 1999), pp. 71–90.

19 Charles H. Long, "Perspectives for a Study of African-American Religion in the United States," in Fulop and Raboteau op. cit., pp. 21–35; and Albert J. Raboteau, "African Americans, Exodus, and the American Israel," in David G. Hackett (ed.), *Religion and American Culture: A Reader* (London: Routledge, 1995), pp. 73–86.

20 Charles H. Long (1997) op. cit.

21 Ibid., p. 26.

22 Mike Phillips and Trevor Phillips, (1998) op. cit., pp. 294–297.

23 Tariq Modood, Richard Berthoud, Jane Lakey, James Nazroo, Patten Smith, Satnam Virdee, and Sharon Beishon (eds.), *Ethnic Minorities in Britain: Diversity and Disadvantage* (London: Policy Studies Institute, 1997).

24 Tariq Modood, "Conclusion: Ethnic Diversity and Disadvantage," in Modood *et al.*, (eds.), op. cit., pp. 339–359.

25 Thomas Tweed, (1992) op. cit., pp. 130–132.

26 Ibid. p. 130.

27 Kenneth K. Tanaka (1998) op. cit.; Gil Fronsdal, "Insight Meditation in the United States," in Prebish and Tanaka (eds.), op. cit., pp. 482–495; G. Victor Sogen Hori,"Sweet-and-Sour Buddhism," *Tricycle: The Buddhist Review* 4, 1 (1994): 48–52.

28 Victor Hori, (1994), op. cit.

29 See, for example, Jack Kornfield, "Psychotherapy and Meditation," in *A Path with Heart: A Guide through the Perils and Promises of Spiritual Life* (London: Rider, 1994), pp. 244–253. Though the contributors to Guy Claxton (ed.), *Beyond Therapy: The Impact of Eastern Religions on Psychological Theory and Practice* (London: Wisdom East-West, Grey Series, 1986) note that psychotherapy has developed on the basis of Western models of the mind, they do not go on to consider what implications this has given the diversity of the West, generally approaching the issue in essentialist terms, regarding it as the interface between an "Eastern spiritual tradition" and "Western thought." For

examples of the extensive work that has considered how Western psychothera-
peutic techniques can be adapted to address the needs of ethnic minorities, see
Derald Wing Sue and David Sue, *Counseling the Culturally Different: Theory
and Practice*, 2nd edition (New York: John Wiley & Sons, 1990) and Dinesh
Bhugra and Kamaldeep Bhui, "Psychotherapy for Ethnic Minorities: Issues,
Context and Practice," *British Journal of Psychotherapy* 14, 3 (1998):
310–326.

30 One work that is an exception to this general phenomenon in taking an ethnic
profile of respondents is Coleman's study of Buddhist groups from various
traditions (James William Coleman, "The New Buddhism: Some Empirical
Findings," in Williams and Queen op. cit., pp. 91–99). But generally, even
major studies such as Wilson and Dobbelaere's excellent survey of Sōka Gakkai
in the United Kingdom, (Bryan Wilson and Karel Dobbelaere, *A Time to
Chant: The Soka Gakkai Buddhists in Britain* [Oxford: Clarendon Press,
1994]) – though asking participants for age and employment status – do not
appear to take account of this issue, despite Sōka Gakkai's uniqueness among
sanghas of convert Buddhists for its diversity. Work by Hammond and
Machacek on Sōka Gakkai in the United States also appears to make the same
omission (Philip Hammond and David Machacek. "Supply and Demand: The
Appeal of Buddhism in America," in Willams and Queen, (eds.)., op. cit., pp.
100–114). The recent *Engaged Buddhism in the West* by Christopher S. Queen
(Somerville, MA: Wisdom Publications, 2000) makes a significant contribution
to increasing the visibility of diversity issues within Western Buddhism.

31 Donald Rothberg, "Responding to the Cries of the World: Socially Engaged
Buddhism in North America," in Prebish and Tanaka (eds.)., op. cit., pp.
266–286; Susan Moon, "Activist Women in American Buddhism," in Queen,
op. cit., pp. 246–268.

32 Donald Rothberg, (1998) op. cit.; Stephanie Kaza, "To Save All Beings:
Buddhist Environmental Activism," in Queen, op. cit., pp. 159–183.

33 Jane Hurst, "Nichiren Shoshu and Soka Gakkai in America: The Pioneer
Spirit," in Prebish and Tanaka op. cit., pp. 79–97; Nattier, op. cit.; Wilson and
Dobbelaere, op. cit. p. 43; Kenneth K. Tanaka, op. cit.; David W. Chappell,
"Racial Diversity in the Soka Gakkai," in Queen, op. cit., pp. 184–217.

34 Chappell, op. cit.

35 Hurst, op. cit. p. 90.

36 . Chappell, op. cit.

37 Wilson and Dobbelaere, op. cit., pp. 53–75.

38 Patrick Kalilombe, "Black Christianity in Britain," in Gerrie ter Haar (ed.),
Strangers and Sojourners: Religious Communities in the Diaspora (Leuven:
Peeters, 1998), pp. 173–193.

39 Nicole Rodriguez Toulis, *Believing Identity: Pentecostalism and the Mediation
of Jamaican Ethnicity and Gender in England*(Oxford: Berg, 1997).

40 Chappell, op. cit., p. 196.

41 Aiken, Bill. "Engaged Buddhism and Diversity–An American Perspective," in
*Buddhism in America: Proceedings of the First Buddhism in America
Conference*, Tuttle Publishing, (1998).http//sgi.org/about/buddhism/aiken.html
Chappell, op. cit.

42 Aiken, op. cit.

43 Wilson and Dobbelaere, op. cit., pp. 14–15.

44 SandraBell, "A Survey of Engaged Buddhism in Britain," in Queen, op. cit., pp.
397–422.

45 "Dharma, Diversity and Race," *Tricycle: The Buddhist Review* 4, 1 (Fall
1994).

46 "Diversity in Our Sanghas," *Turning Wheel: Magazine of the Buddhist Peace Fellowship* (Summer 1999), *passim*.
47 Charles. Johnson, "A Sangha by Another Name." *Tricycle: The Buddhist Review* 9, 2 (1999): 43–47 and 110–113.
48 Moon, op. cit.
49 Dharmacharini Muditasri, "Unity in Diversity: A Black Buddhist Speaks," in Dharmacharini Kalyanavaca (ed.), *The Moon and Flowers: A Woman's Path to Enlightenment* (Birmingham: Windhorse Publications, 1997), p. 233.
50 Information available from <http//www.buddhismandracism.org/>
51 Personal communication from Diana Winston, coordinator of Buddhist Alliance for Social Engagement (BASE).
52 Winston, Diana. "Buddhists of Color Sangha," in *Touching Base: A Newsletter for the BASE (Buddhist Alliance for Social Engagement) Community* I, 3 (Fall 1999).
53 Cited in Fields, op. cit., p. 198.
54 These can be found at blackbuddhists@yahoogroups.com and buddhists–of–color@yahoogroups.com> respectively.
55 Moon, op. cit.
56 Personal communication from Diana Winston, co-ordinator of Buddhist Alliance for Social Engagement (BASE).
57 Prebish, op. cit. p. 109.

12

SYMBOL AND NARRATION IN BUDDHIST PRISON MINISTRY

Virginia Cohn Parkum and J. Anthony Stultz

Buddhists from all the major traditions are very active in Western prison ministries, bringing the Dharma to inmates and staff in such varied ways as correspondence, providing books and worship supplies, supporting zendo and other in-prison worship sites, visitation and instruction, offering meditation courses, AIDS hospice work, and legal aid concerning freedom of religion issues.[1] Great difficulties are encountered, however, in obtaining permission to offer the courses or services in prisons and in the severe challenges the prison environment presents all sentient beings.

Giving the teachings in this setting is extremely challenging. The history of Buddhism over 2,500 years has shown that ways of teaching are not so much carved in stone as written in water. Prison chaplains act in the spirit of *The Flower Ornament Scripture* when it advises enlightening beings to practice skill-in-means while "generating great compassion for bad sentient beings who are mean and fixed on error."[2] However, Ken Kraft has asked if, in effect, some ways of presenting the Dharma may muddy the waters: "We must ask, without prejudging the answer: When is the stretch from traditional Buddhism to engaged Buddhism too big?"[3] "When do fresh interpretations, often in the service of engagement, distort Buddhism's past inauthentically?"[4] He specifically asks those active in prison work if it is acceptable to use the Buddha's disciple Angulimala, who had been a murderer, as the patron saint of a modern prison reform movement, i.e. Angulimala, the Buddhist prison chaplaincy organization of Great Britain.[5] This critique may be extended to include the use of other traditional figures with violent or criminal pasts, such as Prince Ajatasatru, Milarepa and the wrathful Fudo as either devotional figures or subjects of teaching stories.

In response to questions about the authenticity of teaching stories and images, Kraft has suggested three guidelines: (1) that they actually are part of the Buddhist literary heritage; (2) that they be used to show aspects of the teachings that they illuminated in the context in which they were first recorded; and (3) that "these wonderful teachings are being shared, and a person does not have to be a Buddhist to use them and benefit from them."[6]

Concerns with authenticity have also been raised in the Buddhist popular media. David Patt writes in *Tricycle*, "What is demanded of those who seek to preserve the authentic teachings is continuous mindfulness of the central values of the tradition, and a present awareness of the context in which we live and practice."[7] However, the Venerable Ajahn Khemadhammo, spiritual director and founder of Angulimala, reminds us all that "behind the exoticism and intellectualization, the need for practical application lies at the core of everything the Buddha said."[8]

The experiences of prison chaplains interviewed for this study put these concerns to a double-edged empirical test:

1 Is the use of hellish-looking images and stories about criminal behavior effective in the prison setting?
2 Are they used in ways that are faithful to their content and intent: are the translation and re-telling accurate and are they used in a way consistent with the Buddha's teaching methodology?[9]

Narration and image in Buddhist prison work

Buddhist prison chaplains must work hard to reach their audience. Pema Chodron, the American teacher of Tibetan Buddhism, notes that sometimes the teachings, coming as they do from unfamiliar cultures, need to be presented in a simple way. We must learn how to speak so that others can hear us rather than causing barriers to go up and ears to close.[10] Parables and stories, with which the Buddha's teachings abound, are a classic way to reach an audience. The Buddha himself taught through conversation. In the *Sermon of the Great Decease* he told his disciples how he attempted to blend into each audience, "becoming a color like unto their color," and "in a voice like unto their voice."[11] William Barbieri asks, "Is there a teacher of ethics who has not on occasion entertained the suspicion that no work of scholarship could ever match the virtuosity of the literary artist in addressing complex moral themes?"[12] In his development of the usefulness of a "narrativist ethics" he finds much potential for religious accounts that incorporate narrative into their ecclesiologies, their church stories.[13] In Asia, rhetoric has consistently been seen as being inseparably interconnected with problems of ethics, psychology, politics, and social relations.[14]

Learning theorist Robert C. Schank notes the power and role of stories as "reminders," enabling people to comprehend events, serving as "the mind's method of coordinating past events with current events to enable generalization and prediction."[15] Finding a relevant past experience that will help make sense of a new experience is at the core of intelligent behavior, Schank writes; human memory being story-based, we easily remember a good story.[16]

Since stories such as that of the serial murderer Angulimala are prominent in the canon, they must be important. The mystery of the symbolic process is basic to the Buddhist conception of reality.[17] Archetypal images, when used under the guidance of a trained prison chaplain, can be very effective in communicating cross-culturally while maintaining their original meaning.

Using art images also has deep roots in Buddhism, as it does in some Western schools of rhetoric. The *ars memorativa* technique employed images in a memory-help system. Rhetoric manuals stressed that an effective memory was a visual memory.[18]

Art can also be revelatory, enabling the viewer to see more deeply within. "The spiritual in art confronts us with what we have forgotten."[19] The symbolic structure of the Buddhist art and literature discussed below can reveal "perceived relationships, or designs, in the phenomena of human life and in the phenomena of the universe, which is our dwelling place."[20] Indeed, the root meaning of "art" is to join or fit together. Buddhism's stories and images of beings who have encountered hellish circumstances, criminal activity, and imprisonment provide a rich heritage upon which all traditions can draw when speaking to people currently facing these very realities.

The great teaching stories: Angulimala

There is perhaps no more intense illustration of the skillful application of traditional imagery to present reality than the red-and-white home page of Great Britain's Angulimala Prison Chaplaincy website.[21] Angulimala writhes in frustration before the serenely sitting Buddha, whom Angulimala had been stalking for hours. The legendary brigand had sought to kill him to complete a gruesome necklace of severed fingers (the meaning of his name) required of him by his sinister guru. Over and over again he had tried to finish the necklace, but he needed one more victim. In the Internet image, bloody hand prints surround him, and one can almost feel his brain squirming like a toad in his skull as he screamed in frustration "Stop, monk, stop!" The moment is captured when the silent traveler halted, turned slowly, and like a compassionate father to his prodigal son, said, "I have stopped, Angulimala, you stop too."[22]

The ancient story appears in the Middle Length Discourses (*Majjhima Nikaya*) of the Pali scriptures, Buddhism's earliest written record. The home page states: "It teaches us that the possibility of Enlightenment may be awakened in the most extreme circumstances." The text provides inspiration for the organization's founding in February, 1985. The Buddha explained his teaching in its simplest and most universal form as "ceasing to do evil, learning to do good, and purifying one's own mind."

Angulimala, converted by the simple words and powerful presence of the Holy One, deeply repented and remained steadfast despite reaping the consequences of his acts. He was distrusted by the villagers, who frequently refused to help him during his alms rounds, pelting him instead with stones. He chose not to react with violence and eventually became an enlightened *arahant*, finally attaining the Way.

The story is ripe with symbols pertinent to people who have committed acts of violence. He was rehabilitated, becoming a productive member of the community in which he lived. The story also clearly teaches that one's actions produce consequences. Spiritual transformation is the core of the story and is another important theme. His birth name was Ahimsaka, "harmless," and he eventually recognized this as indeed his True Nature, his Buddha Nature:

> "Non-harmer" is the name I bear,
> Who was a harmer in the past,
> The name I bear is true today,
> I hurt not any one at all.[23]

Both of these themes were emphasized by Randi Getsushin Brox, a chaplain affiliated with the Dharma Rain Zen Center in Portland, Oregon, as reasons the Angulimala story was so appropriate in her work with death row inmates: "They knew they had to experience the suffering they caused, and many then wanted to reach out to the families they had harmed."[24] She felt the story also resonated deeply in her own life, as did a number of the other chaplains.

Non-harming or nonviolence (*ahimsa*) is at the heart of the Buddha's teachings. That this was Angulimala's birth name symbolizes that from birth we all have Buddha Nature, that we are born with Original Blessing, not Original Sin. Co-author Anthony Stultz, in his twelve years as chaplain and counselor in county, state, and federal prisons in Pennsylvania and Massachusetts, found this teaching very important to prisoners, who feel that they are morally defective. It is an aspect of what Buddhist ministry offers that is distinctly Buddhist. The Judeo-Christian ethic posits an outside being as necessary for entering the good life, and if one does not obey and recognize this, one is condemned forever to Hell. Prisoners already deeply feel such dualism, having often been subjected to situations in which others have the power to satisfy their desires and needs if only they obey (abusive parents, school administrators, prison authorities). They obey until the outside "being" either cannot meet their needs or they are no longer afraid of the power the outside force can exert. Buddhism presents them instead with an inner morality and the teaching that we are all interdependent and interrelated. This leads to the realization that the power to not harm lies within themselves, it is a decision made from the realization of this interdependence, from the "conversion experience" to the feeling of *bodhichitta*, of their at-oneness with all beings. In the liturgy he developed for the Blue Mountain Lotus Society of Harrisburg, Pennsylvania, Stultz states these ideas in the form of moral precepts: "We take complete responsibility for our own life and all of our actions," and, "We affirm our own being and acknowledge it as a path to awakening and freedom." Angulimala recognizes all this as he seeks the truth of his original name, his Buddha Nature, good and pure. For prisoners, this recognition is a liberating experience.

In turn, Angulimala's vow of non-harming is at the heart of the story's effectiveness in the prison setting. Here, with these particular people, vows are the glue that holds the teachings together, according to Stultz. A prisoner wrote: "Recently I found myself on the receiving end of a physical assault during which I chose not to fight back … and only block his blows. This is in no small part due to my vow not to harm anyone."[25]

Many Buddhist chaplains offer Angulimala as a great example for prisoners. He transgressed. His response to anxiety was to murder people to gain his goal. He is an example of someone who seemed beyond redemption, beyond rehabilitation. A real patron saint for prisoners needs to be someone who has conquered a problem. A patron saint image should not cut anyone out. It should draw everyone back into the fold. People's negative response to him could have turned him back into a murderer. This is certainly the way many people view those in prison: rehabilitate them but don't let them live in my backyard; let's rehabilitate them but I'm not going to hire them; they're not going to date my daughter. He exemplifies the hard fact that just because you're awakened, everyone isn't going to love you, a reality former inmates have to face daily. He suffered but was free from continuing it within himself and from extending it to others. The Buddha's teaching to Angulimala, and Angulimala's message to those who have committed criminal acts is: "I can stop. I can change the way things manifest and how I respond to them. From now on I will bring love and creativity to life instead of harm and destructiveness."

Prisoners are looking for a new identity, a new way of understanding themselves. They loath themselves, and society has labeled them as loathsome. The Angulimala story and the accompanying teachings show that you can change your identity positively and choose to act out of this new identity. In Sensei Stultz's experience, recidivism was more related to whether the person decided to have a new identity than to participation in education or other help programs. The decision to change themselves is what helped them deal with whatever came along when they were released.

The Reverend Karuna Dharma of the International Buddhist Meditation Center, Los Angeles, has corresponded with close to 1,000 prisoners throughout the United States. She uses Angulimala frequently and finds no problem with using stories that involve some violence. She often uses them in her letters, "as prisoners are often quite frank, and violence has been a part of their lives." Such stories are appropriate "as long as you understand where the prisoner is coming from and they understand where you are coming from."[26]

It should be noted that even many early sangha members feared criminals and did not all respond favorably to the Buddha's welcoming Angulimala. The *Mahavagga*, part of the *Vinaya Pitaka* or monastic rules, states that after Angulimala, no one may enter the order who wears the emblems of criminal deeds can be a monk (I.41), has escaped from jail (I.42), been punished by scourging or branding (I.44–45), or identified as a robber (I.43), debtor (I.46), or runaway slave (I.47).[27] This would seem to preclude many who benefit from Buddhist prison work today. However, this collection of rules for the Hinayana monastics was composed for those who were leaving society and taking on a new identity as a community narrowly devoted to the path of the *arahant*. The Theravadin communities developed a canon law that was probably written in the second century bce. As a rejection of lay life, this canon was very strict and replete with sectarian bias, distortions, additions, and omissions. In time, a schism developed which eventually led to the creation of the Mahayana community, which had a more lay-oriented approach to the Dharma.[28]

Milarepa, Queen Vaidehi, and Prince Ajatasatru

The Vajrayana tradition of Tibet, which grew out of the Mahayana tradition in India in the seventh and eighth centuries ce, contains the story of the famous saint Milarepa, 1040–1123 ce. Milarepa had been a sorcerer but sought the transformative teachings of the Dharma from Marpa, after being plagued with feelings of remorse and guilt when he caused the death of thirty-five relatives with his black magic. Marpa forced him to undergo terrible ordeals to cleanse his negative momentum, driving him to the point of suicide. After twelve years in contemplative retreat in the high Himalayas, he became a perfectly enlightened adept. He then traveled all over Tibet, teaching thousands, singing his profound teachings in a folksong format. He serves as an example of an ordinary man who became a great sinner and then through sincere practice and great ordeals became enlightened and a great teacher.[29]

Milarepa's tale is perhaps not quite as appropriate for use with prisoners as Angulimala's. Angulimala made an adult decision and repeated his actions over and over, calculating each murderous act and ignoring the pleas of his victims for mercy. Milarepa's crimes were motivated by revenge against a wicked uncle who had mistreated his widowed mother. His remorse and quest for inner transformation contrast with Angulimala's sudden conversion by the Buddha. Milarepa is very popular among the many prisoners served by today's Vajrayana ministries. One wrote of a new prison study group: "We decided upon the name Milarepa Buddhist Community because the example of Je Mila is especially dear and relevant to us."[30]

Deeply significant to the Jodo-Shinshu, or Pure Land tradition of Japan is the story of Queen Vaidehi and her son Prince Ajatasatru, who lived during the Buddha's lifetime. Her narrative is contained in the Meditation Sutra (*Kanmuryoju-kyo*), one of the three Pure Land Sutras, known as the Sutra on Meditation on the Buddha of Immeasurable Life.

King Bimbisara, a patron of the Buddha, and his Queen Vaidehi were imprisoned by their son Prince Ajatasatru, who wanted to become king himself. Ajatasatru was under the sway of the Buddha's scheming cousin Devadatta, who wished to harm the work of the Buddha. When Queen Vaidehi begged the Buddha for help, he sent two disciples, one of whom was his beloved cousin and personal attendant, Ananda. Then the Buddha himself appeared, visiting the Queen in prison like today's prison chaplains. The Queen prostrated herself, asking to be shown a land of no sorrow and no affliction where she could be reborn. The Buddha then taught her the method of visualizing the Pure Land.

Prince Ajatasatru's story, as set forth in the Great Nirvana Sutra, continues as King Bimbasara starves to death in prison. Rather than enjoying the fruits of kingship, Ajatasatru begins to feel remorse, and eventually, when his body breaks out in painful sores, he cries, "I always thought hell was something distant and in the future but it is the most terrible of hells in which I am now living."[31]

In agony, the prince went to the Buddha for help. The Buddha gave him teachings on interdependence, karma, and the mind's power to create a living hell for those imprisoned in their own deeds. "If you cannot be freed from this crime, nobody – including I, Sakyamuni – can be free. Nobody can find peace – not even the Buddha!"[32] Recognizing his ability to repent, Ajatasatru found the peace he sought and vowed to help others do likewise, whatever pain it might cause himself. He became a model for those who feel they have "rootless faith" – who, though never having responded to such words previously and feeling themselves unable to control themselves, mentally or physically, can find their faith awakened and their hearts and minds transformed. The Buddha joyfully exclaimed, "Ajatasatru, thanks to you, future generations will receive faith from me, the hopeless will be rescued, the helpless freed."[33] These are inspiring words indeed to those who suffer and to the chaplains and other teachers who minister to them – a story of transformation and skillful means.

Shinran Shonin (1173–1262 ce), the founder of the Jodo-Shinshu school, held these stories in deepest regard. "The Mahayana Nirvana Sutra, in which Ajatasatru's story is told, is the only sutra besides the

Larger Pure Land Sutra where I say Namu-amida-butsu [the *nembutsu,* "Praise to the Buddha"] at the end of every chapter." The Reverend Shoji Matsumoto, a Pure Land chaplain today, declares that "everything you want to know about yourself is in this story."[34]

Shinran himself was treated as a criminal during his lifetime. The Judo-Shinshu tradition was being persecuted, and in 1207 its leaders, including Shinran, were banished, deprived of their monkhood, and given secular names. Some were condemned to death. For Shinran, Queen Vaidehi was a model of steadfastness under difficult circumstances and of single-minded devotion.[35]

The Queen's story was illustrated in the great Taima Mandala, a tapestry based on the Meditation Sutra. Woodblock copies were made and distributed throughout Japan and China. Copies were widely used as "etoki," explanations of the teachings by picture.[36] Even those who break the five precepts and constantly pollute their streams of birth and death are liberated, as was Queen Vaidehi, in a single moment upon encountering the wisdom of the Buddha. Her example also showed that one need not be a monastic for this practice of praising the Buddha's name (*nembutsu*), but the practice is available to all lay people regardless of status or condition, she herself being in prison. She is mentioned in Shinran's *Shoshinge,* chanted daily by Shin Buddhists. Her story accompanied Japanese-American Shin Buddhists imprisoned unjustly in internment camps in the American West during World War II.[37]

Bodhisattva stories: Fudo, Kannon, and Jizo

Buddhist prison chaplains often use devotional figures of three bodhisattvas who display wrathful aspects or appear in hell. The bodhisattva images may be considered as archetypes, "fundamental models of dominant psychic aspects of the enlightening beings, according to Daniel Taigon Leighton."[38] Archetypes themselves are "Crystallizations of components of the psyche, and catalysts to self-understanding."[39] They can serve as models or guides for the beholder's own life, when introduced by the appropriate teachings.

The Japanese Fudo-Myo-o (Sanskrit: *Achalanatha Vidya Raja*) is the Immovable King of Light, the wrathful aspect of Dainichi (Vairochana) Buddha. His visage is fierce, with glaring eyes and fangs. Holding a sword and rope, often wearing ankle chains, and sometimes surrounded by flames, Fudo is a very formidable figure. Correctly presented, he represents steadfast will to enlightenment, standing with determination in the flames of ignorance, anger, and greed. With training, the flames may come to represent to the student the cleansing fire of Truth. The ankle chains represent his vow to stay in hell and help all beings pass through safely. The rope signifies the precepts, and the diamond-bladed *vajra,* sword of wisdom, cuts through all delusion. He offers these tools for people to use, without force or coercion. In the words of the Hymn to Achalanatha, "By our own wills and vigilance, may we cut our fetters away."[40]

Chaplain Stultz, who uses a small devotional statue of Fudo in his prison work, finds it extremely relevant and meaningful. The ankle chains represent Fudo's determination to stay in a hellish environment to save beings. In turn, the Fudo image helped prisoners transform their notion of chains as something imposed from the outside to one of determination to maintain their True Nature in the hellish prison environment – to transform their prison from a penal colony to a spiritual colony.

The image of Fudo in the flames of hell was also very powerful to the inmates. The hell for them was not necessarily just the prison environment. It was often their early life, the environment they came out of, the knowledge of the pain and suffering they caused others. By identifying their new identity as a bodhisattva with their own Buddha Nature, they were able to embrace Fudo as one who shared their own sufferings.

Fudo is a strong figure for difficult times and situations. He represents resolution, firm commitment and resolve, a person who has made a vow and lives that vow regardless of the cost. As the inmates say, "There is no BS about him." Some of these prisoners will never get out, have a family life, and a well-paying job. So the ability to accept the reality of being in that hell and turn it into something good, something that protects and nurtures what is whole, is exceedingly important. Not causing harm is always a choice. Fudo makes us aware of that. Fudo reminds us all that we must make a choice in this respect to have an immovable mind. The Reverend Kyogen Carlson, of the Dharma Rain Zen Center, also uses Fudo with positive results. For him, Fudo represents cutting through self-deception and confusion wherever these arise. His will to be steadfast and vigilant in the midst of all conditions has special meaning in the context of prison.[41] Again, Fudo "reminds us all to have immovable resolve to be clear-eyed and accepting."[42]

In contrast, two chaplains felt Fudo's image was too intense. One prisoner asked Sensei Geoffrey Shugen Arnold of Zen Mountain Monastery, New York, head of the National Buddhist Prison Sangha, "Why are you bringing that in here? We have enough of that in our lives." Arnold no longer uses Fudo.[43]

Another minister, who does not use Fudo but does use the Angulimala story, felt inmates may misinterpret the wrathful-looking images. Sometimes published descriptions are themselves inaccurate, such as one calling Fudo a "scourge of the sinful."[44] In one instance of Japanese history an unusual version showing Fudo running, sword held behind and high, was supposedly used by Emperor Kameyama in a prayer for deliverance from the Mongol armies.[45] However, most who have used Fudo were effusive in praising his effectiveness in the prison setting. Carlsen responded that in overemphasizing on the passive, we throw out something of value if we are not careful. It seems that the choice of stories and images requires of bodhisattva practice of skillful means, as some are not suitable for particular teachers or students.

The Japanese Jizo (Sanskrit: *Kshitigarbha*; Chinese: *Ti-ts'ang*) is another bodhisattva mentioned by prison chaplains. One of his aspects is that of the bodhisattva who saves beings even from the depths of hell. Jizo vowed to assume whatever forms and employ whatever means necessary to deliver all suffering creatures, wherever they reside (*Sutra of the Past Vows of Kshitigarbha Bodhisattva*). In paintings he is often shown in hell, standing by and comforting the afflicted, working ceaselessly to release beings from their sufferings. Hell is not seen as a permanent, eternal destiny. Hell can be a physical location such as prison or a psychological state experienced as a consequence of unwholesome actions.[46] The chaplain who avoided Fudo was more comfortable with Jizo on the prison altar and used his example as a teaching story.

Kannon or Kanzeon (*Avalokiteshvara* in Sanskrit, *Quanjin* in Chinese), who assumes many different forms, is the best-known Bodhisattva of compassion. Two parts of his/her being are especially relevant in prison work. "The Universal Gateway of the Bodhisattva Regarder of the Sounds of the World" chapter of the *Lotus Sutra*, verse 11, relates "If the jail-keeper locks you in a yoke, manacles your hands, and shackles your feet, let your thought dwell on the power of Kwannon. The chains will drop off and let you go free."[47]

Again, the symbol of transformation is important. Kyogen Carlson interprets the verse to mean that when we are physically bound in chains, the real shackles are reactions like anger, denial, and self-pity. If one stops trying to escape the reality of the physical condition of being in prison, the shackles can end up being "the very things that truly set us free."[48]

Kannon shows the power of all-acceptance. In prison that means to accept fully, without flinching, all the causes and conditioning that led to where you are now, letting all excuses and self-pity drop away. Anthony Stultz states the Fourth Precept as: "We embrace all aspects of our being, including our shadow, so that they may be transformed." Acceptance and transformation echo throughout the scriptures and are vital to a successful practice wherever it is done.

Kannon, in the form of Bato-Kannon (Horse-Headed Avalokiteshvara) also appears as a fierce, wrathful figure, quite a different picture than the gentle human face usually shown. Yet this expresses an aspect of compassion, as some beings need such incitement to awaken or be helped.[49] This is a "tough love" aspect of skillful means, an operational philosophy advocated by various help groups today, including one bearing that name, devoted to aiding parents of delinquent or severely troubled children.

Tara, Avalokiteshvara's female counterpart in the Vajrayana pantheon, is widely venerated as the female bodhisattva of compassion. Death row inmate Jarvis Masters, on the day of his Buddhist empowerment (refuge) ceremony, conducted through a glass window in the prison visitation room by Chagdud Tulku Rinpoche, described the experience: "I just sat still, repeating the prayer to Red Tara. 'Illustrious Tara, please be aware of me, remove my obstacles and quickly grant my excellent aspirations.'"[50] Rinpoche instructed: "Visualize Tara's blessings in the form of light and nectar washing you, cleansing you, filling you with bliss. Pray and visualize the light and nectar blessing you and all beings."[51] Palden Gyatso, a Tibetan monk imprisoned for thirty-one years by the Chinese in Tibet, found both gentle humor and deep appropriateness in American prisoners envisioning Tara, thousands of miles and a cultural time warp from where he had grown up with her practices.[52]

The timelessness of skillful means

Ken Kraft notes that "as engaged Buddhist thinkers continue to refine methodologies, the concept of skillful means will itself be subjected to new tests. On this, Western scholars and Buddhist practitioners agree: a good method must also be a self-reflective one."[53]

Using stories of people with criminal histories or those affected by crime goes back to the very roots of Buddhism, the original sangha and the Buddha's teachings and teaching methodology. These narratives are as forceful now as it was when they were first told in the various traditions. The stories of Angulimala, Queen Vaidehi, Prince Ajatasatru, and Milarepa and the images of bodhisattvas Fudo, Jizo, and Kannon pass the empirical tests of effectiveness in the prison setting and faithfulness to the tradition. This conclusion is based on analysis of the development of the stories and a distillation of the experiences of chaplains from the major Buddhist traditions. Using the stories to convey the transformative and tough-love aspects of the Buddha's teachings and the inescapability of karma, are all seen by Kraft as authentic for the prison setting.[54]

Returning to the *Flower Ornament Scripture* and the vow of Universal Goodness:

> Those who have committed hellish crimes
> Under the sway of ignorance
> Will quickly put an end to them all
> When this practice of good is expounded.[55]
> I will expound the teaching
> In the languages of gods and dragons,
> In the languages of demons and humans,
> And of all living beings.[56]

These images and stories are for when times are tough, when life is hell. "The spiritual in art makes its contribution to the pilgrim's halting progress. It is a resource for those who look beyond, understand that there is work to do, and undertake it."[57]

The attraction of today's teachers to these various ancient skillful means was also born out in doing the research for this chapter. Roshi Robert Aitken, with years of prison ministry experience, was so taken with hearing how Fudo was being used that he had copies of the first draft of this chapter made and sent to Diamond Sangha members currently working with prisoners.[58] The Reverend Karuna Dharma wanted to further explore the work and stories of the Shin chaplains.

Is Angulimala suitable as a patron saint of prison chaplains and others engaged in the various aspects of Buddhist prison ministry, or indeed as the original ancestor of a lineage of those engaged in this vital work, including the prisoners themselves, bravely living the teachings in hell? Pema Chodron's words are ringingly resonant:

> We become part of a lineage of people who have cultivated their bravery throughout history, people who, against enormous odds, have stayed open to great difficulties and painful situations and transformed them into the path of awakening. We *will* fall flat on our faces again and again, we *will* continue to feel inadequate, and we can use these experiences to wake us up, just as they did.[59]

The answer can only be "yes."

Notes

1 For an extensive discussion of these activities, see Virginia Cohn Parkum and J. Anthony Stultz, "The Angulimala Lineage: Buddhist Prison Ministries," in Christopher S. Queen (ed.), *Engaged Buddhism in the West* (Boston: Wisdom Publications, 2000), pp. 347–371.

2 Thomas Cleary (trans.), *The Flower Ornament Scripture: A Translation of the Avatamsaka Sutra* (Boston: Shambhala, 1993), p. 1093.

3 Kenneth Kraft, "New Voices in Engaged Buddhist Studies," in Queen, op. cit., pp. 485–511.

4 Ibid., p. 503.

5 To visit the Angulimala website http//www.users.zetnet.co.uk/phrakhem/ang. htm.

6 Kenneth Kraft, in a telephone interview with Virginia Cohn Parkum, June 14, 2001.

7 David Patt, "Who's Zoomin' Who?," in *Tricycle* 10, 4 (Summer 2001): 96.

8 Angulimala website.

9 In-depth interviews were conducted with eleven Buddhist prison chaplains from the Zen, Shin, Tibetan, SGI, Vipassana, and Theravadan traditions. An extensive review of works by or about Buddhist prison ministers was done. Several former prisoners were also interviewed and prisoner writings reviewed.

10 Pema Chodron, *Awakening Compassion: Meditation Practice for Difficult Times* (Boulder, CO: Sounds True, 1995), Tape 5B, audio cassettes.

11 Robert T. Oliver, *Communication and Culture in Ancient India and China* (Syracuse, NY: Syracuse University Press, 1971), p. 72. Oliver quotes the Sutra passage from T.W. Rhys Davids (trans.), *Buddhist Sutras* (Oxford: Clarendon Press, 1900), pp. 48–49.

12 William A. Barbieri, Jr., "Ethics and the Narrated Life," *The Journal of Religion* 78, 3 (July, 1998): 369.

13 Ibid.

14 Oliver, op. cit., p. 11.

15 Roger C. Schank, *Tell Me a Story: Narrative and Intelligence* (Evanston, IL: Northwestern University, Press, 1990), pp. 1–2.

16 Ibid., p. 12.

17 Ibid., pp. 11–12.

18 Peter Parshall, "The Art of Memory and the Passion," *The Art Bulletin* 81:3 (September, 1999): 456.

19 Roger Lipsky, *An Art of Our Own: The Spiritual in Twentieth Century Art* (Boston: Shambhala, 1997), p. 14.

20 John A. Kouwenhoven, *Half a Truth Is Better Than None: Some Unsystematic Conjectures About Art, Disorder, and American Experience* (Chicago: The University of Chicago Press, 1982), p. 208.

21 Angulimala web site.

22 Hellmuth Hecker, *Angulimala: A Murderer's Road to Sainthood* (Kandy, Sri Lanka: Buddhist Publication Society, 1984).

23 Ibid., p. 21, from the *Theragatha*, verse 879.

24 Randi Getsushin Brox, Dharma Rain Zen Center, Portland, Oregon, in a telephone interview with Virginia Cohn Parkum, June 12, 2001.

25 Geoffrey Shugen Arnold and the inmates of the National Buddhist Prison Sangha, "There Has to be a Better Way to Live," *The Mountain Record* 17, 1 (1998): 27.

26 The Reverend Karuna Dharma, International Buddhist Meditation Center, Los Angeles, California, in a telephone interview with Virginia Cohn Parkum, June 17, 2001.

27 T.W. Rhys Davids and Hermann Oldenberg (eds), *Vinaya Texts: Part 1* (Delhi: Motilal Banarsidass, 1968), pp. 196–199.

28 Richard H. Robinson and Willard L. Johnson, *The Buddhist Religion* (Belmont, CA: Wadsworth, 1997), pp. 51–54, 82–85.

29 Robert A.F. Thurman, *Essential Tibetan Buddhism* (Edison, NJ: Castle Books, 1997), pp. 28–31.

30 *Mandala* (November/December, 1997), http//www.cuenet.com/~fpmt/mandala.

31 Shoji Matsumoto and Ruth Tabrah, *Ajatasatru: The Story of Who We Are* (Honolulu, Hawaii: Buddhist Study Center Press, 1988), p. 5. This beautiful translation is modern in both language usage and terminology.

32 Ibid., p. 28.

33 Ibid., pp. 34–35. See also Shinran, *The Collected Works of Shinran* (Kyoto, Japan: Jodo Shinshu, Hongwanji-Ha, 1997), pp. 140–150.

34 Ibid., p. i.

35 Alfred Bloom, *Shoshinge: The Heart of Shin Buddhism* (Honolulu, Hawaii: Buddhist Study Center Press, 1986), p. 85.

36 The mandala and detailed discussions of it are available at http//www.odn.ne.jp/pureland-mandala/con-ex.htm. Professor Hisao Inagaki kindly provided color printouts of parts of the mandala from this web site.

37 Kenneth K. Tanaka, *Ocean: An Introduction to Jodo-Shinshu Buddhism in America* (Berkeley, CA: Wisdom Ocean Publications, 1997), pp. 96–97.

38 Taigen Daniel Leighton, *Bodhisattva Archetypes: Classic Buddhist Guides to Awakening and Their Modern Expression* (New York: Penguin Arkana, 1998), p. 3.

39 Ibid., pp. 3–4.

40 *Shasta Abbey Buddhist Supplies Catalog* (Mt Shasta, California: 1997), p. 31.

41 Kyogen Carlson, "Facing the Storm," *Gateway* 1:3 (Winter, 1996): 11–12. Available at the Engaged Zen Foundation's website, <http//www.engaged-zen.org>.

42 Sensei Kyogen Carlson, Dharma Rain Zen Center, Portland, Oregon, in a telephone interview with Virginia Cohn Parkum, June 7, 2001.

43 Sensei Geoffrey Shugen Arnold, Zen Mountain Monastery, Mt Tremper, New York, in a telephone interview with Virginia Cohn Parkum, June 7, 2001.

44 Sherman E. Lee, *A History of Far Eastern Art* (Englewood Cliffs, NJ: Prentice Hall and New York: Harry N. Abrams, 1964), p. 332.

45 Ibid., pp. 332–333.

46 See Daniel Leighton, *Bodhisattva Archetypes*, pp. 208–242, for a thorough discussion of the various aspects of Jizo.

47 Richard Robinson (trans.), *Chinese Buddhist Verse* (London: John Murray, 1954), p. 38.

48 Carlson, op. cit., p. 12.

49 Leighton, op. cit., pp. 164–165.

50 Jarvis J. Masters, *Finding Freedom: Writings From Death Row* (Junction City, CA: Padma Publishing, 1997), p. 124.

51 Ibid., p. 128.

52 Palden Gyatso in an interview, April 8, 2000 with Virginia Cohn Parkum, Carlisle, Pennsylvania.

53 Kraft, "New Voices," p. 506.

54 Kraft, interview.

55 Cleary, op. cit., p. 1517.

56 Ibid., p. 1513.

57 Lipsky, op. cit., p. 16.

58 Roshi Robert Aitken, interview with Virginia Cohn Parkum, Kaimu, Pahoa, Hawaii, March 7, 2000.

59 Pema Chodron, *Start Where You Are: A Guide to Compassionate Living* (Boston: Shambhala, 1994), p. 49.

IV

THREE CRITIQUES

13

ENGAGED BUDDHIST ETHICS
Mistaking the boat for the shore

James E. Deitrick

> Bhikkhus, I shall show you how the Dhamma is similar to a
> raft, being for the purpose of crossing over, not for the
> purpose of grasping... When you know the Dhamma to be
> similar to a raft, you should abandon even good states, how
> much more so bad states.
>
> (Majjhima-nikaya 1.134–135)

Given Max Weber's still widely touted characterization of Buddhism as an
"anti-political status religion"[1] and Melford E. Spiro's insistence that
Buddhism is normatively concerned solely with the soteriological needs of
individuals conceived in other-worldly terms,[2] questions naturally arise
about the credibility of engaged Buddhism's appeal to the Buddhist tradition for support of its social and political activities. It is not unreasonable
to ask, for instance, whether or not engaged Buddhist social ethics can
legitimately be called "Buddhist" at all. As Daniel B. Stevenson asks in
regard to American forms of Buddhism generally, "Is there a point at
which institutional and conceptual change begins to threaten the integrity
of that tradition or to stretch it beyond recognition?"[3] Are they not, as
Christopher S. Queen has asked, something akin to Buddhist "heresies"
clothing essentially liberal Protestant notions of social service and activism
in the language and symbols of Buddhism? After exploring the central
characteristics of socially engaged Buddhism, I will address the question of
whether or not its social ethics may be considered anything more than
nominally Buddhist.[4]

Defining engaged Buddhism

Socially engaged Buddhism is a diverse phenomenon – or, perhaps more
accurately, a network of diverse phenomena. On the one hand, the term
"socially engaged Buddhism" is merely a convenient analytic construct
that allows scholars to understand similar, though distinct socio-religious

stirrings throughout Buddhist Asia and the West that share an interest in it relating Buddhism to contemporary social issues. On the other hand, many of these movements have also recognized their commonalities and have joined together through such institutions as the International Network of Engaged Buddhists to organize a cohesive, international social movement that sets as one of its goals the creation of "an ecumenical World Buddhism."[5] Thus, "socially engaged Buddhism" is at once a term used to refer to diverse Buddhist movements that manifest similar qualities, as well as a term used to describe a loosely organized global socio-religious phenomenon.

Examples of socially engaged Buddhist movements in Asia include: (1) the anti-war movement among Vietnamese Buddhist monks and nuns, such as Thich Quang Duc, the monk who first immolated himself in protest against the War in 1963, and Thich Nhat Hanh – the monk who is credited with coining the term "engaged Buddhism," who was exiled for his peace activism during the war, nominated by Martin Luther King, Jr. for the Nobel Peace Prize, and continues to exert influence as a Buddhist peace activist around the world; (2) the human rights activism of the four-teenth Dalai Lama of Tibet, Tenzin Gyatso; (3) the Burmese people's movement led by Buddhist scholar and statesperson, Aung San Suu Kyi, who, along with Tenzin Gyatso, has been awarded the Nobel Peace Prize; (4) the conversion to Buddhism by Dr. Bhimrao R. Ambedkar and millions of his "untouchable" followers in India as a political protest against caste discrimination in that country; (5) the Sri Lankan *Sarvodaya Shramadana* community development movement engineered by educator A. T. Ariyaratne; (6) the social reformism of the Siamese (Thai) Buddhist layperson, Sulak Sivaraksa; and (7) the efforts by both men and women in many parts of Asia and the West to restore full ordination to women and to rebuild the nuns' order in Theravada Buddhism. Each of these figures and movements is discussed elsewhere and need not be elaborated upon here.[6] For our purposes, it is enough to consider the characteristics they share in common.

Engaged Buddhism as cultural interpenetration

In attempting to lay out the defining characteristics of engaged Buddhism, it is useful first to consider what Christopher Queen means by referring to these movements as novel products of Asian and Western "cultural inter-penetration." Although it is possible to point to examples of Buddhist social engagement throughout Asian Buddhist histories, Queen argues that the "shape and style of contemporary engaged Buddhism" is a recent phenomenon, made possible by the infusion of Euro-American religious and political thought into the veins of Buddhist Asia. According to Queen:

it is only in the late nineteenth-century revival of Buddhism in Sri Lanka – and particularly in its two principal figures, the American Theosophist, Col. Henry Steel Olcott (1832–1907) and his protégé, the Sinhalese Anagarika Dharmapala (1864–1933) – that we first recognize the spirit and substance of the religious activism we call "socially engaged Buddhism." And it is only in this context that we first meet the missing ingredient – in effect, the primary explanation for the appearance of socially engaged Buddhism in its contemporary form following the arrival of Colonel Olcott and Madame Blavatsky in Ceylon on May 17, 1880. This ingredient is the influence of European and American religious and political thought (and perhaps equally important, western methods of institutional development and public communication) on the evolution of modern Buddhism.[7]

Accordingly, Queen regards the "Protestant Buddhism"[8] of Olcott and Dharmapala as the result of a "profound cultural interpenetration":

> deeply derivative of the Victorian Christianity which Olcott and Dharmapala encountered and imported from the West ... [and] also, significantly, a *protest* against Victorian religion and the political dominance it represented in preindependence South Asia. Thus, ... we cannot consider the Buddhist revival in South Asia in purely Buddhist terms. We are forced to acknowledge and to trace the ways in which Buddhist and Christian – Asian, European, and American – traditions have become inextricably intertwined in the brief history of socially engaged Buddhism.[9]

Significant for the development of engaged Buddhism, therefore, is the fact that Olcott and Dharmapala were "high-profile personalities whose careers straddled and sometimes blended East and West."[10] As noted by Queen, each was educated in English-speaking schools, and each traveled widely throughout Asia and the West. Perhaps more significant is the fact that the Buddhism that Olcott first encountered in Ceylon (Sri Lanka) and subsequently exported to the West through his best-selling book, *A Buddhist Catechism*, was already itself an "amalgam of Eastern and Western elements."[11] Queen cites Thomas A. Tweed's observation that "Buddhist apologists" like Olcott

> stood united with American critics, travelers, and scholars in implicitly or explicitly affirming the role of religion in stimulating effective economic, political, and social activity. Almost all participants in Victorian culture and contributors to the public discourse about Buddhism agreed: whatever else true religion was, it was

optimistic and activistic. In many ways, then, nineteenth-century Euro-American Buddhist sympathizers had more in common with their mainline Protestant contemporaries than with nineteenth-century Asian-American or twentieth-century Caucasian Buddhists [e.g., the Beat poets].[12]

The point here is that Buddhism was already understood as activistic – or, we might say, "socially engaged " – by certain segments of late nineteenth-century Victorian culture, and it was this activist Buddhism that Olcott "found" when he traveled to Asia. Anticipating the question to which we will turn shortly, Queen rightly concludes that:

> whether we are justified in speaking of a localized Buddhist "heresy," of an emerging "heterodoxy" encompassing several cultural areas, or of a "new Buddhism of truly global significance," it becomes clear that a complex interpenetration of spiritual, intellectual, and behavioral habits ... from Buddhist and Christian societies has evolved.[13]

The cultural interpenetration responsible for the rise of engaged Buddhism in Asia is not only "spiritual, intellectual, and behavioral," however, but can also be interpreted materially. Just as with the Christian Social Gospel in the United States, the primary impetus for the rise of these movements has not been only the presence of new ideas and forms of social engagement – these are, in a sense, but mere tools – but, rather, the impact of modernity and its attendant forces of industrialization and urbanization on Asian societies. Robert N. Bellah and Donald K. Swearer have both sought to understand the impact of modernization on Buddhist Asia, and their insights are useful for interpreting engaged Buddhism.[14]

Bellah observes that as religions in Asia have been confronted by the challenges of modernity and Western ideas and values they have typically responded in two ways. On the one hand, "neotraditionalist" movements have arisen that espouse ideologies "designed to keep change to a minimum and defend the *status quo* as far as possible."[15] According to Bellah, these movements use "modern ideas and methods to defend traditional cultural values, which are held to be superior to those of any other tradition."[16] On the other hand, "reformist" movements advocating significant change have also arisen that rely on "a return to the early teachers and text, a rejection of most of the intervening tradition, [and] an interpretation of the pristine teaching ... as advocating social reform and national regeneration."[17]

Similarly, Swearer, writing specifically about Buddhism in Southeast Asia, suggests that Buddhism in that area has responded to modernity in two "seemingly opposed" ways. The first he labels "fundamentalism or fundamentalist-like" and the other "liberal and reformist." "Both trends," he says:

> lament the loss of a Buddhistically defined moral community but differ in their approach, analysis and solution. The fundamentalist solution often seems doctrinally simplistic and moralistic, advocating a return to an idealized personal piety that either ignores or misunderstands the nature of systemic economic, social, and cultural problems and tensions. The reformist solution, on the other hand, engages head-on the tensions, dislocations and "evils" of the contemporary age, applying creative interpretations of traditional beliefs and practices as part of their solution.[18]

According to these paradigms, we may say that Asian socially engaged Buddhist movements are, most generally, "reformist" in the senses explicated by both Bellah and Swearer, though, as Sallie B. King makes clear, we cannot say this without some qualification.[19] Nevertheless, they certainly represent efforts by Buddhists to engage the "tensions, dislocations and 'evils'" of modernity head-on by "applying creative interpretations of traditional beliefs and practices as part of their solution."

In sum, socially engaged Buddhism is the product of the interpenetration of Euro-American and Asian cultures and has arisen in Asia in response to the material forces of modernity, industrialization, and urbanization. This only begins to describe the movements being discussed here, however. We must go further than merely saying that engaged Buddhism is a "reformist" response to modernity informed by both Asian and Western cultures and note the particular contours that differentiate this response from other Buddhist movements that also might be characterized as novel, reformist products of Asia's interaction with modernity and the West. Most basically, according to Queen and others, it is the common pairing of "inner peace and world peace," which enjoins a conjunction of spiritual and political practice, that is the "distinguishing mark of contemporary engaged Buddhism"[20] in both Asia and the West. Beyond this, Queen also likens engaged Buddhist movements in Asia to other so-called Third World religiously based (especially Christian) liberation movements. Citing Deane William Ferm's general observations about Christian liberation theologies as (1) "stress[ing] liberation from all forms of human oppression: social, economic, political, racial, sexual, environmental, religious";[21] and (2) "insist[ing] that theology must be truly indigenous,"[22] Queen notes that engaged Buddhist movements in Asia are similar with respect to the first, but not the second; that is, Asian engaged Buddhist movements typically seek to provide release from all forms of oppression – or as they would put it, "suffering" – but, unlike their Christian cousins, they work explicitly toward the formation of an "ecumenical World Buddhism"; thus, they tend to see their insights and methods as universally applicable and not necessarily bound to one culture or geographical region.

Echos of the three jewels

Queen also notes that, beyond the drive to end suffering in all of its forms and the tendency toward universalism, Asian engaged Buddhist movements also share three common traits which are related to the personal, doctrinal, and institutional dimensions of the movements, and echo, in turn, the three jewels or refuges of Buddhist spirituality: Buddha, Dharma, and Sangha. First, Queen observes that Asian engaged Buddhist movements have all "coalesced around a popular leader or leaders whose identity and mission are understood by followers to be distinctively *Buddhist*."[23] Moreover, these Buddhist leaders tend to come from relatively affluent backgrounds, are well educated, and most have made a choice against "the most traditional role for Buddhist leaders in the past, that of the forest or temple monk."[24] Queen also remarks, however, that, despite their relative affluence:

> each one has had to confront and overcome daunting obstacles. Ambedkar's childhood (and perhaps more painfully, his adulthood) as an Untouchable was the source of his moral authority and his attraction to Buddhism. The activist women, especially in South Asia, have confronted staunch resistance to change from lay and ordained sectors of Buddhist society. Other leaders have had great personal sadness to bear: for the Dalai Lama, exile and the near extinction of his culture; for Thich Nhat Hanh, the protracted civil and superpower war in his country; ... for Sulak Sivaraksa, imprisonment and exile for denouncing the Thai throne; [and] for leaders of the Ambedkarite movement in central India and the Sarvodaya Shramadana movement in Sri Lanka, the intractable poverty and backwardness of rural and urban slum populations.[25]

For all of these leaders, these hardships have no doubt contributed to their passion to bring release from suffering to others.

Second, according to Queen, engaged Buddhist movements are similar in that each has offered novel interpretations of traditional Buddhist doctrines, especially "those of selflessness, interdependence, the five precepts, the four noble truths, nondualism, and emptiness."[26] This novelty cannot be over-stressed. One of the most distinctive innovations of these movements is their tendency to interpret Buddhist "liberation" in this-worldly terms. Theirs is not merely the other-worldly psycho-spiritual liberation from the kind of suffering (*dukkha*) traditionally understood by Buddhists to arise from egoistic attachments. Rather, engaged Buddhists typically pursue a kind of "mundane awakening" that includes "moral, cultural, spiritual, social, political, and economic dimensions."[27] Queen thus concludes:

> that a profound change in Buddhist soteriology – from a highly personal and other-worldly notion of liberation to a social, economic, this-worldly liberation – distinguishes the [socially engaged] Buddhist movements in our study. The traditional conceptions of karma and rebirth, the veneration of the bhikkhu sangha, and the focus on ignorance and psychological attachment to account for suffering in the world (the second Noble Truth) have taken second place to the application of highly rationalized reflections on the institutional and political manifestations of greed, hatred, and delusion, and on new organizational strategies for addressing war and injustice, poverty and intolerance, and the prospects for "outer" as well as "inner" peace in the world.[28]

Notably, it is these "innovations" that lead to our present questions about the relationship of engaged Buddhist social ethics to more traditional Buddhist social ethics.

Finally, according to Queen, not only have engaged Buddhists provided new understandings of Buddhist liberation, they have also developed new ("skillful") means for its achievement. Focusing on the mundane causes of worldly suffering, they have also sought methods for achieving release from that suffering that involve social and political dimensions. These methods often utilize "education, mass communication, political influence and activism, jurisprudence and litigation, and yes, even fund-raising and marketing [to achieve their goals]." With regard to education, for instance, some of these leaders and movements have started vocational schools to train adults in a particular skill and pre-schools that allow parents to engage in full-time work or attend school themselves. Others have founded primary and secondary schools, and still others, universities.[29] With regard to the use of mass media and marketing, many of these leaders and movements have cultivated relationships with politicians, other religious leaders of renown, publishers, and even celebrities and film producers to bring international attention to their causes and activities. Consider, for instance, the public relationships of the Dalai Lama with actor Richard Gere, and those of Thich Nhat Hanh with the late Trappist monk, Thomas Merton, and civil rights leader, Martin Luther King, Jr.[30] Also note the spate of popular movies that have recently been produced that sympathetically depict the oppression of Tibetans by the Chinese, as well as the inordinate number of books that have been published by engaged Buddhist leaders –

Thich Nhat Hanh having produced over sixty titles alone.[31] Queen continues:

> The printing press, the public address system, and the speaking tour have [all] been skillfully employed by Asian Buddhist liberation movements and leaders [to promote their causes]; ... yet some of them have gone considerably farther. By staging highly newsworthy media events and by associating – or "networking" – with celebrated personalities to reach a worldwide audience, engaged Buddhists have sought to bring international pressure on governments and individuals perpetrating violence and suffering. Was this not, after all, the effect of the self-immolations in Saigon in 1963 ...? If Mahatma Gandhi used street theater, newsreel, and print media to communicate with his adversaries during the Indian struggle for independence, now television, fax, and e-mail make it possible for engaged Buddhists to enter the offices and homes of the rich and powerful: heads of government and multinational corporations, and the middle class who rule by checkbook and ballot box.[32]

Thus, Queen observes, "contemporary Buddhist liberation movements are as likely to apply their interpretive and organizational efforts to the critique and reform of social and political conditions as they are to propose and practice new spiritual exercises."[33]

In sum, Asian engaged Buddhist movements are typically alike (1) in forming around affluent and well-educated leaders who have had to overcome their own "mundane suffering"; (2) in producing novel interpretations of Buddhist doctrines that focus on the mundane aspects and causes of suffering; and (3) in developing novel means for combating that mundane suffering that involve social and political activity. They are, in short, according to Queen, Buddhist liberation movements, that is, "voluntary association[s] of people, guided by exemplary leaders and a common vision of a society based on peace, justice, and freedom."[34]

What is Buddhism?

In addressing Stevenson's question mentioned above as to whether or not the institutional and conceptual change of socially engaged Buddhism stretches the Buddhist tradition beyond recognition, it is important to point out that Buddhism is a notoriously malleable tradition that, as many scholars have noted, almost defies definition. Still, if the term "Buddhism" is to retain any meaning, we must have some working definition that implies a certain set of shared characteristics. In the pursuit of definitions of long-standing religions, such as Buddhism, that have been transmitted not only through the course of millennia but also across numerous social and cultural boundaries, we are cautioned to remember that our definitions must reflect the complexities of the religions they seek to define. In the process, however, we must also avoid tautological definitions that merely declare that which goes by the name of "Buddhism" to be Buddhism, for example, Buddhism is what Buddhists do or what Buddhists are. Such a method is tempting for many, I think, because of the legitimate desire not to exclude people from the religious traditions with which they identify. Thus, it is often regarded as best to respect the self-definition of a religious group's constituency and to study every such group as a positive instance of the religion with which its members identify – perhaps best reckoned as a "transformed" instance of the religion. As already noted, however, such a method is based on a mere tautology which is insufficient, at least for our present purposes, in that it does not allow us adequately to distinguish between the core and peripheral aspects of a religion, and thereby to render a complete analysis of the tradition. We are thus prevented from asking, as Queen does, "if the 'deep structure' of Olcott's [and, by implication, socially engaged] Buddhism is Protestant ..., must not the faith be called Christian, not Buddhist?"[35] In the study of comparative religious social ethics, this is hardly an unimportant question, and is deserving of, at the very least, a provisional answer and hopefully extended discussion.

Another way to define "Buddhism" would be to delineate critical aspects of the religion that have generally been agreed upon as constituting the core of the tradition by the religion's central proponents and by scholars of Buddhism. Notably, such a method does not necessarily need to assume or iterate a rigid "essence" of Buddhism. Rather, we might look for that which is "basic" to Buddhism, some characteristic or set of characteristics that constitutes a necessary, though not necessarily sufficient, condition of something's being called "Buddhism." This would allow us to differentiate between what we might call "nominal" and "basic" Buddhism.[36] It would also free us from the hazard of offering up too narrow a definition of Buddhism. Indeed, for the present analysis, it may suffice to locate even one characteristic that is necessary or basic to Buddhism, and use it as a minimal standard of comparison for judging whether engaged Buddhism in Asia ought rightly to be regarded as a novel application of Buddhist principles to contemporary social problems or a "heretical" movement that misapplies the term Buddhism to its theories and practices.

It should, of course, be noted that if engaged Buddhism possesses this basic characteristic, we may not thereby conclude that it is necessarily a positive instance of Buddhism, for its possessing of that characteristic is not sufficient for such an identification. On the other hand, however, if it lacks even that one characteristic, then we might be forced to conclude that it is not basically Buddhist. Though it may possess other elements that are also common or even necessary characteristics of Buddhism, such as the practice of meditation, its lack of this one necessary characteristic may prohibit us from using the term "Buddhism" in reference to engaged Buddhism in anything more than a nominal sense. At the least, we should conclude that engaged Buddhism is in need of revision if it wished to maintain continuity with traditional modes of Buddhism.

Buddhist suffering is personal, not social

In keeping with this method of defining Buddhism, I suggest that among other things necessary or basic to Buddhism is the fundamental insight, reliably attributable to Siddhartha Gautama, the Buddha, that life within the causal nexus of *samsara* is essentially unsatisfactory, or "suffering," and this suffering is caused by the human propensity to form attachments to things and existence as it is experienced from the perspective of ego-centeredness. Buddhist "suffering," then, is an intrinsically personal and psychological affair. The remedy for this suffering, according to basic Buddhist teachings, is to rid oneself of attachments and achieve the individual experience of liberation. I suggest, then, that theoretical, practical, and sociological accordance with the teachings of the Four Noble Truths is a necessary, though not necessarily sufficient, condition for a given religious group or movement to be esteemed basically Buddhist.[37]

Before ascertaining whether engaged Buddhism meets this minimal standard, however, it is important to note that there is a difference in asserting against Weber *et al.* that Buddhism does indeed possess an intrinsic social ethics, and identifying that ethics with the social ethics of engaged Buddhism. It merely suggests that any social ethics that may be considered basically Buddhist must accord with the Four Noble Truths.[38] This point is hinted at by Bardwell L. Smith when he says:

> The primary goal of Buddhism is not a stable order or just society but *the discovery of genuine freedom (or awakening) by each person*. It has never been asserted that the conditions of society are unimportant or unrelated to *this more important goal*, but *it is critical to stress the distinction between what is primary and what is not*. For Buddhists to lose this distinction is to transform their tradition into something discontinuous with its original and historic essence.[39]

This point cannot be over-stressed. Buddhism has been far from unconcerned with the affairs of society and state, even from its inception. Rather, it early developed a social ethics that was consistent with its ultimate goal of "genuine freedom" for all individuals. It did not in the process, however, see that social ethics as anything more than an expedient measure designed to create and maintain the kind of social conditions wherein individuals might pursue the more important goal of their own liberation.

In sum, the whole of Buddhist morality, individual and social, is based on the pragmatic distinction between "wholesome" and "unwholesome" (*kushala* and *akushala*) actions, that is, actions that are or are not conducive to liberation.[40] According to Russell F. Sizemore and Donald K. Swearer, then, "the justification for social action [in Buddhism] is primarily religious. The instruction for action is based on a theory of what is conducive to salvation (for the entire society),[41] not on an independent norm of social cooperation or nonreligious rationality."[42] While they go on to admit that "one might say critically that *Buddhism's single concern is with religious salvation, not social welfare... [and that] the material well-being of society's members pales in comparison to the supreme value of spiritual enlightenment*," they nevertheless note, with deference to Robin W. Lovin's[43] insights, that:

> Buddhist social ideals are no less social for this religious justification, nor are they any less connected to traditional moral concerns of social harmony. Social welfare and religious advancement are not in conflict, and Buddhist methods for directing society envision their mutual achievement.[44]

Thus, we may conclude that *Buddhism's singular concern is with religious salvation of individuals and that its social theory is pragmatically related to this supreme and, for Buddhists, noble goal.* In a sense, then, Weber and Spiro are correct in arguing that Buddhism abandons society. What they fail to recognize, however, is that society is ideally abandoned only after it has served its function of leading its populace toward liberation.[45]

What is important to observe here is that neither the *sangha* nor the state bear the responsibility within Buddhism of eradicating suffering. This is most fundamentally due to the manner in which suffering is conceived within Buddhism. As we saw above, suffering is a psychological state brought on by individuals' attachments. It is not the direct and necessary result of external conditions, but rather the result of the manner in which those conditions are responded to. As Andrew Olendski explains in his analysis of the stress reduction techniques employed by the Mindfulness-Based Stress Reduction movement:

> The content of our experience is entirely benign – the sights and sounds, flavors, odors, and physical contacts that make up the data of our experienced world are never, in themselves, causes of suffering. Similarly, our thoughts and perceptions merely convey cognitive information, which in each case may then be experi-

enced as either pleasurable or painful (or sometimes neither of these) in affective tone. But how we respond to this experience, to what extent we succumb to the motivation to pursue pleasure and avoid pain by clinging in various ways – this is the crucial point at which it is determined whether we suffer, or claim our freedom to simply be aware of our experience in all its natural diversity. It is in this sense that the expression is used by a number of modern meditation teachers, "Pain is inevitable, but suffering is optional."[46]

The same might be said about the societal oppression with which many engaged Buddhists are – rightly, I think – so concerned. Suffering is not, from a Buddhist point of view, a necessary outcome of oppression, and because of this cannot be eliminated solely by eradicating the mundane causes of oppression.

Work toward the creation of a good society, therefore, holds no intrinsic value for Buddhism. Rather, the achievement of such a goal is penultimately related to, and infinitely relativized by, Buddhism's ultimate goal – the liberation of every individual from society and the world. Accordingly, Buddhism does not allow that one could ever attain liberation for another; rather, the most one can do for others is to strive to create the conditions within which they may work effectively to achieve their own liberation. While such work might entail seeking and introducing cures for the mundane ills of individuals, societies, and even nature, this work cannot be understood as intrinsically good and simultaneously be regarded as basically Buddhist. From a Buddhist perspective, such work is regarded as good only insofar as it serves the ultimate goal of liberation for all individuals from the world of *samsaric* suffering.[47]

Conclusion

Our brief survey of engaged Buddhism above, however, suggests that it often concerns itself with something other than creating the conditions within which others might pursue their own liberation from suffering. Rather, with its focus on "mundane awakening" and its attempts to locate "the *causes, varieties* and *remedies* of worldly suffering and oppression,"[48] it appears to forget the most basic of Buddhism's insights, that *suffering has but one cause and one remedy*, that is, attachment and the cessation of attachment (the Second and Third Noble Truths). As noted above, suffering for Buddhism is not typically equated with physical pain or societal oppression, at least not in the deepest sense of the term *dukkha*. Rather, it is the sense of lack of satisfaction that comes with the perverse human tendency to cling to the self and other ostensibly illusory objects in an ever-changing world.

Having understood this truth, and further, having extinguished his own desires, the Buddha is said to have been tempted to remain in an enlightened state of *nirvanic* bliss, completely detached from the world, and to leave the world behind for good. But, it is also said that he regarded this as a temptation to be overcome, and looking out across the world, was able to see that there were others capable of achieving the same realization that he had achieved and who would benefit from his teaching. He therefore resolved out of compassion for others to dedicate the rest of his life to the teaching of the *dharma*, the truth of his enlightenment, and to the creation of social institutions conducive to the attainment of enlightenment by others. The religion that developed around him and his teachings, therefore, has been correctly characterized by John Ferguson as "a world-renouncing religion that nonetheless lays stress on the service to others in this world to help them to escape."[49] As numerous scholars have pointed out, the Buddha and his early followers were not by vocation social reformers. Rather, as Richard Gombrich notes, "[the Buddha's] concern was to reform individuals and help them to leave society forever, not to reform the world."[50]

Granting these points, Queen nevertheless affirms the continuity of engaged Buddhist movements in Asia with the Buddhist tradition. This he is able to do because he assumes a tautological definition of Buddhism as discussed above. For Queen, "the refuge formula, expressing homage to Buddha, Dharma, and Sangha, offers a standard for regarding a thinker or movement as 'Buddhist,' *regardless of the presence of non-Buddhist cultural elements, and regardless of the absence of other traditional teachings.*"[51] Thus, he concludes that when:

> [the] principles and techniques [of engaged Buddhism], *regardless of their provenance*, are proclaimed and practiced in the name of the Awakened One, in accord with the teachings of wisdom and compassion, and in the spirit of the unbroken community of those seeking human liberation – that is, in harmony with the ancient refuges of Buddha, Dharma, and Sangha – then we may regard the catechism of the transplanted Civil War colonel, the Biblical cadences of Anagarika Dharmapala, ... and the sacrifice of the Ven. Thich Quang Duc as authentically Buddhist.[52]

As noted, Queen's definition of Buddhism as "expressing homage to Buddha, Dharma, and Sangha" is insufficient in that it is seems to be nothing more than a variation of the tautological definition I alluded to above.[53] Although one might argue that, from a Buddhist perspective, paying homage to Buddha, *dharma*, and *sangha* has positive karmic consequences that allow one to make progress toward the ultimate goals of enlightenment and liberation, it still remains true that the ultimate and true release from suffering envisioned by the Buddha consists of nothing less than the individual's realization of the basic truths of Buddhism discussed above. Homage is mere expediency: the boat, but not the shore. So, for that matter, is alleviating the many causes and varieties of worldly oppression. It still remains for the individual to step freely off the boat and to grasp the liberation that can only be arrived at on one's own.

I would argue, then, that engaged Buddhist movements do not typically make clear distinctions between the "worldly" or "mundane" suffering which is caused by temporal conditions, and the more profound "spiritual" suffering (*dukkha*) that is the result of individuals' attachments. Though engaged Buddhist groups may share some or even many commonalities with traditional forms of Buddhism (for example, the practice of meditation, compassion for others, taking refuge in the Buddha, *dharma*, and *sangha*, etc.), their social ethics, nevertheless, tend to lack the necessary characteristic of theoretical, practical, and sociological accordance with the basic teachings of the Four Noble Truths noted above. Engaged Buddhist social ethics are, therefore, probably best regarded as nominally Buddhist. It should again be stressed, however, that this does not mean that traditional Buddhist social ethics has regarded the elimination of mundane suffering and oppression as unimportant. It is, rather, a matter of priority that has significant ramifications for the development of a Buddhist social ethics relevant to the contemporary world. Thus, the distinction between "temporal" and "spiritual" suffering is crucial and should not be overlooked by engaged Buddhists if they wish to maintain a sense of continuity with the Buddhist tradition.

Finally, it is important to note that while the social character of engaged Buddhism's soteriological vision and its mundane understanding of suffering seriously militate against considering its ethics as basically Buddhist, the movement is in a sense only a relatively small step away from establishing itself more firmly within the Buddhist tradition. If engaged Buddhists were to amend their theories in such a way as to suggest that all their strivings for peace and social justice were intended to create the conditions within which others – as well as themselves – might pursue their own liberation from the world of *samsaric* suffering, then they might be in a position to begin moving toward the creation of a distinctively Buddhist social ethics relevant to the contemporary world. With this suggestion I mean to emphasize that I agree with engaged Buddhists that Weber and his followers are mistaken in their characterization of Buddhism as essentially inimical to social ethics. Indeed, as I have suggested above, there exists in historical Buddhism not only the nascence of a social ethics, but a complex and developed one. Perhaps, if engaged Buddhists were to attend in greater detail to the historical development of this ethics, they would be in a better position truly to bring a distinctively Buddhist perspective to contemporary social problems.

Notes

1 Max Weber, *The Religion of India* (Glencoe, IL: The Free Press, 1958), p. 206.
2 See Melford E. Spiro, *Buddhism and Society: A Great Tradition and its Burmese Vicissitudes* (New York: Harper and Row, 1970).
3 Daniel B. Stevenson, "Tradition and Change in the *Sangha*: A Buddhist Historian Looks at Buddhism in America," in Charles Wei-hsun Fu and Sandra A. Wawrytko (eds), *Buddhist Ethics and Modern Society: An International Symposium* (New York: Greenwood Press, 1991), p. 247.
4 Although engaged Buddhism has also established an impressive presence in the West, given both the similarities of Western engaged Buddhism with Asian engaged Buddhism, as well as the natural expectation that Asian engaged Buddhist movements would accord more deeply with traditional forms of Buddhism than their Western cousins, I limit my discussion here to Asian engaged Buddhist movements. For discussion of engaged Buddhism in the West, see Christopher S. Queen (ed.), *Engaged Buddhism in the West* (Boston: Wisdom Publications, 2000).
5 See Christopher S. Queen, "Introduction: The Shapes and Sources of Engaged Buddhism," in Christopher S. Queen and Sallie B. King (eds), *Engaged Buddhism: Buddhist Liberation Movements in Asia* (Albany: State University of New York Press, 1996), p. 23.
6 See Queen and King, op. cit.
7 Queen, "Introduction," p. 20.
8 The now-popular term, "Protestant Buddhism," as used by Queen, was first used by Gananath Obeyesekere to refer to the Buddhism of Olcott and Dharmapala in "Religious Symbolism and Political Change in Ceylon," in Bardwell L. Smith (ed.), *The Two Wheels of Dhamma: Essays on the Theravada Tradition in India and Ceylon* (Chambersburg, PA: American Academy of Religion, 1972), p. 62, where he offers the following definition of the expression:

> The term "Protestant Buddhism" in my usage has two meanings. (a) As we have pointed out many of its norms and organizational forms are historical derivatives from Protestant Christianity. (b) More importantly, from the contemporary point of view, it is a protest *against* Christianity and its associated Western political dominance prior to independence.

9 Queen, "Introduction," p. 21.
10 Ibid., p. 33; italics deleted.
11 Ibid., p. 31.
12 Thomas A. Tweed, *The American Encounter with Buddhism: 1844–1912* (Bloomington, IN: Indiana University Press, 1992), p. 155, quoted in Queen, *Engaged Buddhism*, p. 30.
13 Queen, "Introduction," p. 31.
14 Robert N. Bellah, "Epilogue: Religion and Progress in Modern Asia," in Robert N. Bellah (ed.), *Religion and Progress in Modern Asia* (New York: Free Press, 1965); and Donald K. Swearer, "Sulak Sivaraksa's Buddhist Vision for Renewing Society," in Queen and King, op. cit.
15 Bellah, p. 213.
16 Ibid., p. 201.
17 Ibid., p. 210.
18 Swearer, op. cit. p. 196.
19 Sallie B. King, "Conclusion: Buddhist Social Activism," in Queen and King, op. cit., pp. 402–404.
20 Queen, "Introduction," p. 5.

21 Deane William Ferm, *Third World Liberation Theologies: An Introductory Survey* (Maryknoll, NY: Orbis Books, 1992), 1, quoted in Queen, *Engaged Buddhism*, p. 5.
22 Queen, "Introduction," p. 5.
23 Ibid., p. 6.
24 Ibid., p. 7.
25 Ibid., pp. 7–8.
26 Ibid., p. 8.
27 Ibid., p. 9.
28 Ibid., p. 10.
29 Ibid., p. 11.
30 It was Thich Nhat Hanh's appeal to Martin Luther King, Jr. to speak out on the war in Vietnam that was purportedly responsible for King's decision publicly to repudiate the war, which he first did in a joint press conference with Nhat Hanh in 1966. Sallie B. King, "Thich Nhat Hanh and the Unified Buddhist Church in Vietnam: Nondualism in Action," in Queen and King, op. cit., pp. 323–324.
31 Ibid., p. 321.
32 Queen, "Introduction," p. 12.
33 Ibid., p. 11.
34 Ibid., p. 19.
35 Ibid., p. 31.
36 I am not unaware of the many discussions that constantly rage concerning "essentialism" and our (in)ability to define religions (or any phenomena, for that matter). These are complex, philosophical arguments that, while not without import, would take us wildly off course if we were to pursue them here. Although I do not support essentialist definitions of religions that regard them as transcendent, transhistorical, or transcultural entities, nevertheless, I believe that if language is to be useful, we must be able to set limits for the categories we employ, and this implies that some claimants to a particular religious appellation are bound to be excluded on the basis our definitions. Nothing of what follows, however, constitutes a judgment about the worth or importance of the movements under consideration. That is, by saying that a movement can or cannot be called "basically Buddhist," I am not saying that that movement lacks worth or importance. My concerns are solely definitional and my goal is simply to understand the relationships of these movements to other "Buddhist" and "non-Buddhist" movements, as well as to the more ephemeral entity that we conventionally refer to as "Buddhism."
37 See Chapter 2 of Noble Ross Reat's *Buddhism: A History* (Berkeley, CA: Asian Humanities Press, 1994) for a discussion of the problem of establishing the earliest records of the Buddhist traditions, and thus of those teachings which may be reliably attributed to the Buddha. There Reat concludes that "on the basis of agreement between the *Salistamba Sutra* and material found in the Pali canon, one may say with confidence that the essence of the historical Buddha's teachings was the Four Noble Truths" (p. 24).
38 Here it should be noted that I am not really even asking whether engaged Buddhism may properly be regarded as Buddhist, but rather, whether its social ethics may be so regarded. It is imaginable that one might be a Buddhist and employ an ethics that is not derivative of one's own religious heritage. Thus, any conclusion I reach with regard to the relationship of engaged Buddhist social ethics to basic Buddhist social ethics should not be regarded as tantamount to saying that engaged Buddhists are not really Buddhists.

39 Bardwell L. Smith, "Sinhalese Buddhism and the Dilemmas of Re-interpretation," in Smith, op. cit., p. 106; italics added.

40 See Reat, pp. 39–40, and David J. Kalupahana, *Ethics in Early Buddhism* (Honolulu: University of Hawaii Press, 1995), p. 114.

41 It is probably better to say for the entire populace, as it is not the society that is to be saved, but the individuals who compose society.

42 Russell F. Sizemore and Donald K. Swearer, Introduction in Sizemore and Swearer (eds.), *Ethics, Wealth, and Salvation: A Study in Buddhist Social Ethics* (Columbia: University of South Carolina Press, 1990), p. 9.

43 Robin W. Lovin, "Ethics, Wealth and Eschatology: Buddhist and Christian Strategies for Change," in Sizemore and Swearer op. cit.

44 Sizemore and Swearer, op. cit., p. 10.

45 Lest it be thought that these ideas exist only within early and Theravada Buddhism and do not form the basis of a Mahayana social ethics, it is instructive to look at Nagarjuna's *The Precious Garland of Advice for the King* (*Rajaparikatha-ratnamala*), purportedly written as advice to his friend, King Udayi of the Satavahana Dynasty of South Central India. It should first be noted that Nagarjuna's advice to the king commences with the council that his own enlightenment far outweighs the importance of any of his kingly duties. The implication here is, no doubt, that the good king is one who rules according to enlightened insight, though the advice that he "renounce the world/For the sake of true glory" not only has obvious parallels with the life of the Buddha, but also accords with the more general Buddhist axiom that the liberation of individuals is the *sine qua non* of Buddhism itself. As king, then, Udayi may do wondrous things for the populace, but his own liberation takes precedence over all else. As Robert A. F. Thurman puts it, "as enlightenment of each one individually is the most important thing for each one, one by one, the enlightenment of any one individual is of supreme importance at any one time"; or again, "he [i.e., Nagarjuna] does not consider any ends of society, achieved by getting the king to follow his policies, to be as important as the king's own self-development and self-liberation" ("Nagarjuna's Guidelines for Buddhist Social Action," in *The Path of Compassion: Writings on Socially Engaged Buddhism*, ed. Fred Eppsteiner [Berkeley, CA: Parallax Press, 1988], pp. 122 and 125). Relatedly, then, even should the king decide to retain his throne, he ought still to dedicate himself to self-development and self-liberation, and should therefore pursue a life of detachment from sensory pleasures and a concomitant dedication to meditative practice. With regard to his sovereign responsibilities, the advice of Nagarjuna on Buddhist statecraft is virtually identical to the social ethics initiated within early Buddhism and refined over time within the Theravada tradition, where primary importance is put on the liberation of individuals, and the role of Buddhist social ethics is seen as pragmatically related to this ultimate goal. The state is thus to rule benevolently and to support the monastic *sangha* so as to provide the conditions wherein individuals may seek their own enlightened liberation.

46 Andrew Olendski, "Meditation, Healing, and Stress Reduction," in Queen, *Engaged Buddhism in the West*, p. 313.

47 For discussions of Buddhist social ethics see, for instance, Uma Chakravarti, *The Social Dimension of Early Buddhism* (Delhi: Oxford University Press, 1987); Bardwell L. Smith (ed.), *The Two Wheels of Dhamma: Essays on the Theravada Tradition in India and Ceylon* (Chambersburg, PA: American Academy of Religion, 1972); Russell F. Sizemore and Donald K. Swearer (eds.), *Ethics, Wealth, and Salvation: A Study in Buddhist Social Ethics* (Columbia:

University of South Carolina Press, 1990); and David J. Kalupahana, *Ethics in Early Buddhism* (Honolulu: University of Hawaii Press, 1992).

48 Queen, "Introduction," p. 11.

49 John Ferguson, *War and Peace in the World's Religions* (New York: Oxford University Press, 1978), pp. 43–42.

50 Richard F. Gombrich, *Theravada Buddhism: A Social History from Ancient Benares to Modern Colombo* (London and New York: Routledge and Kegan Paul, 1988), p. 106.

51 Queen, "Introduction," p. 32; italics added.

52 Ibid., 33; p. italics added.

53 It is conceivable that Queen has identified a necessary characteristic of Buddhism, and one to which engaged Buddhism does, in fact, conform. As noted, however, such conformity does not guarantee that engaged Buddhism is basically Buddhist. There may be other necessary characteristics that engaged Buddhism lacks, as indeed, I suggest it does.

14

DOES BUDDHISM NEED
HUMAN RIGHTS?

Derek S. Jeffreys

In 1995, the *Journal of Buddhist Ethics* held an on-line conference on Buddhism and human rights.[1] Responding, in part, to the "Declaration towards a Global Ethic," drafted at the 1993 Parliament of the World's Religions, this conference produced a lively exchange. Some insisted that Buddhism needs human rights, while others rejected them as ill-suited to Buddhism. In 2000, this same journal hosted a second on-line conference, this time devoted to engaged Buddhism.[2] What emerged from this discussion was the close link between engaged Buddhism and human rights. In fact, some insisted that human rights are an integral element of the engaged Buddhism Movement.

For those familiar with Anglo-American political theory, this uncritical embrace of human rights is puzzling. Those discussing Buddhism and human rights rarely acknowledge some significant criticisms of a human rights ethic. For example, few show any awareness of the debates provoked by the great political theorist Leo Strauss.[3] Without argument, they assume that the concept of human rights is univocal, a claim Strauss famously challenged with his distinction between ancient and modern notions of rights. Similarly, engaged Buddhists largely ignore recent critics like Alasdair McIntyre, Michael Sandel, Jean Bethke Elshtain and Mary Ann Glendon.[4] These thinkers urge us to abandon a human rights ethic, which they see as a confused product of the European Enlightenment. Unfortunately, engaged Buddhists seem oblivious to this critique. Finally, many engaged Buddhists often criticize a simplistic account of human rights. Repeatedly, we are treated to descriptions of human rights as presupposing the "atomistic" individual, an isolated and freestanding island with little connection to other people. Undoubtedly, thinkers like Thomas Hobbes endorse this conception of rights, but others like Martha Nussbaum and Alan Gewirth reject the individualism often associated with human rights.[5]

Rather than focusing on these deficiencies in engaged Buddhism's presentation of the contemporary human rights debate, however, in this essay, I will consider a Buddhist critic of human rights, the Thai monk,

270

Phra Prayudh Payutto. A scholar of the Pali Canon, Phra Payutto has written extensively on social, economic, and political topics. Drawing on his work, I will suggest that grounding human rights in Buddhism is philosophically problematic. First, I consider Damien Keown's attempt to develop a Buddhist conception of human rights. One of the more philosophically sophisticated thinkers in the Buddhism and human rights debate, Keown derives human rights from Buddhist duties. Second, I summarize Phra Payutto's 1993 address to the Parliament of the World's Religions, in which he sharply criticizes the concept of human rights. Third, drawing on his criticisms, I demonstrate difficulties in Keown's position. His argument requires a stable agent who possesses rights, and Phra Payutto demonstrates that this concept is merely conventional. Ascribing rights to persons requires that we revise Buddhist ontology, a move Phra Payutto would never endorse. Fourth, I consider objections to Phra Payutto's argument, responding to doubts about linking metaphysics and ethics, concerns about human rights and value, and arguments that engaged Buddhism must be practical, not philosophical. I conclude by urging scholars to reconsider their quest for a Buddhist theory of human rights.

Damien Keown and human rights

Despite heated controversies, the 1993 Parliament of the World's Religions affirmed the importance of human rights. In its documents, it maintained that they provide a common *ethical* currency that can unite different religious traditions. It urged religious leaders to support human rights, and unite around common ethical and political goals. This challenge met with both praise and condemnation. Among Buddhists, some welcomed it, arguing that Buddhism can and should support human rights. Others, however, expressed skepticism that Buddhism and human rights could ever be reconciled.

In 1995, Damien Keown responded to this skepticism by philosophically defending a Buddhist theory of human rights. In an article entitled "Are There Human Rights in Buddhism?" he carefully defines human rights, noting that a human right is not merely a moral principle. Historically, a right originally referred to justice and proper relations in a community.[6] However, it then developed into an entitlement claim linked to individuals. Keown notes several key elements of this idea. First, a right is something that an individual *possesses*. Analogically, we can apply it to states or other entities, but primarily, it refers to individuals. Second, a right is something to which a person is *entitled*, creating a corresponding *obligation* on the part of others. Third, rights can take the form of either "claim-rights" or a "liberty-rights."[7] With a claim-right, a person claims a good that others are obliged to provide. For example, when I have a right to life, I claim the good of life, and others have an obligation to abstain from killing me. With a liberty-right, a person claims a liberty to act. For example, when I claim a right to free speech, others have an obligation to allow me to speak freely. In summary form, Keown defines a right as "a benefit which confers upon its holder either a claim or a liberty."[8] Importantly, he notes that unlike other moral idioms, it "provides a particular perspective on justice, in that the right-holder always stands in the position of beneficiary."[9]

After defining a human right, Keown reviews potential Buddhist justifications for human rights. First, he considers human dignity as a potential source of rights. Dignity is the ethical ground for human rights found in the 1948 United Nations "Universal Declaration of Human Rights." However, Keown notes that the concept of human dignity appears rarely in the Pali Canon and not at all in the Four Noble Truths. Moreover, *prima facie*, the language of dignity conflicts with Buddhist ideas like the impermanence of all conditioned things and the no-self doctrine.[10]

Instead of human dignity as a source of human rights, some contemporary thinkers appeal to Dependent Origination or *paticcasamuppada*. Often, we hear that all things are interdependent, and therefore, we ought to value both human and non-human life. Keown dismisses this argument, at one point calling it a "conjuring trick."[11] In his view, it begins with a factual claim about relations between things, and then illegitimately derives a claim about values.[12] Such an enterprise succumbs to the Naturalistic Fallacy, made famous by David Hume and G. E. Moore. To be technical, such a fallacy occurs when an argument's conclusion contains a normative element that is absent from its premises. Keown thinks this problem dooms any attempt to derive human rights from *paticcasamuppada*.

In contrast, Keown grounds human rights in a conception of goodness. Rather than focusing on the first two of the Four Noble Truths, he develops a conception of the good from the last two. Human rights acknowledge that human value "lies nowhere else than in the literally infinite capacity of human nature for participation in goodness."[13] They are, Keown maintains, prerequisites for developing the "human good-in-community," defining what is necessary for human beings to lead fulfilled lives in society.[14] Without rights, "the opportunities for the realization of human good are greatly reduced."[15] Keown insists that despite significant differences, competing religious and philosophical traditions can acknowledge "a substructure known as 'human rights,'" a complex of fundamental rights and liberties which are the preconditions for the realization of particular opportunities made available by competing ideologies."[16]

How does Keown move from this general claim about the good of human-flourishing-in-community to human rights? He acknowledges that the concept of human rights rarely appears explicitly in Buddhist texts.

Yet, he agrees with Alan Gewirth, who argues that it can be implicit in the moral traditions of a society.[17] Drawing on this idea, Keown links the Buddhist Five Precepts or *Panca Sila* with human rights, arguing that we can translate them into rights.[18]

Keown's translation occurs as follows. First, he maintains that in "taking the precepts," a Buddhist acknowledges a duty to others arising from the *Dhamma*. Second, he adopts the familiar idea that a duty is correlative with a right, establishing rights linked with the Five Precepts.[19] Finally, he describes these rights as claim-rights, thus concluding that people have a claim to the goods recognized by them. To take one example, in the first precept, a person states, "I undertake the precept to abstain from taking life."[20] This precept expresses a duty to refrain from taking life, which we can correlate with a right to life. Persons can then claim this right over against others and political authorities.

In concluding his argument, Keown states that the apparent difference between the Five Precepts and human rights is "one of form rather than substance."[21] Drawing on the "logic of moral relations," he thinks that we can extrapolate human rights from central Buddhist ideas. Thus, from the Five Precepts, he derives a right to life, property and marital fidelity. Keown insists that these rights are not alien imports from Western political theory, but are present implicitly in Buddhist thought.

Phra Payutto and the poverty of human rights

Turning to Phra Payutto, amidst the euphoria over human rights at the 1993 Parliament of World's Religions, Phra Payutto issued some caveats that, unfortunately, few took very seriously. Through a proxy, he gave an address devoted to international politics in the twenty-first century.[22] The end of the Cold War overturned the international order, but many people were, nevertheless, optimistic that we would enter an era of peace and prosperity.[23] Unfortunately, events in the early 1990s dashed these hopes. Ethnic wars, genocide, environmental destruction, terrorism, and the HIV/AIDS epidemic plagued international politics.

To address these terrible problems, Phra Payutto notes how some turn to human rights. The 1948 UN "Universal Declaration of Human Rights," subsequent human rights agreements during the Cold War, and human rights documents that religious bodies produced all seem to provide an ethical idiom we can use to solve international problems. Phra Payutto recognizes the value of these agreements and documents, viewing them as legal constructs that provide a modicum of order in a fractured and violent world. Yet, he insists that the importance of human rights is based on a "world still under the influence of divisive ways of thinking."[24] They establish a minimal guarantee that we will not destroy each other, yet this is a far cry from the ethical ideal they represent for so many people.

Why does Phra Payutto reject human rights as an *ethical* foundation for the international order? In his speech, he presents three arguments in summary fashion. First, like many non-Buddhists, he traces the origins of human rights to the sixteenth- and seventeenth-century European wars of religion. In these difficult times, human rights provided a moral minimum that prevented Protestants and Roman Catholics from murdering each other. Yet, Phra Payutto maintains that they represent an uneasy and imperfect compromise. Marked by a grudging surrender of power, it creates attitudes of resignation and dissention.[25]

In his second criticism of human rights, Phra Payutto distinguishes between conventional and ultimate truth. Ultimate truth is grounded in the *Dhamma*, reflecting an accurate understanding of reality. Conventional truth lacks this ground, yet is useful because it helps us navigate our way around our environment. For Phra Payutto, human rights are "a convention, purely human inventions which do not exist as a natural condition."[26] In this startling sentence, he departs from the Western tradition of natural rights, so powerfully articulated by the great European and American rights theorists of the eighteenth and nineteenth centuries. By removing their natural basis, he places human rights on a precarious footing, acknowledging that they need legal protection in order to have any meaning.

In a final criticism of human rights, Phra Payutto rejects them as "merely conventions for social behavior."[27] Undoubtedly, they control our behavior, and thus are valuable tools for preventing harm. However, they do nothing to get at the deeper causes of human suffering. Rehearsing the familiar Buddhist triad of greed, hatred and delusion, Phra Payutto suggests that a human rights ethic fails to uproot these deep motivations. Focusing primarily on outward behavior, it avoids any reference to our mental life. For Phra Payutto, such an ethic will never alleviate human suffering.

Are human rights merely conventional?

Although inadequately developed, Phra Payutto's critique of human rights reveals some significant difficulties in Keown's argument. His view that human rights are divisive is unexceptional. One can find similar claims in the work of Mary Ann Glendon and other critics of human rights language. Moreover, many in the liberal tradition, such as Alan Gewirth, have responded to this charge, insisting that human rights are perfectly compatible with pursuing the common good.[28] On this score, Phra Payutto has little to add, and there is nothing distinctively Buddhist about his argument.

His more important contribution lies in his claim that human rights are purely conventional. Throughout his writings on science and economics, he distinguishes between conventional and ultimate truth. For example, in his major work, *Buddhadhamma*, he defines conventional truth or *sammuti-sacca* as knowledge according to the five senses, which is considered relative or conventional.[29] In contrast, ultimate or higher truth, *paramattha-sacca*, originates from wisdom, providing insight into impermanence, suffering, and the no-self doctrine. Repeatedly, Phra Puyutto argues that distinguishing between these kinds of truth is indispensable for ending human suffering.

Often, he applies this distinction to the no-self doctrine, and this doctrine is what I think creates serious problems for Keown. For Phra Payutto, any conception of the self belongs to conventional truth. Naturally, we need names and other conventions to assist us in navigating our environment. However, ontologically, the self does not exist. Unfortunately, we cannot accept this idea, and adopt self-conceptions that produce repeated and severe suffering. In discussing the self, Phra Payutto outlines the five *khandas*, and then, in good Buddhist fashion, insists that they are merely causally linked elements. There is no person, agent, or self lurking behind them. Instead, we have a rapidly changing "integrated form composed of various elements."[30] Phra Payutto emphasizes both the *ontological* and *ethical* importance of the no-self doctrine. Ontologically, it helps us to achieve *panna* or wisdom about reality. Ethically, he enables us to overcome our pernicious attachments to self.

Returning to Keown's translation of *Dhammic* duties into rights, we can see why the no-self doctrine undermines it. In its light, we ought to think of the Five Precepts as outlining duties toward momentarily changing combinations of the five aggregates. Their peculiar instantiation in human beings makes humanity very special, and loving kindness, compassion, and other ethical concepts acknowledge this special character. Human beings have the extraordinary capacity to engage in intentional action, thus enabling them to shape their future in skillful ways. This capacity can ultimately lead to *nibbana*.

However, this analysis differs fundamentally from a claim that the five aggregates, embodied in a human form, possess a right. In fact, Keown's argument only works if there is a self. Recall, he insists that what is distinctive about a human rights ethic is that it "provides a particular perspective on justice, in that the right-holder always stands in the position of beneficiary."[31] In Western ethics and political theory, this idea makes a great deal of sense. In fact, most modern rights theorists devote considerable energy to defining the person and exploring action theory. For example, Alan Gewirth meticulously derives human rights from human freedom and well-being, which are for him, essential attributes of moral agency.[32] Similarly, Pope John Paul II, a vigorous supporter of human rights, insists that they can only receive a secure conceptual foundation if we anchor them in an adequate conception of the person.[33] Likewise, as

Keown acknowledges, the preamble to the 1948 UN "Universal Declaration of Human Rights" grounds human rights in the dignity of the person.

Many of these defenses of human rights presuppose a *substantial* view of the person. Persons are not merely a series of causal events, but have an enduring presence through time. Naturally, substance theorists differ on how to understand substance, with thinkers like Aristotle, Thomas Aquinas, Descartes and Edmund Husserl all offering competing conceptions of it. However, what characterizes them all is a commitment to something with properties that endure across time. As philosopher Richard Swinburne nicely puts it, a substance is anything "traceable through time under a form (that is, a system of essential properties which it has to preserve in order to be that substance)."[34]

Prima facie, this idea clashes with the Buddhist no-self doctrine, and the history of Buddhism's engagement with the idea of substance reflects this clash.[35] The key difficulty for Keown and a Buddhist human rights ethic is to define the rights-holder. Without a substance, who claims a right? Any answer to this question falls prey to the standard objections to the existence of the self, found throughout the Pali Canon and other Buddhist texts.[36] For example, we should ask Keown precisely which of the five aggregates possesses and claims a right. *Rupa* or corporeality changes instantly, making it ill-suited to be the rights possessor. Moreover, few human rights theorists are willing to accord rights on the basis of physical constitution. Because they also change constantly, any of the other *khandas* are equally incapable of playing the role Keown accords to the rights-claimant. We cannot identify the rights-holder with momentary sensations (*vedana*), or rapidly changing perceptions (*sanna*).

One candidate for what possesses a right might be the consciousness or cognition aggregate (*vinnana*). For many Buddhists, cognition is intentional in the Brentano sense.[37] Intentionality is the "aboutness" of consciousness, the idea that it takes an object. Perhaps for a moment, we can say that it takes as its object a right, thus yielding a rights-claim. Yet, like all the other *khandas*, cognition changes immediately, and it is unclear how we can ascribe a right to a brief moment of intentionality.

Perhaps the strongest candidate for the rights-holder is the formations *khanda*. Among many formations is *cetana* or intention, which shapes our future. If we identify *cetana* and the accumulated results with the rights-holders, we might then have a stable center of agency to which we could attribute rights. However, how does this center of agency differ from a self? Does it change constantly, or endure for some period of time? If it changes, what precisely is it that possesses a right?

Keown never addresses these questions, and his argument is therefore philosophically problematic. Illegitimately, his translation of duties to rights assumes the existence of an enduring agent, but without this presupposition, it fails. As Phra Payutto warns, we should never confuse ultimate and conventional truths. At most, Keown has shown that human rights are conventionally true. This Phra Payutto affirms, acknowledging that a regime of human rights reduces suffering. However, this affirmation of conventional truth differs radically from what we find in the 1948 UN "Universal Declaration on Human Rights," the Parliament of the World's Religions' "Declaration towards a Global Ethic," or similar statements about human rights from engaged Buddhists. These documents contain language of personhood that *prima facie* clashes with the no-self doctrine. Lacking a response to this incompatibility, we ought to resist an easy translation of Dhammic duties into human rights.

Objections

Some mitigate these difficulties by refusing to see the no-self doctrine as an ontological claim, by divorcing ethics from metaphysics, or by maintaining that engaged Buddhism should be entirely practical. To consider the first objection, Charles Strain contributed a paper to the *Journal of Buddhist Ethics* human rights conference in which he compares engaged Buddhism and Roman Catholic Social Ethics. At one point, he notes how the no-self doctrine creates problems for a human rights ethic, yet hastens to add that "the truth of the not-self is a skillful means for healing what ails our very lives rather than an absolute metaphysical category to which we might cling."[38] However, he provides no arguments to support this startling claim, and thus, it appears to be simply a way of avoiding complex philosophical issues. Unfortunately, this rejection of *anatta* as a metaphysical concept is common among some scholars of Buddhism. As Steven Collins notes in his superb book, *Selfless Persons*, such a rejection was very common among European scholars in the late nineteenth and early twentieth centuries.[39] Many simply could not believe that Buddhism included the no-self doctrine, and to eliminate their conceptual discomfort, they found various devices to explain it away.

Undoubtedly, as Strain suggests, the no-self doctrine has the pragmatic function of helping us reduce craving and clinging. In *Buddhadhamma*, Phra Payutto notes this function, and explores the benefits of *anatta*. Yet, he never implies that it is *only* a pragmatic doctrine, and to infer this from his work requires importing alien metaphysical baggage into it. Instead, he warns us not to become attached to ontological concepts. Sometimes, Phra Payutto cites those texts in the Pali Canon where the Buddha refuses to answer speculative questions. Yet, he locates them within a dialogical context, avoiding the mistake of reading them as absolute prohibitions against metaphysical speculation. Such speculation must play its *proper* role in the Buddhist life. It should never become an end-in-itself, a kind of attachment that Phra Payutto calls attachment to views or *ditthi*.[40]

Nevertheless, for him, this danger cannot become a licence to eliminate ontology altogether.

Another objection to considering *anatta* and human rights appears scattered throughout Keown's excellent book, *The Nature of Buddhist Ethics*. After noting that Buddhism provides "sufficient criteria for personal identity to allow the identification of subjects within a moral nexus," he insists that "to pursue the issue of the ultimate ontological constitution of individual natures in this context is to confuse ethics with metaphysics, and does not make a fruitful line of enquiry."[41] His suggestion seems to be that we can divorce ethics and metaphysics. Indeed, when discussing *upaya* in Mahayana Buddhism, he criticizes the "attempt to argue to an ethical conclusion from metaphysical premises, or from a fact to a value."[42] This procedure is suspect because although facts may be important for ethics, "they have no priority, and ethical issues must be addressed with ethical arguments; they cannot be brushed aside by reference to facts of a scientific, ontological, or metaphysical nature."[43]

What, precisely, is problematic about deriving ethics from ontology? While discussing Aristotle and the soul, Keown maintains that to "derive judgments of value from a factual description of the soul would be a form of the Naturalistic Fallacy."[44] Following John Finnis, he states that a purely descriptive, non-evaluative understanding of humanity "cannot deal in the currency of human good; by itself, it provides only a thin, one-dimensional picture of human nature."[45] In sum, Keown suggests that ethics should be an autonomous discipline, which avoids deriving its conclusions from ontology.

Without considerable development, these remarks cannot resolve the problems *anatta* creates for a Buddhist human rights theory. Appeals to the Naturalistic Fallacy effectively respond to ethics grounded entirely in science, such as Sociobiology. Often, these approaches do derive evaluative claims from non-evaluative premises. Whether crude or sophisticated, by itself, an appeal to what nature dictates cannot ground an ethic. However, we cannot use the Naturalistic Fallacy to dismiss an ethic grounded in well-developed metaphysic. For example, in describing the human being, Buddhism does not, as Keown alleges, offer a "purely descriptive, non-evaluative understanding of humanity." Instead, its account of the natural world and our place in it is evaluative, with value linked to certain states of affairs. Repeatedly, in his writings on economics and science, Phra Payutto rejects the scientific and social-scientific tendency to posit a morally-neutral set of "facts."[46] Bemoaning this modern penchant, he insists that we reconnect values and scientific inquiry. Reality, as the sciences explain it, always contains value. This kind of axiology is immune from charges of the Naturalistic Fallacy. The Naturalistic Fallacy states that we cannot derive an evaluative conclusion from an argument containing only factual claims. However, because the Buddhist conception of persons contains evaluative elements, any ethical conclusion we draw from it avoids this logical blunder.

Moreover, by invoking this fallacy, Keown shelters his argument from metaphysical objections, constructing an artificial division between ethics and metaphysics. Often, with devices like the Naturalistic Fallacy, contemporary Anglo-American ethics separates ethics from larger questions of value and ontology. The result has been a facile dismissal of the metaphysical issues integral to any ethics.[47] Why is life *dukkha*? How are we linked to other beings? Are we selves? What is causality? For Phra Payutto and other Thai Buddhists, these questions are central to human existence, and should be part of any ethical inquiry. Contrary to what Keown asserts, pursuing them within the context of ethics is "a fruitful line of enquiry." One of the satisfying elements of Phra Payutto's work is that he sees no difficulties in making ontological claims. In fact, they are so important that they occupy much of the early chapters of *Buddhadhamma*. In reading this work, we do not find Wittgensteinian claims about language-games or historicist arguments about the linguistic character of all human knowledge. Instead, we see a refreshing engagement with central metaphysical issues that have been part of Buddhism for centuries. The title of *Buddhadhamma*'s first chapter summarizes this engagement well; ontological questions are among the "things that must be understood first."[48]

However, if we reject the ethical ideal of human rights, are we then left in a sea of cultural relativism that prevents us from seeking social justice? Engaged Buddhists often argue that in an interdependent and rapidly changing world, human rights are the only way of avoiding catastrophe. They show a genuine aspiration for social justice, yet imply that Buddhism without human rights is ethically deficient. In fact, many in the current debate openly suggest that this is the case. For example, in a startling sentence, Keown states that for "an intellectually dynamic tradition, Buddhism is a lightweight in moral and political philosophy."[49] Similarly, Christopher Queen wonders:

> in light of the widespread conditions of human misery in our world today, whether rule-based morality, mental cultivation, individualized good works, and generalized vows to save all beings will be enough to prevent the spread of political tyranny, economic injustice, and environmental degradation in the era to come.[50]

He answers this question in the negative, insisting that through the concept of human rights, engaged Buddhism recognizes "the inalienable value of the human person, whatever his or her level of achievement or standing in the community."[51]

The idea that Buddhism without human rights is ethically substandard is an audacious claim to make about a tradition with centuries of philo-sophical development. It may or may not have a tradition of human rights, but does it follow that it is ethically deficient? Without serious argument, this conclusion is completely unwarranted. To return to Phra Payutto, drawing on concepts like *metta* and *karuna*, he writes extensively on Buddhist social ethics, rarely discussing human rights. Moreover, he applies these traditional concepts to contemporary economic and social problems. Undoubtedly, in the face of globalization, we need creative thinking that applies Buddhist concepts to new problems. For example, the 1997 Asian financial crisis led many Thai thinkers to begin serious reflec-tion about Buddhism and the morality of the market. Yet, in their work, they often employ traditional Buddhist concepts in creative ways, without adopting human rights language. To say that these ethics are conceptually sub-standard is an ambitious thesis, which in my view, has yet to be substantiated in any serious way.

Nevertheless, can we base a human rights ethics on the understanding of value implicit in Buddhist thought? In a thoughtful article, Sallie B. King suggests that the idea of the potential for enlightenment in Tharavada Buddhism and the notion of a Buddha-nature in Mahayana Buddhism can ground human rights. Human rights, she maintains, acknowledge that each individual is "of great, perhaps absolute value," an idea rooted in the "notion that a human birth is a rare and precious birth, the direct implica-tion of which is that a human life is a rare and precious thing, a thing of great value."[52] Arguing that this axiology is compatible with human rights, King shows how it can support human rights activism of various kinds.

King ably illustrates how we can ground a Buddhist theory of value in the precious character of a human birth. However, she fails to adequately derive human rights from this axiology. To quote Keown again, a human right is particular kind of moral idiom that "provides a particular perspec-tive on justice, in that the right-holder always stands in the position of beneficiary."[53] Establishing a Buddhist ground for valuing human life is crucial, but deriving rights from it requires further argument. King omits any discussion of how this argument would proceed. Like Keown, she ignores the problem of the agent claiming rights, never telling us how we can ascribe rights to the five *khandas*.

Part of the difficulty here is that King simply assumes the viability of a human rights ethic, without acknowledging challenges to it. For example, at one point, she suggests that:

> it might be best to drop the separate terms "rights" and "responsi-bilities" and speak in a unified way of a community of "mutual obligation" in which our individual Goods and the social Good co-inhere such that my obligation to you is also my obligation to

myself. While this would be philosophically more accurate from a Buddhist perspective, the Buddhist community will probably continue to speak with the larger world using "rights" language, since this is the language to which we have become accustomed in international discourse.[54]

I find this paragraph very puzzling. If, as King suggests at the end of her essay, a Buddhist ethic grounded in the value of a human birth "constitutes a provocative conceptual alternative to the better established Western theories of social ethics," why adopt human rights language at all?[55] What seems to prevent King from drawing this conclusion is her commitment to the "language to which we have become accustomed in international discourse." However, without serious philosophical argument, this preference for the *status quo* is utterly arbitrary. In contemporary religious and secular ethics, there are some deep misgivings about what we have become "accustomed to" in modernity. Like some others in the engaged Buddhism movement, King seems oblivious to the philosophical and religious challenges to modernity. In light of the horrible crimes of the twentieth century, many have concluded that key elements of modern ethics are profoundly harmful. In South-east Asia, in particular, some Buddhists have become deeply skeptical of contemporary ethical justifications of market economics. Some of this critique radically challenges our modern presuppositions about human rights. Unfortunately, however, King shows little recognition of these concerns, and clings to the familiar language of human rights so pervasive among engaged Buddhists.[56]

A final objection to the argument I have made is that it is unnecessarily abstract, and has little impact on social practice. If Phra Payutto affirms human rights as important legal devices, what does it matter if they are incompatible with the no-self doctrine? Buddhists can sign on to human rights documents, and people of good will can unite to pursue concrete proposals for social justice. In a world marked by profound suffering, some suggest that discussing ontological niceties is a dangerous waste of time, an impediment to positive social change.

We should acknowledge the value of international law and human rights agreement. However, by dismissing ontological claims, we do an injustice to Buddhism's extraordinary analysis of the mind. In human rights, engaged Buddhists claim to have discovered a universal ethical idiom that transcends religious difference. However, in embracing them, they too easily overlook fundamental religious and philosophical differences about the nature of persons. Recall, in his third criticism of a human rights ethics, Phra Payutto focuses on mental motivation. For him, the primary subject matter of ethics ought to be the link between mental motivation and action. To understand this connection, one must understand how the mind works, and this naturally leads to the no-self doctrine,

Dependent Origination, and other central Buddhist doctrines. These ideas are *not* a peripheral addition to a human rights ethics, some element of a *particularistic* ethic as opposed to the universalism of human rights.[57] Rather, they are an integral part of the *Dhamma*, a universal teaching open to all human beings. To ignore them in order to pursue some allegedly universal moral idiom called human rights is to neglect the beauty and strength of Buddhist ethics.

Conclusion

In closing, let me be clear about what I have and have not argued in this chapter. First, I have *not* maintained that human rights are an imperialistic imposition on Buddhist thought. Clearly, there are Buddhists like the Dalai Lama, Thich Nhat Hanh, and Sulak Sivaraksa who argue for a Buddhist human rights ethic. Moreover, whether or not the concept of human rights is implicit in the Pali Canon is an extremely complex exegetical issue, one that I am not competent to consider. Second, with Phra Payutto, I have affirmed the value of the legal regime of human rights, which has been very important for people throughout the world. Nothing I have said should be taken as a criticism of brave political activists opposing oppression in Southeast Asia and elsewhere. Instead, I have argued that, *prima facie*, a human rights *ethic* is incompatible with the no-self doctrine. Although skillfully presented, Damien Keown's argument for human rights requires an enduring self, an idea that Phra Payutto and many other Buddhists reject. Like others in this Buddhism and human rights debate, Keown ignores the extensive discussion about human rights in Western political theory. Going back to Leo Strauss and his generation, much of this debate focused on the nature of the self. What becomes clear from it is that a metaphysic of substance underlies many modern ideas of human rights. Once we eliminate this substance ontology, it becomes doubtful that we can retain the same ethic. Rather than despairing of this outcome, we ought to acknowledge it, and begin to explore the particulars of Buddhist ethics. Abandoning the pursuit of an elusive Buddhist human rights theory, we might then begin to appreciate Buddhism's fascinating understanding of the mind, a philosophical gem that has much to teach us.[58]

Notes

1   Most of these papers have been collected in *Buddhism and Human Rights*, ed. by Damien V. Keown, Charles Prebish, and Wayne R. Husted (Surrey: Curzon Press, 1998).
2   The papers from this conference are available at <http//jbe.la.psu.edu>.
3   For his most famous statement of this thesis, see Leo Strauss, *Natural Right and History* (Chicago: The University of Chicago Press, 1953).

4 See Jean Bethke Elshtain, *Democracy on Trial* (New York: Basic Books, 1995); Mary Ann Glendon, *Rights Talk: The Impoverishment of Political Discourse* (New York: The Free Press, 1993); Alasdair MacIntyre, *After Virtue: A Study in Moral Theory* (Notre Dame, IN: The University of Notre Dame Press, 1981); Alasdair MacIntyre, *Whose Justice? Which Rationality?* (Notre Dame, IN: The University of Notre Dame Press, 1988); and Michael Sandel, *Liberalism and the Limits of Justice* (Cambridge: Cambridge University Press, 1982); also by Michael Sandel, *Democracy and its Discontents: America in Search of a Public Philosophy* (Cambridge, MA: Harvard University Press, 1997).

5 For one example of the charge of atomistic individualism, see Sallie B. King's recent essay on Buddhism and human rights, in which she charges Western human rights thought with embracing the idea of an "autonomous individual." Sallie B. King, "Human Rights in Contemporary Engaged Buddhism," in Roger R. Jackson and John J. Makransky (eds), *Buddhist Theology: Critical Reflections by Contemporary Buddhist Scholars* (Surrey: Curzon Press, 2000), 294. I will return to her discussion later in this chapter.

6 Keown, in Keown *et al.*, op. cit. p. 17.

7 All references in this paragraph are to Keown, 1998, p. 19.

8 Keown, op. cit., p. 19.

9 Ibid.

10 Ibid., pp. 24–25.

11 Ibid., p., 27.

12 Ibid,. pp. 28–29.

13 Ibid., p. 30.

14 Ibid., p. 30.

15 ,Ibid., p. 31.

16 Ibid.

17 Ibid., p. 20. For Gewirth's argument, see Alan Gewirth, *Human Rights: Essays on Justification and Applications* (Chicago: The University of Chicago Press, 1982).

18 Keown, op. cit., p. 31.

19 Ibid., p. 32. In developing this idea, Keown draws heavily from John Finnis' work, see John Finnis, *Natural Law and Natural Rights* (Oxford: Clarendon Press, 1980). In a response to Keown, Craig K. Ihara maintains that the "central flaw in the arguments given by Keown and Finnis is to assume that every kind of 'ought' or 'duty' entails a corresponding right." I agree with this point, but will not pursue it in this paper. For Ihara's discussion, see Craig K. Ihara "Why there Are No Rights in Buddhism: A Reply to Damien Keown," in *Buddhism and Human Rights*, 1998, pp. 43-52.

20 To understand the Five Precepts, I have consulted Hammalawa Saddhatissa's *Buddhist Ethics* (Boston, MA: Wisdom Publications, 1997).

21 Keown, op. cit., p. 32.

22 All of my references to this address will be to Phra Prayudh Payutto, *Buddhist Solutions for the Twenty-First Century* (Bangkok, Thailand: Buddhadhamma Foundation, 1996). For a recent discussion of Phra Payutto's work, see Pirob Udomittipong and Chris Walker (eds), *Socially Engaged Buddhism for the New Millennium: Essays in Honor of the Ven. Phra Dhammapitaka (Bhikkhu P.A. Payutto) on his 60th Birthday* (Sathirakoses–Nagapradipa Foundation and Foundation for Children, 1999). Soraj Hongladarom carefully compares Phra Payutto and Sulak Sivaraksa on human rights, in "Buddhism and Human Rights in the Thoughts of Sulak Sivaraksa and Phra Dhammapidok (Prayudh Payutto)," in *Buddhism and Human Rights*, 1998, pp.97-110.

23 Payutto, op. cit., p. 63.
24 Ibid., p. 70.
25 These attitudes impede fraternity, an important element of a just social order. In several essays devoted to liberty, Phra Payutto decries the absence of fraternity in American politics. For him, the language of human rights is an important cause of our divisive politics. For one of his discussions of fraternity, see ibid., Chapter 3.
26 Ibid., p. 71.
27 Ibid., p. 71.
28 See Alan Gewirth, *The Community of Rights* (Chicago: The University of Chicago Press, 1997).
29 Phra Payudh Payutto, *Buddhadhamma: Natural Laws and Values for Life*, trans. by Grant Olson (Albany, NY: State University of New York Press 1995), p. 284 n. 101.
30 Payutto, 1995, p. 53.
31 Keown, op. cit., p. 19.
32 Alan Gewirth, *Reason and Morality* (Chicago: The University of Chicago Press, 1978), see also Gewirth, 1982.
33 Pope John Paul II discusses human rights in many of his works. For one such discussion, see "Evangelium Vitae," sections 19–21, in Joseph Donders (ed.), *The Encyclicals in Everyday Language* (Maryknoll, NY: Orbis Press, 1996).
34 Richard Swinburne, *The Christian God* (Oxford: Clarendon Press, 1994), p. 13.
35 In understanding this engagement, I have been helped by two excellent works. In his *On Being Mindless*, Paul J. Griffiths discusses substance in the context of Buddhist practice of the "cessation of consciousness"; see Paul J. Griffiths, *On Being Mindless: Buddhist Meditation and the Mind-Body Problem* (La Salle, IL: Open Court Press, 1986). In a detailed study that has, unfortunately, never been published, Matthew Kapstein explores substance and personal identity.
36 Phra Payutto presents some of these standard arguments in the early pages of *Buddhadhamma*, Payutto, 1995, pp. 53–60.
37 In the nineteenth century, Franz Brentano revived and developed the medieval notion of intentionality, and his student, Edmund Husserl, focused heavily on intentionality. I have taken the idea of applying Brentano intentionality to Buddhist cognition from Paul J. Griffiths; see Paul J. Griffiths, *An Apology for Apologetics: A Study in the Logic of Interreligious Dialogue* (Maryknoll, New York: Orbis Press, 1991), p. 92. In *On Being Mindless*, he explores some interesting possible exceptions to the idea that consciousness is intentional, (Griffiths, 1986).
38 Charles R. Strain, "Socially Engaged Buddhism's Contribution to the Transformation of Catholic Social Teachings on Human Rights," in *Buddhism and Human Rights*, p. 164.
39 See Steven Collins, *Selfless Persons: Imagery and Thought in Theravada Buddhism* (Cambridge: Cambridge University Press, 1982), Chapter 1.
40 Phra Payutto discusses *ditthi* at length. For one example, see Payutto, 1995, p. 132.
41 Damien V. Keown, *The Nature of Buddhist Ethics* (London: Macmillian, 1992),p. 19.
42 Ibid., p. 161.
43 Ibid., p. 162.
44 Ibid., p. 210.
45 Ibid. In adopting Finnis' argument, Keown embraces an ethic that is very controversial among Roman Catholics. Some criticisms of it focus on the

Naturalistic Fallacy, which Neo-Thomists maintain poses no difficulties for a metaphysically sophisticated natural law theory. For one such discussion, see Russell Hittinger, *A Critique of the New Natural Law Theory* (Notre Dame, IN: The University of Notre Dame Press, 1989).

46 See Phra Prayudh Payutto, *Buddhist Economics: A Middle Way for the Market Place* (Bangkok, Thailand: Buddhadhamma Foundation, 1992).

47 Several contemporary scholars bemoan this tendency. For one excellent treatment of it in medical ethics, see Gilbert Meilaender, *Body, Soul, and Bioethics* (Notre Dame, IN: The University of Notre Dame Press, 1995).

48 Payutto, 1995, Part 1, Chapter 1.

49 Keown, 1998, p. 15.

50 "Introduction: A New Buddhism." This essay is available at http//jbe.la.psu.edu.

51 Both quotes are from "Introduction: A New Buddhism." This essay is available at <http//jbe.la.psu.edu>.

52 King, 2000, p. 304.

53 Keown, 1998, p. 19.

54 King, 2000, p. 300.

55 Ibid., p. 308.

56 I am grateful to Christopher Queen for suggesting I read Sallie King's article.

57 Keown implies this distinction between a universal and particular ethic when he contrasts "comprehensive conceptions of the good" articulated by religious traditions with the universal "minimum conditions" for human flourishing defined by human rights charters, see Keown, 1998, p. 31.

58 This chapter was originally given as a paper at the Annual Meeting of the American Academy of Religion, November 20, 2000. I thank Professor Christopher Queen for his helpful response to my presentation. I have also benefited from on-line discussions during the "Journal of Buddhist Ethics" 2000 conference on Socially Engaged Buddhism, and the perceptive comments of Paul J. Griffiths of the University of Illinois, Chicago.

15

ENGAGED BUDDHISM

New and improved? Made in the USA of Asian materials

Thomas Freeman Yarnall

In recent decades a movement of "engaged Buddhists" has begun to sweep the globe. This movement is comprised of a wide range of individuals from diverse cultural backgrounds. Inspired by Buddhist values, they are united by a common drive to lessen the suffering of the world, in particular by "engaging" (as opposed to renouncing) the various social, political, and economic institutions, structures, and systems in society. Such engagement can take many forms (e.g., voting, lobbying, peaceful protest, civil disobedience), but it is always aimed at actively challenging and changing those institutions which are perceived as perpetuating suffering through various forms of oppression, injustice, and the like.

The term "engaged Buddhism" appears originally to have been coined by the Vietnamese Buddhist teacher, Thich Nhat Hanh, in 1963, and the expanded term "socially engaged Buddhism" emerged during the 1980s.[1] However, apart from the usage of these relatively new labels, scholars are divided as to when, where, and how a politically or socially engaged Buddhism actually first began.

One group of scholars maintains that Buddhists have never accepted a dualistic split between "spiritual" and "social" domains. To engage in the spiritual life necessarily includes (though it cannot be reduced to) social engagement. Thus, for them, since the time of Shakyamuni the Buddhadharma has *always* had a more-or-less fully articulated socio-political dimension in addition to its (supposedly "other-worldly") spiritual/soteriological dimension. Modern forms of Buddhism (engaged Buddhism or otherwise) are essentially continuous with traditional forms, in spite of any superficially apparent differences. Due to this emphasis upon continuity with Buddhism's traditional past, I will refer to members of this group as "*traditionists*."[2]

A second group takes a very different approach and arrives at a decidedly different conclusion. While this group admits that there have been doctrines and practices with socio-political relevance *latent* in Buddhism since its inception, it insists that these latencies have always remained relatively untapped, that they have not been (or often *could* not have been) fully realized until Buddhism's encounter with various Western elements unique to the modern era. Modern engaged Buddhism may share some essential features with traditional forms of Buddhism, but it also contains enough substantive differences to warrant calling it a relatively "new" form of Buddhism unique to the modern era.[3] Thus, due to their emphasis upon discontinuity with the past, I will refer to members of this group as "*modernists*."[4]

In addition, most members of these groups have tacitly considered their own position to be relatively natural or self-evident, and thus (until the last couple of years) neither group has taken the other's position very seriously – or at least they have given this impression by spending a minimum amount of time discounting the other group's position.[5] Traditionists have charged that modernists simply do not understand the essence or spirit of Buddhism, and that such modernists have thus been pre-disposed to miss the social theories and practices of Buddhists throughout the ages. Modernists, on the other hand, have dismissed traditionists as method-ologically naïve and historically reconstructive, insisting that traditionists peer unwittingly through a modern lens at ancient/traditional teachings.

As I have examined the burgeoning writings from these two groups I have become increasingly interested in the question of why these groups take the positions they do (both have some good arguments, and neither presents a completely self-evident position). What motivates these authors? Who are their intended audiences? Do the different scholars in these groups claim to represent these engaged movements, to be spokespersons ordained to provide a theoretical/historical basis for the activities of engaged Buddhists "on the ground"? Or do these authors seem to want to maintain a stance of "scholarly objectivity," merely describing these move-ments to others? In either case, how might traditional Asian Buddhists respond to these scholarly opinions? And how might different self-styled engaged Buddhists themselves respond to these opinions? (Or is it even possible to separate the "practitioners" of this movement from the theo-reticians who would shape their very understanding of who they are and what they are doing?) Thus, this present examination of the phenomenon of socially engaged Buddhism represents such a meta-level investigation (and ultimately a philosophical/methodological critique) of the society of scholars who themselves claim to represent (or describe) this social move-ment.

In particular, and in spite of their claims to methodological superiority, I have been continually struck by how ideologically motivated the modernists persistently seem to be. Much of what they write seems "natural" when read quickly and uncritically; but upon closer analysis this group of authors often appears almost obsessed with demonstrating, for example, what they perceive to be the *newness* of Buddhism's socially engaged dimension. The demonstration of this "newness" (and the corresponding emphasis on its previous "latency") seems to be not an observation but a *necessity*. Indeed, in reviewing the relatively short history of modernist writings on engaged Buddhism, it has often seemed that earlier vague descriptions of what it meant to be socially engaged were fine-tuned and developed over time in tacit response *to* emerging (traditionist) claims that Buddhism historically had been engaged. As traditionists have presented evidence of past Buddhist activities which met the modernists' criteria for engagement, it seems that modernists have been driven to modify their criteria precisely in order to continue to construe socially engaged Buddhism as something new.

It is important to underscore at the outset that in this present study I will not be primarily engaged with assessing these authors' (historical) truth claims (though to do so is clearly an important desideratum): it is simply beyond the scope of this study to thoroughly research and present the variety of historical evidence that would have to be amassed in order to address (or refute) the many shifting modernist definitions of what it means to be socially engaged. Instead, the present chapter will attempt to address some of the theoretical and methodological issues mentioned above, particularly as they regard the majority modernists. Nor will I be arguing (at this meta-level) that the modernists' insistence on discontinuity with the past is entirely "wrong" (one can, with good reason, easily choose to emphasize either continuities or discontinuities with the past). Rather, I will be striving to accomplish the following two limited objectives. First, I hope to demonstrate that the discontinuity which the modernists emphasize is just that, an emphasis – it is less of an "observation" than it is an ideologically motivated *construction*. Second, I hope to reveal some of these unarticulated ideological motives which underlie this modernist choice of emphasis, and to call into question the value of this choice.

This present study was originally completed in 1997. As of that time there was relatively little discussion of these meta-level issues – as mentioned above, modernists and traditionists simply ignored or dismissed each other's views (while – *significantly* – often practicing some form of engaged Buddhism side-by-side). In the short time since 1997 the field of engaged Buddhist studies has developed a fair amount, and I have tried to update this chapter accordingly to reflect some of these developments. As we shall see in the section on Christopher Queen near the end of this chapter, one significant development has been the identification of the continuity/discontinuity issue (the "newness" question) as an important question in its own right. Indeed, the call for papers for the 2000 *JBE* conference included the following invitation: "Papers dealing with ... the question of whether social engagement is a modern innovation or inherent in the tradition, are also encouraged." Nor should this "newness" question be considered merely an "academic" question – as Kenneth Kraft observes after an examination of the merits and demerits of stressing either continuity or discontinuity: "The process of articulating a field is not only an avenue to understanding; it can also be a type of engagement."[6]

However, in spite of these promising developments, the legacy of the views and attitudes that predominated in this field prior to the early to mid-1990s still has a great deal of momentum, and the ideological commitments, paradigms, and biases prior to this time have their own inertia. Thus, I believe that many of the observations and critiques below – focused as they are on pre-1997 writings – may be still relevant and useful to today's dialogue. Again, in the later section on Queen *et al.*, I will review and critique some of the more recent developments in engaged Buddhist studies.

To accomplish the objectives mentioned above (to show that discontinuity is only one possible emphasis, and to suggest some of the ideological motivations that may underlie such an emphasis) will require a close examination of many textual passages published by these authors. We will first look at a few passages representative of the traditionists, followed by a few from the modernists. This will provide us with enough raw material to begin to observe some of the patterns of thought characteristic of these two groups. As engaged Buddhist authors themselves tend to be relatively short on methodology, I will next bring in some methodological strategies and observations from some Buddhist scholars writing on topics *other* than engaged Buddhism. Armed with these tools, we will then examine in greater detail further passages representative of the modernists' views, biases, presuppositions, agenda, etc. We will be focusing our critique on the modernists because it is they who claim the methodological higher ground, even though (I hope to show) they are no *less* ideologically driven than are the traditionists whom they claim are so naïve. In particular, I will argue that the modernists' views may be seen to stem from a subtle form of neo-colonial, neo-Orientalist bias. By the end of this chapter I hope to have synthesized some methodological approaches which may have the potential to bear more fruitful conclusions concerning the status of Buddhist social teaching and practice.

Overview of the traditionists

Traditionist engaged Buddhist scholars are comprised of some scholars from historically Buddhist cultures as well as a few from Western cultures. Representatives of the former include Thich Nhat Hanh, Silak Sivaraksa, Walpola Rahula, Ven. Khemadhammo, Kato Shonin, and H.H. the Dalai Lama. Representatives of the latter include Patricia Hunt-Perry, Lyn Fine, Paula Green, Joanna Macy, Stephen Batchelor, Bernard Glassman Roshi, and Robert Thurman, among others.

The essence of Buddhism

As mentioned above, traditionists maintain that the very "essence" or "spirit" of Buddhism involves a commitment to social engagement. Thus, they discern a continuity between modern forms of Buddhism (including so-called "engaged Buddhism") and the Buddhisms of the past. Since Buddhists have always been socially engaged, a "socially engaged Buddhism" is nothing new. Indeed, even Thich Nhat Hanh, who is himself credited with coining the very term "engaged Buddhism," does not seem to consider the "engaged" aspect of Buddhism to be anything new – as Kenneth Kraft reveals: "At times [Nhat Hanh] ... even dismisses the term he coined as a misnomer: 'Engaged Buddhism is just Buddhism. If you practice Buddhism in your family, in society, it is engaged Buddhism.'"[7]

And in a contribution to *Engaged Buddhism in the West* entitled "All Buddhism is Engaged: Thich Nhat Hanh and the Order of Interbeing,"[8] Patricia Hunt-Perry and Lyn Fine write:

> The fundamental premise of this chapter is that, for Thich Nhat Hanh and the Order of Interbeing, peacemaking and socially engaged Buddhism encompass all aspects of life... The basic tenets of engaged Buddhism in the tradition of Thich Nhat Hanh that we have identified include: (1) *"Buddhism is already engaged. If it is not, it is not Buddhism."*[9]

Elsewhere Nhat Hanh himself clearly indicates that engagement (here "nonviolent struggle" or "action") is a "natural" impulse (which, by implication, could not be anything new or unique to the modern era):

> The essence of nonviolence is love. Out of love and the willingness to act selflessly, strategies, tactics, and techniques for a nonviolent struggle arise naturally.[10]

> You cannot prefabricate techniques of nonviolent action and put them into a book for people to use. That would be naive. If you are alert and creative, you will know what to do and what not to do. The basic requisite is that you have the essence, the substance of nonviolence and compassion in yourself. Then everything you do will be in the direction of nonviolence.[11]

The Thai reformer Sulak Sivaraksa (protégé of Thai scholar-monk Buddhadasa Bhikkhu) echoes this contention about the nature or essence of Buddhism:

> Religion means deep commitment, and personal transformation. To be of help we must become more selfless and less selfish. To do

this, we have to take more and more moral responsibility in society. This is the essence of religion, from ancient times right up to the present.[12]

If "moral responsibility in society" has been the very "essence" of Buddhism "from ancient times right up to the present," then it goes without saying that social engagement could be nothing new in Buddhism – that "good" Buddhists, at least, have always been socially engaged.

In an interview with Christopher Queen, Bernie Glassman Roshi gives us a Zen echo to Nhat Hanh's and Sivaraksa's sentiments. Glassman asks rhetorically, "How did [the Buddha] benefit mankind by sitting in meditation?" He answers his own question:

> This is a problem with the term "engaged Buddhism" in a broad sense... Anything one is doing to make themselves whole in their own life, or realizing the Way, or becoming enlightened – whatever term you would use – these are all involved in service, because if we realize the oneness of life, then each person is serving every other person and is reducing suffering.[13]

And later in the same interview he comments:

> I still feel – maybe it's wrong – that if you keep on practicing, even in the cave, there is no way of not working on social issues, only the method might be different... Social action is established now [in Buddhism in America]. It was always amazing to me how people could think it wasn't an element of Buddhism, but I don't hear that anymore.[14]

Paula Green reports on Kato Shonin, instrumental in developing Nichidatsu Fujii's "Nipponzan Myohoji" order of Nichiren Buddhism in America:

> In reflecting on Buddhism and social engagement, Kato Shonin believes that since the Buddha turned the Wheel of Dharma on this earth, this earth is where we obtain his teachings and reach enlightenment... If individuals practice the *Lotus Sutra* correctly, Kato Shonin says, "life itself is engagement and we do not need to separate into engaged and not-engaged Buddhism"... Every moment of life is engagement; every moment of life is Buddhist.[15]

Stephen Batchelor – well trained as a Buddhist monk in both the Tibetan and Korean traditions – also invokes an "engaged essence" in Buddhism in a personal communication to Sandra Bell in 1997:

Leaving aside language of engagement – or its opposite – Buddhist practice, in essence, is one in which a person tries to seek and balance ... wisdom ... with compassion... Traditionally these have been seen as the two wings of a bird... [A] tension between insight and understanding on the one hand and a compassionate response to the world on the other ... is a classic tension. If one starts from there the whole notion of making an issue out of engagement becomes superfluous.[16]

Historically ancient origins

Most (if not all) traditionists make arguments similar to those above in their writings.[17] If the very essence of Buddhism includes social responsibility and engagement, then that essence must be clearly evidenced *throughout* Buddhism's history. The great Sinhalese scholar Walpola Rahula wrote a whole book (*The Heritage of the Bhikkhu*) defending this very point. Christopher Queen tells us: "'Buddhism is based on service to others,' wrote Walpola Rahula ... in 1946 ... Rahula ... argued on historical grounds that political and social engagement was the 'heritage of the bhikkhu' and the essence of Buddhism."[18]

In an anthology dedicated to socially engaged Buddhism, *The Path of Compassion*, Joanna Macy reveals her own surprise at discovering that traditional Sri Lankan monks found an "engaged Buddhism" to be nothing new:

Some fellow scholars of Buddhism, whom I had consulted, considered Sarvodaya's[19] reinterpretation of doctrine – such as in its version of the four noble truths – to be a new-fangled adulteration of Buddhism, lacking doctrinal respectability. To present release from suffering in terms of irrigation, literacy, and marketing cooperatives appears to them to trivialize the Dharma. When I asked very learned Buddhist monks in Sri Lanka what they thought of this recasting of the four noble truths, I did so with the expectation that they, too, would see it as a corruption of the purity of the Buddha's teachings. Instead, almost invariably, they seemed surprised that a Buddhist would ask such a question – and gave an answer that was like a slight rap on the knuckles: "But it is the same teaching, don't you see? Whether you put it on the psychospiritual plane or on the socio-economic plane, there is suffering and there is cessation of suffering."[20]

In a contribution to another "engaged" anthology, *Inner Peace, World Peace: Essays on Buddhism and Nonviolence*, Robert Thurman expresses the opinion that Buddhist social activism began with Shakyamuni himself:

"[Certain scholars] ... are overlooking the nonviolent strategy and social policy instituted by Shakyamuni Buddha ... Buddhist activism began when the Buddha decided, 'No, I will not run a kingdom. Instead, I'm going to start a Sangha, a monastic army.'"[21]

He further explicitly states:

> Shakyamuni's original strategy for conquering violence through non-violence was intended to operate not only on an individual level but also on the scale of an entire society. If we reconsider the history of Buddhism from this perspective, we see that the creation of a monastic order was a precisely planned nonviolent movement.[22]

And finally, in *The Path of Compassion*, Thurman unequivocally states:

> The primary Buddhist position on social action is one of total activism, an unswerving commitment to complete self-transformation and complete world-transformation. This activism becomes fully explicit in the Universal Vehicle (*Mahayana*)... But it is also compellingly implicit in the Individual Vehicle (*Hinayana*) in both the Buddha's actions and in his teachings... Thus, it is squarely in the center of all Buddhist traditions to bring basic principles to bear on actual contemporary problems to develop ethical, even political, guidelines for action.[23]

In the conclusion to this essay he argues that "individualistic transcendentalism ..., pacifism ..., educational universalism ..., and socialistic sharing of wealth ... encompass mainstream Buddhist social practice, as counseled by [those at least as far back as] Nagarjuna."[24]

Disengagement as a Western misperception

In "The Social Teachings of the Buddha" (excerpted from *What the Buddha Taught*), Rahula wrote:

> Buddhism does not consider material welfare as an end in itself: it is only a means to an end – a higher and nobler end. But it is a means which is indispensable, indispensable in achieving a higher purpose for human happiness.
>
> The Buddha did not take life out of the context of its social and economic background; he looked at it as a whole, in all its social, economic, and political aspects. His teachings on ethical, spiritual, and philosophical problems are fairly well known. But little is known, particularly in the West, about his teaching on social,

economic, and political matters. Yet there are numerous discourses dealing with these scattered throughout the ancient Buddhist texts.[25]

Sivaraksa not only agrees that Westerners have been relatively ignorant of Buddhism's social dimension, but he further maintains that if Buddhism has appeared disengaged to Westerners, this appearance itself has in fact been due to Western influences:

> Many people, particularly in the West, think that Buddhism is only for deep meditation and personal transformation, that it has nothing to do with society. This is not true. Particularly in South and Southeast Asia, for many centuries Buddhism has been a great strength for society ... But things have changed, due mainly to colonialism, materialism, and western education.[26]

> Some Westerners want to become Buddhist monks only to escape from the world of turmoil, to benefit only themselves. My own experience over the last 30 years clearly indicates that Buddhism in the West has been practiced by many who did not want to get involved with society.[27]

Joanna Macy echoes Sivaraksa's and Rahula's contention that a *disen-gaged* Buddhism is a *Western* construction:

> Early Western scholars of Buddhism, beginning with Max Weber, have perceived Buddhism as "other-worldly" and without specific formulations of social ethics. They understood the release from this world as Buddhism's goal. Yet the Pali scriptures abound in passages where the Buddha deals explicitly with social ethics, and many more cases where the social implications are certainly obvious.[28]

Indeed, it is not only "*early* Western scholars of Buddhism" such as Max Weber that have construed Buddhism as "'other-worldly' and without specific formulations of social ethics," for as Christopher Queen contends in his 1996 anthology: "Today, after eighty years of new research, many specialists are inclined to agree with Weber that, in its essence, primitive Buddhism was not based on service to others, but on the quest for individual enlightenment."[29]

In a footnote to this claim, Queen cites "Weber, Kitagawa, Bardwell Smith, and others" as being among these "many specialists" supposedly in this (modernist) Weberian lineage who share a "negative assessment of Buddhism's contribution to social and political thought." However (ironically), in a 1999 review of Queen's 1996 book, Bardwell Smith himself objects to "[Queen's] contention that scholarly discussions of Buddhism have typically characterized this tradition as one of 'personal liberation' to the subordination, if not the neglect, of any social message," and he particularly objects to being associated with any such (modernist) scholars:

> as is accurately indicated in the other essays (including Queen's own chapter on Ambedkar), these two thrusts [personal and social] in Buddhist teachings and practice were never intended to be separated, however much they may be distinguished. Ironically, though I am cited as among those who provide this negative assessment, I agree fully with what Queen and the others are saying about the connection between personal and social liberation... If some interpreters of Buddhism, as cited by Queen, separate these goals, this has never been my position.[30]

From this we can see that the "disengaged" label is not only misapplied (according to traditionists) *to traditional Buddhism* by certain (i.e., modernist) Western Buddhologists, but that it can also be misapplied *to other Western Buddhologists* themselves! (We can likewise watch out for misapplications of the modernist "engaged" label.)

Overview of the modernists

Modernist engaged Buddhist scholars are comprised of a few scholars from historically Buddhist cultures and what would appear to be the vast majority of scholars from Western cultures. Some Modernists include Robert Aitken, Cynthia Eller, Nelson Foster, Richard Gombrich, Ken Jones, Joseph Kitagawa, Kenneth Kraft, Christopher Queen, English-born Sangharakshita, Gary Snyder, Judith Simmer-Brown, and Max Weber, among others.

Traditional Buddhism has not been socially engaged

Modernists make either the strong assertion that historically Buddhism (and especially early Buddhism) has *not* been socially interested at all, or the somewhat moderated assertion that it has been only *indirectly* or *latently* so interested. Joseph Kitagawa makes the stronger claim in "Buddhism and Social Change: An Historical Perspective" when he writes:

> [In early Buddhism] neither the monastics nor the laity seemed to have given much thought one way or the other to the norms and

structures of the social or political order, which to them had no immediate religious significance.[31]

[T]he kingship and the state ... had no religious significance to the early Buddhist.[32]

And Kitagawa's assessment of Buddhist social engagement in East Asia is not much better: "Chinese Buddhism contributed very little in the way of guiding principles to the Chinese society and nation ... Similar observations may be made regarding the influence of Chinese Buddhism on the socio-political order in general."[33]

Likewise, Ken Jones states that "present-day interest in Buddhist activism has little warranty in scripture, history and tradition ..."[34] Such activism is historically unwarranted, he claims, because Buddhist philosophers have in fact never been interested in the social realm. To back up this contention he quotes Gary Snyder:

Historically, Buddhist philosophers have failed to analyse out the degree to which ignorance and suffering are caused or encouraged by social factors, considering fear-and-desire to be given facts of the human condition. Consequently the major concern of Buddhist philosophy is epistemology and "psychology" with no attention paid to historical or sociological problems.[35]

Nelson Foster, interestingly, seems to be willing to admit that early (Pali) Buddhism may have been socially involved (or at least "aware"), but he claims that the East Asian Buddhism which he studies was not: "[I]t is clear from the Pali texts ... that early Buddhism was aware of itself as a force for social good... As Buddhism moved into China, however, its social orientation changed quickly and thoroughly."[36] Foster then describes this quick and thorough East Asian "change," also using Gary Snyder as an authority:

Gary Snyder has probably gone to the heart of the matter in observing that the Chinese world view (and later the Japanese) precluded a significant social role for Buddhism... Chinese society effectively bottled up the social impulse in Buddhism and thereby set the direction of Zen.[37]

It is perhaps more common for modernist scholars to make the slightly moderated claim that there *may* be discernible social implications *latent* in Buddhist teachings. For example, in the introductory essay to the anthology *The Path of Compassion*, Kenneth Kraft writes:

When ... [the contributors to this volume] examine Buddhism's 2,500-year-old heritage, these authors find that the principles and even some of the techniques of an engaged Buddhism have been latent in the tradition since the time of its founder.[38]

And in *Inner Peace, World Peace*, Cynthia Eller states her own opinion, backed by Jones and Foster:

[A] "socially engaged" nonviolence – prompted by Buddhism's encounter with the Christian demand for social relevance – is ... difficult to uncover. The elements of a socially engaged nonviolence are latent in the Buddhist tradition, but an overall concept of social engagement is not at the forefront, and advocates of modern Buddhist nonviolence are frank about admitting this. As Ken Jones laments, "Buddhism has no explicit body of social and political theory comparable to its psychology or metaphysics." Or as Nelson Foster comments, "It is remarkable that Zen lacks a clear tradition of social action. One searches in vain for a body of teaching equivalent to the 'social gospel' of Christianity."[39]

Jones himself, who at times adopts the stronger negative position, refers in the following passages to social activism as being an "extension" or an "amplification" of what is (he argues elsewhere in the same book) only latent in Buddhist teachings:

Buddhist social activism – "Engaged Buddhism" – is ... seen ... simply as the logical extension of the traditional teachings of morality and compassion to twentieth-century conditions.[40]

A socially engaged Buddhism needs no other rationale than that of being an amplification of traditional Buddhist morality, a social ethic brought forth by the needs and potentialities of present-day society.[41]

As all of the above passages indicate, the modernists' views indeed seem to reflect a resurgence of Weberian thought. In support of his contention that "after eighty years of new research, many specialists are inclined to agree with Weber,"[42] Queen quotes another one of these "specialists," Richard Gombrich (apparently a stronger example than Bardwell Smith!), who takes the strongest possible position: "[Buddha's] concern was to reform individuals and help them to leave society forever, not to reform the world ... He never preached against social inequality, only declared its irrelevance to salvation."[43]

The modern world faces unprecedented socio-political problems

Another factor that modernists like to stress is how "unique" or "different" our modern circumstances and problems are. For example, in "To Enter the Marketplace," Nelson Foster laments: "The ancient teachers did not live in a world as ruined and miserable and precarious as ours. We cannot know how they would have responded had they felt the urgency of the atomic age."[44]

Likewise, in "Speaking Truth to Power: The Buddhist Peace Fellowship," Judith Simmer-Brown quotes BPF co-founder Robert Aitken Roshi as saying: "The Buddha did not live in a time like ours, when dangerous competition between nations threatens to blow up the world. He was not faced with the probability of biological holocaust ... I wonder what he would say today."[45]

In an excellent special issue of the *Journal of the American Academy of Religion* dedicated to articles on the theme of "Religious Responses to Problems of Population, Consumption, and Degradation of the Environment," Rita Gross writes:

> [T]he key question is what values and practices would convince people to consume and reproduce less when they have the techno-logical ability to consume and reproduce more. The world's religions have not previously faced this situation, which explains why ecological ethics have not been in the forefront of religious thinking in any tradition.[46]

And in the Introduction to his 1992 anthology, Kenneth Kraft writes:

> In cases such as the treatment of animals in scientific research, classic Buddhist tenets are being applied to situations that differ greatly from the contexts in which those tenets were originally conceived. The Buddhist creed of nonviolence that once func-tioned as a personal moral code for monks in ancient India is now expected to provide guidelines for dealing with complex social and political dilemmas. Though such leaps may seem dubious from certain scholarly or religious standpoints, they are earnestly being attempted nonetheless. Graphic reminders of the discrepancies between ancient and modern worldviews are furnished by the traditional stories cited in these pages.[47]

Modernists consider the unique problems of the modern world to have spawned some unique solutions. For example, in the same 1992 introduc-tion Kraft first cautiously writes:

An essayist in the *New Yorker* magazine recently observed that nonviolence "ranks as one of the few great modern discoveries." At first, this remark may appear short-sighted: Jainism and Buddhism have stressed nonviolence for millennia, and the Sermon on the Mount was not preached last Sunday.[48]

But he then continues, highlighting the significance of the modern (mostly Western) contributions in this area:

Yet the point is well taken. The twentieth century has witnessed Gandhi ..., Martin Luther King ..., and the nonviolent reversals of ... Communist party power[s]... Though we tend to associate the concept of nonviolence with ancient Asian thought, some of the most notable instances of nonviolent political action have occurred in the West during this century. Gene Sharp argues in his essay that the political potential of this "modern" discovery has yet to be fully appreciated.[49]

When traditionists counter that many such "modern solutions" are in fact evident in ancient Buddhist teachings, modernists simply dismiss such traditionist contentions as methodologically naïve and historically "reconstructive." These modernists tend to be well aware of the scriptural "evidence" that the traditionists cite (Nagarjuna's *Jewel Garland*; Ashoka's edicts; the *Cakkavati-*, *Kutadanta-* and *Sigala-suttas*; etc.), but they claim that too much has been read back into such sources. For example, in *The Social Face of Buddhism: An Approach to Political and Social Activism*,[50] Ken Jones levels the "reconstructionist" critique at what I have been calling the traditionists (what he here calls 'modernists'!):

We believe that it is unscholarly to transfer the scriptural social teaching uncritically and without careful qualification to modern societies, or to proclaim that the Buddha was a democrat and an internationalist.[51]

[I]t is not legitimate to find instant scriptural and historical authority for contemporary secular ideas and ideologies (like democracy or Marxism) by *reading them back* into the evidence from scripture and history, whilst ignoring both the spiritual significance of that evidence and/or its culture-bound meaning. This is a common device of ... reductive modernism ...[52]

Concerned to make Buddhism manifestly relevant to the social and political requirements of the post-colonial era, these [reductive] modernists tend to read the scriptures in terms of certain dominant contemporary ideas, as if they were originally a programme for social reform; their over-arching spiritual and existential context and significance is lost beneath a burgeoning humanistic rationalism. Meanings are read into them which are at best arguable and at worst extravagant and tendentious.[53]

Likewise, in his introduction to the anthology *Engaged Buddhism: Buddhist Liberation Movements in Asia*, Christopher Queen levels a similar charge at what he discerns to be two types of "reconstructionists." Thus, following good Buddhist style, having first convincingly presented his *purvapaksha* (the opponent's view – primarily Rahula's), he then presents a lengthy argument in which he attempts to refute this view by formulating his own definition of "social engagement" in such a way that he can admonish us to reject the "two extremes of historical reconstruction." These (traditionist) extremes are (1) "the extreme of a primitive Buddhist counterculture bent on social reform," as exemplified, presumably, by those such as Thurman, and (2) "the extreme of a sangha directing social change from its position within the power elite," as exemplified by Rahula.

While Queen focuses the bulk of his critique on his second extreme, Kenneth Kraft takes on (at least implicitly) what Queen has identified as the first extreme – here with reference to the essay by Thurman cited above:[54]

According to Robert Thurman, certain Mahayana texts reveal the outlines of a society that is "individualistic, transcendentalist, pacifist, universalist, and socialist." Carried to an extreme, such interpretations envision an ideal Buddhism too far removed from its actual historical development. But the thrust of the argument is constructive: to show that the Buddhist tradition contains untapped resources for skillful social action and peacemaking, accessible to Buddhists and non-Buddhists alike.[55]

Here, of course, the implication is that Thurman has carried his interpretation to an idealistic, ahistorical extreme (he has "read back," in Jones' terms) – for, as we saw above, he certainly does *not* maintain that the Buddhist tradition contains merely "*untapped* resources for skillful social action."

Western/Buddhist social engagement

Having thus dismissed traditionists' views as naïve and "reconstructionist," and having emphasized the unprecedented uniqueness of our contemporary problems, modernists finally stress the uniqueness and modern-ness (and Western-ness) of their solution, engaged Buddhism. So, with regard to this "nascent movement," Kraft beams: "Qualities that were inhibited in pre-modern Asian settings ... can now be actualized through Buddhism's exposure to the West, where ethical sensitivity, social activism, and egalitarianism are emphasized."[56] Nelson Foster reflects and magnifies this confident beaming, producing an image of a Western Zen permeated with an excited anticipation of what could be:

> Fortunately, prajñā itself does not die, and as long as zazen and realization are taught, an opportunity exists to renew the tradition we inherited. Indeed, as Zen moves west again, it enters a relatively open environment that may allow the sangha to live out its politics to a greater extent than ever before. With external constraints amounting to little more than the loose demands of neighborly courtesy and local ordinances, American Zen seems free to develop according to the lights of prajñā. Already American sanghas can be seen shattering some of the strictures that have bound Zen in Asia.[57]

In fact, Foster does not merely think that such a development *might* occur – rather, he considers the Western "environment" to be so optimal that the "organic development of Western Zen" is "inevitable."[58]

In "The Impact of Christianity on Buddhist Nonviolence in the West," Cynthia Eller writes in a similar vein:

> Buddhism in the West is in constant interaction with the Judeo-Christian tradition – if only because most of its practitioners were raised in homes and/or a culture dominated by these religions ... When the search for a genuinely Buddhist nonviolence is filtered through the latent demands of predominantly Christian conscience, what emerges is a new Buddhism and a new Buddhist ethics, no less valid than the many new Buddhisms that have been produced in the 2,500 years of the Dharma's movement eastward around the globe.[59]

Likewise, Robert Aitken Roshi traced the roots of contemporary engaged Buddhism to the Judeo-Christian West when in 1984 he wrote, "We do not find Buddhist social movements developing until the late nineteenth century, under the influence of Christianity and Western ideas generally."[60] Queen is even more specific about the origins of this modern East-West blend. He maintains that it is "[only] once we have rejected two extremes of historical reconstruction" (cited above), that "we recognize that the shape and style of contemporary engaged Buddhism does not appear in Buddhist history until about the year 1880."[61] In particular, he states:

It is only in the late nineteenth-century revival of Buddhism in Sri Lanka – and particularly in ... Olcott ... and ... Dharmapala – that we first recognize the spirit and substance of the religious activism we call "socially engaged Buddhism." And it is only in this context that we first meet the missing ingredient... This ingredient is the influence of European and American religious and political thought (and perhaps equally important, western methods of institutional development and public communication) on the evolution of modern Buddhism.[62]

Thus he concludes that in fact such an engaged Buddhism is necessarily an "amalgam of Eastern and Western elements."[63] (We will be returning to these arguments in the section on Queen *et al.*, and in the Conclusion.)

Summary of the modernists' views

The above views and methodologies tend to be commonly shared (to varying degrees) among all modernists. These modernist positions may be summarized as follows:

1   *Traditional Buddhism has not been socially engaged.* Traditional (Asian) forms of Buddhism have emphasized the "spiritual" concerns of individual liberation from the world; they may have had *latent* social teachings (particularly in Mahayana), but these have always taken a back seat to soteriological concerns. Social teachings have rarely (if ever) been fully articulated or actualized in these traditional societies. (Ashoka is frequently cited as *the one* main exception to this – but the importance of his example is minimized, as we shall see).

2   *The modern world faces unprecedented socio-political problems.* In addition, the problems facing the modern world (social, political, economic, ecological, military, medical, etc.) are unique to this time; the Buddhisms embedded in traditional societies have never had to face such intricate, complex, and inter-related problems.

3   *Modern Western socio-political theory presents unique and unprecedented analyses and solutions – it must not be "read back" into Buddhism – "historical reconstruction" must be avoided.* Unlike traditional Asian Buddhist societies, modern (nineteenth–twentieth century) Western societies *have* developed a sophisticated understanding of the systemic and institutional forms and causes of suffering. This understanding has given rise to unique social and political theories and practices relating to human rights, democracy, civil disobedience, etc. These insights have developed due to historical circumstances unique

302

to the modern era (especially in the West), and we must not "read back" such theories into traditional Buddhism where they are in fact lacking or at best only indirectly implied.

4   *Traditional Buddhism is therefore not an adequate model for engagement.* Therefore, given (1), (2) and (3), although we may draw spiritual inspiration from traditional forms of Buddhism, such forms (as they stand) can never serve as an adequate model for social engagement in the modern world.

5   *Modern Western socio-political theory can be used to activate Buddhism's latent potential to create a new amalgam: Western /Buddhist engagement.* Nevertheless, modern "Western" social and political theories and practices may benefit from some of Buddhism's spirit and inspiration (and *vice versa*). Therefore, modern Western insights and traditional "Eastern" Buddhist insights should be brought to bear on each other in order to bring about a *new*, revitalized form of Buddhism (and social theory) more 'relevant' to the problems of the modern world. Such a blending of the best of West and East should be embraced, not feared – it may be our only hope. The nascent "engaged Buddhist" movement may well be just the amalgam we now need.

Methodological issues

Before we undertake our detailed critique of certain modernists' views, we must first develop some methodological tools and vocabulary. As mentioned above, we will borrow some insights from discussions taking place outside of the engaged Buddhist dialogue. In particular, we will examine two essays from *Curators of the Buddha: The Study of Buddhism Under Colonialism*[64] which address methodological concerns which can be very usefully applied to our study of socially engaged Buddhism. This will enable us to begin to explore the possibility that these modernists' views might in fact be the heirs to an entrenched neo-colonial, neo-Orientalist bias among Buddhologists (and Western scholars in general). Finally, we will end this methodological section with some brief observations concerning Westerners' construction of their own identity.

Orientalist emphases and isolates – constructed dualities

The first pertinent essay is the "Introduction" by editor Donald Lopez, Jr. In this overview essay, Lopez makes the following relevant observations about the emphasis and focus in the early European study of Buddhism:

[M]uch of the representation of Buddhism to the west, both by western scholars and Asian apologists, has centered on philosophical doctrines... Buddhism has typically been studied as a thing apart from the rest of the intellectual and cultural history of India (or China or Japan).[65]

And:

[T]he Buddhism that largely concerned European scholars was an historical projection derived exclusively from manuscripts and blockprints, texts devoted largely to a "philosophy," which had been produced and had circulated among a small circle of monastic elites. With rare exception, there was little interest in the ways in which such texts were understood by the Buddhists of Asia, less interest in the ways in which such texts were put to use in the service of various ritual functions.[66]

In other words, according to this critique, early European Buddhologists who saw Buddhism as a "philosophy" (as *opposed* to, e.g., a "religion") unwittingly projected their form of "philosophical" Buddhism by means of the "historical" lenses and filters they employed. In particular, as the above passages show, they accomplished their historical reconstruction by:

1   Prejudicing *texts* over other types of historical evidence.
2   Prejudicing a specific, narrow spectrum of texts over other types of texts.
3   Prejudicing the past (fixed texts) over the present (living oral interpretations) by disregarding contemporary Asian Buddhists' own understandings of their texts (let alone their overall tradition).[67]
4   Prejudicing the philosophical uses of those texts by disregarding any of their non-philosophical (e.g., ritual) uses.

Thus, the early European Orientalists can be criticized for having constructed Buddhism as a "pure philosophy" through their having studied it as "a thing apart from the rest of the intellectual and cultural history of [Asia]." Or, more accurately perhaps, they should be criticized not for having adopted a "philosophical" focus which ignored, e.g., the "ritual" uses of Buddhist texts, but *for having constructed a dubious, dualistic "philosophical/ritual" split in the first place.*[68] According to such a critique, one can charge that the Orientalists first created such a dualistic philosophical/ritual split, then isolated the "philosophical" side of this split as "pure, classical Buddhism" (having dismissed any ritual elements as later, degenerate, superstitious folk accretions), and finally identified medieval and modern Asian Buddhists as having corrupted the "pure essence" of their own tradition precisely by mixing these philosophical and ritual dimensions. Through such dualistic constructions and strategies the Orientalists thus inappropriately wrested from Asian Buddhists the authority to interpret their own tradition.[69]

Now, if we substitute "socio-political activities" for "ritual functions" in the above discussion, we can derive a critique that I will argue is as appropriate to contemporary modernist engaged Buddhists as it was to early European Orientalists generations ago. For example, if we make such substitutions in Lopez's final sentence above, we get:

> With rare exception, among modernist engaged Buddhists there has been little interest in the ways in which texts have been understood by the contemporary Buddhists of Asia, less interest in the ways in which such texts have been put to use in the service of socio-political activities.

In other words, I believe it can be argued that modernist engaged Buddhists who see Buddhism as having been historically "*dis*engaged" may have unwittingly projected *their* form of "disengaged" Buddhism by means of the "historical" lenses and filters *they* have employed. In such a case, paralleling the early European Orientalists, they can be criticized for having constructed Buddhism as socially "disengaged" through their having studied it as "a thing apart from the rest of the intellectual and cultural [and socio-political] history of [Asia]." Or, again more accurately perhaps, they should be criticized not for having critiqued Buddhism's soteriological drive – assumed to be directed at other-worldly concerns, and thus socially disengaged – but rather for having constructed a dubious, dualistic "soteriological (disengaged)/social (engaged)" split *in the first place.*[70] In particular, modernists might be said to have created such a split when they charge that living traditionist Asian Buddhists (Rahula, Sivaraksa, Macy's Sri Lankan monks, H.H. The Dalai Lama, Thich Nhat Hanh, etc.) – who claim that their texts (and practices) have always had direct social significance, utility, and impact – are naïvely reconstructing their own history, and when they conclude that these traditionists are to be dismissed as having "read" contemporary ideas "into" the past and as having over-idealized the "not-so-engaged legacy" of their tradition.[71] I would thus caution that the modernists themselves may have constructed a disengaged history for Buddhism in order to appropriate for themselves the title of "inventor of engaged Buddhism." Such a modernist appropriation of interpretive power would indeed be reminiscent of the Orientalists generations ago; and such a neo-Orientalist bias must be seen to be ironic, of course, given that it is the modernists who routinely accuse the traditionists of "historical reconstruction."

The unavowed colonial stance: recognition, appropriation, and distancing

The other pertinent essay from *Curators of the Buddha* is "Oriental Wisdom and the Cure of Souls: Jung and the Indian East" by Luis O. Gómez. In this essay, Gómez brings into sharp focus many observations regarding the biases evident in Carl G. Jung's theories and writings. While Gómez's essay accords appropriate respect to Jung for making many valuable contributions to psychology and for engendering a powerful interest in "the East," it nevertheless lays bare many of Jung's Orientalist biases and unacknowledged neo-colonial agenda. In particular, Gómez clearly demonstrates how Jung himself misread Asian texts in such a way as to construct an Eastern "Other" to serve as a foil to an (equally constructed) Western "Self." Thus, Jung wrote of the "Eastern mind" (with its "psychic aspect" and its tendency toward an "inordinate amount of abstraction") as *opposed* to the "Western mind" (with its penchant for "scrupulously accurate observation"),[72] and he constructed many of his psychological theories on the basis of such manufactured polar dichotomies.

Many of Gómez's observations regarding Jung will also be of immense value and relevance to our present study. Lopez summarizes several of these important observations in his Introduction:

> Gómez's essay examines how Jung created his own colonial economy during his repeated ventures into translations of Asian texts. He judged the raw materials of Asian religion to be valuable, but unusable and even dangerous to the European in their unrefined form. He therefore removed them from their cultural and historical contexts and then manufactured theories from them for Europeans, to be used to remedy deficiencies in their own souls... In his writings he also exported Asian symbols (such as the mandala) back to Asia, attempting to explain (in the sense of leveling) to Asians the true nature of their own symbols and psyches... The healing power of Asia can only heal when mediated through Jung's theories, with Jung serving as the intermediary between East and West, both as diagnostician and healer.[73]

This is a powerful critique. As above, we can rework this latter paragraph to address our present issue as follows:

> Modernists create their own neo-colonial economy during their repeated ventures into translations of Buddhist texts. They judge the raw materials of Buddhism to be valuable, but unusable and even dangerous (or irrelevant) to the modern Westerner in their unrefined form. They therefore (subtly) remove them from their cultural and historical contexts and then manufacture theories

from them for modern Westerners (especially engaged Buddhists), to be used to remedy deficiencies in their own identities and socio-political circumstances... In their writings they also export Buddhist symbols and 'history' ... back to Asia, attempting to explain (in the sense of leveling) to Asian Buddhists the true nature (or a more pertinent use) of their own symbols ... and socio-political history... The socially transformative power potentially *latent* in Asian Buddhism can only transform society when activated by and mediated through the Western modernists' socio-political theories, with the Western modernist serving as the intermediary between East and West, both as strategist and social activist.

Gómez summarizes the methodological observations implicit throughout his own essay when he explicitly draws out what he calls the "Orientalist bias and the unavowed colonial stance." This involves "the three movements of recognition, appropriation, and distancing." This concise but potent threefold analysis will be of the greatest use to us in our study. In Gómez's own words:

We should ask ... what defines the Orientalist bias, and the unavowed colonial stance, in Jung's writings on Asia... This stance is clearly outlined in the three movements of recognition, appropriation, and distancing. The European maintains his control over Asia first by conceding authority to the alien culture, then by assuming that authority for himself, and last by asserting the difference that separates him from the other.[74]

We can now discern these three movements in the above reworked passage concerning the modernist engaged Buddhists:

1   *Recognition*: Modernists ... judge the raw materials of Buddhism to be valuable...

2   *Appropriation*: They therefore (subtly) remove them from their cultural and historical contexts and then manufacture theories from them for modern Westerners (especially engaged Buddhists), to be used to remedy deficiencies in their own identities and socio-political circumstances... In their writings they also export Buddhist symbols and "history" ... back to Asia, attempting to explain (in the sense of leveling) to Asian Buddhists the true nature (or a more pertinent use) of their own symbols ... and socio-political history...

3   *Distancing*: The socially transformative power potentially *latent* in Asian Buddhism can only transform society when mediated through the Western modernists' socio-political theories, with the Western

modernist serving as the intermediary between East and West, both as strategist and social activist.

Thus, the typical Orientalist moves are: (1) *Recognition*: to hail the alien tradition as (at least *potentially*) valuable; (2) *Appropriation*: to mine one's sources (texts, "native informants," etc.)[75] for sufficient information to feel as though one has learned enough about the tradition that one can speak authoritatively *for* the tradition; and (3) *Distancing*: to claim that, due to one's position as "other," and due to one's learning, one has in fact earned a *privileged* (more "objective") perspective on the alien tradition, and that one is thus uniquely positioned to critique and explain this tradition. Distancing will also usually involve the further claims that, due to having been illumined by the "other," one has a unique insight into one's *own* tradition, and that one is thus uniquely disposed to be the authoritative intermediary between the two traditions.

The Orientalists' moves and claims may not at first seem to be so unreasonable. After all, who *other* than one trained in both traditions might validly claim to be an authoritative spokesperson or intermediary? Indeed, I would suggest, one making such a claim *may* be relatively justified in doing so. The key to what would make it a problematical claim – an *Orientalist* claim – would seem to lie in Gomez's initial 'recognition' phase. As I would elaborate it, the recognition phase involves more than just an acknowledgment that the "other" tradition is valuable: it also *necessarily* involves a *construction* of the "other" tradition that is supposedly being merely "recognized" in the first place. Moreover, for this phase to qualify as truly Orientalist, and for the next two phases to ensue, this constructive process must remain relatively unconscious (thereby masking various self-identity agenda).

Furthermore, assuming that the constructive process underlying the recognition phase *does* remain unconscious, we can note that the appropriation and distancing phases will be inter-related in a particular way. Precisely *because* the Orientalist appropriates the authoritative voice *from* an alien position (the self-position constructed in the recognition phase, in fact), he will be unlikely to use that voice to speak as an insider or apologist for the tradition (to do so would be to have "gone native," to have rejected the self-identity initially constructed in the recognition phase). Rather, he will want to consciously distance himself from the tradition (at least somewhat) by assuming the voice of a critic (if even a sympathetic one). The more he appropriates the power to speak for the tradition, the more he will tend to distance himself from it; and the more he distances himself, the more authoritative power he will tend to appropriate. Thus, the Orientalist's "recognition" (self–other *construction*) creates the initial context for an appropriation that will inevitably result in a distancing; this distancing will further solidify the original dual self–other construction, which will in turn lead to greater appropriation, and so on.

Western assumptions: new is improved; ours is better; actions speak louder than words

It would seem that it is an integral part of the self-description and identity of many contemporary Westerners (especially *Americans*) to be "new, innovative, original, forward-looking, ground-breaking, paradigm-shifting," etc. We see ourselves as competitive innovators. Anything we don't invent ourselves we can certainly improve upon – if we get it from them, we can make a newer version that will necessarily be better than theirs. We are certain that *to be new is to be improved*. In addition, we generally describe ourselves as "active" or "engaged" (we make things happen, we get the job done), and even as "pro-active" (we have the freedom and foresight to keep a step ahead of what will need to be done next). For some strange reason – I will leave it to others to trace the historical (or karmic?) roots – this is just who we tell ourselves we are; it is our identity.

Given this, it should come as no surprise that many Westerners should automatically construct their "Other" – in our present case, Asians, and especially Buddhists – as "ancient, traditional, ever looking toward the past, conservative," etc. In addition, such uncritical Westerners will likewise generally describe "them" as "passive" or "responsive." If such Westerners are inclined to be disillusioned with (or simply critical of) their own Western tradition, then such constructions will take on a positive, exotic spin: Asian Buddhists are the keepers of an ancient, timeless wisdom, and are "passive" in the sense of being non-violent, etc. On the other hand, if they are inclined to identify with their own Western tradition (as most are), then such constructions will take on a negative, "third-world" spin: Asian Buddhists are stuck with out-moded models and theories, and are "passive" in the sense of being disengaged and ineffectual. This latter attitude is related to what Thurman has called "temporal chauvinism:"

> Americans, and modern people in general, are often afflicted with what I call temporal chauvinism – the assumption that anything devised or conceived before 1960 is primitive and useless ... [W]e might be the ones who get hit by the big [nuclear] bang. Thus we should do a great thing and figure out how to transmute the world into a state of nonviolence. It is assumed that no one in the past has tackled this problem with any degree of success. As for Buddhist monks wandering around in poor Third World countries, the usual reaction is: "Never mind them, their countries are

in such bad shape they couldn't possibly have thought of anything."[76]

If the above observations are valid, then in order for most of us Westerners to accept and use ("practice") Buddhism, we must appropriate it as *ours*, and to do that we must *necessarily* improve upon it. To do this we can either (a) *fully* develop some previously *underdeveloped*, *key* component of Buddhism; (b) *add* some *new*, *key* component to Buddhism; or (c) both. For the modernist engaged Buddhists, of course, this key component is "active engagement" itself – one of *our* "own" identity-formations, after all. For this project to succeed – that is, for "our" Western Buddhism to be termed "engaged Buddhism" – then any claim that Buddhism has been engaged in the past must *immediately* be refuted. If it appears to some contemporary readers that the words enshrined in various ancient Buddhist texts have social ramifications, modernists must contend either that these texts were not understood this way by traditional Asian Buddhists, or, to the extent to which they were so understood, that those Buddhists could not (or simply historically did not) act accordingly. The active engagement evident *now* among Buddhists must be proven to be the new (or at least the fully developed) contribution which *we* have made. Our contemporary engaged *actions* must be shown to speak louder than their mere ancient, scriptural *words*.

Analysis of the modernists' arguments

We are finally ready to begin our analysis and deconstruction of the modernists' arguments in some detail. Toward this end we will first examine the writings of Kitagawa and Jones as representative examples of earlier (1980s') modernist tendencies. (It should be recalled that these earlier views have had an enduring influence into the present.) In particular, we will seek to reveal the different dualities which each of these authors unwittingly constructs, on the basis of which each can recognize something potentially positive in Buddhism, appropriate the authority to explain it, and finally distance himself from it (and place himself above it). Thus, we will see that Kitagawa assumes (i.e., constructs) it to be natural that early Buddhists perceived both a "religious" and a "non-religious" domain, and that they were, of course, only interested in the former. Likewise, we will see that Jones makes a very *sharp* distinction between "transcendent, spiritual" truths and "social, secular" realities, and that he portrays Buddhism as being properly interested only in the former. Thus, in each case we will be reminded of the spiritual/social split typical of Orientalists discussed above and in each case we will see how these authors engage in the threefold movement of recognition, appropriation, and distancing. Finally, we will turn our attention to a detailed analysis of some of the more recent, nuanced developments in engaged Buddhist theory, focusing on the contributions made by Christopher Queen in his two edited anthologies.[77]

Joseph Kitagawa : "Buddhism and Social Change"

We can begin by recalling that modernists generally insist that "early" Buddhists in particular (including Shakyamuni himself) were completely socially disinterested.[78] Kitagawa acknowledges that, "As to the actual relation of Buddhism to the Indian society during the early days of Buddhism, there is no agreement among scholars" (true enough!). His own opinion, however, is decidedly clear:

> [C]ontrary to the popular notion that the Buddha was a crusading social reformer, fighting for the cause of common man against the establishment of his time, there is no evidence that he attempted, directly at any rate, to change society. He seems to have accepted the various forms of socio-political order known to him... It was taken for granted by him that the transformation of "society," which significantly included all living beings, would come only as a by-product of the religious transformation of individual beings in this world (loka).[79]

Though the tone here is descriptive, this is clearly quite interpretive (constructive),[80] for, as we saw before, it can just as easily be argued that the Buddha's abdication of his socio-political duties as a kshatriya crown-prince, as well as his establishment of a major social institution (the monastic order) which deliberately ignored India's primary socio-political ordering schema (the caste system), do not indicate that he "accepted the various forms of socio-political order known to him"!

Kitagawa, like most modernists, points to King Ashoka as perhaps the first truly (at least partially) engaged Buddhist. Kitagawa tells us that "in retrospect" (i.e., from our privileged vantage point) we can discern that "Ashoka found two levels of meaning in Buddhism." The first of these levels involves the usual "religious" or soteriological meanings of the Three Jewels. "On another level," Kitagawa adds, "Ashoka found in the Buddhist teaching an ethical, social and cultural guiding principle, i.e., Dharma, which is applicable both to religious and non-religious domains, as well as to all men, Buddhist and non-Buddhist alike."[81] As is often the case with such statements, this sounds innocuous enough until it is scruti-nized more carefully. Was Ashoka really the first to find an "ethical, social and cultural guiding principle" in the Dharma? Should we join Kitagawa in calling this "the Ashokan turn"? And if we can discern this "in retro-spect," are we to infer that Ashoka himself was not fully aware of his own

311

"discovery"? If he *was* the first, are we to infer that, strangely, Shakyamuni Buddha himself did not understand (or for some reason did not act on) the social implications of his own Dharma? Furthermore, were not Shakyamuni's wandering missionary *bhikkhu*s expected to give spiritual advice and guidance to the laity, and might not this have likely included "ethical, social and cultural guiding principles"? Finally, and most significantly, were there *really* two distinct "domains" for the early Buddhists, one "religious" and one "non-religious"? One could perhaps imagine that certain early Buddhists might have used some such categories heuristically, but was there really a domain, a sphere of activity, a physical place in which actions (*karma*) had no soteriological significance for them?

In a manner similar to the Orientalists' construction of a philosophy / ritual split, Kitagawa has here constructed a dualistic split between a "religious" and a "socio-political" sphere, a split which may well have seemed unnatural (or even unacceptable) to the subjects for whom he is presuming to speak. Nevertheless, once such a split has been created, it presents a gap which must be bridged. Kitagawa hails Ashoka as the first to attempt such a feat:

> [T]he novelty of Ashoka's contribution to the history of Buddhism was his attempt to locate religious meaning in the social and political institutions of this world, so that the kingship and the state, which had no religious significance to the early Buddhist, came to be regarded as the instruments "to protect according to the Dharma."[82]

Now it is indeed true that Ashoka may have been the first Buddhist king to have been in a position to *implement* the idea that the institutions of kingship and of the state should be used as instruments "to protect according to the Dharma," but Kitagawa engages in sheer speculation when he asserts that Ashoka was the first to *have* the very idea. Moreover, he is quick to appropriate the voices of all Buddhists prior to Ashoka when he asserts that such institutions "had no religious significance to the early Buddhist."

Kitagawa seems further disappointed that the abstract, disengaged, religious sphere of Dharma which he has constructed in contrast to the "real" socio-political world was never really bridged with any "middle principles" by any Buddhists *after* Ashoka either:

> We can also observe that while Buddhism had lofty universal principles (Dharma) as well as moral codes for individual life, it made little effort in developing what might be called "middle principles" to mediate between universal principles and the empirical socio-political and economic situations in any given society. In the main,

Buddhism depended primarily on the idealised notion of the Buddhist king, based on the memory of king Ashoka, as the most feasible link between the religious and non-religious spheres of life.[83]

An idealized "memory of King Ashoka" was all that later Buddhists would have to depend on. Ashoka's valiant attempt to bridge the gap (which he, Kitagawa, himself created) was not only the first such attempt but also essentially the last (and hence *only*) successful attempt in the succeeding two millennia of Buddhism's history throughout Asia: "Ashoka's way of dealing with the two levels of reality provided the only tangible norm for the relation of Buddhism to the socio-political order that was acceptable to many Buddhists ..." that is, of course, "until the modern period."[84]

Ken Jones: The Social Face of Buddhism

In 1989 Ken Jones published *The Social Face of Buddhism*, one of the earliest monographs on engaged Buddhism. This is one of the richest, most nuanced studies on this topic, filled with many useful insights and discussions. Nonetheless, if we first look at what he says Buddhism is *not* (or should not be), so that we can then better appreciate what he thinks it is (or should be) – we will in this way be able see how his own categories force him, too, into an extreme Orientalist-style dualism.

Jones is strongly critical of certain attitudes and practices of modern engaged Buddhists. Though I will be arguing shortly that Jones himself constructs and appropriates Buddhism for his own unspoken (modernist) aims, here (ironically) we see Jones making the accusation that it is Western Buddhists who engage in improper appropriation:

> Buddhism in the West is part of the personal cultural equipment of quite a lot of people who value it as a system of ideas and orientation, and this is an important fact in any discussion of Buddhist activism... It is, however, something that has been appropriated and *used*, rather than something that has profoundly engaged the personality as in the case of the dedicated practitioner. The flavour is different.[85]

In particular, such Westerners have "appropriated and used" Buddhism in a way which reduces it to a *mere* socio-political tool. So, Jones hears these reductionists "talking in terms of personal change being necessary [merely] to facilitate fundamental social change, as if spirituality were no more than the handmaiden of truly profound and human social revolution."[86]

Later on Jones identifies such objectionable reduction and appropriation as the process of "secularization": "What is being contested is the secularization of both scriptural meaning and engaged spirituality by annexing both to contemporary social categories and perspectives confined within superficial and secular consciousness."[87]

And finally, in the following passage, Jones defines "secularization" and identifies it with what he calls "reductive modernism":

> *Secularization* is here the process by which spirituality is denied in a culture as well as the stripping down of formal, exoteric religion in society. As we saw ... secularization also inverts and reduces spirituality to being a handmaiden and auxiliary in projects for social change, in psychotherapy and in other areas wherein a lower level of consciousness and a secular perspective prevail... *"Reductive modernism"* is the term used here for that movement in religion which in effect secularizes religion from within.[88]

So far, so good. It does seem that the processes of secularization and the movement of reductive modernism, aptly described by Jones, do indeed occur (we will return to this in the section on Queen, *et. al.*, below). And I have no doubt that many Westerners are, to some degree, guilty of such appropriative excesses. However, we can recall from our overview above that when Jones speaks in terms of "*the* present-day interest in Buddhist activism," he seems to imply that *all* modern Buddhist activists must be naïvely engaging in such secular appropriation: "[T]he present-day interest in Buddhist activism has little warranty in scripture, history and tradition and is in effect a covert form of twentieth-century secularization grafted onto the traditional Dharma."[89]

Such universal condemnations would seem to insinuate that *any* present-day Buddhist activist who sees *any* signs of social engagement in Buddhism's history is mistakenly "reading back" her own "secular" agenda (and at times, at least, whether intentionally or not, it does seem like Jones maintains such a strong stance). In any event, as we now turn to look at how Jones *himself* describes true "spirituality" or Buddhism (his constructed "Other"), we will see why his constructs might force him to reject the views of the *vast majority* of Buddhist activists.

To begin with, Jones divides religion into an "esoteric" and an "exoteric" form as follows:

> The so-called esoteric part of religion is its gnostic or spiritual part. This comprises a diagnosis of the human disease and systems of psycho-physical training whereby individuals can realize their True Nature... The exoteric part of religion comprises dogmas, moral codes, institutions, and other means for readily communicating, manifesting and sustaining religion in society. These will include some kind of economic base, charitable and educational

activities, the affirmations of public worship and ritual and the exercise of political influence.[90]

Two initial points should be noted here. First, what he calls exoteric religion is *not* the same as what he criticizes as secularized religion. These two are entirely unrelated, and he is not interested in critiquing the exoteric part of religion. Second, he clearly states that the *exoteric* part of religion (to the extent to which he may think it constitutes "religion" at all) already *does* include socially and politically engaged elements.

Next, he associates *true* Buddhism with the "esoteric, gnostic, spiritual" element of religion. Thus, he frequently makes reference to the "primary," "existential," "perennial," or "epistemological" nature of Buddhism. In the following passage he contrasts the approach of reductive modernism with that of "a Buddhist interpretation" (which he describes as being a "spiritual and root-existential" one), and he then defines the Buddhist approach as "*transcendental* modernism":

> "Modern Buddhism" can be modern in two opposed senses. It can either be the contemporary culture's interpretation of Buddhism, and this inevitably tends to reduce Buddhism to a rational humanism (reductive modernism). Or else it can be a Buddhist interpretation of the contemporary culture, which gives us a spiritual and root-existential understanding of that culture (transcendental modernism).[91]

Here we clearly see that the secular/spiritual dichotomy which Jones had earlier constructed forces him to adopt the strong stance that members of contemporary culture will "*inevitably*" engage in reductive modernism.

Now if, as we saw in Jones' definition just above, an esoteric religion such as Buddhism must concern itself with *individual, spiritual* soteriology (a "training whereby *individuals* can realize their *True Nature*"), then Jones' project will have to be to determine how such a religion *could* develop a *socially* engaged element *without* succumbing to secular reductive modernism. Jones raises this methodological issue when discussing the subject of the *validation* for Buddhist activism, which raises the question: "on what basis, on what foundation, is Buddhist social analysis, and the activism derived from it, to be grounded?" Jones contrasts his method with "*the* other method" (that of the reductive modernists, of course):

> My method of validation can be characterized by terms such as primary, existential, perennial, epistemological. It contrasts with the other method of validating Buddhist social analysis and justifying social activism, which is secondary, exegetical, culture-bound and contingent in character, relying on specific scriptural evidence

and historic Buddhist practice to give direct and prescriptive guidance.[92]

The way in which Jones uses the labels "primary" and "secondary" here is very revealing. Most post-modern, "critical" thinkers, ever insistent on highlighting the contextuality of everything, would certainly insist on reversing these labels (as would I). "Specific scriptural evidence and historic Buddhist practice" should be considered the *primary* source (the raw data, so to speak) *on the basis of which* various *secondary* "existential" or "epistemological" *interpretations* can be formulated. For Jones to think that his methodology is "perennial" and *not* "exegetical" is naïve in the extreme, as even any *pre*-modern Buddhist hermeneutist would attest! But, of course, his adoption of the label "primary" is necessary if he is to *appropriate* the authority to speak for the Buddhist tradition, and his adoption of labels such as "existential," "epistemological" and "perennial" are necessary if he is to construct an historically *dis*engaged Buddhism from which he can *distance* (exalt) his own, innovative engaged hybrid.

When discussing Lopez and Gómez above, we saw how the Orientalists of the colonial and post-colonial period created a philosophy/ritual split in order to appropriate Buddhism as a pure philosophy. Jones makes a similar observation when he notes that post-colonial Buddhist intellectuals created a religion/politics split, this time in order to appropriate a politically engaged legacy for Buddhism:

> [As illustrated by H. Bechert and Demieville,] Western cultural colonialism was challenged by those [Asian Buddhists] who had already unknowingly succumbed to it, but who professed to find in the Buddhist scriptures and traditions such secular Western ideals as scientific rationalism and state socialism. These could then be claimed as having been all along a part of the Eastern cultural heritage.[93]

Certainly such examples of false consciousness[94] or inappropriate "reading back" did occur, and were perhaps even rampant. And certainly the following also occurred:

> In the heady post-colonial period, Buddhist intellectuals were concerned to present the Dharma as a national, humanistic, democratic, and even socialist ideology for today... Buddhism was ... claimed to be no less rational, scientific and "modern" (and there-

fore *relevant*) than either the technological capitalism or the
Marxian scientific socialism which challenged it.[95]

However, I should *not* want to assume that *all* such claims were necessarily
examples of naïve appropriation fostered by false consciousness. Many
legitimate, sober comparisons were no doubt drawn as well. But Jones will
not be so generous; he states a little further on:

> This kind of reductive modernism in my view overemphasizes and
> misinterprets the significance of the social teachings of the Pali
> canon... Concerned to make Buddhism manifestly relevant to the
> social and political requirements of the post-colonial era, these
> [reductive] modernists tend to read the scriptures in terms of
> certain dominant contemporary ideas, as if they were originally a
> programme for social reform; their over-arching spiritual and exis-
> tential context and significance is lost beneath a burgeoning
> humanistic rationalism. Meanings are read into them which are at
> best arguable and at worst extravagant and tendentious.[96]

Jones here confidently criticizes these Buddhists for reading their own
scriptures "as if they were originally a programme for social reform," as if
he, Jones, can authoritatively say that they were *not*. Furthermore, he
proceeds to tell them what the true significance of their scriptures *is*, a
significance which is to be recovered from what *Jones* discerns to be their
"over-arching spiritual and existential context" – a significance and
context which he says the Buddhists have "lost." It seems that, in the
heady post-*modern* period (obsessed with revealing ever more context and
eschewing dubious comparisons), Orientalism is alive and well.

Thus, in a manner similar to Jung, Jones constructs an Asian "Other"
which is essentially the opposite of (and complementary to) his Western
"Self" image. For Jones, Buddhism becomes primarily an enlightened spiritual tradition which has always been relatively disinterested in social and
political issues. We stand to learn much from its spiritual wisdom, but its
socio-political disinterest must be considered naïve or even dangerous in
today's modern world. Conversely for Jones, we in "the West" have developed a strong socio-political awareness and tradition, though we have
done so for the most part in isolation from our own spiritual traditions.
Buddhists stand to learn much from our socio-political wisdom, but our
modern spiritual nihilism must be considered naïve or even dangerous in
today's modern world. Having set up this Self/Other (socio-political / spiritual) dichotomy, Jones perceives that we now have a unique and
unprecedented opportunity to attempt to forge a union of these two great
traditions:[97]

The traditional Buddhist picture of personal delusion karmically sustained over many lifetimes must now be supplemented and seen also as a social process sustained through successive historical cultures. Society in the Buddha's time lacked the kind of dynamism and complexity that might have stimulated such awareness. This only came into existence in the West in comparatively recent times, with the emergence of the social sciences.[98]

However, he regularly implies that recent attempts on the part of both Buddhists and Western activists sympathetic to Buddhism seem inevitably to have resulted in some form of reductive modernism, that "secularized shell of public Buddhism"[99] which combines, not the best, but elements of the *worst* of each tradition.

Jones suggests that the *"transcendental modernism"* developed in his book provides the elusive formula needed to effectively combine the *best* of both. In the following remarkable passage Jones (1) recognizes the (essence of) Dharma as (beneficial) "light;" (2) appropriates the authority to (a) reveal this light from behind its thick, cultural "encrustations,"(b) determine (presumably) what is and what is not an "archaic," "misleading," "obsolescent," etc. encrustation; and (c) speak "both for many dedicated Buddhists and for the great mass of socially concerned people;" and (3) distances his transcendental modernism from Buddhism's currently encrusted state:

> [T]o explain the modern world in the light of Dharma, various cultural encrustations of time may need to be gently scraped off. Archaic and misleading modes of presentation, obsolescent institutions, and extrinsic secondary beliefs may have so dimmed the light that only the most sensitive and dedicated can still read by it. When the light has become feeble and the encrustations thick, then the whole apparatus may become *widely* understandable only in secular terms. And this makes of it something altogether different. It is the task of transcendental modernism to prevent this happening and, with humility and sensitivity, to help keep open access by all to the essential Dharma. Writing this book is an exercise of this kind, in a world in which Buddhism as a spirituality at present lacks direct social significance, both for many dedicated Buddhists and for the great mass of socially concerned people.[100]

Overall, I am generally quite sympathetic to Jones' warnings about the contemporary tendency toward secular "reductive modernism." The *problem* (and it is a big one) with his otherwise insightful observations is that he far over-extends his critique: just about *everybody* who describes

Buddhism as having had a history of social engagement seems to be accused of being a reductive modernist. This critique is enabled by his elaboration of what *he* considers the essence of Buddhism to be – a perennial set of truths intended to address the *existential* (but not the socio-political) sufferings of beings. For Jones, it is only now, in the modern era, that we have developed the mature perspective (and the urgent need) to bring out the socio-political *implications* latent in the Buddha's perennial teachings. However, unfortunately, everyone who has tried to do this has gone too far, inadvertently reducing Buddhism to a hollowed-out shell of secular, localized, socio-political ideologies, thereby losing Buddhism's original, transcendental, perennial essence. Jones seems to find only himself to be uniquely qualified to speak for what an engaged Buddhism could and should be. It should be evident that in all of these respects, and in spite of his otherwise excellent contributions, Jones is clearly a classic example of what I have herein described as a modernist.

Christopher Queen *et al.*

As I suggested in the introduction, in the last couple of years "engaged Buddhist studies" has begun to show the mature signs of a great deal more critical self-reflection. One such sign has been the conscious identification of the "newness" issue as one needing serious study and debate. For example, in his Preface to the anthology *Engaged Buddhism: Buddhist Liberation Movements in Asia*, editor Christopher Queen identifies this issue as "the central question" which he will explore in his Introduction:

> The central question examined in the introduction concerns whether the activist impulse of contemporary Asian Buddhism is historically new – a series of responses to uniquely modern conditions and historical forces – or whether there exist substantive precedents for such engagement with social and political concerns in Buddhist history.[101]

The essay to which this Preface alludes is entitled "Introduction: The Shapes and Sources of Engaged Buddhism." This title itself is appropriately exploratory in tone; as we have already seen previously, the central thesis which Queen develops therein (as well as the conclusion which he reaches) is decidedly modernist. Four years later, the title of his introductory essay for the anthology *Engaged Buddhism in the West* asserts his modernist thesis up front: "Introduction: A New Buddhism."

Indeed, Queen can perhaps be credited with *making* this newness question an issue in its own right. Other writers (both in Queen's anthologies and elsewhere) have certainly stressed either continuity or discontinuity in their elaborations of engaged Buddhism, but they have generally done so in passing – it has not been their main topic. What I will attempt to show in this section is that Queen has analyzed and then defined both of the terms "engaged" and "Buddhism" in such a way as to not only (a) fore-ground the newness issue *as* a central issue, but also so as to (b) favor the conclusion that engaged Buddhism is new. In brief, he has defined engage-ment as relating to "this-worldly" concerns, especially institutional and systemic causes and forms of suffering, and he has characterized "tradi-tional" Buddhism as other-worldly (following Weber). I will examine each of these in turn. First, I will argue that his narrowing and specifying of the term "engagement," although extremely interesting, valuable, and useful, may go so far as to make engaged Buddhism susceptible to Jones' criticism regarding secular reductive modernism. (Moreover, in the Conclusion I will suggest some reasons why his insistence that "engagement" – as he defines it – is *necessarily* recent and Western may be unfounded or at least counterproductive.) Second, I will argue that his characterizations of tradi-tional Buddhism as other-worldly (which he routinely makes in passing, perhaps influenced by his greater familiarity with Theravadin forms of Buddhism)[102] are entirely incompatible with most forms of Buddhism (especially Mahayana), both doctrinally as well as historically.

What is engagement?

Prior to the mid-1990s *most* (not all) scholars were fairly vague about the two or three terms involved in the label "(socially) engaged Buddhism." Although certain authors were occasionally more precise in their defini-tions, the range of definitions varied so greatly between authors that the possibility of meaningful dialogue was often obscured. As we have seen, this vagueness enabled both modernists and traditionists alike to indulge in either mutual myopia or in quick, dismissive, polemical rhetoric. In *The Social Face of Buddhism* Ken Jones offered a description sufficiently broad (and vague) that most would have probably accepted it:

> By "social action" we mean the many different kinds of action intended to benefit human kind. These range from simple, indi-vidual acts of charity, teaching and training, organized kinds of service, "Right Livelihood" in and outside the helping professions, and through various kinds of community development as well as to political activity in working for a better society.[103]

However, later in the same book Jones refracts this single, broad "range" of meanings into three distinct types of socially engaged Buddhism:

1 *Alternative Societal Models* (for example, monastic and quasi-monastic communities) and particularly "right livelihood."

2   *Social Helping, Service and Welfare*, both in employment and voluntarily.
3   *Radical Activism* (directed to fundamental institutional and social changes, culminating in societal metamorphosis).[104]

This spectrum spans from what he later calls a "soft end" to a "hard end." In a personal communication to Sandra Bell, Jones explains this "taxonomy":

> At the soft end are individuals and organizations who see Engaged Buddhism as ranging from being kind to your neighbors to promoting a society based on the principles of the Dharma. The hard enders do not deny the irrefutable logic of this, but claim that it robs Engaged Buddhism of a sufficiently clear definition... Hard enders believe governments and other institutions should be included in the active concerns of Buddhist morality.[105]

Citing this same passage from Jones, Queen[106] also implicitly bemoans the past vagueness of definition (as "robbing of sufficient clarity") and offers his own parallel spectrum from "mindfulness-based" to "service-based" engagement. Just as Jones (ahead of his time) clearly identified with the "hard end,"[107] Queen clearly identifies the "service-based" end as his primary subject (it is, after all, the form of engaged Buddhism which he feels he can argue is "new").

Although neither Jones nor Queen originated it, Queen has probably been the most vocal and articulate advocate of this narrower, more specific definition of engagement, as well as the most aggressive proponent of its "newness." As he describes it in his 1996 Introduction: "It is this new awareness of the social and institutional dimensions of suffering and the liberation from suffering that has contributed to the rise of contemporary Buddhist liberation *movements*."[108] Although he was quite clear and consistent about this definition in that first book, he emphasizes and develops this theme much more in his 2000 anthology:

> The essence of the new outlook is a recognition of (1) the inalienable value of the human person, whatever his or her level of achievement or standing in the community, (2) the social and collective nature of experience, shaped in particular by cultural and political institutions that have the power to promote good or evil, fulfillment or suffering, progress or decline, and (3) the necessity of collective action to address the systemic causes of suffering and promote social advancement in the world.[109]

Other engaged Buddhists have also recently sought to identify with this type of narrower definition of engagement.[110] These refinements are indeed extremely valuable and useful, and they have advanced considerably the discussions of issues central to the concerns of all engaged Buddhists. But exactly how "new" are such definitions? As such definitions draw on and are expressed in terms of recent Western (critical, Marxist) theories of political economy, social analysis, and so forth, modernist engaged Buddhists who adopt such language certainly insist that they are new. But could one trace *similar* developments in social theory in Buddhist discourse prior to the modern era, and if so might other (traditionist) engaged Buddhists be justified in emphasizing more continuity? I will explore one useful (perhaps conciliatory) approach to the question of determining the criteria for similarity *vs.* newness (continuity/discontinuity) in the concluding section on Ruegg's methodological observations.

The real issue before us presently is to clarify how *Queen* specifies and then applies such narrower definitions. In particular, how "this-worldly" must such an engaged approach be? More importantly, what does "this-worldly" itself mean and entail? What, if anything, does it exclude? In the following section we will see that Queen is able to magnify the perceived disjunction between traditional Buddhism and engaged Buddhism precisely by exaggerating both the "other-worldliness" (and individual orientation) of the former as well as the "this-worldliness" (and social/collective orientation) of the latter. When taken to an extreme, this drive to emphasize radical disjunction misrepresents both sides and runs the serious risk of disjointing the two halves of engaged Buddhism itself: traditional Buddhists are made out to be so other-worldly that they are not engaged, while engaged Buddhists are made out to be so this-worldly that (I will argue) they come dangerously close to not being Buddhists!

What is Buddhism? What is liberation?

While Queen never ventures a *definition* of Buddhism (a daunting task for anyone, to be sure!), his frequent, passing characterizations of various types of Buddhists are quite revealing. Two examples from his earlier anthology will suffice:

> The social engagement of Buddhist liberationists may indeed be seen as a rejection of the other-worldly asceticism of the tradi-

tional monk and the routinized devotionalism and merit-making of the lay masses...

[N]ineteenth-century Asian-Americans (Chinese and Japanese immigrants) were occupied in the ritual observance of their imported faiths.[111]

These passages present a surprisingly stereotypical, negative caricature of Buddhists. Among the "traditional Buddhists" the ordained are disconnected "other-worldly ascetics," and the lay are a naïve and mechanistic "mass" engaged in "routinized devotion." The East Asian Mahayana Buddhist immigrants seem dull and hapless, "occupied" as they are with "observing" the "rituals" dictated by their blindly accepted "faiths." In just a few words Queen, like Jung, constructs the quintessentially passive Eastern "Other" – one which opposes, of course, a conversely active and assertive Western "Self," namely, "the mainstream Protestant Buddhist sympathizers and adherents who forged the conception of an activist, socially engaged Buddhism."[112]

These cultural and religious reifications are continued in his 2000 anthology:

For Buddhists and practitioners of the other world faiths, it is no longer possible to measure the quality of human life primarily in terms of an individual's observance of traditional rites, such as meditation, prayer, or temple ritual; or belief in dogmas such as "the law of karma," "buddha-nature," the will of God," or "the Tao."[113]

Here it seems fair to ask – sticking to the Buddhist case – has it *ever* been possible to measure the quality of life *primarily* in terms of the "observance" of "rites" or the "belief" in "dogmas"? As with the earlier example, the verbs "to observe" and "to believe" suggest very passive behavior, and "rites" and "dogmas" are again terms for very rigid, routinized things to which practitioners automatically adhere. Are we really to believe that this is how Buddhists have always made this measurement (until now, now that unique modern circumstances have dictated that "it is no longer possible")?

We must equally question the implication in the above passage that Buddhists measure the quality of life exclusively in terms of an *individual's* actions and beliefs. This implication is made explicit in the following passage (here with respect to the ultimate quality of life, liberation): "it is no longer possible to see the individual as the sole "unit" of liberation or salvation... – ... the prime beneficiary of self-cultivation – separate from the complex of roles and relationships that make up his or her life-world."[114]

323

Again, we must ask, has this *ever* been possible? Would not any Individual Vehicle practitioner well-educated in the basic teachings on selflessness and interdependence have found it impossible to see the "individual" as a "separate unit" of anything? Certainly any Universal Vehicle practitioner well-educated in Central Way philosophy (*Madhyamaka*) would have understood that insofar as "individual selves" may be said to exist, they exist not as "separate units" but *precisely as* "complexes of roles and relationships," that is, they exist conventionally, as dependent designations, as relationalities. Moreover, Universal Vehicle treatises never assert or imply that an individual self could be the "prime beneficiary" of liberation. Rather, "liberation" (which in the Universal Vehicle context necessarily entails full "enlightenment" or Buddhahood)[115] involves the full development of both a Buddha's Truth Body as well as a Buddha's Form Body, which provide, respectively, the complete fulfillment of both "one's own benefit" (*sva-artha, rang don*) *and* "others' benefit" (*para-artha, gzhan don*).

Indeed, whether in the ethical, philosophical, or socio-political sphere, it often seems that the "new" and modern innovations that Queen discerns as distinguishing "engaged Buddhism" from "traditional Buddhism" are little more than a reformulation of the classical differences distinguishing Universal Vehicle Buddhism from Individual Vehicle Buddhism.[116] For example, in the *ethical* sphere he states, "Now it is necessary to consider the effects of personal and social actions on others," qualifying this in the *philosophical* sphere by saying, " 'The others' affected by these [personal and social] actions must be understood not only as unit selves, but as significant collectivities: families, neighbors, ... international populations ... and ecosystems."[117] These sound like traditional Universal Vehicle concerns and insights. Also in the philosophical sphere he states: "We may conclude that a profound change in Buddhist soteriology – from a highly personal and other-worldly notion of liberation to a social, economic, this-worldly liberation – distinguishes the Buddhist movements in our study."[118]

Again, it can be argued that this is precisely the "profound change" that occurred between the Individual Vehicle and Universal Vehicle articulations of liberation (we will explore this more in the next section). Finally, in the *socio-political* sphere he speaks of "the democratization, if not the transformation, of spiritual practices – for example, meditation and ritual initiations as now appropriated by lay practitioners."[119] Again, this is what historically occurred with Universal Vehicle (especially Vajra Vehicle) Buddhism in India and Tibet.

For now, suffice it to say that Queen understands traditional Buddhism (without reference to Vehicle) to be concerned with such "a highly personal and other-worldly notion of liberation," and he considers modern engaged Buddhism, by contrast, to be revolutionary in its focus on liberating beings from "concrete" and "worldly" conditions. He shows that such a worldly focus has characterized Christian liberation theology, and he argues that "the worldly perspective of [Christian] liberation theologies ... is fully consistent with the Buddhist liberation movements..."[120] This perspective is, he maintains, what defines a liberation movement as such: "It is, finally, their focus upon the relief of concrete economic, social, political, and environmental ills that qualifies these [Buddhist] movements as 'liberation movements?'[121]

Moreover, in the engaged Buddhism of contemporary Asia: "the liberation sought has been called a 'mundane awakening' (*laukodaya*), which includes individuals, villages, nations, and ultimately all people (*sarvodaya*), and which focuses on objectives that may be achieved and recognized in this lifetime, in this world."[122]

What remains to be explored here is just what this "this-worldly focus" entails. Whether or not it is truly new (as Queen insists it is), does Queen consider this focus on a "worldly liberation" to be (a) a secondary but important *supportive complement* to more "traditional" elaborations of liberation; (b) the new *primary* focus and goal; or (c) the new *exclusive* goal of self-proclaimed engaged Buddhists. Leaving aside the newness question, (a) would seem perfectly acceptable. On the other hand, (c) would seem unacceptably non-Buddhist.[123] The remaining option, (b), presents somewhat of a gray area – *how* primary is "worldly liberation" presented to be? There would seem to be a spectrum of possibilities here. As the primacy of the status of "worldly liberation" is emphasized ever more, the status (or relevance) of "traditional" elaborations of liberation – whether or not it is justified to characterize them as "other-worldly" – becomes ever more remote, representing more of an "unrealistic" goal; this moves (b) dangerously close to (c), opening it to Jones' critique regarding secular reductive modernism. It is this gray option (b) that Queen clearly discerns as characteristic of engaged Buddhism:

> We have noted that the most distinctive shift of thinking in socially engaged Buddhism is from a transmundane (*lokuttara*) to a mundane (*lokiya*) definition of liberation.
>
> Accompanying this shift is a de-emphasis on the stages of transmundane liberation ... and a new focus on the causes, varieties, and remedies of worldly suffering and oppression.[124]

Finally, in the following passage Queen indeed pushes (b) precariously close to (c):

> *The traditional conceptions* of karma and rebirth, the veneration of the bhikkhu sangha, *and the focus on ignorance* and psychological attachment to account for suffering in the world (the second

Noble Truth) *have taken second place to* the application of highly rationalized reflections on *the institutional and political manifestations of greed, hatred, and delusion*, and on new organizational strategies for addressing war and injustice, poverty and intolerance, and the prospects for "outer" as well as "inner" peace in the world.[125]

Returning now to the ethical sphere, Queen discerns three "distinctive styles" of traditional Buddhist ethics, *discipline*, *virtue*, and *altruism*, and he then proposes that *"engagement"* itself be adopted as the term for a fourth, new style of Buddhist ethics, characteristic of engaged Buddhism.[126] He then rightly surmises: "The reader may be wondering at this point how a final style of Buddhist ethics could improve upon the altruism of the Mahayana"[127] His explanation and defense of this "newness" is as follows:

It would be wrong to argue that the first three styles of Buddhist morality are not productive of a more peaceful and prosperous society, as well as happier individuals. But one may wonder, in light of the widespread conditions of human misery in our world today, whether rule-based morality, mental cultivation, individualized good works, and generalized vows to save all beings will be enough to prevent the spread of political tyranny, economic injustice, and environmental degradation in the era to come. Such a question itself reflects a critical shift in thought and practice that distinguishes Buddhist leaders and communities today from their predecessors in traditional Asian societies.[128]

In this passage Queen adopts one of the modernist strategies we discussed above, emphasizing that the modern (and future) context is something historically unique and unprecedented. More troubling, however, is his characterization of Mahayana altruism as "generalized vows to save all beings." Once again, through an extremely reductive (mis)portrayal of a passive Eastern "Other," room is made for the activist Western "Self" and its new ethic of engagement. For we can note that "generalized vows to save all beings" represent only one side – the first step – of Mahayana altruism (*bodhicitta*), what is called "aspirational bodhicitta" (*pranidhi-bodhicitta, smon pa'i byang sems*). The other essential side – the follow-through, the heart of daily practice – is what is precisely called *"engaged* bodhicitta" (*prasthaana-bodhicitta, 'jug pa'i byang sems*)![129] Nevertheless, Queen describes his proposed fourth ethic of "engagement" as radically new and different: "As the fourth style of Buddhist ethics, engaged Buddhism is radically different from the Mahayana path of altruism because it is directed to the creation of new social institutions and social relationships."

Regarding this radical newness, he acknowledges that "there are indeed harbingers of socially engaged practice in the annals of Buddhist history" such as (of course) Ashoka in India and some others in China, but he contends that "these are exceptions to the practices of individual discipline, virtue, and altruism advocated in the tradition."[130]

Having "recognized" (constructed) that in all three spheres (ethical, philosophical, and socio-political) traditional and engaged forms of Buddhism occupy opposite ends of an (equally constructed) transcendent-worldly spectrum, Queen then distances his newly appropriated "world-engaged" Buddhism as far as possible, taking it to its logical (modernist) conclusion: he boldly proposes that "engaged Buddhism be thought of as a fourth yana."[131] He suggests several terms for the "New Vehicle" (*Navayana*, following Ambedkar) of the "new Buddhism," including "Earth Vehicle" (*Terrayana*, following Kraft, 2000), and "World Vehicle" or "Global Vehicle" (*Lokayana*).[132] On page 1 of his "Introduction: A New Buddhism" he alerts us that:

> Inasmuch as ... concepts [of human rights, distributive justice, and social progress] have had few parallels in the classical formulations of ... Hinayana ...,Mahayana ..., ... and ... Vajrayana ..., I shall argue that the general pattern of belief and practice that has come to be called "engaged Buddhism" is unprecedented, and thus tantamount to a new chapter ... a new paradigm ... a "new vehicle."[133]

And later on when he actually makes this argument he says:

> This [New Vehicle] Buddhism is endowed with many, if not all, of the themes and techniques from the past... But it is also endowed with a sensitivity to social injustice, institutional evil, and political oppression as sources of human suffering, that has not been central to Buddhist analysis in the past.[134]

Now others such as Joanna Macy[135] and Franz-Johannes Litsch[136] have suggested that engaged Buddhism should be considered a "new turning of the wheel of Dharma," so Queen is certainly not alone in wanting to appropriate traditional Buddhist hermeneutical schema to give the highest possible status to what he sees as a truly revolutionary, new development in Buddhism. In fact, none of these contemporary Western Buddhists are alone, for Asian Buddhists throughout history have repeatedly made such controversial attempts at re-definition and re-classification – *the very attempt to define a "New Vehicle" or a "new turning of the wheel of Dharma" is itself nothing new!*[137] A substantial body of literature exists regarding such controversies,[138] so it would seem most sensible for engaged Buddhists wanting to make such claims to consult this material for precedents. On the other hand, since making such radical claims is often more of a political act than a hermeneutical one, perhaps it behooves such attempts to keep this material in the shadows!

Universal Vehicle liberation

We will now look more closely at Universal Vehicle Mahayana elaborations of "the world" and of "liberation (from 'the world')" to determine whether or not the more "worldly" dimensions of "engagement" are as new as they are claimed to be.

So exactly how "this-worldly" is the Universal Vehicle notion of "liberation," really? Let us clarify the premise and the question. Charles Prebish suggests that Nhat Hanh's notion of "engagement" was influenced by French post-war existentialist concepts of engagement (*l'engagement, engagé*), particularly by Sartre's notion that (in Prebish's words) "to be 'engaged' is to actualize one's freedom by ... acknowledging one's inescapable involvement in the world."[139] So to restate the question: Does Universal Vehicle theory admit "one's *inescapable* involvement in the world?" If so – if one *cannot* escape – then what could 'liberation' possibly mean? *These are in fact classical Universal Vehicle themes.*

The answer to these questions depends, of course, on a subtle analysis of what is meant (or even could be meant) by "this world" and by "liberation." Ever since Nagarjuna, Universal Vehicle proponents have relentlessly critiqued the naïve notion that liberation (*moksha, nirvana*) is (*or logically even could be*) another realm, a "goal" to "reach" somehow dualistically *apart* from this world (*loka, samsara*). As Nagarjuna says in his *Mulamadhyamakakarika* (XXV: 19–20):

> There is not the slightest difference
> Between cyclic existence and nirvana.
> There is not the slightest difference
> Between nirvana and cyclic existence.
>
> Whatever is the limit of nirvana,
> That is the limit of cyclic existence.
> There is not even the slightest difference between them,
> Or even the subtlest thing.[140]

Garfield himself comments on these verses:

> To be in samsara is to see things as they appear to deluded consciousness and to interact with them accordingly. To be in nirvana, then, is to see those things as they are – as merely empty,

dependent, impermanent, and nonsubstantial, but not to be somewhere else, seeing something else.[141]

The nonduality (*advaya, gnyis med*) of samsara and nirvana has been
one of the *central* themes explored and developed throughout all of
Universal Vehicle literature (Prajñaparamita-sutras, Vimalakirti-sutra,
Madhyamaka shastric literature, etc.). Now it is very important to stress
that in these treatises the "nonduality" of any two things is clearly distinguished from their "unity." Characterizations of the "unity," "monism,"
or "oneness" of two things invariably *conflate* or *reduce* one of those
things to the other. Thurman (following Tsong Khapa's interpretation of
Nagarjuna) has discussed these dangers at length. Coining the terms
"monistic absolutist" and "existential relativist" for two possible extreme
interpretations, Thurman says: "The former hold the message of the
central way to be that *samsara* is *Nirvana*. The latter hold it to be that
Nirvana is *samsara*."[142]
He then acknowledges that, "Either of these positions may be partially
correct," that "Each has its own evidence, arguments, and advantages,"
and he cites numerous Indian, Tibetan, and Western interpreters who may
be said to fall into these two camps. (We might add that Queen *et al.*,
would seem to fall into the existential relativist camp.) But then, after a
lengthy defense of the merits of each of these views, he tells us that "Tsong
Khapa insists that these would-be Dialecticist Centrists, or interpreters of
the school, are in fact the chief antagonists (*purvapaksin*) of the
school!"[143] After an equally lengthy discourse on Tsong Khapa's refutation
of these two extreme positions and on his Centrist solution, Thurman
concludes by citing the verse above by Nagarjuna (XXV, 19) and then
emphasizing the half-truths present in each of those two extreme positions:

> The absolutist is correct; there is an overriding soteric aim. There
> is a Nirvana, a supreme bliss. But salvation is not "mystic," a
> "leap into the void" having discarded reason, and Nirvana is not a
> place outside the world; it is a situation that includes the world
> within its bliss. Samsara cannot be distinguished from it. It is in
> Nirvana that samsara is embraced completely ... But the relativist
> is also correct. "Perfection" is always correlated with "imperfec-
> tion"; there is no escape from inevitable relativity. Nirvana ... is
> just here now, and the full experiential acceptance of that is libera-
> tion, which is not a going elsewhere. But truly being "here" is not
> an abandonment of the Absolute, a capitulation to the mysterious-
> ness of meaninglessness, a relative meaninglessness. It is rather an

Absolute being here, a triumphal commitment to sensible duality. For part of relativity is the ideal of the Absolute.[144]

If Thurman and Tsong Khapa are correct, then from the Universal Vehicle perspective liberation has always entailed *both* a transcendent, transmundane, "other-worldly" (*lokottara*) aspect *as well as equally* an immanent, mundane, "this-worldly" (*lokiya*) aspect. Both aspects exist together, nondually, without either aspect collapsing into the other.

Bringing this lofty philosophical discussion on the nature of liberation back down to Buddhist liberation movements "on the ground" (so to speak), José Cabezón tells us in Queen's own anthology:

> [T]he Buddhist social philosophy emerging out of the Tibetan liberation movement is not envisioned as a radical rethinking of traditional Buddhist philosophy. Although suggesting a new reading of Buddhist texts, a new hermeneutical lens, it does not do so at the expense of the traditional understanding of Buddhist scripture ... [I]t stresses continuity with the tradition rather than rupture ... In the Tibetan case it is not that the traditional goals of Buddhism (e.g., *nirvana*, the universal emancipation of all beings, and so on) are discarded in favor of action in the world. Instead, the two goals, worldly and supramundane, are seen as reinforcing each other.[145]

Moreover – and of great relevance to our discussion on Queen's possible sources and influences – in a footnote to this passage Cabezón *contrasts* this nondual Mahayana approach with a more dualistic Theravadin one (as developed, e.g., in the earlier writings of Bardwell Smith):

> This [Tibetan Buddhist social theory] is in marked contrast to the theory of the development of a Buddhist social ethic that assumes the kammatic/nibbannic distinction, in which social action belongs in the kammatic, that is, "secular," realm, and is therefore related primarily to the goal of higher rebirth, as opposed to the nibbanic aspect of the religion whose goal is emancipation from all rebirth. In the Tibetan setting, and perhaps more generally in Mahayana Buddhism, the case can convincingly be made that such a distinction is unwarranted. Social action is as much the cause of *nirvana* as monastic discipline is; and vice versa, typically "nibbannic" practices such as wisdom and compassion are as relevant to properly acting within the world as is the concept of *karma*.[146]

Thus, we may now *hazard* a guess at a possible genealogy of modernist engaged Buddhist views. A Buddhist with a more dualistic background (perhaps Theravadin) *may* be predisposed to misunderstand (or to miss altogether) certain key nondual elements within the Mahayana traditions. Initially missing the specific "worldly" implications within various Mahayana doctrines (implications well-known and even explicit within the Mahayana tradition itself), such a Buddhist, upon glimpsing such implications, might think they were radically new (which for him they would be). However, without fully appreciating the Mahayana view (of emptiness, relativity, and nonduality), he would certainly be prone to misunderstanding the subtleties of the implications which he now no longer *completely* missed. He would then most likely fall to one extreme or another, and "existential relativism" (which overemphasizes the reality of samsara, "the world") would be the most likely option for a postmodern global citizen (whether Asian or Western). A "Buddhism" founded by such a Buddhist would thus tend to de-emphasize transcendence and to (over)emphasize a type of world-engagement which was perceived to be unprecedented and "new." Voilà – modernist engaged Buddhism.

Conclusion

It is well known that in the history of Buddhist studies in the West there have been numerous evolutions in understanding. Thus, for a long time Pali (Theravada) Buddhism was seen to be the "pure, original" form of Buddhism of which Mahayana Buddhism was a "later, degenerate" form. Discontinuity was stressed as Mahayana was seen to be a radically separate form of Buddhism "made up" by ingenious and deceitful Indians half a millennium after the "historical Buddha." Eventually, however, this clear-cut picture was eroded as more and more continuities were discerned and as a more nuanced understanding emerged of how Buddhists themselves variously understood Buddhism (or *buddhavacana*) throughout their own histories. Similar evolutions in scholarly thinking have developed with respect to Indian tantric Buddhism (originally seen as a complete degeneration, now often respected as continuous with "mainstream" Mahayana Buddhism), and with respect to Tibetan Buddhism in general (originally seen as degenerate "Lamaism," now seen as unique but nonetheless continuous with Indian forms of Buddhism). The present chapter has merely sought to suggest that a similar evolution in common scholarly awareness has yet to occur with respect to the possible *continuities* between modern forms of engaged Buddhism and Buddhism's past.

Nor do I wish to *over*emphasize such possible continuities. I do not wish to have left the impression that all of the modernists' conclusions are "wrong." Many of their interpretations *may* turn out to be plausible, given further research and dialogue (and I believe that *much* more of both are needed). I have rather tried herein to demonstrate that many modernists have arrived at their "conclusions" far too hastily, that they may have only "discovered" what were in fact tacit *foregone* conclusions.

The Queen challenge

As I see it, the modernists have put out an articulate, healthy challenge to the community of Buddhist scholars. As Queen put it in 1996: "[F]ew contemporary scholars have successfully challenged the conventional wisdom that, until recent times, Buddhism focussed on personal liberation, not on social transformation."[147]

And more recently in 2000:

> In lieu of a concerted argument that engagement, as we have defined it, has co-evolved with the ethics of discipline, virtue, and altruism in Buddhist history, however, one must conclude ... that it is the product of dialogue with the West over the past one hundred years or so.[148]

In this present chapter I have tried to problematize many of the suppositions in such formulations: Whose "conventional wisdom" are we talking about? What is meant by "personal liberation" and "social transformation," and what is the relationship between them? Must we accept "engagement" as you have defined it? Must we accept your four types of ethics?

But these methodological questions notwithstanding, the basic challenge is still there, and it is a good one. While we must always continue to ask such questions, it is time to begin digging into the "data." Interested scholars (both traditionists as well as open-minded modernists) *should* now revisit the history of premodern Buddhist Asia with the *express* purpose of discovering examples of "engagement" as defined (more or less) by Queen and/or other modernists. For this analysis to be "concerted" it must be undertaken by a variety of scholars specializing in a variety of disciplines (including, but not limited to, "Buddhist Studies") spanning vast temporal, cultural, and geographical domains. Scholars will want to re-investigate theories and arguments found in Buddhist texts, but they must also examine less traditional textual sources including political and legal documents, census reports, economic surveys, etc., as well as non-textual sources included in the archaeological record, and so forth. In addition, it will be necessary to consult non-Buddhist (e.g., Hindu or Muslim) accounts as well as non-indigenous accounts (e.g., Chinese accounts of India). If after such a concerted effort sufficient evidence is *not* found, then the modernists' contentions regarding the discontinuity between modern "engaged" Buddhism and premodern "traditional" (disengaged) Buddhism must be conceded (the question of how such a "new" Buddhism should be related to traditional forms [a new vehicle?] – including what it means to call it "Buddhism" – will, however, remain). However, if sufficient evidence *is* found, then a *well-documented* and "concerted argument" can be formulated in favor of traditionists' insistence on continuity.

Gimme distance

I have proposed that many Westerners do not seem to be able (or willing) to assimilate Buddhism organically, that Buddhism's many and varied seeds *cannot* be allowed to simply take root on our soil! We *must* tinker with those foreign seeds, genetically re-engineer them, clone and graft them to make our *own* hybrid, indigenous forms. If they are made "*new*" in this way, it seems we assume, they will *necessarily* be "improved." Of course, if we did allow for a more organic transfer they would still become uniquely ours (I certainly do not subscribe to the perennialist notion that Buddhism is a set of eternal, unchanging principles that are transferred intact throughout the centuries from country to country). A variety of Buddhism would still adapt and become uniquely "American" (for example) for the simple fact that they would be growing in American soil, in the diversity of American climates, nourished by American nutrients, etc. But for some reason this is not enough for us – it seems we *must* make Buddhism over in our own image. In short, having *recognized* (constructed) something in Buddhism that we want, we must *appropriate* it and then *distance* ourselves from its original (Asian) sources.

Due to the force of this strong inclination, modern Western engaged Buddhists are being told (and are telling themselves) that they can have their seeds and eat them too: they can have their Buddhism and not call it "Buddhism."[149] Or, in the terms of the present essay, they can appropriate their Buddhism and distance themselves too. Thus, as Kraft declared in one of his earlier essays: "Nor is any conversion to Buddhism required. The ideas and practices offered here are assumed to be effective whether or not a Buddhist label is attached to them."[150] Kraft is of course correct about this, but I wonder if modernist engaged Buddhists, with their zeal for newness, aren't *too* eager to throw off the "Buddhist label" (and any possible continuities that may have been associated with it). Much is lost in this process. The entire past is lost in this process.

Continuity or discontinuity?

We saw that many modernists are quick to emphasize the differences between the "simpler" times of the Buddha and our own, more "complex" times, and that they use such differences to assert that, e.g., "it is unscholarly to ... proclaim that the Buddha was a democrat and an internationalist."[151] Likewise, many (not all) of the papers submitted to the first *JBE* online conference argued that the concept of "human rights" is a uniquely modern, Western innovation.

However, in an essay entitled "Some Reflections on the Place of Philosophy in the Study of Buddhism," David Ruegg offers some very useful methodological observations that suggest an alternative to such a rigid prohibition of "source-alien terminology." He writes:

> [H]owever much a philosophical insight or truth transcends, *in se,* any particular epoch or place, in its expression a philosophy is perforce conditioned historically and culturally.
>
>   But when saying that it is historically and culturally conditioned, I most certainly do not mean to relativize it or to espouse reductionism – quite the contrary in fact. The often facile opposition relativism vs. universalism has indeed all too often failed to take due account of the fact that what is relative in so far as it is conditioned in its linguistic or cultural expression may, nonetheless, in the final analysis have a very genuine claim to universality in terms of the human, and hence of the humanities. It seems that this holds true as much when we postulate some "Western" or "Eastern" philosophy of this or that period as when we consider what is now termed human rights, which by definition must transcend specific cultures in time and place.[152]

Thus, it may well be valid to say that the Buddha *did* espouse "democracy," "internationalism" or "human rights," regardless of the fact that what he espoused may not have been *exactly* "the same as" what we now mean by those terms. But for that matter, one cannot say that all people in different times and places throughout the modern era have used those terms in exactly (or sometimes even approximately) "the same" way! A similar observation could be made about the use of the term "engagement" in general.[153]

Ruegg then makes some very useful and relevant comments about K. L. Pike's "emic" and "etic" approaches to source studies[154] which further draw out the implications for the use of "source-alien terminology." First, he explains that an "emic" approach involves studying a tradition systemically and structurally, by "making use of their own intellectual and cultural categories and seeking as it were to 'think along' with these traditions." By contrast an "etic" approach involves the intentional use of one's own interpretive strategies and categories for the purpose of "generalizing and comparative" analysis.[155] Then, he observes:

> The distinction between the "emic" and "etic" approaches ... is no doubt parallel to the distinction drawn between the use of

author-familiar as opposed to author-alien terminologies for the purposes of comparison and exposition. But ... it may still be possible to employ author-alien terminologies even within an approach that is committed to "emic" analysis and understanding. For example, in explaining the Buddhist theory of spiritual classes or "lineages" (*gotra*) to the extent that it is based on a biological metaphor, one might evoke the idea of a (spiritual) "gene"... Of course, ... the modern biological term "gene"... [is] alien to our Indian and Tibetan sources, in which no lexeme is to be found with precisely the meaning of... [this] modern word... Yet it seems possible to invoke, *mutatis mutandis*, the ideas expressed by ... [this] new term ... when seeking to explicate the ... [theory] in question. In other words, author-alien (or source-alien) terminology could very well be compatible with an "emic" approach to understanding, and it does not necessarily bring with it an exclusive commitment to the "etic" approach. (Conversely, it would in principle be possible to employ source-familiar terminology and still misconstrue and misrepresent a doctrine, thus infringing the requirement of an "emic" approach.) Furthermore, ... the use of source-familiar terminology need not stand in the way of proceeding from "emic" to "etic" approaches.[156]

Likewise, if evidence is obtained which warrants it, it should be entirely possible to describe traditional Buddhists as "engaged," as "internationalists," etc. Moreover, I would strengthen Ruegg's parenthetical statement that "it would in principle be possible to employ source-familiar terminology and still misconstrue and misrepresent a doctrine, thus infringing the requirement of an 'emic' approach" by saying that "*it is in practice quite common* to employ source-familiar terminology and still misconstrue and misrepresent a doctrine..." – for that is exactly what I have suggested many modernists do when they insist that "historically" Buddhism has always been "*dis*engaged."

And finally, Ruegg suggests that the careful application of an "emic" approach can help us to avoid the type of subtle (often unconscious) "neo-colonialism" that we have discussed at length herein:

Structural and systemic analysis is in a position to allow due weight to the historical as well as to the descriptive, that is, it may be diachronic as well as synchronic. Here the observation might be ventured that *careful "emic" analysis can provide as good a foundation as any for generalizing and comparative study, one that will not superimpose* from the outside extraneous modes of thinking and interpretive grids in a way that sometimes proves to be scarcely distinguishable from *a more or less subtle form of neo-colonialism.*[157]

Choices, choices

One can choose to stress the continuities between the beliefs and practices of contemporary Buddhists and those of the past, or one can choose to stress the discontinuities. If such choices are not made consciously and carefully, then they are always made unconsciously. Either way, they usually represent more of an ideological or political disposition (or move) than an historical "observation." While we may agree with Queen that in principle "to stress the discontinuity of engaged Buddhism with its classical and medieval predecessors ... is not to *discredit* its authority,"[158] it nevertheless seems that for Queen (and other modernists) "to stress the discontinuity" (to recognize, then distance) is often to *appropriate* its authority.

On the other hand, if some modernists do consciously and carefully choose to emphasize discontinuities with the past, then certainly other contemporary Buddhists need not be threatened by what those modernists may construe as their new "innovations." Buddhism has always been adaptive and fluid – as Thurman has stated, Buddhism has a *"tradition of originality."*[159] It *is* traditional to *be* original in Buddhism! So the traditionists can relax in the face of the modernists' "adaptations."

But equally importantly (and almost never noted, from what I have seen) is the fact that modernist Buddhists need not be threatened when traditionists consciously and carefully choose to emphasize continuities with the past. Buddhism has had a much longer and more diverse history than modernists typically acknowledge – many of our "contemporary" problems (and solutions) may not be so "new." The modernists' rhetoric of "newness" seduces us into prematurely abandoning the rich mine of the Buddhist tradition and cheats us out of many jeweled resources from which we could have greatly profited. Again, Thurman's comments make this very simple point:

> The Buddhist monastic way of life that has been carried down through history in various Asian countries contains a great deal of knowledge concerning the ways that minds and societies work. Without it, we cannot expect to have a Buddhism that stands up to the militarism of the age in which we live.[160]

Even the possibility of the total destruction of our habitat or of "life as we know it" can be seen to be not quite as "new" or "modern" as we are continually told to believe. Although it is true that the various *technologies* of destruction (nuclear, chemical, mass environmental pollution and exploitation, etc.) are truly new and unprecedented, we should not under-emphasize the very real threats and realities that many premodern civilizations have endured, including the annihilation of *their* "entire world" (their entire society, culture, and habitat – life as they knew it) by other means (invading hoards of armies, etc.). There is much we *still* stand to learn from this rich human history. Our situation may be unique, but it is no *more* unique than anyone else's in the past! So if modernist engaged Buddhists are truly concerned with transforming the world in which we all live, they might do well to relax and let go of their need to appropriate, own, and reinvent Buddhism from the ground up.

What would be most productive for those of us interested in the socio-spiritual welfare of living beings (both as individuals and as societies) is greater patience, a renewed readiness to respect and dialogue with one another (including "the natives"!), more sophisticated methodological approaches, and a much keener self-awareness of the reasons and agenda motivating our many enterprises.

Notes

1 Cf. Kenneth L. Kraft (ed.), *Inner Peace, World Peace: Essays on Buddhism and Nonviolence* (Albany: State University of New York Press, 1992), p. 18; Christopher S. Queen and Sallie B. King (eds.), *Engaged Buddhism: Buddhist Liberation Movements in Asia* (Albany: State University of New York Press, 1996), p. 34, note 6; and Charles S. Prebish, *Luminous Passage: The Practice and Study of Buddhism in America* (Berkeley, CA: University of California Press, 1998), p. 273.

2 Of course, the very term "tradition" (or "*the* Buddhist *tradition*") itself empha-sizes continuity with the past.

3 Modernists are often vague about the exact time-frame for their espoused "modern-ness." When they do specify it they generally refer to "the past one hundred years or so." Christopher S. Queen (ed.), *Engaged Buddhism in the West* (Boston: Wisdom Publications, 2000), p. 30, note 34; and Robert Aitken, *The Mind of Clover* (San Francisco: North Point Press, 1984), p. 164, cited in Queen, 2000, p. 17. Queen offers the most specific dates when he suggests that engaged Buddhism emerged after 1880 or 1881 (Queen, 1996: 20), or even only after the 1940s (Queen, 1996, pp.18–19).

4 Note that I will be using these terms "traditionist" and "modernist" to desig-nate *only* the views just described. These terms of course carry other connotations, none of which are to be inferred herein. I will thus be employing these somewhat awkward and inadequate labels only for lack of a better set of terms.

5 As I will mention shortly, this mutual myopia has been rectified somewhat since 1997, as demonstrated for example by some of the essays in Queen (2000). Earlier exceptions to this observation would include Ken Jones, "Buddhism and Social Action: An Exploration," in Fred Eppsteiner (ed.), *The Path of Compassion: Writings on Socially Engaged Buddhism* (Berkeley, CA: Parallax Press, 1988), pp.65–81; and some of the authors in Queen (1996).

6 Kenneth L. Kraft, "New Voices in Engaged Buddhist Studies," in Queen, 2000, p. 506.

7 Kenneth L. Kraft, *Inner Peace*, p. 18. Here Kraft is citing a comment Nhat Hanh made in *BPF Newsletter* 11:2 (Summer, 1989), p. 22.

8 It is worth noting that in his Introduction to this anthology, modernist editor Christopher Queen refers to this title as "provocative," Queen, 2000, p. 7.

9 Queen, 2000, pp. 35–36. Here the authors are citing Nhat Hanh's own words in *Love in Action: Writings on Nonviolent Social Change* (Berkeley, CA: Parallax Press, 1993).

10 Thich Nhat Hanh, "Love in Action," in Arnold Kotler (ed.), *Engaged Buddhist Reader* (Berkeley, CA: Parallax Press, 1996), p. 57.

11 Ibid., p. 62.

12 Sulak Sivaraksa, "Buddhism in a World of Change," in Eppsteiner (ed.), *The Path of Compassion*, p. 12.

13 Bernie Glassman Roshi, as quoted by Queen, 2000, p. 104.

14 Glassman, as quoted by Queen, 2000, p. 122. It should be noted that Glassman himself does not just "practice in the cave" to "realize the Way," etc. As Queen's interview essay reveals, Glassman is quite active and directly engaged in many social arenas. And as Queen himself says in his Introduction to the anthology: "*Service-based engaged Buddhism* is my term for the results-oriented practice of teachers like Bernie Glassman and many of the Buddhist environmentalists, prison chaplains, and peace activists profiled in this book" (Queen, 2000, p.10). However, it can also be noted that when Glassman is asked, "Can a meditator on a retreat in a cave be an engaged Buddhist?" Queen (the quintessential modernist) says he is "confounded" by Glassman's affirmative answer (ibid., p. 10)! Queen concludes (we can surmise he finds this paradoxical), "With Glassman Roshi, the continuum from mindfulness-based to service-based engaged Buddhism becomes a full circle" (ibid., p. 11).

15 Paula Greene, "Walking for Peace: Nipponzan Myohoji," in Queen, *Engaged Buddhism in the West*, pp. 153–154.

16 Batchelor, as quoted by Sandra Bell, "A Survey of Engaged Buddhism in Britain," Queen, *Engaged Buddhism in the West*, p. 413.

17 H. H. The Dalai Lama XIV and Thich Nhat Hanh are perhaps the most well-known examples.

18 Queen, 1996, p. 14.

19 The Sarvodaya Shramadana Sangamaya movement was begun by A. T. Ariyaratne in Sri Lanka in 1958. For more on this "engaged" movement, cf. Macy, 1988, p. 174ff, and the essay by George D. Bond entitled "A. T. Ariyaratne and the Sarvodaya Shramadana Movement in Sri Lanka" (Chapter 4 in Queen, 1996).

20 Joanna Macy, "In Indra's Net: Sarvodaya & Our Mutual Efforts for Peace," in Eppsteiner, *The Path of Compassion*, p. 179.

21 Kraft, 1992, pp. 84–85.

22 Ibid., p. 86.

23 Robert A. F. Thurman, "Nagarjuna's Guidelines for Buddhist Social Action," in Eppsteiner, *The Path of Compassion*, p. 120.

24 Ibid., p. 142.

25 Walpola Rahula, "The Social Teachings of the Buddha," in Eppsteiner, *The Path of Compassion*, p. 104.

26 Sivaraksa, in Eppsteiner, 1988, p.12.

27 Ibid., p. 15.

28 Macy, in Eppsteiner, 1988, p. 173.

29 Queen, 1996, p. 17.

30 Bardwell Smith, Review of *Engaged Buddhism: Buddhist Liberation Movements in Asia* (Queen, 1996), in *Journal of the American Academy of Religion* 67,2 (summer 1999): 501.
31 Joseph M. Kitagawa, "Buddhism and Social Change: An Historical Perspective," in *Buddhist Studies in Honor of Walpola Rahula*, ed. by Somaratna Balasooriya *et al.* (London: Gordon Fraser, 1980), p. 89.
32 Ibid., p. 91.
33 Ibid., p. 97.
34 Ken Jones, *The Social Face of Buddhism: An Approach to Political and Social Activism* (London: Wisdom Publications, 1989), p. 207.
35 Ibid., pp. 207–208.
36 Nelson Foster, "To Enter the Marketplace," in Eppsteiner, 1988, p. 49.
37 Ibid., p. 50.
38 Kenneth L. Kraft, "Engaged Buddhism: An Introduction," in Eppsteiner, 1988, pp. xii–xiii. This generalization is somewhat strange, since this anthology contains essays by several outspoken traditionists.
39 Cynthia Eller, "The Impact of Christianity on Buddhist Nonviolence in the West," in Kraft, *Inner Peace, World Peace*, p. 102.
40 Jones, 1989, p. 21.
41 Ibid., p. 194.
42 Cf., p. 9.
43 Richard Gombrich, as quoted by Queen, 1996, p. 17.
44 Foster, in Eppsteiner, 1988, p. 51.
45 Robert Aitken Roshi, as quoted by Judith Simmer-Brown, "Speaking Truth to Power: The Buddhist Peace Fellowship," in Queen, 2000, p. 81. In her preface to this passage Simmer-Brown herself states that the "BPF ... analyzes ... especially suffering caused by social, economic, and political structures," then unabashedly concludes that "This analysis goes beyond the Buddha's."
46 Rita M. Gross, "Toward a Buddhist Environmental Ethic," *Journal of the American Academy of Religion* 65, 2 (1997): 335.
47 Kraft, 1992, p. 6.
48 Ibid.
49 Ibid., p. 7.
50 This is one of the earliest book-length studies of "Engaged Buddhism," and while it is largely modernist in tone, it is perhaps one of the most sophisticated and well-balanced works on this topic. We will be returning to his arguments extensively below.
51 Jones, 1989, p. 66.
52 Ibid., pp. 197–198. We will be discussing Jones' notion of "reductive modernism" below.
53 Ibid., p. 237.
54 Cf. p. 8.
55 Kraft, 1992, p. 13.
56 Kraft, in Eppsteiner, 1988, p. xiii. It is significant to note that this 1988 essay, as bold (or extreme) as it may sound, has had an important and enduring history of its own in publications on engaged Buddhism. It was selected for inclusion and reprinted essentially unchanged in the 1996 *Engaged Buddhist Reader*, pp. 64–69, and the very passage cited here was also quoted by Queen in the culminating paragraph of his Introduction to his 1996 *Engaged Buddhism*.
57 Foster, in Eppsteiner, 1988, pp. 51–52.
58 Ibid., p. 56.
59 Eller, in Kraft, 1992, p. 91.

60 Robert Aitken, *The Mind of Clover: Essays in Zen Buddhist Ethics* (San Francisco: North Point Press, 1984), p. 164, as cited by Queen in (Queen, 2000, p. 17).

61 Queen, 1996, p. 20.

62 Ibid.

63 Ibid., p. 31.

64 Donald S. Lopez Jr. (ed.). *Curators of the Buddha: The Study of Buddhism Under Colonialism* (Chicago: University of Chicago Press, 1996).

65 Ibid., p. 8.

66 Ibid., p. 7.

67 Indeed, earlier in his essay Lopez quotes an article published by Hodgson in 1828 which clearly shows "the ambivalence of trust and suspicion of the native that would come to characterize the study of Buddhism in the west," in Lopez, 1996, p. 3.

68 On the untenability of a "theory/practice" split, cf. Catherine Bell's *Ritual Theory, Ritual Practice* (New York: Oxford University Press, 1992).

69 It should be noted that modern Buddhologists have widely (if not universally) deconstructed and discredited at least *this particular* Orientalist formulation (real Buddhism = pure philosophy).

70 Such a dubious split parallels the *nirvana/samsara* split clearly refuted by Nagarjuna, among others. It must be admitted that such a naïve, dualistic split certainly *was* maintained by certain "early Buddhists" (the ones Nagarjuna was claiming to refute); but it must equally be admitted that there were probably "early Buddhists" who did *not* accept such a split (the ones Nagarjuna would have been claiming to side with – for Nagarjuna himself did not claim to be an innovator, but rather claimed to be speaking *within* and *for* the Buddhist tradition).

71 Modernists might "expect" that scholars from historically Buddhist countries would naïvely misconstrue their own history in this way, but they would also probably "expect" that Western scholars such as Thurman or Macy "should know better."

72 Luis O. Gómez, "Oriental Wisdom and the Cure of Souls: Jung and the Indian East," in Lopez, 1996, p. 208.

73 Lopez, 1996, p. 17.

74 Gómez, in Lopez, 1996, p. 229.

75 Note that to refer to "*my* sources, *my* texts, *my* native informants," etc., is already to engage in a subtle act of appropriation.

76 Robert A. F. Thurman, "Tibet and the Monastic Army of Peace," in Kraft (ed.), *Inner Peace, World Peace*, p. 83.

77 Queen, 1996; Queen, 2000.

78 Cf. p. 10

79 Kitagawa, in Balasooriya, 1980, p. 87.

80 cf. Andrew P. Tuck, *Comparative Philosophy and the Philosophy of Scholarship: On the Western Interpretation of Nagarjuna* (New York: Oxford University Press, 1990), pp. 10–11 on the significance of a descriptive tone which sounds as if something has been discovered or observed rather than interpreted or constructed.

81 Kitagawa, in Balasooriya, 1980, p. 90.

82 Ibid., p. 91.

83 Ibid., p. 100.

84 Ibid., p. 92.

85 Jones, 1989, p. 134.

86 Ibid., p. 124.

87 Ibid., p. 198.
88 Ibid., pp. 128–129.
89 Ibid., p. 207.
90 Ibid., p. 130.
91 Ibid., p. 271.
92 Ibid., pp. 196–197.
93 Ibid., p. 273.
94 I am here using "false consciousness" in the most generic sense, as nicely defined in the *Cambridge Dictionary of Philosophy* ed. Robert Audi, (Cambridge: Cambridge University Press, 1996), p. 262: "lack of clear awareness of the source and significance of one's beliefs and attitudes concerning society, religion, or values."
95 Jones, 1989, p. 235.
96 Ibid., p. 237.
97 A similar East–West dichotomy (and the need for a similar synthesis) is espoused by Eller in 1992: Some ... thinkers suggest that ... 'social gospel' or 'social and political theory' is precisely what the West (or Christianity) has to offer to Buddhism. Through a melding of these two traditions, they believe, a more complete philosophy of life and the world will come to light. Gary Snyder takes this position when he says, "The mercy of the west has been social revolution; the mercy of the east has been individual insight into the basic self/void. We need both" (Cynthia Eller, "The Impact of Christianity on Buddhist Nonviolence in the West," in Kraft, *Inner Peace, World Peace*, p. 102).

Here *both* "West" and "East" are construed as having had (presumably always) intrinsically "incomplete philosophies," each waiting to find the other to "complete" itself. This stereotypical portrayal seems again motivated by the kind of neo-colonial, "appropriative" disposition we have been discussing: East and West may be said to complete each other, but the final synthetic hybrid is accomplished by Western practitioners, defined in Western terms, used in a Western way, on Western soil (primarily), etc.
98 Jones, 1989, pp. 37–38.
99 Ibid., p. 275.
100 Ibid., pp. 271–272.
101 Queen, 1996, p. xi.
102 Queen says of himself, "As one trained in the Theravada practice lineage that produced American Dharma teachers Jack Kornfield, ... [etc.], I imagine myself as a 'hinayanist'" Queen, 2000, p. 31, note 52.
103 Jones, 1989, p. 65.
104 Ibid., p. 216.
105 Jones, as quoted by Sandra Bell, in Queen, 2000, p. 405.
106 Queen, 2000: 8–10.
107 Jones, 1989, p. 222. Here he notes that the main subject of his book has been the third type, "radical activism."
108 Queen, 1996, p. 10.
109 Queen, 2000, p. 3. It is impossible for me to see how Queen could consider (1) to be part of a "new" outlook. However, as the main topic of our discussion here is really (2) and (3), we shall leave the issue of (1) aside.
110 Thus, Jones and Queen are certainly not the only engaged Buddhists to have recently sought to associate engaged Buddhism specifically with the challenging of the *institutionalized* and *structural* forms of suffering. For example, as Simmer-Brown tells us, the Buddhist Peace Fellowship, active since 1978, "[has recently] engaged in a 'future process' designed to refine strategies concerning institutional and "structural *dukkha*" (suffering), its sources, and

the actions and realizations that might lead to its relief" (Judith Simmer-Brown "Speaking Truth to Power: The Buddhist Peace Fellowship," in Queen, 2000, p. 78). Simmer-Brown then cites a 1997 BPF document as stating: "We feel our particular responsibility is to address structural and social forms of suffering, oppression, and violence. These are not abstractions – war, racism, sexism, economic oppression, denial of human rights and social justice, and so many other ills cause great fear and suffering for all beings..." And she concludes: "In this analysis, BPF is expressing the core of its most current theoretical contribution to engaged Buddhism in America: that meditation practice and training the mind directly relate to diminishing our personal suffering, but that practitioners will not have fully addressed the suffering of the world if they do not address the social, economic, and political structures that legitimize violence and suffering"(Queen, 2000, p. 80.)

111 Queen, 1996, p. 30.
112 Ibid., p. 31.
113 Queen, 2000, p. 1.
114 Ibid., p. 3.
115 This is a common Universal Vehicle contention. See, for example, Tsong Khapa's 15th century Tibetan discussion of this in *Tantra in Tibet* in the section entitled "All the Divisions [of scriptures, paths, or vehicles] Are Ultimately Branches of the Process of Fullest Enlightenment," pp. 101–104. Therein he argues that everything the Buddha taught is necessarily something that leads to Buddhahood, even if certain paths (e.g., Individual Vehicle paths) are determined to have incomplete methods and are thus only a *part* of the process leading to Buddhahood.
116 Again, this is perhaps due in part to his greater familiarization with Theravadin forms of Buddhism (see above, note 102).
117 Queen, 2000, p. 3.
118 Queen, 1996, p. 10.
119 Ibid., p. 11.
120 Queen, 1996, p. 5. In the same anthology José Cabezón discusses Christian liberation theology at great length, characterizing it in much the same way as Queen. However, Cabezón comes to a decidedly different conclusion about its consistency with Buddhist liberation movements in José Ignacio Cabezón, "Buddhist Principles in the Tibetan Liberation Movement," in Queen, 1996, p. 311.
121 Queen, 1996, pp. x–xi.
122 Ibid., p. 9.
123 This should be fairly obvious. There are many *sutras* in which the Buddha declares that everything he teaches is solely for liberating beings. See also note 115 above.
124 Queen, 1996, p. 11.
125 Ibid., p. 10.
126 Queen, 2000, pp. 11–17.
127 Ibid., p. 15.
128 Ibid., p. 16.
129 There are countless Mahayana treatises which discuss these two sides of *bodhicitta*. See for example Shantideva's *Bodhisattva-carya-avatara*, I, pp. 15–16, or verse 19 of Atisha's *Bodhi-patha-pradiipa*, etc.
130 Queen, 2000, p. 17.
131 Ibid., p. 24.
132 Ibid., p. 23. *Lokayana* might perhaps better be translated as "Worldly Vehicle" to parallel the adjectival form "Global" and to suggest the focus on

"worldly" (*lokiya*) liberation which he asserts to be characteristic of liberation movements.

133 Queen, 2000, pp. 1–2.

134 Ibid., p. 25.

135 Cited in Stephanie Kaza, "To Save All Beings: Buddhist Environmental Activism," in Queen 2000, p. 160.

136 Franz-Johannes Litsch, "Engaged Buddhism in German-Speaking Europe," in Queen 2000, p. 423.

137 Another example that comes to mind was the attempt by Dol-po-pa (1292–1361) to legitimize his controversial *gzhan stong* interpretation of emptiness by invoking the language of "Councils" in one of his key texts on the subject (*The Great Calculation of the Doctrine, Which has the Significance of a Fourth Council*). See Cyrus Stearns, "The Buddha from Dol po and His Fourth Council of the Buddhist Doctrine," (PhD dissertation, University of Washington (Seattle), 1996).

138 In an excellent essay entitled "Tibetan Hermeneutics and the yana Controversy," Nathan Katz demonstrates with abundant scriptural citations and penetrating analysis that "Examples of this yana discourse could extend almost indefinitely, as virtually all Mahayana sutras have something to say on the subject" Nathan Katz, "Tibetan Hermeneutics and the yana Controversy," in *Contributions on Tibetan and Buddhist Religion and Philosophy [Proceedings of the Csoma de Koros Symposium, 1981]*, vol. 2, editors Ernst Steinkellner, and Helmut Täuscher (Wiener Studien zur Tibetologie und Buddhismuskunde, 1983), p. 113.

See also the extended discussions in *Tantra in Tibet* on this very subject (esp. the discussions surrounding pp. 48, 55, 60, 92, 100–104). Therein, Tsong Khapa and H.H. The Dalai Lama argue that a difference in vehicles must be posited with respect to a difference in either wisdom or means (or effect/cause, or fruit/means). This analytical perspective is then used to elucidate why Hinayana and Mahayana are different yanas, why Perfection and Mantra Vehicles are different yanas (within the Mahayana), but why, for example, Cittamatra and Madhyamaka are not different yanas, or why other partial sub-paths within a given yana are not considered separate yanas, or why different paths and teachings geared toward different levels of disciples are not considered different yanas, and so on.

139 Charles S. Prebish and Kenneth K. Tanaka, *The Faces of Buddhism in America* (Berkeley, CA: University of California Press, 1998), p. 273.

140 *The Fundamental Wisdom of the Middle Way: Nagarjuna's Mulamadhyamakakarika*, trans. with commentary by Jay L. Garfield (Oxford: Oxford University Press, 1995), p. 75.

141 Garfield, 1995, p. 332.

142 Robert A. F. Thurman, *The Speech of Gold* [Reprint of *The Central Philosophy of Tibet*, Princeton, NJ: Princeton University Press, 1984], (Delhi: Motilal Banarsidass, 1989), p. 150.

143 Thurman, 1989, p. 155.

144 Ibid., p. 159.

145 José Ignacio Cabezón, in Queen, 1996, p. 311.

146 Ibid., p. 317, note 57.

147 Queen, 1996, p. 41.

148 Queen, 2000, p. 30, n. 34.

149 An attitude often revealed in the rhetoric of pop Zen, or as suggested by the title of Stephen Batchelor's recent book, *Buddhism Without Beliefs* (New York: Riverhead Books 1997).

150 Kraft, in Eppsteiner, 1988, p. xv.

151 Jones, 1989, p. 66.

152 David S. Ruegg, "Some Reflections on the Place of Philosophy in the Study of Buddhism," *Journal of the International Association of Buddhist Studies* 18, no. 2, 1995, p. 155.

153 Ruegg's elucidation and application of the notion of "family resemblance" or of "topos" to such discussions is also extremely illuminating here. See his *Buddha-nature, Mind and the Problem of Gradualism in a Comparative Perspective* (London: School of Oriental and African Studies, 1989), pp. 2, 5, 13, 109, 123–24, etc. Therein he notes:"The notion of family resemblance was made use of in philosophy by L. Wittgenstein ... [I]n a polythetic arrangement or chain no single feature is essential, or sufficient, for membership in the classification in which all the individual do *not* share one single characteristic feature ... [W]hen we consider Buddhism in its various traditions in India, China and in Tibet ... the question may even arise as to whether the name "Buddhism" denotes one single entity rather than a classification embracing (more or less polythetically) a very large number of strands held together by family resemblances"(Ibid., p. 2).

154 See Ducrot, Oswald and Tzvetan Todorov (trans. Catherine Porter), *Encyclopedic Dictionary of the Sciences of Language* (Baltimore: Johns Hopkins University Press, 1994), p. 36 for further explanation of these terms and an extensive bibliography.

155 Ruegg, 1995, p. 157. These "emic" and "etic" approaches may be seen to be related to the useful distinction Wayne Proudfoot makes in *Religious Experience* (Berkeley, CA: University of California Press, 1985) between "description" and "explanation," respectively.

156 Ruegg, 1995, pp. 158–159.

157 Ibid., p. 157.

158 Queen, 1996, p. 31.

159 Thurman, 1989, p. 8.

160 Thurman, in Kraft, 1992, p. 89.

INDEX